INDIANA
SCIENCE
FUSION

fusion [FYOO • zhuhn] a combination of two
or more things that releases energy

This **Interactive Student Edition** belongs to

_____

Teacher/Room

_____

HOLT McDOUGAL

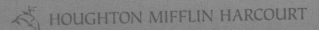

HOUGHTON MIFFLIN HARCOURT

Consulting Authors

Michael A. DiSpezio

Global Educator
North Falmouth, Massachusetts

Michael DiSpezio is a renaissance educator who moved from the research laboratory of a Nobel Prize winner to the K–12 science classroom. He has authored or co-authored numerous textbooks and written more than 25 trade books. For nearly a decade he worked with the JASON Project, under the auspices of the National Geographic Society, where he designed curriculum, wrote lessons, and hosted dozens of studio and location broadcasts. Over the past two decades, he has developed supplementary material for organizations and shows that include PBS *Scientific American Frontiers, Discover* magazine, and the Discovery Channel. He has extended his reach outside the United States and into topics of crucial importance today. To all his projects, he brings his extensive background in science and his expertise in classroom teaching at the elementary, middle, and high school levels.

Marjorie Frank

*Science Writer and
Content-Area Reading Specialist*
Brooklyn, New York

An educator and linguist by training, a writer and poet by nature, Marjorie Frank has authored and designed a generation of instructional materials in all subject areas, including past HMH Science programs. Her other credits include authoring science issues of an award-winning children's magazine; writing game-based digital assessments in math, reading, and language arts; and serving as instructional designer and co-author of pioneering school-to-work software for Classroom Inc., a nonprofit organization dedicated to improving reading and math skills for middle and high school learners. She wrote lyrics and music for *SCIENCE SONGS,* which was an American Library Association nominee for notable recording. In addition, she has served on the adjunct faculty of Hunter, Manhattan, and Brooklyn Colleges, teaching courses in science methods, literacy, and writing.

Acknowledgments for Covers

Front cover: *satellite dishes* ©Robert Glusic/Photographer's Choice RF/Getty Images; *gecko* ©Pete Orelup/Flickr/Getty Images; *mountain biker* ©Jerome Prevost/TempSport/Corbis; *digital screen* ©Michael Melford/Stone/Getty Images; *Giant's Causeway* ©Rod McLean/Alamy.

Back cover: *fossils* ©Yoshishi Tanaka/amana images/Getty Images; *cells* ©Todd Davidson/Getty Images; *tarsier* ©Bruno Morandi/The Image Bank/Getty Images; *x-ray* ©Lester Lefkowitz/Taxi/Getty Images.

Printed in the U.S.A.

ISBN 978-0-547-43844-3

8 9 10 0877 19 18 17 16 15 14

4500502950   BCDEFG

Michael R. Heithaus

Director, School of Environment and Society
Associate Professor, Department of Biological Sciences
Florida International University
North Miami, Florida

Mike Heithaus joined the Florida International University Biology Department in 2003. He has served as Director of the Marine Sciences Program and is now Director of the School of Environment and Society, which brings together the natural and social sciences and humanities to develop solutions to today's environmental challenges. While earning his doctorate, he began the research that grew into the Shark Bay Ecosystem Project in Western Australia, with which he still works. Back in the U.S., he served as a Research Fellow with National Geographic, using remote imaging in his research and hosting a 13-part *Crittercam* television series on the National Geographic Channel. His current research centers on predator-prey interactions among vertebrates, such as tiger sharks, dolphins, dugongs, sea turtles, and cormorants.

Donna M. Ogle

Professor of Reading and Language
National-Louis University
Chicago, Illinois

Creator of the well-known KWL strategy, Donna Ogle has directed many staff development projects translating theory and research into school practice in middle and secondary schools throughout the United States. She is a past president of the International Reading Association and has served as a consultant on literacy projects worldwide. Her extensive international experience includes coordinating the Reading and Writing for Critical Thinking Project in Eastern Europe, developing an integrated curriculum for a USAID Afghan Education Project, and speaking and consulting on projects in several Latin American countries and in Asia. Her books include *Coming Together as Readers; Reading Comprehension: Strategies for Independent Learners; All Children Read;* and *Literacy for a Democratic Society.*

Program Advisors/Reviewers

PROGRAM ADVISORS

Rose Pringle, Ph.D.
Associate Professor
School of Teaching and Learning
College of Education
University of Florida
Gainesville, FL

Carolyn Staudt, M.Ed.
Curriculum Designer for Technology
KidSolve, Inc./The Concord Consortium
Concord, MA

CONTENT REVIEWERS

Paul D. Asimow, Ph.D.
Associate Professor of Geology and Geochemistry
Division of Geological and Planetary Sciences
California Institute of Technology
Pasadena, CA

Nigel S. Atkin son, Ph.D.
Professor of Neurobiology
Section of Neurobiology
The University of Texas at Austin
Austin, TX

Laura K. Baumgartner, Ph.D.
Postdoctoral Researcher
Pace Laboratory
Molecular, Cellular, and Developmental Biology
University of Colorado
Boulder, CO

Sonal Blumenthal, Ph.D.
Science Education Consultant
Austin, TX

Monica E. Cardella, Ph.D.
Assistant Professor
School of Engineering Education
Purdue University
West Lafayette, IN

Eileen Cashman, Ph.D.
Professor
Department of Environmental Resources Engineering
Humboldt State University
Arcata, CA

Shanna R. Daly, Ph.D.
Research Fellow and Lecturer
College of Engineering and the Design Science Program
University of Michigan
Ann Arbor, MI

Program Advisors/Reviewers *(continued)*

Elizabeth A. De Stasio, Ph.D.
Raymond H. Herzog Professor of Science
Professor of Biology
Department of Biology
Lawrence University
Appleton, WI

Heidi A. Diefes-Dux, Ph.D.
Associate Professor
School of Engineering Education
Purdue University
West Lafayette, IN

Julia R. Greer, Ph.D.
Assistant Professor of Materials Science and Mechanical Engineering
Division of Engineering and Applied Science
California Institute of Technology
Pasadena, CA

John E. Hoover, Ph.D.
Professor
Department of Biology
Millersville University
Millersville, PA

Charles W. Johnson, Ph.D.
Chairman, Division of Natural Sciences, Mathematics, and Physical Education
Associate Professor of Physics
South Georgia College
Douglas, GA

Ping H. Johnson, Ph.D.
Associate Professor
Department of Health, Physical Education, and Sport Science
Kennesaw State University
Kennesaw, GA

Tatiana A. Krivosheev, Ph.D.
Associate Professor of Physics
Department of Natural Sciences
Clayton State University
Morrow, GA

Louise McCullough, M.D., Ph.D.
Associate Professor of Neurology and Neuroscience
Director of Stroke Research and Education
University of Connecticut Health Center & The Stroke Center at Hartford Hospital
Farmington, CT

Mark Moldwin, Ph.D.
Professor of Space Sciences
Department of Atmospheric, Oceanic, and Space Sciences
University of Michigan
Ann Arbor, MI

Hilary Clement Olson, Ph.D.
Research Scientist Associate V
Institute for Geophysics,
Jackson School of Geosciences
The University of Texas at Austin
Austin, TX

Russell S. Patrick, Ph.D.
Professor of Physics
Department of Biology, Chemistry, and Physics
Southern Polytechnic State University
Marietta, GA

James L. Pazun, Ph.D.
Professor and Chairman
Chemistry and Physics
Pfeiffer University
Misenheimer, NC

L. Jeanne Perry, Ph.D.
Director (Retired)
Protein Expression Technology Center
Institute for Genomics and Proteomics
University of California, Los Angeles
Los Angeles, CA

Senay Purzer, Ph.D.
Assistant Professor
School of Engineering Education
Purdue University
West Lafayette, IN

Kenneth H. Rubin, Ph.D.
Professor
Department of Geology and Geophysics
University of Hawaii
Honolulu, HI

Michael J. Ryan, Ph.D.
Clark Hubbs Regents Professor in Zoology
Section of Integrative Biology
The University of Texas at Austin
Austin, TX

Brandon E. Schwab, Ph.D.
Associate Professor
Department of Geology
Humboldt State University
Arcata, CA

Miles R. Silman, Ph.D.
Associate Professor
Department of Biology
Wake Forest University
Winston-Salem, NC

Marllin L. Simon, Ph.D.
Associate Professor
Department of Physics
Auburn University
Auburn, AL

Kristin Walker, Ph.D.
Assistant Professor of Physics
Department of Chemistry and Physics
Pfeiffer University
Misenheimer, NC

Matt A. Wood, Ph.D.
Professor
Department of Physics and Space Sciences
Florida Institute of Technology
Melbourne, FL

Adam D. Woods, Ph.D.
Associate Professor
Department of Geological Sciences
California State University, Fullerton
Fullerton, CA

TEACHER REVIEWERS

Kimberly Elpers, M.Ed.
Sts. Peter and Paul School
Haubstadt, IN

Amy Hamann, M.El.Ed. & M.Sci.Ed.
Barker Middle School
Michigan City, IN

Krista Harrison, M.Ed.
Carmel Middle School
Carmel, IN

Jane Hunn
Tippecanoe Valley Middle School
Akron, IN

Kevin McBride
Colonel John Wheeler Middle School
Crown Point, IN

Mark McCollom, M.Ed.
Lakeview Middle School
Warsaw, IN

Sharon McElroy
East Washington Middle School
Pekin, IN

Matt Moller, M.Ed.
Carmel Middle School
Carmel, IN

Tracey Streit, M.Ed.
Franklin Township Middle School East
Indianapolis, IN

Daniel Wray, M.S.
Lakeview Middle School
Warsaw, IN

Contents in Brief

Plants use the sun's energy to produce food.

Program Overview xii

Indiana Standards xvi

Unit 1
Nature of Science 1

Unit 2
Matter 67

Unit 3
Energy 117

Unit 4
The Solar System 147

Unit 5
The Earth-Moon-Sun System 241

Unit 6
Ecology 283

The Design Process 339

Look It Up! Reference Section R1

Glossary R39

Index R46

It takes a change in temperature to pop popcorn!

Contents

	Assigned	Due
Unit 1 Nature of Science 1	☐	_____
Citizen Science 2	☐	_____
DP 6.5, DP 6.10		
Lesson 1 What Is Science? 4	☐	_____
NOS 6.1		
Lesson 2 Scientific Knowledge 14	☐	_____
Lesson 3 Scientific Investigations 24	☐	_____
NOS 6.1, NOS 6.2, NOS 6.3, NOS 6.4, NOS 6.5, NOS 6.6, NOS 6.7, NOS 6.8, NOS 6.9, NOS 6.10		
Lesson 4 Representing Data 38	☐	_____
NOS 6.3, NOS 6.7, NOS 6.8, NOS 6.11		
Think Science Making Conclusions from Evidence ... 48	☐	_____
NOS 6.3, NOS 6.8		
Lesson 5 Science and Society 50	☐	_____
Unit Summary 62	☐	_____
ISTEP+ Review 63	☐	_____

Unit test date: _____

Modern agriculture allows us to grow plants anywhere. Plants can even grow without soil!

			Assigned	Due
Unit 2 Matter	67	☐	_____
Citizen Science	68	☐	_____
♩ DP 6.1, DP 6.2, DP 6.4			
Lesson 1 Introduction to Matter	70	☐	_____
Lesson 2 States of Matter	84	☐	_____
♩ 6.1.1, 6.1.2			
Think Science Planning an Investigation	94	☐	_____
♩ NOS 6.2, NOS 6.4			
Lesson 3 Changes of State	96	☐	_____
♩ 6.1.3			
Unit Summary	112	☐	_____
♩ **ISTEP+ Review**	113	☐	_____

Unit test date: _____

Assignments:

_____
_____
_____
_____
_____
_____
_____
_____
_____
_____

Devices such as this spring scale measure weight.

Contents (continued)

Kinetic energy depends on speed. So, a cheetah has more kinetic energy when it's running than when it's walking.

		Assigned	Due
Unit 3 Energy	117	☐	_____
Citizen Science	118	☐	_____
♪ DP 6.1			
Lesson 1 Kinetic and Potential Energy	120	☐	_____
♪ 6.1.4, 6.1.5, 6.1.6, 6.4.3			
Focus on Engineering The Right Tool	130	☐	_____
♪ 6.4.1, 6.4.2, 6.4.3			
Lesson 2 Forms of Energy	132	☐	_____
♪ 6.1.5, 6.1.7			
Unit Summary	142	☐	_____
♪ **ISTEP+ Review**	143	☐	_____

Unit test date: _____

© Houghton Mifflin Harcourt Publishing Company • Image Credits: ©Steve Bloom Images/Alamy

			Assigned	Due
Unit 4 **The Solar System**		147	☐	_____
Citizen Science		148	☐	_____
♪ DP 6.10				
Lesson 1 **Historical Models of the Solar System**		150	☐	_____
♪ 6.2.3				
People in Science Sandra Faber		160	☐	_____
Lesson 2 **Gravity and the Solar System**		162	☐	_____
♪ 6.2.2				
Think Science Determining Relevant Information		176	☐	_____
♪ NOS 6.8				
Lesson 3 **The Sun**		178	☐	_____
♪ 6.2.3				
Lesson 4 **The Terrestrial Planets**		190	☐	_____
♪ 6.2.4				
People in Science A. Wesley Ward		204	☐	_____
Lesson 5 **The Gas Giant Planets**		206	☐	_____
♪ 6.2.4				
Lesson 6 **Small Bodies in the Solar System**		218	☐	_____
♪ 6.2.4				
Unit Summary		234	☐	_____
🔵 **ISTEP+ Review**		235	☐	_____

Unit test date: _____

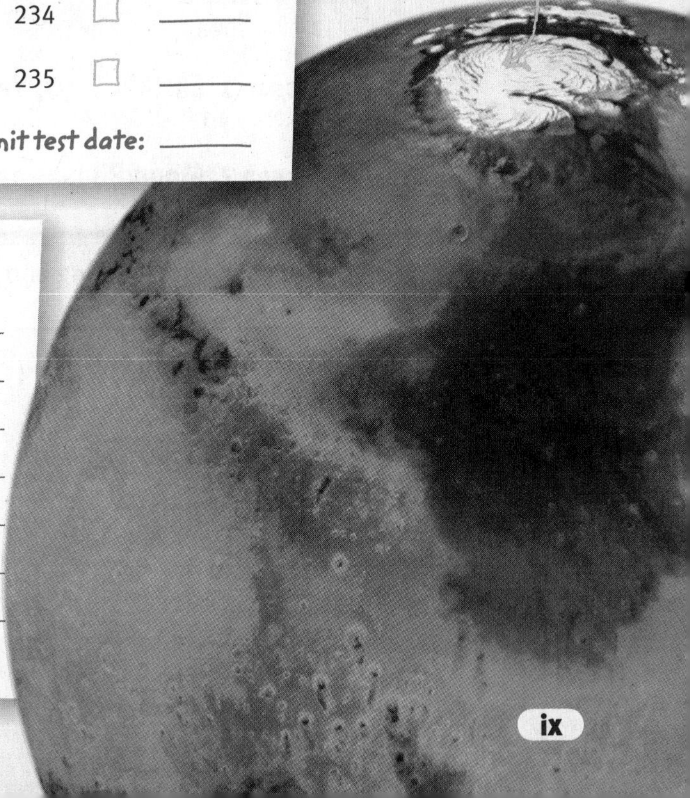

Mars's northern polar ice cap changes with the seasons.

Assignments:

_____
_____
_____
_____
_____
_____

Contents (continued)

A lunar eclipse takes several hours. You can see Earth's shadow move across the Moon!

	Assigned	Due
Unit 5 The Earth-Moon-Sun System 241	☐	_____
Citizen Science 242	☐	_____
🎵 DP 6.1, DP 6.2, DP 6.4, DP 6.5		
Lesson 1 Earth's Days, Years, and Seasons 244	☐	_____
🎵 6.2.1, 6.2.5		
Lesson 2 Moon Phases and Eclipses 254	☐	_____
🎵 6.2.1		
Think Science Testing and Modifying Theories 264	☐	_____
🎵 NOS 6.8		
Lesson 3 Earth's Tides 266	☐	_____
🎵 6.2.2		
Unit Summary 278	☐	_____
🏛 **ISTEP+ Review** 279	☐	_____
	Unit test date:	_____

		Assigned	Due

Unit 6 Ecology .... 283 ☐ _____

Citizen Science .... 284 ☐ _____
  🔖 DP 6.1

  Lesson 1 Introduction to Ecology .... 286 ☐ _____
  🔖 6.3.2, 6.3.3

  People in Science Kenneth Krysko .... 296 ☐ _____

  Lesson 2 Roles in Energy Transfer .... 298 ☐ _____
  🔖 6.3.4, 6.3.5, 6.3.6

  Lesson 3 Interactions in Communities .... 310 ☐ _____
  🔖 6.3.1, 6.3.5

  **Lesson 4 Photosynthesis and
  Cellular Respiration** .... 320 ☐ _____
  🔖 6.3.4, 6.3.5, 6.3.6

Unit Summary .... 334 ☐ _____

🔷 **ISTEP+ Review** .... 335 ☐ _____

Unit test date: _____

The Design Process 339

Look It Up! Reference Section R1

Glossary R39

Index R46

Assignments:
_____
_____
_____
_____
_____
_____
_____
_____
_____

Puffins are part of a coastal food web. They get their energy from eating herring.

Power up with Science Fusion!

Your program fuses...

Online Virtual Experiences

Inquiry-Based Labs and Activities

Active Reading and Writing

...to generate energy for today's science learner — *you.*

Active Reading and Writing

Be an active reader and make this book your own!

You can answer questions, ask questions, create graphs, make notes, write your own ideas, and highlight information right in your book.

By the end of the school year, your book will become a record of the knowledge and skills you learned in science.

Inquiry-Based Labs and Activities

ScienceFusion includes lots of exciting hands-on inquiry labs and activities, each one designed to bring science skills and concepts to life and get you involved.

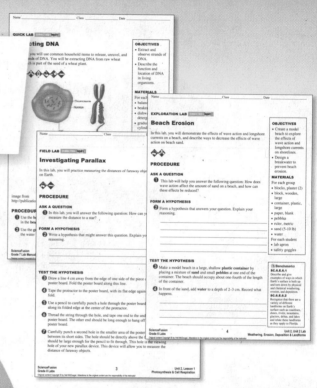

By asking questions, testing your ideas, organizing and analyzing data, drawing conclusions, and sharing what you learn...

You are the scientist!

Online Virtual Experiences

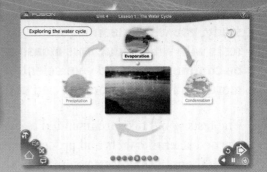

Explore cool labs, activities, interactive lessons, and videos in the virtual world—where science comes alive and you make it happen.

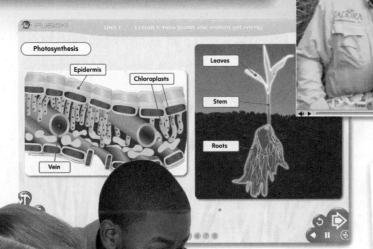

See your science lessons from a completely different point of view—a digital point of view.

Science Fusion! is a new source of energy... just for YOU!

Indiana Standards

An Overview and What It Means to You

This book and this class are structured around the Indiana Academic Standards for Science. As you read, experiment, and study, you will be learning what you need to know to take the tests with which educators measure your progress. You will also be continuing to build your scientific literacy, which makes you a more skillful person both in and out of school.

The tests you'll take are intended to measure how well you learned scientific facts and procedures, and how well you can apply them to situations you might find in the real world. What you remember long after the tests, called enduring understandings, will help you see, measure, interpret, and evaluate many more situations you encounter in life.

The Indiana Academic Standards for Science describe major themes and overarching concepts in science. The standards appear throughout your book. Look for them on the opening pages of each Unit and Lesson.

The next few pages address several questions, including:

- What are the standards underlying the instruction?
- Where is each standard found in this book?
- What makes the standards relevant to you now?
- What kinds of questions will you be asked on the tests?

Notice the **Essential Question** on the Lesson opener. This question is a hint to the enduring understanding you may take away from this lesson, long after you've studied it and passed a test and perhaps forgotten some of the details.

Find the **Core Standards** for the unit on the Unit opener.

Find the **standards** for each lesson on the Lesson opener.

UNIT 1

Nature

Nature of Science

Students gain scientific knowledge by observing the natural and constructed world, performing and evaluating investigations and communicating their findings. These principles should guide student work and be integrated into the curriculum along with the content standards on a daily basis.

Lesson 1

What Is Science?

ESSENTIAL QUESTION

How is science different from other fields of study?

By the end of this lesson, you should be able to distinguish what characterizes science and scientific explanations from other forms of knowledge and recognize creativity in science.

Today, we know that Earth is a sphere.

A scientist studies the genetic code. To most people, this looks impossible to understand. To her eyes, it's a wealth of information.

Indiana Standards

NOS 6.1 Make predictions and develop testable questions based on research and prior knowledge.

4 Unit 1 Nature of Science

1

Nature of Science

Students gain scientific knowledge by observing the natural and constructed world, performing and evaluating investigations and communicating their findings. These principles should guide student work and be integrated into the curriculum along with the content standards on a daily basis.

What It Means to You

If you suddenly found yourself somewhere that you had never been before, you would probably look around yourself with curiosity. You'd compare what you saw, heard, smelled, and felt to what you knew about other places. You might experiment a little and then draw some conclusions. Then you would be able to describe your surroundings to someone else. You would be thinking like a scientist.

Hiker in hills

Standards

NOS 6.1 Make predictions and develop testable questions based on research and prior knowledge.
Where to Check It Out Unit 1, Lessons 1 & 3

NOS 6.2 Plan and carry out investigations as a class, in small groups or independently often over a period of several class lessons.
Where to Check It Out Unit 1, Lesson 3; Unit 2 Think Science

NOS 6.3 Collect quantitative data with appropriate tools or technologies and use appropriate units to label numerical data.
Where to Check It Out Unit 1, Lessons 3 & 4; Unit 1 Think Science

NOS 6.4 Incorporate variables that can be changed, measured or controlled.
Where to Check It Out Unit 1, Lesson 3; Unit 2 Think Science

NOS 6.5 Use the principles of accuracy and precision when making measurement.
Where to Check It Out Unit 1, Lesson 3; Look It Up! Reference Section

NOS 6.6 Test predictions with multiple trials.
Where to Check It Out Unit 1, Lesson 3

NOS 6.7 Keep accurate records in a notebook during investigations.
Where to Check It Out Unit 1, Lessons 3 & 4

NOS 6.8 Analyze data, using appropriate mathematical manipulation as required, and use it to identify patterns and make inferences based on these patterns.
Where to Check It Out Unit 1, Lessons 3 & 4; Unit 1 Think Science; Unit 4 Think Science; Unit 5 Think Science

NOS 6.9 Evaluate possible causes for differing results (valid data).
Where to Check It Out Unit 1, Lesson 3

NOS 6.10 Compare the results of an experiment with the prediction.
Where to Check It Out Unit 1, Lesson 3

NOS 6.11 Communicate findings using graphs, charts, maps and models through oral and written reports.
Where to Check It Out Unit 1, Lesson 4

Sample Question   Circle the correct answer.

1 Scientists use different tools to investigate how and why things happen. Some examples of tools that can be used to gather data are: a graduated cylinder, a measuring cup, and a graduated beaker. Which unit might be used for data obtained using ALL of these tools?

A. meter

B. kilogram

C. milliliter

D. grams per liter

The Design Process

As citizens of the constructed world, students will participate in the design process. Students will learn to use materials and tools safely and employ the basic principles of the engineering design process in order to find solutions to problems.

This chair is designed to be portable.

What It Means to You

You are thinking like a scientist when you plan and carry out investigations to solve a problem or answer a question. For example, you use the proper tools and materials in a safe way. And you gather and analyze data and report your findings to the rest of the class.

Standards

DP 6.1 Identify a need or problem to be solved.
Where to Check It Out Units 2, 3, 5, & 6, Citizen Science; The Design Process

DP 6.2 Brainstorm potential solutions.
Where to Check It Out Units 2 & 5, Citizen Science; The Design Process

DP 6.3 Document the design throughout the entire design process so that it can be replicated in a portfolio/notebook with drawings including labels.
Where to Check It Out The Design Process

DP 6.4 Select a solution to the need or problem.
Where to Check It Out Units 2 & 5, Citizen Science; The Design Process

DP 6.5 Select the most appropriate materials to develop a solution that will meet the need.
Where to Check It Out Units 1 & 5, Citizen Science; The Design Process

DP 6.6 Create the solution through a prototype.
Where to Check It Out The Design Process

DP 6.7 Test and evaluate how well the solution meets the goal.
Where to Check It Out The Design Process

DP 6.8 Evaluate and test the design using measurement.
Where to Check It Out The Design Process

DP 6.9 Present evidence using mathematical representations (graphs, data tables).
Where to Check It Out The Design Process

DP 6.10 Communicate the solution including evidence using mathematical representations (graphs, data tables), drawings or prototypes.
Where to Check It Out Units 1 & 4, Citizen Science; The Design Process

DP 6.11 Redesign to improve the solution based on how well the solution meets the need.
Where to Check It Out The Design Process

Sample Question

2 Selena is going camping soon, and she wants to bring some board games to play in the evening. However, some of her board games are in bulky boxes which are hard to pack in her camping bag. What is another problem that Selena might face if she brings traditional board games on a camping trip?

_____

_____

_____

Select a traditional board game and describe how the board and pieces can be modified to solve both problems.

_____

_____

_____

_____

_____

_____

Selena decides to make a prototype of a modified board game to address the problems. Use the space below to draw the prototype and label its modifications.

Indiana Standards *(continued)*

Physical Science

 Core Standards

Explain that all objects and substances in the natural world are composed of matter in different states with different properties.

Understand that there are different forms of energy with unique characteristics.

What It Means to You

If you leave a water bottle outside in cold weather, you might return to find that the water in the bottle is frozen. What has happened to the water inside? What would you have to do to get it back to its liquid form? The answer involves heat, which is the energy transferred between objects at different temperatures.

You might already know that energy in the form of heat moves from warmer substances to cooler substances—such as from room-temperature water to colder air or from hot cocoa to your tongue. A refrigerator, air conditioner, freezer, furnace, and stove top transfer energy in the form of heat for different results. Behind these appliances is a series of conversions—with coal, gas, oil, wind, water, or steam as starting sources—that help provide the energy needed in your daily life.

Standards

6.1.1 Understand that the properties and behavior of matter can be explained by a model which depicts particles representing atoms or molecules in motion.
Where to Check It Out Unit 2, Lesson 2

6.1.2 Explain the properties of solids, liquids and gases using drawings and models that represent matter as particles in motion whose state can be represented by the relative positions and movement of the particles.
Where to Check It Out Unit 2, Lesson 2

6.1.3 Using a model in which matter is composed of particles in motion, investigate that when substances undergo a change in state, mass is conserved.
Where to Check It Out Unit 2, Lesson 3

6.1.4 Recognize that objects in motion have kinetic energy and objects at rest have potential energy.
Where to Check It Out Unit 3, Lesson 1

6.1.5 Describe with examples that potential energy exists in several different forms (gravitational potential energy, elastic potential energy, and chemical potential energy, among others).
Where to Check It Out Unit 3, Lessons 1 & 2

6.1.6 Compare and contrast potential and kinetic energy and how they can be transformed within a system from one form to another.
Where to Check It Out Unit 3, Lesson 1

6.1.7 Explain that energy may be manifested as heat, light, electricity, mechanical motion, and sound and is often associated with chemical reactions.
Where to Check It Out Unit 3, Lesson 2

Sample Question Circle the correct answer.

3 Which properties of all SOLIDS are based on the motion and position of their particles?

  A. a changing shape and a changing volume

  B. a changing shape and a definite volume

  C. a definite shape and a changing volume

  D. a definite shape and a definite volume

Earth Science

Core Standard

Understand the relationships between celestial bodies and the force that keeps them in regular and predictable motion.

Milky Way galaxy

What It Means to You

The sun and moon are more than just objects in the sky. The gravitational attraction of the sun causes Earth to move around the sun in a regular and predictable motion. Earth's gravity causes the moon to orbit Earth in a regular and predictable manner. In addition, the way in which the sun, moon, and Earth move in relationship to one another affects everyday events on Earth. Their motions cause night and day, the seasons, and the tides.

Standards

6.2.1 Describe and model how the position, size and relative motions of the earth, moon, and sun cause day and night, solar and lunar eclipses and phases of the moon.
Where to Check It Out Unit 5, Lessons 1 & 2

6.2.2 Recognize that gravity is a force that keeps celestial bodies in regular and predictable motion, holds objects to earth's surface, and is responsible for ocean tides.
Where to Check It Out Unit 4, Lesson 2, Unit 5 Lesson 3

6.2.3 Understand that the sun, an average star where nuclear reactions occur, is the central and largest body in the solar system.
Where to Check It Out Unit 4, Lessons 1 & 3

6.2.4 Compare and contrast the planets of the solar system with one another and with asteroids and comets with regard to their size, composition, distance from sun, surface features and ability to support life.
Where to Check It Out Unit 4, Lessons 4, 5, & 6

6.2.5 Demonstrate that the seasons in both hemispheres are the result of the inclination of the earth on its axis which in turn causes changes in sunlight intensity and length of day.
Where to Check It Out Unit 5, Lesson 1

Sample Question Circle the correct answer.

4 Eclipses are predictable solar system events. The answer choices below list relative positions of Earth, the sun, and the moon. Which list represents the position of Earth, the sun, and the moon during a lunar eclipse?

A. sun, Earth, moon

B. Earth, sun, moon

C. sun, moon, Earth

D. moon, sun, Earth

Life Science

Core Standards

Describe that all organisms, including humans, are part of complex systems found in all biomes (freshwater, marine, forest, desert, grassland, tundra).

Understand that the major source of energy for ecosystems is light produced by major nuclear reactions in the sun.

What It Means to You

You and all of the living things around you are part of a large, complex system. For example, plants store energy from sunlight. Animals eat plants and other animals to get the energy they need to live. Where on the Earth plants and animals live affects how they live.

Desert sun

Standards

6.3.1 Describe specific relationships (predator/prey, consumer/producer or parasite/host) between organisms and determine whether these relationships are competitive or mutually beneficial.

Where to Check It Out Unit 6, Lesson 3

6.3.2 Describe how changes caused by organisms in the habitat where they live can be beneficial or detrimental to themselves or the native plants and animals.

Where to Check It Out Unit 6, Lesson 1

6.3.3 Describe how certain biotic and abiotic factors, such as predators, quantity of light and water, range of temperatures, and soil composition, can limit the number of organisms that an ecosystem can support.

Where to Check It Out Unit 6, Lesson 1

6.3.4 Recognize that plants use energy from the sun to make sugar (glucose) by the process of photosynthesis.

Where to Check It Out Unit 6, Lessons 2 & 4

6.3.5 Describe how all animals, including humans, meet their energy needs by consuming other organisms, breaking down their structures, and using the materials to grow and function.

Where to Check It Out Unit 6, Lessons 2, 3 & 4

6.3.6 Recognize that food provides the energy for the work that cells do and is a source of the molecular building blocks that can be incorporated into a cell's structure or stored for later use.

Where to Check It Out Unit 6, Lessons 2 & 4

Sample Question Circle the correct answer.

5 Remoras are small fish that attach to sharks but do not harm them. When sharks tear prey apart, remoras eat the leftovers. What statement about the relationship between remoras and sharks is TRUE?

A. Remoras and sharks have a predator-prey relationship

B. The relationship between remoras and sharks is an example of mutualism.

C. The relationship between remoras and sharks is an example of parasitism.

D. The relationship between remoras and sharks is an example of commensalism.

Science, Engineering and Technology

Core Standard

Apply a form of energy to design and construct a simple mechanical device.

What It Means to You

You see objects in motion around you every day—from cars and bikes to bats and balls. Sometimes you or someone else is moving the object. Other times, such as when a rock tumbles down a hill, things look like they are moving on their own. These objects are being moved by invisible forces such as gravity. Motion is a characteristic of matter that you can see, describe, and measure.

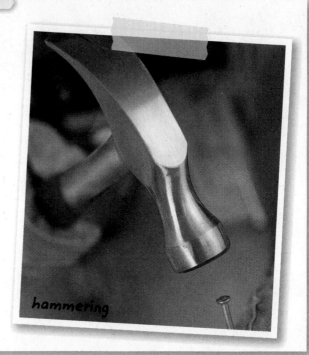

hammering

Standards

6.4.1 Understand how to apply potential or kinetic energy to power a simple device.
Where to Check It Out Unit 3, Focus on Engineering

6.4.2 Construct a simple device that uses potential or kinetic energy to perform work.
Where to Check It Out Unit 3, Focus on Engineering

6.4.3 Describe the transfer of energy amongst energy interactions.
Where to Check It Out Unit 3, Lesson 1, Unit 3, Focus on Engineering

Sample Question   Circle the correct answer.

6 The Wilson family put some solar-powered night-lights in their back yard. The lights turn on at dark. They run all night from a battery that charges during the day. What transfer of energy stores the energy that powers the lights?

A. electromagnetic to thermal

B. chemical to mechanical

C. electromagnetic to chemical

D. electrical to thermal

Nature of Science

People used to think that because Earth was flat, you would fall off the edge if you got too close.

Nature of Science

Students gain scientific knowledge by observing the natural and constructed world, performing and evaluating investigations and communicating their findings. These principles should guide student work and be integrated into the curriculum along with the content standards on a daily basis.

What do you think?

Careful observations and experiments provide us with new information that may change or confirm what we know about the world we live in. What is one way in which science has changed your view of the world?

Today, we know that Earth is a sphere.

Unit 1
Nature of Science

Lesson 1
What Is Science?.....................4
NOS 6.1

Lesson 2
Scientific Knowledge..............14

Lesson 3
Scientific Investigations..........24
NOS 6.1, NOS 6.2, NOS 6.3, NOS 6.4, NOS 6.5,
NOS 6.6, NOS 6.7, NOS 6.8, NOS 6.9, NOS 6.10

Lesson 4
Representing Data.................38
NOS 6.3, NOS 6.7, NOS 6.8, NOS 6.11

Think Science.....................48
NOS 6.3, NOS 6.8

Lesson 5
Science and Society...............50

Unit Summary.....................62

ISTEP+ Review...............63

Indiana Standards

As citizens of the constructed world, students will participate in the design process. Students will learn to use materials and tools safely and employ the basic principles of the engineering design process in order to find solutions to problems.

DP 6.5 Select the most appropriate materials to develop a solution that will meet the need.

DP 6.10 Communicate the solution including evidence using mathematical representations (graphs, data tables), drawings or prototypes.

CITIZEN SCIENCE

Things Change

People used to have strange ideas about the world they lived in. How science has changed some of those ideas is shown here.

1687
People used to think the sun and planets revolved around Earth. In 1687, Newton described gravity and how it affects objects. His work explained why all of the planets, including Earth, must revolve around the much larger sun. Newton's work finally convinced people that the sun and not Earth was at the center of the solar system.

Sir Isaac Newton

Louis Pasteur

1950s

In 1915, people didn't believe Alfred Wegener when he proposed that the continents were moving slowly. It wasn't until the 1950s that advances in technology provided four different lines of evidence, which proved that continents do move. Wegener was right.

Water ice on Mars

1861

People used to think that living things could come from nonliving things, such as flies and beetles from rotting meat. This idea was called *spontaneous generation*. It was Pasteur's experiments that finally disproved this idea.

Modern continents used to be a part of Pangaea.

2008

People used to think that there were Martians on Mars. However, probes and landers have replaced ideas of little green men with real information about the planet. In 2008, we discovered water ice there.

Create Your Own Timeline

① Think About It

Choose a favorite science topic and write it down below.

Moon, Sun, Earth

② Conduct Research

Here are some questions to ask as you research your topic:

• What famous people contributed to the development of your topic and when?

_____

_____

_____

• What images can you use to illustrate the changes that occurred to your topic over time?

_____

_____

_____

③ Make A Plan

Sketch out how you would like to organize your information in the space below, including time, people involved, pictures, and brief passages showing the changes in your topic.

Take It Home

Describe what you have learned to adults at home. Then, have them help you create a poster of how your topic has changed over time.

What Is Science?

ESSENTIAL QUESTION

How is science different from other fields of study?

By the end of this lesson, you should be able to distinguish what characterizes science and scientific explanations from other forms of knowledge and recognize creativity in science.

Indiana Standards

NOS 6.1 Make predictions and develop testable questions based on research and prior knowledge.

A scientist studies the genetic code. To most people, this looks impossible to understand. To her eyes, it's a wealth of information.

1 Predict Check T or F to show which statement is true or false.

T	F	
☑	☑	Science can determine what book you will enjoy.
☑	☐	Scientists can often be creative when designing experiments.
☑	☐	Because they are well educated, scientists do not need to make many observations before coming to a conclusion.
☑	☐	Scientific results can be proven incorrect.

2 Contrast The pottery in the photo is known for its unique appearance. This is partly because of the glaze used on it. What is one question a scientist might ask about this pottery and one question a nonscientist might ask?

_____

_____

_____

_____

_____

_____

 **Active Reading**

3 Apply Use context clues to write your own definition for the underlined word.

Example sentence
Having watched frogs in ponds her whole childhood, Reilley had a lot of <u>empirical</u> evidence about how they behaved.

empirical

_____

_____

_____

_____

Vocabulary Terms

- science
- empirical evidence

4 Identify As you read, place a question mark next to any words that you don't understand. When you finish reading the lesson, go back and review the text that you marked. If the information is still confusing, consult a classmate or teacher.

Science Is Everywhere

What does science study?

One way to define **science** is as the systematic study of natural events and conditions. It is a logical, structured way of thinking about the world. Scientists ask questions about nature. They try to give explanations to describe what they observe. Any explanation a scientist gives must rely on information available to everyone. It must be an explanation others can test.

You probably have done science yourself without knowing it. If you have looked around you and tried to explain what you saw in a way that could be tested, you have done science.

Active Reading

5 Apply As you read, underline examples of subjects that can be studied by science.

The Natural World

Science is subdivided into different branches. Each branch considers a different part of the world. Each branch, however, studies the world in the same logical and structured way.

Biology, or life science, is the study of all living things, from the smallest, one-celled organisms to mammals. Geology, or earth science, studies Earth, from the materials that make it up to the processes that shape it. Astronomy, the study of objects in outer space, often is included under Earth science. Physical science is the study of energy and all nonliving matter. Physical science includes both physics and chemistry.

These branches of science can and often do overlap. You might hear a scientist called a *biochemist* or *geophysicist*. Such terms refer to those whose work falls a little in each branch.

Think Outside the Book *Inquiry*

6 Infer List three questions you would like to have answered. Categorize them as scientific or nonscientific. For the nonscientific questions, can you rephrase them in a scientific way? Do you think you can answer every question scientifically?

Testable Ideas

What are types of questions scientists ask? Scientists ask questions that can be tested. They ask questions that have answers they can measure in some way. An explanation in science is usually agreed upon by many people and not just someone's opinion.

One way to understand how scientific thinking differs from other activities is to think of a sculptor making a piece of art. For example, consider the ice sculptor on the next page. Different people can have different ideas of the value of the art. Some may think it is beautiful. Others may find it ugly. Still another may think it's beautiful one day and ugly the next. These are all opinions. No one's opinion is more correct than another's. The types of books you like, the clothes you like to wear, or the foods you like to eat are not questions science normally addresses.

However, now think of other things the sculptor or onlooker might wonder about the piece. How long will an ice sculpture like this last before it melts? Might the sculpture stay frozen longer if something is used to treat the ice? Would using warmer tools make sculpting ice easier? Questions like these have testable answers. The results can be measured and compared. More important, they can be proved false. This is what distinguishes scientific questions from other kinds.

Visualize It!

7 Apply This sculptor wonders whether the piece may start to melt before it's finished. Is this a question he can investigate scientifically? Explain.

_____

_____

_____

_____

_____

8 Explain This sculptor wonders if making the wings thinner would make the sculpture look more graceful. Is this a question that could be tested by science? Explain.

_____

_____

_____

_____

_____

Tools like this thermometer help scientists make measurements.

9 Discriminate What other testable questions might one ask about the statue?

_____

_____

"Give me an explanation . . ."

What is a scientific explanation?

A scientific explanation describes a natural process. It relies heavily on evidence gained from direct observation and testing. It is an explanation that others can test and refute.

Evidence gained from observation is empirical evidence. **Empirical evidence** includes observations, measurements, and other types of data scientists gather. Scientists use these data to support scientific explanations. Personal feelings and opinions are not empirical evidence.

A scientist never should hide any evidence he or she claims supports a scientific explanation. Whatever that evidence might be, the scientist must disclose all of it, if he or she wants to be taken seriously. If one scientist does an experiment, other scientists must be able to do the same experiment and get the same results. This openness is what makes scientific explanations strong.

Scientific explanation can be complex and, perhaps, even unintelligible to nonscientists. This should not discourage you from at least trying to evaluate explanations you hear like a scientist would.

For example, what makes popcorn pop? You most likely have seen it pop. You probably even have some idea as to how it happens. Here is a scientific explanation for it you can evaluate.

The corn pops because of a change in temperature. All plants contain water. Maybe the rise in temperature causes that water in the shell to boil. When the water turns into a gas, it pushes the kernel apart. The popcorn "pops" when the hard outer shell explodes. This is an explanation you can evaluate.

Active Reading **10 List** Give two examples of things that are not empirical evidence.

_____

_____

EVIDENCE

LOGIC

TESTS

How is a scientific explanation evaluated?

Now that you have an explanation for what makes popcorn pop, you can try to evaluate it as a scientist might. Here is how you might proceed. For each step, some sample responses are provided. Try to think of others.

First, look at any empirical evidence. Think of all the evidence that might support the explanation. Think of the times you've seen popcorn pop. What have you noticed?

Second, consider if the explanation is logical. Does it contradict anything else you know? What about it don't you understand? What else might you also wish to know?

Third, think of other tests you could do to support your ideas. Could you think of a test that might contradict the explanation?

Last, evaluate the explanation. Do you think it has stood up to logic and testing? What about it might be improved?

> **The Scientific Explanation:**
> Popcorn pops because the rise in temperature causes the water in it to expand and "pop" the kernel outward.

The Evidence

For the first step, identify all the evidence you can think of for what causes popcorn to pop.

11 Identify What have you observed about how and when popcorn pops?

- Pops when placed in a microwave
- Pops on a stove top

Inquiry

The Logic

Second, consider if the explanation is consistent with other evidence you have seen.

12 Infer Describe how well your explanation agrees with all of the evidence you have and with all that you know.

- See that water does turn to a gas when heated
- Other things expand when heated

The Tests

Think of other tests you could do that would support the explanation.

13 Predict What other ways might you pop popcorn if this explanation is correct?

- Could pop it in a solar cooker
- Could pop it using hot air

The Conclusion

Last, evaluate the explanation. Describe its strong points. Describe how it might be improved.

14 Evaluate How strong do you think the explanation is? How might it be improved?

Creative Expression

How do scientists show creativity?

Scientists must rely only on what they can observe. They must always try to think logically. Indeed, this might seem dull. However, the best scientists are very creative. They can be creative both in the experiments they design and in the explanations they draw from them.

Active Reading

15 Apply Underline examples of creative solutions used by scientists to solve problems.

In Designing Experiments

How might creativity help in designing experiments? In one case, environmental scientists in the Washington, DC, area were looking for a method to detect harmful substances in drinking water. It would be too dangerous to have people drink the water directly, so they had to be creative.

Scientists knew bluegills are very sensitive to some contaminants. The fish "cough" to expel dirty water from their gills. Some scientists thought to use the fish coughing to identify contaminated water. They set bluegills in tanks in different locations. Sensors hooked up to the tanks detected the fishes' coughing and alerted monitors to potential harm. To ensure each fish's safety, a fish stayed in the tank only a short time.

The bluegill's "coughing" expels contaminants from its gills.

16 Infer How does the bluegill example illustrate creativity in designing experiments?

_____

_____

_____

_____

In Explaining Observations

Sometimes, a creative mind can put old evidence together in a new way. New explanations can often be as important as new observations.

Isaac Newton claimed the law of gravity came to him when he saw an apple fall. He reasoned that some force, gravity, pulled the apple to the ground. The question was why didn't gravity pull the moon to the ground as well?

Newton claimed it did. He explained the moon just didn't reach the Earth because it was moving too fast. To understand the idea, think of what would happen if you threw an apple as hard as you could. The harder you throw it, the farther it goes before gravity pulls it to the ground. What if you threw it so hard that it would travel once around the Earth before it reached the ground? This is what is happening to the moon. As it moves, Earth's gravity attracts it. It just moves too fast to fall to the ground.

Newton's explanation changed the understanding of motion forever. He had taken something many had seen, the fall of an apple, and explained it in a new way.

17 Devise Write a caption for this figure explaining how Newton related the moon to an apple falling to the ground.

_____

_____

_____

_____

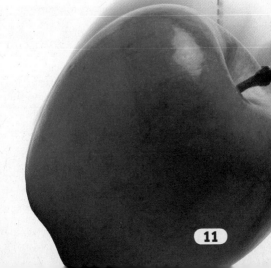

Visual Summary

To complete this summary, circle the correct word or phrase. Then use the key below to check your answers. You can use this page to review the main concepts of the lesson.

What Is Science?

Science is the systematic study of the natural world.

18 The natural sciences are normally divided into the life, earth, and physical / behavioral branches.

19 Science can / can't explain why you think a particular sculpture looks good.

Scientific explanations are supported by empirical evidence.

20 Empirical evidence includes observations / personal beliefs.

21 Scientific explanations are / are not able to be proved false.

Science can seem to be very dull work, but scientists are often very creative people.

22 Scientists are often creative in designing / comparing experiments.

23 Creative explanations must / need not rely on new observations.

Answers: 18 physical; 19 can't; 20 observations; 21 are; 22 designing; 23 need not

24 Hypothesize Why is it important that a scientist be both very logical and very creative?

Vocabulary

Fill in the blanks with the term that best completes the following sentences.

1 The study of _____ involves the study of the natural world.

2 Science uses _____ to support its explanations.

Key Concepts

3 Distinguish You just bought a book titled *The Most Beautiful Artworks of the Century*. Is this likely to be a science book? Explain.

_____
_____
_____

4 Determine A manufacturer claims its cleanser works twice as fast as any other. Could tests be performed to support the claim? Explain.

_____
_____
_____
_____

5 Contrast What is empirical evidence and what is it not?

_____
_____
_____
_____

6 Identify What are two ways in which scientists can show creativity?

_____
_____
_____

Critical Thinking

Use this table to answer the following questions.

Color of flower	Number of butterfly visits	Number of moth visits
Red	11	0
Yellow	13	1
White	0	24

7 Distinguish For a science fair project, Ina wanted to investigate if flower color influenced the attraction of butterflies and moths. She made the table after observing the visits of butterflies and moths over a one-day period. Did she collect empirical evidence? Explain.

_____
_____
_____
_____

8 Infer Ina concludes that color does influence the attraction of butterflies and moths. Do you think this was a logical conclusion? Explain.

_____
_____
_____
_____

9 Judge Does being creative in doing science mean that a scientist should make things up? Why?

_____
_____
_____
_____

Scientific Knowledge

ESSENTIAL QUESTION

How do we know about the world we live in?

By the end of this lesson, you should be able to identify examples of scientific knowledge and describe how they may change with new evidence.

This scientist is a paleontologist. She is very carefully removing small pieces of rock from fossilized bones. She is trying to uncover the fossil without damaging it.

Engage Your Brain

1 Conclude Fill in the blank with the word or phrase that you think correctly completes the following sentences.

A scientific _____describes a basic principle of nature that always occurs under certain conditions.

A scientific model doesn't need to be something physical. It can also be a mathematical _____

A good scientific theory is one that _____ the most evidence.

2 Predict Look at the two plants in the photo. What is different about the plant on the left? What do you think may have happened to it? How do you know this?

_____
_____
_____
_____

Active Reading

3 Apply Many scientific words, such as *model*, also have everyday meanings. Use context clues to write your own definition of the word *model*.

Example sentence

The **model** introduced by the automaker this

year was a great improvement.

_____
_____

Example sentence

Rita was a **model** student.

_____
_____
_____
_____

Vocabulary Terms

- theory
- model
- law

4 Identify This list contains the vocabulary terms you'll learn in this lesson. As you read, circle the definition of each term.

Explain That!

What are some types of scientific explanations?

5 Identify As you read, underline examples of scientific theories and models.

Science attempts to explain the world around us. Scientists make observations to collect information about the world. They then develop explanations for the things we see around us. Examples of scientific explanations are theories, models, and laws.

Theories

A scientific **theory** is a well-supported explanation about the natural world. Scientific theories have survived a great deal of testing. Theories explain the observations scientists have made. Scientists also use theories to make predictions about what they may not have seen yet. Theories are powerful things in science. They are much stronger than a hunch made by only one person.

Plate tectonics (playt tek•TAHN•ikz) is an example of a scientific theory. It states that Earth's outer layer is divided into individual plates. The plates move over Earth's surface and carry the landmasses with them.

The theory changed the study of Earth science greatly. Scientists found it could explain many things about the forces that shape Earth's surface. For example, they observed that most major earthquakes occur close to where plates meet and press against each other. In fact, scientists have yet to observe anything that opposes the theory. Plate tectonics helped scientists understand many natural events, such as mountain formation, volcanic eruption, and earthquake activity. It is a powerful scientific theory.

At this plate boundary in northeast Iceland, you can see the ground splitting.

© Houghton Mifflin Harcourt Publishing Company • Image Credits: © Geoff Renner/Robert Harding/World Imagery/Corbis

Models

A scientific **model** is a representation of something in the natural world. Models allow scientists to study things that may be too large, too small, or in some way too difficult to study.

Again, be careful of how you think of a model. In science, models do not need to be physical things. A model can be a computer program or a mathematical equation. A model is anything familiar that helps scientists understand anything not familiar. Scientists use models to help them understand past, present, and even future events.

For example, if the land masses on Earth are moving, Earth's surface would not have looked the same millions of years ago. Scientists cannot know for sure what Earth's surface looked like. They can, however, attempt to make a model of it.

Maps are one example of a scientific model. Below are maps of what Earth's surface looks like today and what scientists think it looked like about 225 million years ago. The model shows that all land was once one big mega-continent. Scientists refer to this continent as *Pangaea* (pan•JEE•uh). The model shows how today's continents once formed Pangaea. Of course, the model of Pangaea does have its limitations. It does not allow scientists to study the "real thing," but it can give them a better sense of what Pangaea was like.

Active Reading

6 Infer What is the theory that can explain the model of Pangaea?

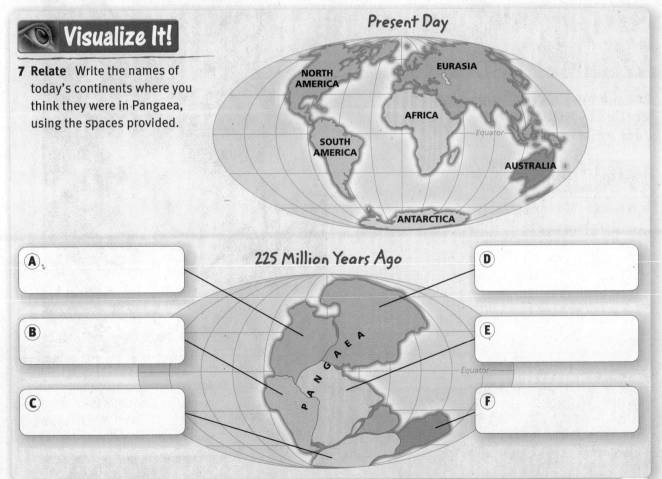

Visualize It!

7 Relate Write the names of today's continents where you think they were in Pangaea, using the spaces provided.

Present Day

NORTH AMERICA
EURASIA
AFRICA
SOUTH AMERICA
AUSTRALIA
ANTARCTICA
Equator

225 Million Years Ago

A
B
C
D
E
F

P A N G A E A

Equator

Laws

Theories and models often are modified as we learn more about the natural world. A scientific **law** describes a basic principle of nature that always occurs under certain conditions.

There are many scientific laws. The law of inertia states that an object in motion or at rest will stay in motion or at rest unless a force acts on it. Charles' law states that, at a constant pressure, as the temperature of a gas increases, its volume increases. Notice that laws simply tell you what to expect. For example, from the law of inertia, you can expect that an object at rest will stay at rest. Unlike a law in society, which is established, enforced, and sometimes changed, scientific laws are eternal and unchangeable.

Laws can be expressed in different ways. A law can be a statement or a mathematical equation. For example, Charles' law can be expressed mathematically as $V_1 T_2 = V_2 T_1$. This is just another way of showing the relationship between the volume and the temperature of a gas at a constant pressure.

Every branch of science has its scientific laws. In geology, the law of superposition states that any one layer of rock is always younger than the layer below it. Therefore, younger layers of rock will always overlie older layers. Again, the law is simply a description of what is seen.

Sedimentary rock is formed by particles carried by wind and water. Layers in the rock build up over time.

Visualize It!

8 Infer Why would the lower layers in the sedimentary rock shown above be older than the upper layers in the same rock?

_____

_____

_____

_____

_____

Think Outside the Book Inquiry

9 Apply Describe how a scientific law is like a societal law. Describe how it is different. Which type of law is more restrictive?

Bending the Law

WEIRD SCIENCE

Mutual Attraction

The law of gravity is a well-known scientific law. It states that the attraction of two masses to each other gets greater the larger the masses are and the closer they are. Isaac Newton first stated the law in the 1600s. He did not give a theory to explain gravity. He just described it.

Over 200 years later, Albert Einstein gave a theory that might explain how gravity works. He suggested that space curved around large masses. You can imagine the effect as similar to putting a heavy ball atop a tightly-stretched blanket. The more massive the ball, the more the blanket will curve. Large objects like stars curve space a great deal.

Bending Space

Scientists have proposed that vast amounts of unseen dark matter exist in outer space based on how its gravity affects the light from distant galaxies. The light appears to curve.

Throw a Curve!

Einstein proposed that large objects, like planets and stars, warped space. Gravity was the result of smaller objects "falling" down this warped space. The illustration shows how a large object, like the sun, warps space.

Extend

Inquiry

10 Identify How was Newton's description of gravity a law and not a theory?

11 Describe Describe a way you might try demonstrating Einstein's theory of gravity to a friend.

12 Infer Using Einstein's theory of gravity, explain why it's hard to notice the attraction of the small things on Earth to each other.

Consider the *Source*

What makes good scientific knowledge?

What makes a good scientific theory or model? Good scientific knowledge does not always last forever. Theories and models often change with new evidence. The best scientific theories and models are those that are able to adapt to explain new observations.

The theory of light is an interesting example of how scientific knowledge can adapt and change. Scientists debated the theory of light for some time. At one time, scientists saw light as particles, and later as waves. The wave theory, however, seemed to explain more about light. For a long time, scientists accepted it. Light is still often depicted as waves.

Today, however, scientists view light as having both a particle nature and a wave nature. In a sense, the particle theory of light did not die. It was good scientific knowledge. It was just incomplete.

Most scientists today probably would agree that all scientific knowledge is incomplete. Even the best theories do not explain everything. Indeed, this is the reason science continues. The goal of science is best described as the attempt to explain as much as possible and to be open to change as new evidence arises. As you study science, perhaps the best advice to remember is that everything we know about the world is simply the best guesses we have made. The best scientists are those that are open to change.

Active Reading

13 Identify As you read, underline two different theories for light.

Visualize It!

14 Apply The figures below model reflection in both the particle and wave theories of light. How might the particle theory have explained light passing through some objects and not others?

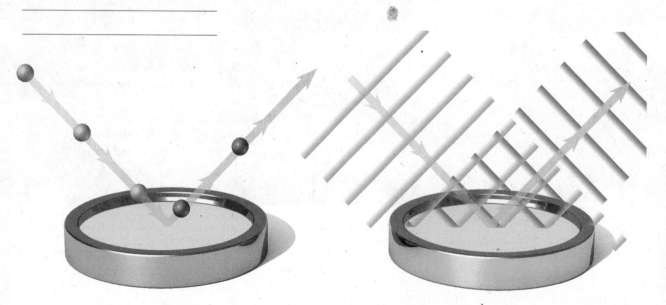

Reflection in the particle theory of light.

Reflection in the wave theory of light.

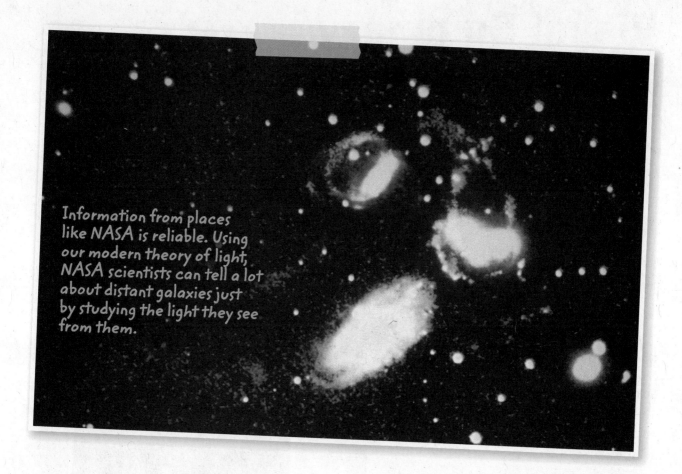

Information from places like NASA is reliable. Using our modern theory of light, NASA scientists can tell a lot about distant galaxies just by studying the light they see from them.

What makes a good source?

Where can you find good scientific knowledge? Because information can easily be sent across the world, you need to be able to separate reliable sources from the unreliable.

In general, you can trust information that comes from a government or university source. Nationally recognized research institutions, such as NASA, the Mayo Clinic, or Salk Institute, are also good sources. These institutions rely on their reputations. They would suffer if their information was found to be not accurate.

You should be cautious with publications more than a few years old. Remember, scientific knowledge changes. You should also be cautious of information made by those trying to sell a product. More often, their motivation is to use science to make money, not to instruct.

15 Evaluate In the table below, check the appropriate box indicating whether information from each source would be reliable, somewhat reliable, or not very reliable. Discuss your choices with others.

Government science agency (.gov site)	☐ reliable ☐ somewhat reliable ☐ not very reliable
Advertising agency	☐ reliable ☐ somewhat reliable ☐ not very reliable
Science textbook from 1985	☐ reliable ☐ somewhat reliable ☐ not very reliable
University (.edu site)	☐ reliable ☐ somewhat reliable ☐ not very reliable
Personal webpage	☐ reliable ☐ somewhat reliable ☐ not very reliable

Visual Summary

To complete this summary, check *true* or *false* below each statement. Then, use the key below to check your answers. You can use this page to review the main concepts of the lesson.

Scientific Knowledge

Models, Theories, and Laws
Models, theories, and laws are three types of scientific knowledge.

16 Any hunch you have is as good as a scientific theory.

☐ True   ☐ False

17 Models can represent things that are too far away or too small to see.

☐ True   ☐ False

18 Scientific laws can be thought of as general descriptions of what we see happening around us.

☐ True   ☐ False

Adaptability of Scientific Knowledge
Scientific knowledge is durable, because it is open to change.

19 Scientific theories can change when new evidence is found.

☐ True   ☐ False

Reliable Sources
Sources for reliable scientific information include government agencies and research institutions, like NASA.

20 You can trust scientific information from advertisers, because they are selling a product.

☐ True   ☐ False

Answers: 16 False; 17 True; 18 True; 19 True; 20 False

---

21 Relate Laws can be explained by theories. If a theory changes, does it mean the law must change? Explain.

Lesson Review

Vocabulary

Fill in the blank with the term or phrase that best completes the following sentences.

1 A(n) _____ is a representation of something in the natural world.

2 Unlike in society, a scientific _____ is simply a description of what we see.

3 A scientific _____ has a lot of support and is more than just a "hunch."

Key Concepts

4 Differentiate How might a theory relate to a model?

_____

_____

_____

5 Discriminate Where might you look on the Internet to find good scientific information about an illness?

_____

_____

6 Identify What two types of scientific knowledge can be expressed as mathematical equations?

_____

_____

7 Analyze Scientific theories can change over time as new information is discovered. If a scientific theory changes, does this mean that it was not a good theory to begin with?

_____

_____

_____

_____

Critical Thinking

The gravity of the sun and the moon affects tides on Earth. The model below shows the positions of the sun, the moon, and Earth during a spring tide. Use it to answer questions 8 and 9.

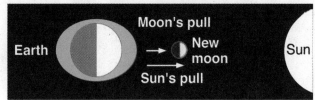

8 Analyze How does this model make it easier for someone to understand the sun's and the moon's influences on the tides?

_____

_____

_____

9 Evaluate What do you think are the limitations of this model?

_____

_____

_____

_____

_____

10 Evaluate Do you agree or disagree with the following statement? Explain your answer. Both theories and laws can be used to predict what will happen in a situation that has not already been tested.

_____

_____

_____

_____

_____

_____

_____

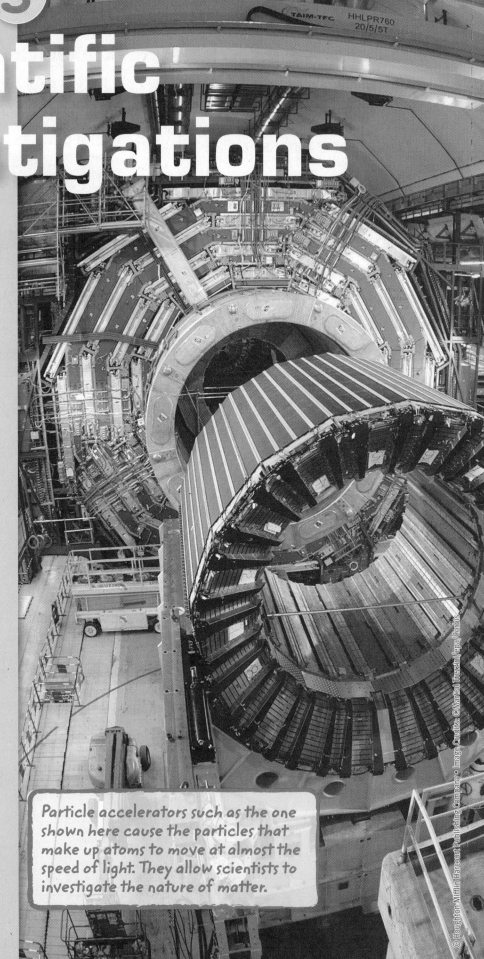

Scientific Investigations

ESSENTIAL QUESTION

How do scientist work?

By the end of this lesson, you should be able to summarize the processes and characteristics of different kinds of scientific investigations.

📘 Indiana Standards

NOS 6.1 Make predictions and develop testable questions based on research and prior knowledge.

NOS 6.2 Plan and carry out investigations as a class, in small groups or independently often over a period of several class lessons.

NOS 6.3 Collect quantitative data with appropriate tools or technologies and use appropriate units to label numerical data.

NOS 6.4 Incorporate variables that can be changed, measured or controlled.

NOS 6.5 Use the principles of accuracy and precision when making measurement.

NOS 6.6 Test predictions with multiple trials.

NOS 6.7 Keep accurate records in a notebook during investigations.

NOS 6.8 Analyze data, using appropriate mathematical manipulation as required, and use it to identify patterns and make inferences based on these patterns.

NOS 6.9 Evaluate possible causes for differing results (valid data).

NOS 6.10 Compare the results of an experiment with the prediction.

Particle accelerators such as the one shown here cause the particles that make up atoms to move at almost the speed of light. They allow scientists to investigate the nature of matter.

1 Evaluate Check T or F to show whether you think each statement is true or false.

T F

☐ ☐ Every scientific investigation is an experiment.

☐ ☐ You could do an experiment to see if eating breakfast helps students raise their grades.

☐ ☐ Scientists need fancy instruments to do experiments.

☐ ☐ Scientists must repeat an experiment for it to be useful.

2 Infer What do you think the scientists who gathered the data for this graph were studying?

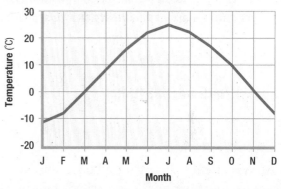

Average Temperature in Minneapolis

_____

_____

_____

_____

Active Reading

3 Synthesize The word *experiment* comes from the Latin word *experiri*, meaning "to try." What do you think the meaning of the word *experiment* is?

_____

_____

_____

_____

Vocabulary Terms

- experiment
- observation
- hypothesis
- variable
- data

4 Apply As you learn the meaning of each vocabulary term in this lesson, write a sentence of your own using the term.

Scientists at Work!

What are some types of scientific investigations?

Scientists carry out investigations to learn about the natural world—everything from the smallest particles to the largest structures in the universe. The two main types of scientific investigations are *experiments* and *observations*.

Scientific Investigations

Experiments

An **experiment** is an organized procedure to study something under controlled conditions. Experiments are often done in a laboratory. This makes it easier to control factors that can influence a result. For example, a scientist notices that a particular kind of fish is becoming less common in a lake near his home. He knows that some fish need more oxygen than others. To find out if this local fish species is being harmed by decreased oxygen levels, he might do the following experiment. First, he measures oxygen levels in the lake. Then, he sets up three tanks of water in a laboratory. The water in each tank has a different level of oxygen. Other factors that might affect fish, such as temperature, are the same in all three tanks. The scientist places the same number of fish in each tank. Then he collects information on the health of the fish.

Active Reading **5 Infer** Why would the scientist in the example want the temperature to be the same in all three tanks?

_____

_____

_____

_____

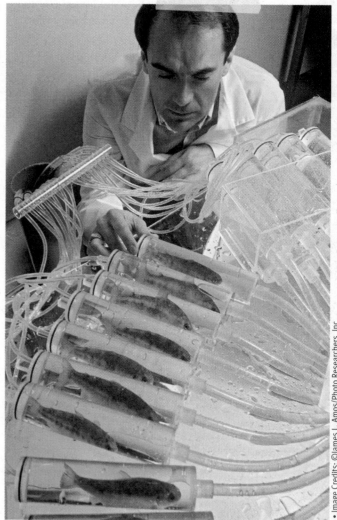

This scientist is studying salmon in a controlled laboratory experiment.

© Houghton Mifflin Harcourt Publishing Company • Image Credits: ©James L. Amos/Photo Researchers, Inc.

Visualize It!

6 Analyze List the factors that the scientists cannot control in the field investigation shown in this picture.

_____

_____

_____

_____

_____

This scientist is observing salmon in their natural environment in Mongolia.

Active Reading

7 Identify As you read, underline reasons why a scientist might choose to do observations that do not involve experiments.

Other Types of Investigations

Observation is the process of obtaining information by using the senses. The word can also refer to the information obtained by using the senses. Although scientists make observations while conducting experiments, many things cannot be studied under controlled conditions. For example, it is impossible to create or manipulate a star. But astronomers can observe stars through telescopes.

Observations of the natural world are generally less precise than experiments because they involve factors that are not controlled by scientists. However, they may give a better description of what is actually happening in nature.

Important scientific observations can be made anywhere. The scientist who experiments with fish and oxygen levels in the example you read on the opposite page might observe a lake to find out which animals and plants live in it. His observations may or may not support the findings of the laboratory experiment.

Another type of investigation is the creation of models, which are representations of an object or system. Models are useful for studying things that are very small, large, or complex. For example, computer models of Earth's atmosphere can help scientists forecast the weather.

Why Ask Why?

What are some parts that make up scientific investigations?

The work that scientists do can vary greatly. Some scientists spend much of their time outdoors. Others mostly work in laboratories. Yet scientific investigations have some basic things in common.

Hypothesis

A **hypothesis** (hy•PAHTH•ih•sis) is a testable idea or explanation that leads to scientific investigation. A scientist may think of a hypothesis after making observations or after reading findings from other scientists' investigations. The hypothesis can be tested by experiment or observation.

For example, imagine that while outside after a snowstorm, you notice that plant leaves seem to be healthy. You wonder how the leaves stayed alive because the temperature was below freezing during the storm. You also know that heat does not pass as easily through snow as it does through air. With this information, you could make the following hypothesis: "The leaves on the plants stayed healthy because the snow cover slowed their loss of heat." This is a hypothesis that could be tested by an experiment.

These scientists are removing a mummy discovered in Peru. Because Peru's climate is so dry, some DNA is preserved.

Mummies such as this one have been preserved by the cold, dry climate of the Andes Mountains in Peru.

Think Outside the Book

8 Apply Think of something you have observed or read about that interests you. Then, write a hypothesis about it.

This scientist is analyzing DNA found in a mummy from Peru.

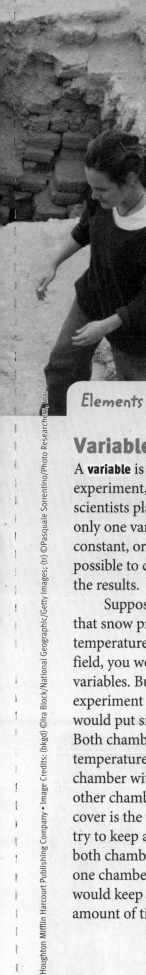

Elements of Investigations

Variables

A **variable** is any factor that can change in an experiment, observation, or model. When scientists plan experiments, they try to change only one variable and keep the other variables constant, or unchanged. However, it may not be possible to control all the variables that can affect the results.

Suppose you decide to test the hypothesis that snow protects leaves from below-freezing temperatures. If you did the experiment in the field, you would not be able to control many variables. But you could set up a laboratory experiment to test your hypothesis. First, you would put similar plants in two chambers. Both chambers would be cooled to the same temperature. You would cover the plants in one chamber with snow and leave the plants in the other chamber without a snow cover. The snow cover is the variable you want to test. You would try to keep all the other variables the same in both chambers. For example, when you open one chamber to pour snow on the plants, you would keep the other chamber open for the same amount of time.

Observations and Data

Data are information gathered by observation or experimentation that can be used in calculating or reasoning. Everything a scientist observes in an investigation must be recorded. The setup and procedure of an experiment also need to be recorded. By carefully recording this information, scientists make sure that they will not forget important details.

The biologist shown in the photo above would record the results of her analysis of mummy DNA. In addition, she would identify the type of tissue that was examined—whether it came from a tooth or bone, for example. She would also record the type of instrument used to examine the tissue and the procedures that she followed. All of these details may be important when she reports her findings. The information will also help other scientists evaluate her work.

9 Identify What kind of data would you record for an experiment testing whether snow protects leaves from cold temperatures?

_____

_____

_____

Many Methods

What are some scientific methods?

Scientific methods are the ways in which scientists answer questions and solve problems. There is no single formula for an investigation. Scientists do not all use the same steps in every investigation or use steps in the same order. They may even repeat some of the steps. The following graphic shows one path a scientist might follow when conducting an experiment.

Visualize It!

10 Diagram Using a different color, draw arrows showing another path a scientist might follow if he or she were observing animals in the wild.

Defining a Problem

After making observations or reading scientific reports, a scientist might be curious about some unexplained aspect of a topic. A scientific problem is a specific question that a scientist wants to answer. The problem must be well-defined, or precisely stated, so that it can be investigated.

Planning an Investigation

A scientific investigation must be carefully planned so that it tests a hypothesis in a meaningful way. Scientists need to decide whether an investigation should be done in the field or in a laboratory. They must also determine what equipment and technology are required and how materials for the investigation will be obtained.

Forming a Hypothesis and Making Predictions

When scientists form a hypothesis, they are making an educated guess about a problem. A hypothesis must be tested to see if it is true. Before testing a hypothesis, scientists often make predictions about what will happen in an investigation.

Identifying Variables

Before conducting a controlled experiment, scientists identify all the variables that can affect the results. Then they decide which variable should change and which ones should stay constant. Some variables may be impossible to control.

Collecting and Organizing Data

The data collected in an investigation must be recorded and properly organized so that they can be analyzed. Data such as measurements and numbers are often organized into tables, spreadsheets, or graphs.

Interpreting Data and Analyzing Information

After they finish collecting data, scientists must analyze this information. Their analysis will help them draw conclusions about the results. Scientists may have different interpretations of the same data because they analyze it using different methods.

Defending Conclusions

Scientists conclude whether the results of their investigation support the hypothesis. If the hypothesis is not supported, scientists may think about the problem some more and try to come up with a new hypothesis to test. When they publish the results of their investigation, scientists must be prepared to defend their conclusions if they are challenged by other scientists.

Use It or Lose It

How are scientific methods used?

Scientific methods are used to study any aspect of the natural world. They can also be used in the social sciences, which focus on human society. It is often harder to control variables in the social sciences. Nevertheless, these fields are made stronger by the methods developed for physical, life, and earth science.

Think Outside the Book Inquiry

11 Plan Suppose that you want to investigate something using scientific methods. First, define a problem. Then, plan a scientific investigation using the methods discussed in the previous pages.

Use of Scientific Methods

Different Situations Require Different Methods

After forming a hypothesis, scientists decide how they will test it. Some hypotheses can be tested only through observation. Others must be tested in laboratory experiments. However, observation and experiments are often used together to build scientific knowledge. For example, if you want to test the strength of a metal used in airplane construction, you may study it in a laboratory experiment. But after conducting the experiment, you may want to inspect airplanes that have flown for a period of time to see how the metal holds up under actual flight conditions.

If an investigation does not support a hypothesis, it is still useful. The data from the investigation can help scientists form a better hypothesis. Scientists may go through many cycles of testing and data analysis before they arrive at a hypothesis that is supported.

12 Apply Give another example of a scientific investigation that would require both observation and experiments.

_____

_____

_____

_____

Scientific Methods Are Used in Physical Science

Physical science includes the study of physics and chemistry. Scientists have used physics to figure out how gecko lizards stick to walls and ceilings.

Various explanations of the gecko's unique ability have been developed. Some scientists thought that static electricity helps geckos stick to walls. Others thought that the gecko produces a kind of glue from its feet. But experiments and observations did not support these hypotheses.

When a team of researchers studied the gecko's feet with a microscope, they found that each foot was covered with hundreds of thousands of tiny hairs. After measuring the force exerted by each hair against a surface, they came up with two possible hypotheses. One hypothesis was that geckos stick to walls because the hairs interact with a thin film of water. The other hypothesis was that the weak forces between the hairs and a surface combine to produce a force great enough to hold the gecko to the surface.

The team designed an experiment to test both hypotheses. The experiment showed that the force of a gecko's hair against a surface was the same whether or not the surface had any water on it. The scientists concluded that the gecko sticks to walls because of the combined forces of the hairs on its feet.

How does this gecko walk on the ceiling?

gecko foot

13 Relate Fill in the flow chart below with examples of the scientific methods used in the gecko investigation.

Defining a Problem

↓

Forming a Hypothesis

↓

Collecting Data

This is a close-up picture of the tiny hairs on a gecko's foot.

Getting It Right

What are some ways to confirm that an investigation is valid?

Scientific investigations should be carried out with great care. But scientists are only human. Sometimes they fail to plan properly. They may make mistakes in collecting or analyzing data because they are in a hurry. On rare occasions, irresponsible scientists produce false results on purpose. Fortunately, there are procedures that help expose flawed investigations.

Evaluating Investigations

Peer Review

Before a study is published, it is read by scientists who were not involved in the investigation. These peer reviewers evaluate the methods used in a study and the conclusions reached by its authors. For example, a reviewer could decide that an experiment was not properly controlled. Or a reviewer might say that the sample used in a survey was too small to be meaningful. Even after a study is published, scientists must answer questions raised by other scientists.

Replication

An important way to confirm an investigation is for other scientists to replicate it, or repeat the investigation and obtain the same findings. To make this possible, scientists must disclose the methods and materials used in the original study when they publish their findings. Not every investigation needs to be replicated exactly. But if a study cannot be supported by the results of similar investigations, it will not be accepted by the scientific community.

WEEKLY

NEWS *Special Edition*

FUSION OR FICTION?

Was this experiment flawed?

WHY CAN'T RESULTS BE REPLICATED?

In 1989 a pair of scientists reported that they had accomplished cold nuclear fusion. The possibility of a cheap source of energy excited the public. However, other scientists considered the claim impossible. Attempts to replicate the findings failed.

Think Outside the Book

14 Evaluate Research the cold fusion news reported in 1989. Write a few paragraphs about the study. Did the study exhibit the characteristics of a good scientific investigation? Explain.

© Houghton Mifflin Harcourt Publishing Company • Image Credits: © Yves Forestier/Sygma/Corbis

How can you evaluate the quality of scientific information?

Scientific information can be found on the Internet, in magazines, and in newspapers. It can be difficult to decide which information should be trusted. The most reliable scientific information is published in scientific journals.

The most reliable information on the Internet is on government or academic webpages. Other sites should be examined closely for errors, especially if they are selling things.

Although the lab reports that you prepare for school might not be published, you should try to meet the same standards of published studies. For example, you should provide enough information so that other students can replicate your results.

Visualize It!

15 Apply List two examples of poor scientific methodology found in this student's lab report.

_____

_____

_____

Problem: How does the amount of sunlight affect the growth of plants?

Hypothesis: Plants that spend more time in the sunlight will grow taller because plants grow taller in warm conditions.

Changed variables: amount of time in the sunlight and type of plant

Constant variables: amount of water

Materials: plants, water, sunlamp, ruler

Procedure: Take the plants and put them under the sunlamp. Leave some of them under the lamp for longer amounts of time than others.

Data Table:

Plant number	Length of time in sunlight per day	Height after 2 weeks
1	5 hours	8 inches
2	8 hours	12 inches

16 Assess Would you believe this result or would you be skeptical of it? Explain your answer.

_____   _____

_____   _____

_____   _____

_____   _____

_____   _____

Visual Summary

To complete this summary, circle the correct word from each set of words. Then, use the key below to check your answers. You can use this page to review the main concepts of the lesson.

Scientific Methods
Scientists use scientific methods to answer questions and solve problems.

19 A problem / hypothesis / variable must be tested to see if it is supported.

20 Scientists must decide which data / hypotheses / variables will stay constant in an experiment.

Types of Scientific Investigations
Scientists carry out investigations through experiments and observation.

17 Scientific investigations that involve testing a single variable are called models / experiments / theories.

18 Hypotheses / Models / Observations are often made before other types of investigations are done.

Scientific Investigations

Characteristics of Good Scientific Investigations
There are procedures that separate good scientific investigations from flawed ones.

21 The findings of experiments are generally not accepted until they are published / proven / replicated.

22 The most reliable scientific information comes from reporters / scientists / companies working in a particular field.

Answers: 17. experiments, 18. observations, 19. hypothesis, 20. variables, 21. replicated, 22. scientists

23 Relate What is the relationship between a scientific problem and a hypothesis?

Lesson Review

Vocabulary

Fill in the blank with the term that best completes the following sentences.

1 A(n) _____ determines what will be tested in a scientific experiment.

2 All of the _____ gathered in an investigation must be recorded.

3 A good scientific _____ can be repeated by someone else and the same results will be found.

Key Concepts

Example	Scientific Method
4 Identify Scientists use instruments to record the strength of earthquakes in an area.	
5 Identify Scientists decide that in an experiment on fish, all the fish will be fed the same amount of food.	

6 Identify What are two key characteristics of a good scientific investigation?

_____

_____

_____

_____

7 Explain Why is it important for scientists to share information from their investigations?

_____

_____

_____

_____

_____

Critical Thinking

Use this drawing to answer the following questions.

water   salt water

8 Analyze Which variable changes in the investigation depicted in the drawing?

_____

_____

9 Conclude Identify one variable that is kept constant for both groups in this experiment.

_____

_____

10 Infer What kind of data might be collected for this experiment?

_____

_____

_____

11 Evaluate Which is less likely to be a reliable source of information, the webpage of a university or the webpage of a scientist who is trying to sell a new invention? Explain.

_____

_____

_____

_____

_____

_____

Representing Data

ESSENTIAL QUESTION

In what ways can you organize data to fully understand them?

By the end of this lesson, you should be able to use tables, graphs, and models to display and analyze scientific data.

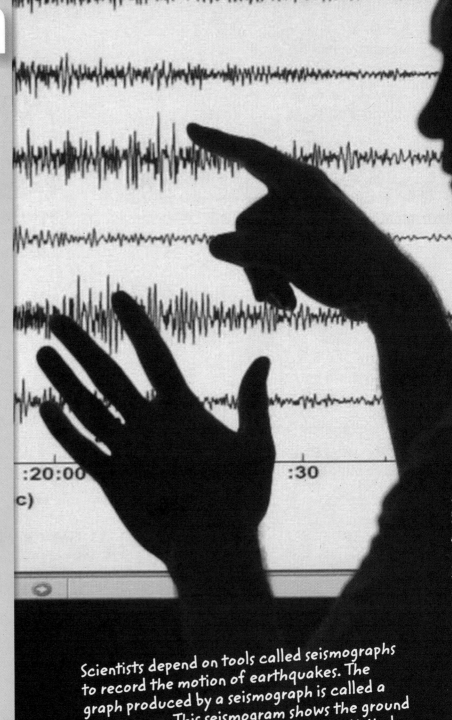

Scientists depend on tools called seismographs to record the motion of earthquakes. The graph produced by a seismograph is called a seismogram. This seismogram shows the ground motion of an earthquake that hit the United Kingdom in 2007.

Indiana Standards

NOS 6.3 Collect quantitative data with appropriate tools or technologies and use appropriate units to label numerical data.

NOS 6.7 Keep accurate records in a notebook during investigations.

NOS 6.8 Analyze data, using appropriate mathematical manipulation as required, and use it to identify patterns and make inferences based on these patterns.

NOS 6.11 Communicate findings using graphs, charts, maps and models through oral and written reports.

Engage Your Brain

1 Predict Check T or F to show whether you think each statement is true or false.

T   F

☐ ☐ Scientific models have been used to show results of scientific experiments.

☐ ☐ Certain types of graphs are better than others for displaying specific types of data.

☐ ☐ Most graphs are confusing and unnecessary.

☐ ☐ If something can be shown in a table, then it should not be shown in a graph.

2 Evaluate Name two things about the model shown that are similar to the object that the model represents. Then name two things about the model that are different.

_____

_____

_____

_____

_____

_____

_____

Active Reading

3 Apply Many words, such as *model*, have multiple meanings. Use context clues to write your own definition for each meaning of the word *model*.

Example sentence
After getting an *A* on another test, Julio's teacher told him he was a <u>model</u> student.

model:

_____

_____

Example sentence
For her science project, Samantha created a <u>model</u> of the solar system.

model:

_____

_____

Vocabulary Term

• model

4 Identify As you read this lesson, underline examples of models.

Crunching Data!

How do scientists make sense of data?

Before scientists begin an experiment, they often create a data table for recording their data. *Data* are the facts, figures, and other evidence gathered through observations and experimentation. The more data a scientist collects, the greater is the need for the data to be organized in some way. Data tables are one easy way to organize a lot of scientific data.

Scientists Organize the Data

A data table provides an organized way for scientists to record the data that they collect. Information that might be recorded in data tables are times, amounts, and *frequencies*, or the number of times something happens.

When creating a data table, scientists must decide how to organize the table into columns and rows. Any units of measurement, such as seconds or degrees, should be included in the column headings and not in the individual cells. Finally, a title must always be added to describe the data in the table.

The data table below shows the number of movie tickets sold each month at a small theater.

Movie Tickets Sold Monthly

Month	Number of tickets
January	15,487
February	12,654
March	15,721
April	10,597
May	10,916
June	11,797
July	18,687
August	18,302
September	16,978
October	10,460
November	11,807
December	17,497

 **Do the Math** You Try It

5 Extend Circle the row in the table that shows the month when the greatest number of tickets were sold. Then circle the row that shows the month when the least number of tickets were sold. Finally, subtract the least number from the greatest number to find the range of the number of tickets sold.

_____ − _____ = _____

greatest number of tickets   least number of tickets   range

Scientists Graph and Analyze the Data

In order to analyze their collected data for patterns, it is often helpful for scientists to construct a graph of their data. The type of graph they use depends upon the data they collect and what they want to show.

A *bar graph* is used to display and compare data in a number of separate categories. The length, or height, of each bar represents the number in each category. For example, in the movie theater data, the months are the categories. The lengths of the bars represent the number of tickets sold each month.

Other types of graphs include line graphs and circle graphs. A *line graph* is often used to show continuous change over time. A *circle graph,* or pie chart, is used when you are showing how each group of data relates to all of the data. For example, you could use a circle graph to depict the number of boys and girls in your class.

Active Reading

6 Interpret What kind of data would you display in a bar graph?

_____

_____

_____

_____

Visualize It!

7 Analyze The data in the graph below are the same as the data in the table at the left. During what three months are the most movie theater tickets sold?

_____

_____

_____

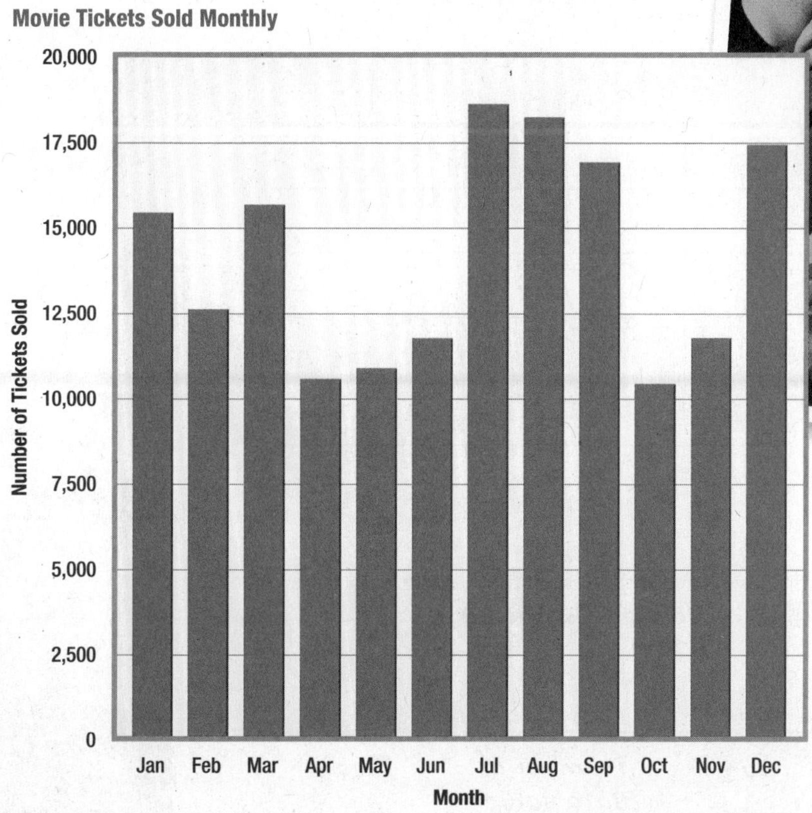

Movie Tickets Sold Monthly

8 Extend What other kind of data could you collect at home that might show differences over the course of a year?

_____

_____

_____

Graph It!

What do graphs show?

Graphs are visual representations of data. They show information in a way that is often easier to understand than data shown in tables. All graphs should have a title explaining the graph.

In certain types of graphs, the data displayed on the horizontal axis are the values of the *independent variable*. This is the variable that is deliberately manipulated in an investigation. For example, if you collect rainfall data over four weeks, the week number is the independent variable because you have chosen to collect data once a week. You have manipulated the time interval between data collections.

The data displayed on the vertical axis are the values of the *dependent variable*. This is the variable that changes as a result of the manipulation of one or more independent variables. For example, the inches of rainfall per week is the dependent variable.

Visualize It!

9 Complete The data at the right show the amount of rain, in inches, that fell in each of four weeks at a school. Use the empty table below to organize the data. Include a title for the table, the column headings, and all of the data.

Week 1: 0.62 in.
Week 2: 0.40 in.
Week 3: 1.12 in.
Week 4: 0.23 in.

Title

Headings

Data

Do the Math You Try It

10 Extend The average, or mean, of the rainfall data is the sum of the data values divided by the number of data values. Calculate the mean of the rainfall data. Round your answer to the nearest hundredth.

$$\underline{\quad} + \underline{\quad} + \underline{\quad} + \underline{\quad} = \underline{\quad}$$

Weeks 1 through 4   Sum

$$\underline{\quad} \div \underline{\quad} \approx \underline{\quad}$$

Sum   Number of   Mean
     data values

How are graphs constructed?

To make a bar graph of the rainfall data at the left, first draw a horizontal axis and a vertical axis. Next, write the names of the categories to be graphed along the horizontal axis. Include an overall label for the axis as well. Next, label the vertical axis with the name of the dependent variable. Be sure to include the units of measurement. Then create a scale along the axis by marking off equally spaced numbers that cover the range of the data collected. For each category, draw a solid bar using the scale on the vertical axis to determine the height. Make all the bars the same width. Finally, add a title that describes the graph.

© Houghton Mifflin Harcourt Publishing Company • Image Credits: (bkgd) ©Comstock Select/Corbis; (br) ©Dorling Kindersley/Getty Images

Active Reading

11 Identify As you read, number the steps used to construct a graph. You may want to rely on signal words that indicate a new step, such as *then* or *next*.

12 Graph Construct a bar graph of the rainfall data at the left. On the lines provided, include a title for the graph and axis labels. Use a scale of 0.20 in. for the horizontal axis, and label the bars on the vertical axis.

Visualize It!

13 Analyze During which week was the rainfall amount approximately twice what it was during week 4? Use your graph to explain.

Title: _____

Amount of Rainfall (in.)

0.0

Week 1 ____ ____ ____

This rain gauge is used to gather and measure liquid precipitation.

Model It!

What types of models can be used to represent data?

A crash-test dummy, a mathematical equation, and a road map are all models that represent real things. A **model** is a representation of an object or a process that allows scientists to study something in greater detail. A model uses something familiar to help you understand something that is not familiar.

Models can represent things that are too small to see, such as atoms. They can also represent things that are too large to see fully, such as Earth. Models can be used to explain the past and the present. They can even be used to predict future events. Two common kinds of scientific models are physical models and mathematical models.

Active Reading

14 Apply As you read, underline different ways that scientists use models.

Physical Models

Physical models are models that you can touch. Toy cars, models of buildings, maps, and globes are all physical models. Physical models often look like the things they represent. For example, this model of Earth shows that Earth is divided into three layers—the crust, the mantle, and the core. The table below shows the estimated densities of each of Earth's layers.

Density of Earth's Layers

Layer	Density (g/cm³)
crust	2.7–3.3
mantle	3.3–5.7
core	9.9–13.1

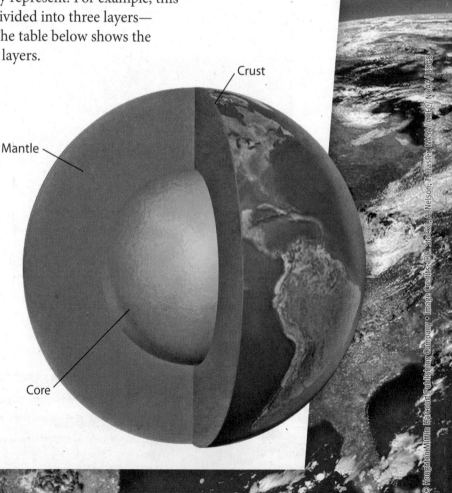

Crust

Mantle

Core

Visualize It!

15 Analyze The table shows the estimated densities of Earth's layers. Write the layers of Earth in order of most dense to least dense.

_____

_____

Mathematical Models

Every day, people try to predict the weather. One way to predict the weather is to use mathematical models. A *mathematical model* is made up of mathematical equations and data. Some mathematical models are simple. These models allow you to calculate things such as how far a car will travel in an hour or how much you would weigh on the moon.

Other mathematical models are so complex that computers are needed to process them. Some of these very complex models, such as population growth, have many variables. Sometimes, certain variables that no one thought of exist in the model. A change in any variable could cause the model to fail.

What are some benefits and limitations of models?

Just as models can represent things that are too small or too large to see, models benefit scientists in other ways. They allow scientists to change variables without affecting or harming the subject that they are studying. For example, scientists use crash-test dummies to study the effects of car accidents on people.

All models are limited because they are simplified versions of the systems that they try to explain. Simplification makes a model easy to understand and use. However, information is left out when a model is made.

Additionally, all models can change. Models can change if a scientist finds new data or thinks about concepts in a new way. Sometimes, new technology challenges existing models. Or, technology may help create new models that allow us to understand the world differently.

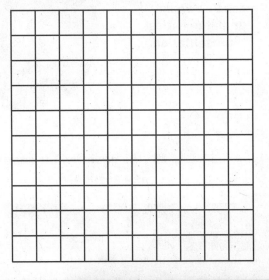

Do the Math You Try It

16 Calculate The air we breathe is made up of 78% nitrogen, 21% oxygen, and 1% other gases. Use three different colored pencils to color the appropriate number of squares in the grid for each of these percentages.

Think Outside the Book Inquiry

17 Apply With a classmate, discuss the benefits and limitations of globes and maps as physical models.

Visual Summary

To complete this summary, check the box that indicates true or false. Then, use the key below to check your answers. You can use this page to review the main concepts of the lesson.

Representing Data

A scientific model can be a visual or mathematical representation.

T   F
☐   ☐   **18** The equation for density is a physical model.

A table can be used to record and organize data as it is being collected.

Density of Earth's Layers	
Layer	Density (g/cm³)
crust	2.7–3.3
mantle	3.3–5.7
core	9.9–13.1

T   F
☐   ☐   **19** Units of measurement should be placed with the column or row headings in tables.

A graph is a visual display of data that shows relationships between the data.

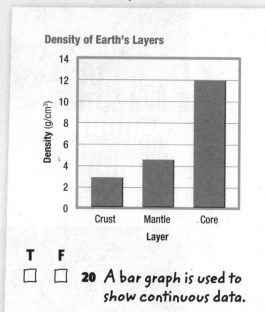

Density of Earth's Layers

T   F
☐   ☐   **20** A bar graph is used to show continuous data.

21 Synthesize Provide an example of something in the natural world that could be depicted in each of the following ways: a table, a graph, and a model. (Use examples not given in this lesson.)

Lesson Review

Vocabulary

Fill in the blank with the term that best completes the following sentences.

1 A(n) _____ can be a visual or mathematical representation of an object or a process.

2 After data are collected, they are often arranged in a(n) _____.

3 Data can be arranged in visual displays called _____ to make identifying trends easier.

Key Concepts

4 Differentiate How is a physical model different from a mathematical model?

_____

_____

_____

5 Identify A data table shows the height of a person on his birthday each year for ten years. What is the dependent variable?

_____

_____

_____

6 Judge Which kind of graph would be best for depicting data collected on the weight of a baby every month for six months?

_____

_____

_____

7 Apply What kind of model would you use to represent the human heart?

_____

_____

_____

_____

Critical Thinking

Use this graph to answer the following questions.

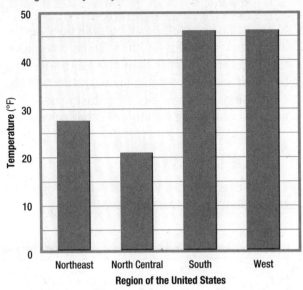

Average January Temperatures

8 Identify Which region of the country has the coldest January temperatures?

_____

9 Estimate How can you use the graph to determine the range of the temperature data? Write the range to the nearest degree.

_____

_____

_____

_____

_____

10 Apply Give an example of a physical model and explain one limitation of the model. Then give an example of a mathematical model and explain one limitation.

_____

_____

_____

_____

_____

Making Conclusions from Evidence

Indiana Standards

NOS 6.3 Collect quantitative data with appropriate tools or technologies and use appropriate units to label numerical data.

NOS 6.8 Analyze data, using appropriate mathematical manipulation as required, and use it to identify patterns and make inferences based on these patterns.

In scientific investigations, you will be asked to collect data and summarize your findings. Sometimes, a set of data can be interpreted in more than one way and lead to more than one conclusion. A reliable investigation will allow you to make conclusions that are supported by the data you have collected, and that reflect the findings of other scientists.

Tutorial

Take these steps as you analyze findings and evaluate a conclusion made from the findings.

Flu Prevention Breakthrough

A medical study has shown that a new drug, Compound Z, protected children from the flu. The results of the study that was conducted last year showed that only 5% of students who were taking Compound Z were affected by the flu. During the same period of time, 20% of the general population was affected by the flu.

Researchers do not know exactly how Compound Z protects children from the flu.

1 What conclusion is made by the study? Identify the conclusion or interpretation of the data that is being made in the study.

2 What evidence or data is given and does the data support the conclusion? Identify all the observations and findings that are presented to support the conclusion. Decide whether the findings support the conclusion. Look for information and data in other studies that replicate the experiments and verify the conclusion.

3 Should other data be considered before accepting the conclusion as true? There may be more than one way to interpret findings of scientific work, and important questions left unanswered. When this happens, plan to make observations, look for more information, or do further experiments that could eliminate one explanation as a possibility.

Other data should be considered before the conclusion above can be supported. For example, data should be gathered to determine the percentage of children who were not taking Compound Z and got the flu. And, within the 20% of the general population who got the flu, what percentage were children?

You Try It!

Climate change is one of the most debated issues in modern science.

In the past 100 years, Earth's average global temperature has risen more than 0.74 °C. In 2008, the cold La Niña current in the Pacific caused the average global temperature to drop, but the global average was still warmer than any year from 1880 to 1996. The concentration of the greenhouse gas carbon dioxide (CO_2), rose from by about 76 parts per million from 1958 to 2008. Many people interpret this to mean that human activity is causing global climate change. However, evidence from the geologic record shows that Earth's climate has experienced even larger climate changes in the past.

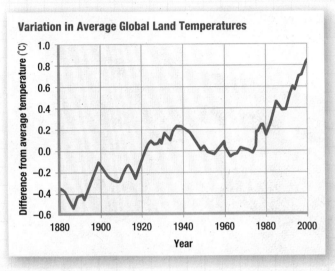

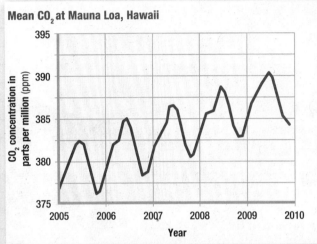

1 Gathering Data The graphs shown above are taken from a study on climate change. Identify trends or patterns that you observe in the graphs.

_____

_____

_____

_____

2 Making a Conclusion Draw a conclusion that is supported by the data you describe. Summarize your conclusion in a single paragraph.

_____

_____

_____

_____

_____

_____

_____

3 Analyzing Data Which conclusions are supported by the data in the graphs? Which conclusions are not supported by the data?

_____

_____

_____

_____

4 Making Predictions What other data do you need to further support your conclusion?

_____

_____

_____

_____

Take It Home

Find an article that makes a conclusion based on a scientific study. Evaluate the conclusion and determine whether the evidence given supports the conclusion. Bring the article to class and be prepared to discuss.

Science and Society

ESSENTIAL QUESTION

How does science affect our lives?

By the end of this lesson, you should be able to describe the impact that science has had on society and the role of scientists throughout history and today.

Science deepens our understanding of the world and improves the quality of our lives. Science also influences the ways we interact with one another.

© Houghton Mifflin Harcourt Publishing Company • Image Credits: © Milk Photographie/Corbis

Engage Your Brain

1 Predict Check T or F to show whether you think each statement is true or false.

T F

☐ ☐ Science has very few career opportunities and does not impact our lives.

☐ ☐ Good scientists are creative, logical thinkers and keen observers.

☐ ☐ Only scientists are capable of scientific thinking.

2 Identify List the first five things you did this morning after you woke up. Put a checkmark next to any of these things that were made possible by the work of scientists.

_____

_____

_____

_____

_____

Active Reading

3 Derive Many English words have their roots in other languages. Use the Latin word below to make an educated guess about the meaning of the word *scientific*.

Latin word	Meaning
scientia	knowledge

Example sentence

After years of <u>scientific</u> experimentation and observation, the researcher reported a major discovery.

Vocabulary

4 Identify As you read, place a question mark next to any words you don't understand. When you finish reading the lesson, go back and review the text that you marked. If the information is still confusing, consult a classmate or a teacher.

scientific:

_____

_____

A Mighty Impact!

What does science affect?

For centuries, people have been asking questions and seeking answers. Even before there were people known as scientists, people engaged in scientific exploration. Science has had a great impact on all of us. Most likely, you can think of ways science affects your life already. You may be surprised to discover how large the influence of science really is.

The Way We Think

How do you see yourself? People used to think that Earth was the center of the universe. They thought the objects in the sky moved around them. They thought the sky existed only for them to look at. These beliefs made people feel very special.

We now know Earth is just one planet in one solar system. Earth orbits the sun and rotates once each day. When people realized this, they had to rethink their place in the universe. They had to rethink just how special they believed themselves to be. Scientific findings affect how we see ourselves.

5 Apply As you read, underline examples of advances in science that have impacted you today.

Space science, 100 BCE

Space science, Today

Visualize It!

6 Explain Why might learning of the vastness of outer space affect how people see themselves?

_____

_____

_____

Modern agriculture is changing where we can grow things. These basil plants are grown using hydroponics on a floating barge!

The Way We Live Our Lives

Our daily activities have been affected by advances in science, too. In industrialized countries, many people enjoy clean water and sanitary living conditions. Scientists frequently find new ways for us to conserve and protect resources. Medicines have eliminated many health concerns. Cars, trains, and airplanes take us where we want to go. Weather forecasts tell us what to expect, and then we can dress appropriately. Satellites and cables allow us to communicate with others from all over the world. Most of these things were not even imaginable just 100 years ago.

Society became more complex with the beginning of farming. People joined together to grow crops for the benefit of all. World population has been able to grow so large today because of advances in farming. We can now grow crops in soil once thought to be infertile. Thanks to science, we can even grow plants with no soil at all! Hydroponics (HY•druh•pahn•iks), or growing plants without soil, may one day allow us to live in outer space.

7 Compare When your grandparents were growing up, they ate mostly foods grown or produced near them. Describe how the food you eat is different from the food your grandparents ate as a result of science's impact on agriculture and transportation.

_____

_____

_____

_____

It Takes All Kinds

Who contributes to science?

Myra Logan was the first female to perform open-heart surgery. She also played piano and contributed to the civil rights movement. Leonardo da Vinci was a great artist. He also drew designs for flying machines and studied human anatomy. Logan and da Vinci are just two of the many people who have contributed to science. People who contribute to science come from all backgrounds, fields of interest, and skill groups. So who contributes to science?

Active Reading **8 Identify** As you read, underline some characteristics of people who do scientific research.

Those Who Do Scientific Research

Scientists are curious, creative, and enjoy solving problems. Scientists do research to answer questions and to investigate and challenge prevailing ideas. Some scientists work in life science, like immunologist Cesar Milstein, who researches viruses like AIDS. Physicist Chien Shiung Wu, a physical scientist, spent time in laboratories with radioactive elements. Mary Leakey, an archaeologist and Earth scientist, unearthed ape fossils in the field.

Leonardo da Vinci and his design for a flying machine

Klaus Radermacher uses robots and computers to make custom prosthetics. Prosthetics are artificial body parts that can replace missing, damaged, or diseased parts.

Visualize It!

9 Predict What problem might Radermacher have been trying to solve when he began his research?

_____

_____

_____

_____

People in Many Fields

The number of men and women who get paid to do scientific research is not very high. However, the opportunities open to those who are willing to learn and think like a scientist in other fields are almost limitless.

Many occupations use science. Medical and dental technicians help doctors and dentists keep people in good health. Architects use the laws of physics to design stable homes and offices. People who dye and style hair use chemistry when mixing hair dye and relaxing solutions. In the growing field of forensics, police officers use science to help them solve crimes. Auto engineers use physics to design aerodynamic cars.

Forensic technician

Auto engineers design vehicles.

10 Infer What might motivate someone to study forensics?

_____

_____

_____

_____

_____

11 Describe Fill in the second column with a description of how a person might use science in each of the careers. Fill in the last row of the table with a career you might like to have.

Career	Science applications
Firefighter	
Pharmacist	
Chef	

Anyone Who Asks Scientific Questions and Seeks Answers

An important point to remember is that anyone can think and act like a scientist and do science. Have you wondered why certain plants always flower at about the same time of year? Have you wondered what the center of Earth is like? Have you wondered why sugar dissolves faster in hot liquids than in cold ones? If you have asked questions and thought about finding the answers, you have acted like a scientist.

Do not be embarrassed to ask impossible questions. A lot of what we take for granted today was once thought impossible. You may even discover that you are asking the same questions many scientists still ask.

Active Reading

12 Identify As you read, underline questions that science can help you answer.

Inquiry

13 Relate Questions about the world can pop into your mind at any time. Write down something you've thought about recently as you've gone about your usual activities. Then write how you might investigate it.

_____

_____

_____

_____

_____

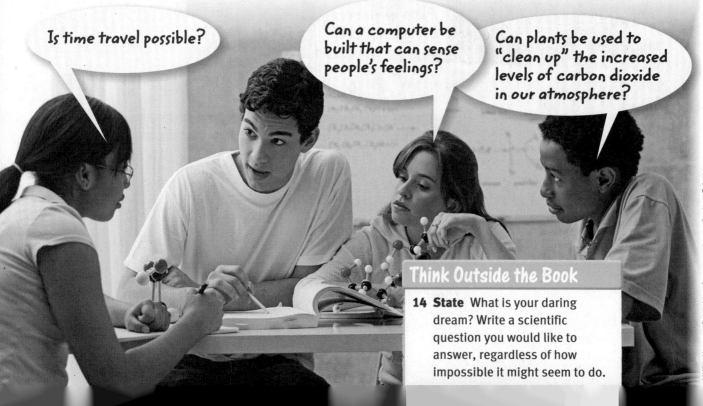

Is time travel possible?

Can a computer be built that can sense people's feelings?

Can plants be used to "clean up" the increased levels of carbon dioxide in our atmosphere?

Think Outside the Book

14 State What is your daring dream? Write a scientific question you would like to answer, regardless of how impossible it might seem to do.

Let the Games Begin

Robotics tournaments, model car races, and science fairs offer opportunities for you to explore and share your interest in science with others. You may even win a prize doing it!

Robot Challenge
This robot was built and operated by students at a San Diego robotics competition. Robots aren't just for competitions, though. Robots can be built for search and rescue missions, manufacturing, and other roles.

Fast and Friendly
This student is racing a model car he built. The car is powered by hydrogen fuel cells. Hydrogen fuel cells may be an environmentally friendly power source for cars of the future!

Extend

Inquiry

15 Select Which would you be most interested in entering: a science fair, a robotics competition, or a model car race? Why?

16 Identify Use the Internet to find a science competition in your area. Consider visiting it!

17 Plan Make a poster, draw a model, or write a paragraph explaining an idea you have for a science competition.

Visual Summary

To complete this summary, check the box that indicates true or false. Then use the key below to check your answers. You can use this page to review the main concepts of the lesson.

Science and Society

Impact of Science

The work of scientists has changed the way we live and think about the world.

	T	F	
18	☐	☐	As science has advanced, technology has advanced.
19	☐	☐	Agriculture and medicine are affected by science.

Who Does Science

Scientists are curious about the world and enjoy exploring it. They may work in laboratories, in the field, or in other locations.

	T	F	
20	☐	☐	Only people who work in science use scientific thinking skills.
21	☐	☐	People from all backgrounds, interests, and cultures can contribute to science.

22 Predict Identify two changes in your world that might occur if funding for scientific research were cut drastically.

© Houghton Mifflin Harcourt Publishing Company • Image Credits: (t) ©Frances Roberts/Alamy; (b) ©Dung Vo Trung/Corbis

Lesson Review

Vocabulary

Fill in the blanks with the term or phrase that best completes the following sentences.

1 A(n) _____ may work in a lab or in the field and conducts research to discover new things.

2 The impact of science on _____ includes improvements in medicine, new technology, and more diverse food sources.

Key Concepts

3 Apply Identify two areas of science or technology that make your life easier, safer, or otherwise better than your grandparents' lives were.

_____

_____

_____

_____

_____

4 List Name three characteristics of scientists that are important to their work but are also found in nonscientists.

_____

_____

Critical Thinking

5 Devise Imagine that one tree outside your school looks unhealthy, although all the other trees seem healthy and strong. Describe how you could apply scientific thinking to the situation.

_____

_____

_____

_____

_____

Use this table to answer the following questions.

Scientists and Their Contributions		
When	**Who**	**What**
1660s	Robert Hooke	Identified and coined the word *cells* using early microscopes
Late 1700s	Antoine Lavoisier	Identified oxygen and oxygen's role in respiration and combustion
Early 1900s	Marie Curie	Experimented with radioactivity and identified new chemical elements
Early 1980s	Luis Alvarez	Used geological evidence to show that a meteor struck Earth and proposed that this led to the extinction of dinosaurs

6 Categorize The main branches of science are life science, physical science, and Earth and space science. Identify a branch of science that was affected by each of these scientists.

_____

_____

_____

7 Justify Why do you think the work of scientists cannot be pinned down to a single year?

_____

_____

_____

8 Debate Do you think the contributions of these scientists are still valuable, even though some were made hundreds of years ago? Explain your answer.

_____

_____

_____

_____

_____

My Notes

Unit 1 **Summary**

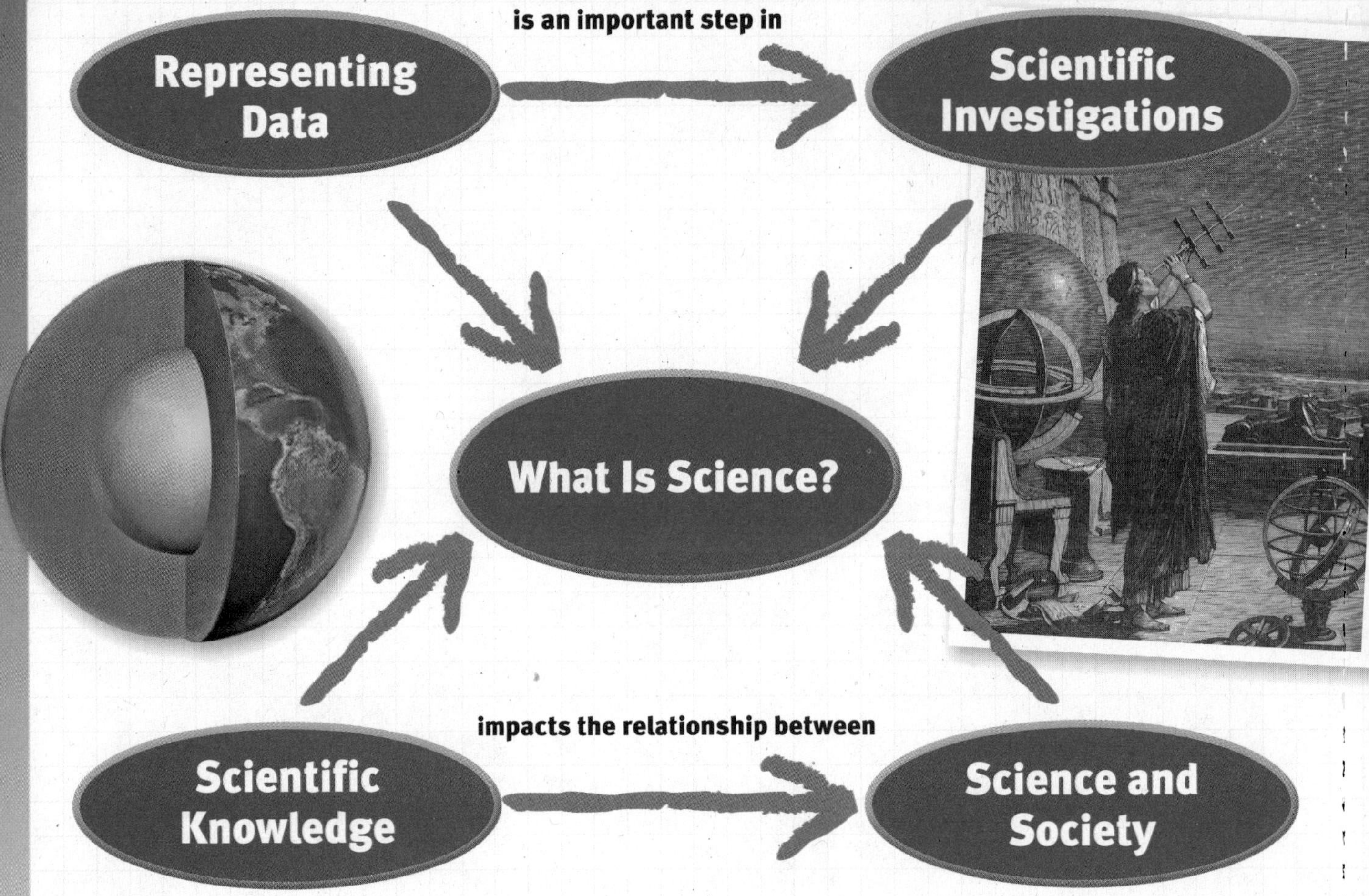

Representing Data

is an important step in →

Scientific Investigations

What Is Science?

Scientific Knowledge

impacts the relationship between →

Science and Society

---

1 Interpret The Graphic Organizer above shows that scientific knowledge can impact society. Explain why this is so.

_____

_____

_____

2 Distinguish Explain the difference between scientific investigations and scientific knowledge.

_____

_____

_____

_____

3 Judge "Representing data is not an important part of scientific investigations." Describe why this statement is incorrect.

_____

_____

_____

4 Support Explain why there is not one "scientific method."

_____

_____

_____

ISTEP+ Review

Name _____

Multiple Choice

1 Scientists do many types of work. Their work often includes making field observations, conducting surveys, creating models, and carrying out experiments. Which must be done BEFORE conducting an experiment?

    A. develop testable questions based on research and prior knowledge

    B. make a physical or mathematical representation of an object or process

    C. observe plants or animals in their natural environment

    D. collect data from the unregulated world for comparative purposes

2 Raul wants to investigate how the angle of a ramp affects the speed of an object rolling down the ramp. He can conduct his investigation in a number of different ways. Which INVESTIGATION should he perform?

    A. observe different bicyclists riding down hills of varying steepness

    B. record the time it takes one bicyclist to ride down hills of varying steepness

    C. perform an experiment in a lab in which the angle of the ramp is controlled and the speed of a rolling cart is measured

    D. observe video of various objects rolling down hills and estimate the angle of the hill and the speed of the object

3 Lida fills two balloons with the same amount of air. Balloon 1 remains at room temperature. Lida places balloon 2 in a freezer. The following diagram shows that the volume of the balloon in the freezer shrinks.

Balloon 1   Balloon 2

Which statement is a LAW that describes the results of Lida's experiment?

    A. decreasing the amount of a gas decreases its temperature

    B. the volume of a gas increases when the temperature decreases

    C. the volume of a gas decreases when the temperature decreases

    D. decreasing temperature decreases the volume of a gas because molecules slow down

4 Ryan made a list of activities that are scientific and activities that are not scientific. Which activity should Ryan classify as NOT SCIENTIFIC?

   A. climbing to the top of a very tall mountain

   B. using a meterstick to measure the height of a plant every day

   C. sorting rocks by color and size

   D. accurately noting how many hours the sun shines each day

5 The diagram shows Niels Bohr's theory about how electrons are arranged in atoms. He thought electrons traveled on specific paths around a nucleus. The current theory is that electrons exist in certain cloudlike regions around a nucleus.

Atom

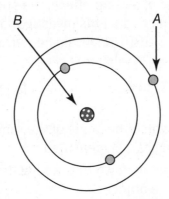

How would a model of the current theory DIFFER from Bohr's model?

   A. it would be the same as Bohr's model

   B. object A would differ from Bohr's model

   C. object B would differ from Bohr's model

   D. both objects A and B would differ from Bohr's model

6 Three lab groups perform experiments to determine the density of samples of iron. They rounded the density to the nearest whole number.

Group	Mass of iron (g)	Volume of iron (cm³)	Density of iron (g/cm³)
1	32	4	8
2	48	6	8
3	?	5	8

What is the MASS of iron for group 3?

   A. 5 g

   B. 8 g

   C. 40 g

   D. 64 g

7   Scientists use different tools to investigate how and why things happen. Here are some examples of tools that can be used to gather data:

- a graduated cylinder
- a measuring cup
- a graduated beaker

Which unit might be used for data obtained using ALL of these tools?

A. meter

B. kilogram

C. milliliter

D. grams per liter

8   A student predicted that black paper will get warmer in sunlight than white paper. He performed an experiment to test his prediction four times. The black paper was warmer three times, and the white paper was warmer once. What might have caused the RESULTS to be DIFFERENT?

A. A thermometer measures temperature differently on white paper and on black paper.

B. Variables other than the color of paper might not have been constant.

C. Results just differ from trial to trial and do not have to be the same.

D. The color of the paper does not affect the temperature of the paper.

Constructed Response

9   A doctor treated a patient for cancer. A scientist discovered a vaccine that prevented a disease.

Who MOST LIKELY used repeated trials to achieve results? Explain.

_____

_____

Which person do you think made more of an impact on society? Explain.

_____

_____

Extended Response

10 The law of superposition states that the rock layer below another layer is older. The diagram below shows layers of rock. The diagonal line shows how the rock layers moved near a fault as the result of an earthquake.

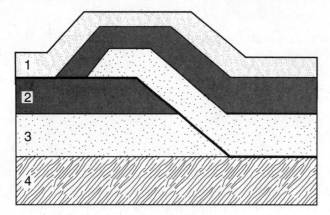

How do you know that layer 3 is older than layer 2?

_____

_____

Which layer most likely contains material that formed other layers? Why?

_____

_____

Explain whether the law of superposition applies to the rock layers around the fault.

_____

_____

_____

Why might a scientist find fossils of organisms that lived at different times in layer 1?

_____

_____

Matter

© Houghton Mifflin Harcourt Publishing Company • Image Credits: (bkgd) ©Sven-Erik Arndt/photolibrary; (t) ©Ken Tannenbaum/age fotostock

Core Standard

Explain that all objects and substances in the natural world are composed of matter in different states with different properties.

What do you think?

A large iceberg floats in water, but an anchor sinks. What is different about these two objects that causes them to behave differently in water?

Unit 2
Matter

Lesson 1
Introduction to Matter 70

Lesson 2
States of Matter 84
6.1.1, 6.1.2

Think Science 94
NOS 6.2, NOS 6.4

Lesson 3
Changes of State 96
6.1.3

Unit Summary.................... 112

🔵 **ISTEP+ Review** 113

🔵 **Indiana Standards**

As citizens of the constructed world, students will participate in the design process. Students will learn to use materials and tools safely and employ the basic principles of the engineering design process in order to find solutions to problems.

DP 6.1 Identify a need or problem to be solved.

DP 6.2 Brainstorm potential solutions.

DP 6.4 Select a solution to the need or problem.

CITIZEN SCIENCE

Deep Freeze

When outdoor temperatures reach 0 °C (32 °F), liquid water can freeze to form a solid. Snow, ice, sleet, and hail are examples of the solid form of water. Understanding the properties of water in its different states helps people to stay safe during icy weather.

1 Think About It

How is liquid water different from solid ice?

_____

_____

_____

_____

This truck is applying salt to an icy road. Do you know what effect this will have on the ice?

② Ask a Question

What precautions should be taken during freezing weather?

Would you believe that the ice on these fruit trees is actually protecting them? The trees are being sprayed with water, which turns to ice in freezing weather. The formation of ice helps to keep the plants warmer. With a partner, research some of the ways in which people protect other areas and living things during icy weather.

Think about the impact that ice could have on

☐ plants

☐ people

☐ bodies of water

☐ pets and other animals

③ Apply Your Knowledge

A List some areas in your community that could be affected by the formation of ice.

_____

_____

_____

B What precautions could your community take before freezing weather arrives to keep these areas safe?

_____

_____

_____

_____

C What could your community do after freezing weather arrives to keep these areas safe?

_____

_____

_____

_____

Take It Home

How do you prepare your home for icy weather? Draw a map of your home and the surrounding area. Identify areas on your map that could become hazardous in freezing conditions. Then, create a plan for protecting these areas.

Lesson 1

Introduction to Matter

ESSENTIAL QUESTION

What properties define matter?

By the end of this lesson, you should be able to relate mass, weight, volume, and density to one another.

Hot air takes balloons aloft because hot air is less dense than the cooler air around it.

Image Credits: (bkgd) ©Christian Kober/John Warburton-Lee Photography/PhotoLibrary

© Houghton Mifflin Harcourt Publishing Company

Engage Your Brain

1 Describe Fill in the blank with the word or phrase that you think correctly completes the following sentences.

A(n) _____ can hold a greater volume of water than a mug.

A hamster weighs less than a(n)

_____ .

A bowling ball is harder to lift than a basketball because _____

_____ .

2 Explain List some similarities and differences between the golf ball on the left and the table-tennis ball on the right in the photo.

_____

_____

_____

_____

_____

Active Reading

3 Apply Many scientific words, such as *matter*, also have everyday meanings. Use context clues to write your own definition for each meaning of the word *matter*.

Example sentence
What is this gooey <u>matter</u> on the table?

Matter:

_____

_____

_____

Example sentence
Please vote! Your opinions <u>matter</u>.

Matter:

_____

_____

_____

Vocabulary Terms

- matter
- mass
- weight
- volume
- density

4 Identify This list contains the vocabulary terms you'll learn in this lesson. As you read, circle the definition of each term.

What's the MATTER?

What is matter?

Suppose your class takes a field trip to a museum. During the course of the day you see mammoth bones, sparkling crystals, hot-air balloons, and an astronaut's space suit. All of these things are matter.

As you will see, **matter** is anything that has mass and takes up space. Your body is matter. The air that you breathe and the water that you drink are also matter. Matter makes up the materials around you.

However, not everything is matter. Light and sound, for example, are not matter. Light does not take up space or have mass in the same way that a table does. Although air is matter, a sound traveling through air is not.

Active Reading 5 **Explain** How can you tell if something is matter?

_____

_____

_____

Visualize It!

6 Identify Name three examples of matter found in this photo.

_____

_____

_____

What is mass?

You cannot always tell how much matter is in an object simply by observing the object's size. But you *can* measure the object's mass. **Mass** describes the amount of matter in an object.

Compare the two balloons at the right. The digital scales show that the balloon filled with compressed air has a greater mass than the other balloon. This is because the compressed air adds mass to the balloon. Air may seem to be made of nothing, but it has mass. The readings on the scale are in grams (g). A gram is the unit of mass you will use most often in science class.

Objects that are the same size can be made up of different amounts of matter. For example, a large sponge is about the same size as a brick. But the brick contains more matter. Therefore, the brick has a greater mass than the sponge.

The readings on these digital scales show that all matter, even air, has mass.

0.010 g

0.005 g

How does mass differ from weight?

The words *weight* and *mass* are often used as though they mean the same thing, but they do not. **Weight** is a measure of the gravitational force (grav•ih•TAY•shuhn•uhl FAWRS) on an object. Gravitational force keeps objects on Earth from floating into space. The gravitational force between an object and Earth depends partly on the object's mass. The greater that the mass of an object is, the greater the gravitational force on the object will be and the greater the object's weight will be.

An object's weight can change depending on the object's location. For example, you would weigh less on the moon than you do on Earth because the moon has less mass—and therefore exerts less gravitational force—than Earth does. However, you would have the same mass in both places. An object's mass does not change unless the amount of matter in an object changes.

The weight of this dachshund on the moon is about one-sixth of its weight on Earth.

Active Reading 7 **Explain** Why do astronauts weigh less on the moon than they do on Earth?

_____

_____

_____

The balance below works by moving the masses on the right along the beams until they "balance" the pan on the left. Moving the masses changes the amount of force the levers exert on the pan. The more massive the object on the pan, the more force will be needed on the levers to balance the two sides.

8 Infer Would this balance give the same value for mass if used on the moon? Explain.

_____

_____

_____

_____

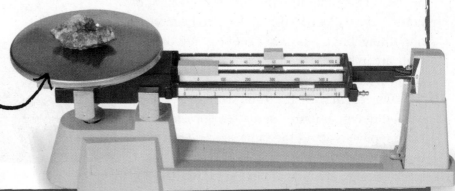

A triple-beam balance can be used to measure the mass of small objects such as this geode fragment.

The spring scale gives weight in pounds (lb).

How are mass and weight measured?

Mass is often measured by using a triple-beam balance such as the one shown above. The balance compares an object's mass to known standards of mass called *countermasses*. The countermasses slide across each of three beams. When the countermasses balance the mass of the object in the balance pan, the pointer will rest at 0. Then, the mass can be read from the position of the countermasses on the beams.

Weight is measured with devices such as the spring scale shown at the left. The spring measures the force between the mass in the pan and Earth. The more massive the object placed in the pan, the more forceful is the attraction between it and Earth, and the more the spring will stretch. Greater stretch means greater weight.

Because weight is a measure of gravitational force, it is given in units of force. You probably are most familiar with weight given in pounds (lb), like the units shown on the scale. The standard scientific unit for weight, however, is the newton (N). A 100-g mass weighs approximately 1 N on Earth. One newton is about one-fourth of a pound.

Measuring Space

How is the amount of space occupied by matter measured?

All matter takes up space. The amount of space that an object takes up, or occupies, is known as the object's **volume.**

Objects with the similar volumes do not always have the same mass. In the photos, the bowling ball and the balloon have about the same volume, but the bowling ball contains a lot more mass than the balloon. You know this because the bowling ball weighs much more than the balloon. The different masses take up about the same amount of space, so both objects have about the same volume.

Active Reading 9 **Define** What does volume measure?

_____

_____

The bowling ball has a lot more mass than the balloon.

The balloon is similar in volume but has much less mass than the bowling ball.

Think Outside the Book Inquiry

10 Infer Big things can look very small when seen from far away. Describe how you know big things far away aren't really small.

How can volume be determined?

There are different ways to find the volume of an object. For objects that have well-defined shapes, you can take a few measurements and calculate the volume using a formula. For objects that are irregularly shaped, such as a rock, you can use water displacement to measure volume. For liquids, you can use a graduated cylinder.

Using a Formula

Some objects have well-defined shapes. For these objects, the easiest way to find their volume is to measure the dimensions of the object and use a formula. Different shapes use different volume formulas. For example, to find the volume of a rectangular box, you would use a different formula than if you were to find the volume of a spherical ball.

To find the volume of a rectangular box, use the following formula:

$$Volume = (length)(width)(height)$$
$$V = lwh$$

The volume of a solid is measured in units of length cubed. For example, if you measure the length, width, and height of a box in centimeters (cm), the volume of the box has units of centimeters multiplied by centimeters multiplied by centimeters, or cubic centimeters (cm^3). In order to calculate volume, make sure that all the measurements are in the same units.

 **Do the Math**   **Sample Problem**

Find the volume of the lunch box.

Identify

A. What do you know?

   length = 25 cm, width = 18 cm, height = 10 cm

B. What do you want to find? Volume

Plan

C. Draw and label a sketch:

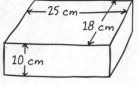

D. Write the formula: $V = lwh$

E. Substitute into the formula: $V = (25 \text{ cm})(18 \text{ cm})(10 \text{ cm})$

Solve

F. Multiply: $(25 \text{ cm})(18 \text{ cm})(10 \text{ cm}) = 4,500 \text{ cm}^3$

G. Check that your units agree: The given units are centimeters, and the measure found is volume. Therefore, the units should be cm^3. The units agree.

Answer: 4,500 cm^3

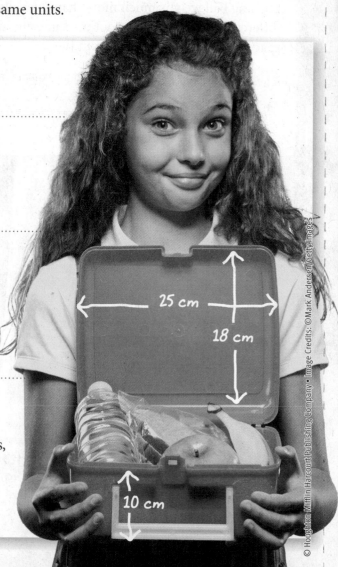

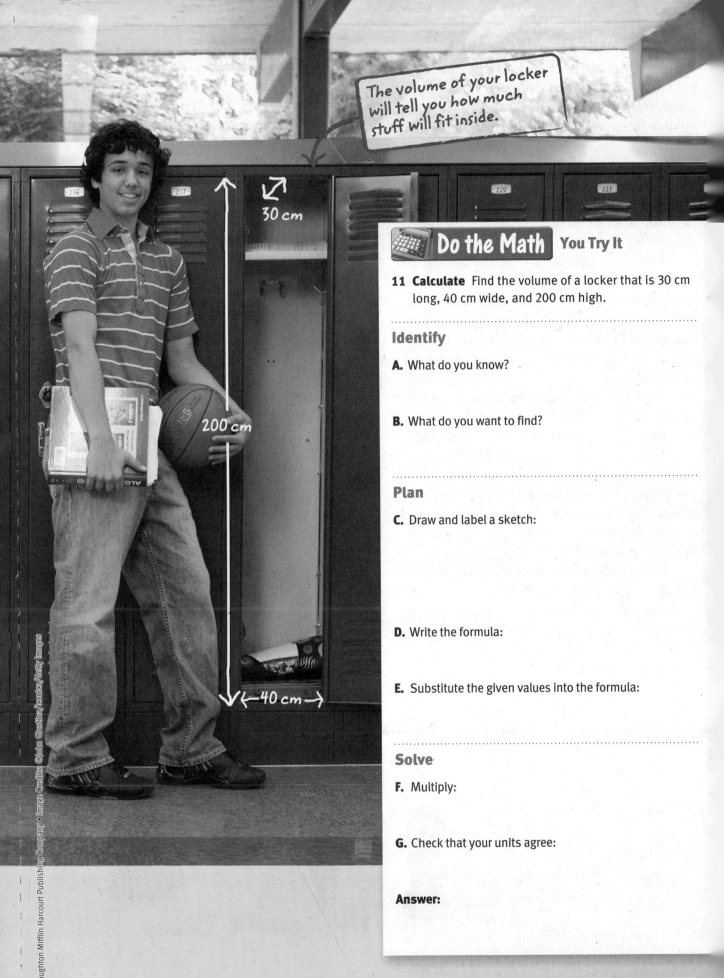

The volume of your locker will tell you how much stuff will fit inside.

30 cm

200 cm

←40 cm→

Do the Math · You Try It

11 Calculate Find the volume of a locker that is 30 cm long, 40 cm wide, and 200 cm high.

Identify

A. What do you know?

B. What do you want to find?

Plan

C. Draw and label a sketch:

D. Write the formula:

E. Substitute the given values into the formula:

Solve

F. Multiply:

G. Check that your units agree:

Answer:

Using Water Displacement

In the lab, you can use a beaker or graduated cylinder to measure the volume of liquids. Graduated cylinders are used to measure liquid volume when accuracy is important. The volume of liquids is often expressed in liters (L) or milliliters (mL). Milliliters and cubic centimeters are equivalent; in other words, 1 mL = 1 cm³. The volume of any amount of liquid, from one raindrop to an entire ocean, can be expressed in these units.

Two objects cannot occupy the same space at the same time. For example, as a builder stacks bricks to build a wall, she adds each brick on top of the other. No brick can occupy the same place that another brick occupies. Similarly, when an object is placed in water, the object pushes some of the water out of the way. This process, called *displacement*, can be used to measure the volume of an irregularly shaped solid object.

In the photos at the right, you can see that the level of the water in the graduated cylinder has risen after the chess piece is placed inside. The volume of water displaced is found by subtracting the original volume in the graduated cylinder from the new volume. This is equal to the volume of the chess piece.

When deciding the units of the volume found using water displacement, it is helpful to remember that 1 mL of water is equal to 1 cm³. Therefore, you can report the volume of the object in cubic centimeters.

Do the Math

You Try It

12 Calculate The two images below show a graduated cylinder filled with water before and after a chess piece is placed inside. Use the images to calculate the volume of the chess piece.

Volume without chess piece = _____

Volume with chess piece = _____

Volume of chess piece = _____

Don't forget to check the units of volume of the chess piece!

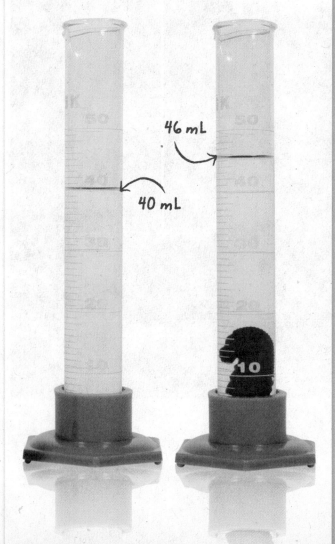

46 mL

40 mL

Packing It In!

What is density?

Mass and volume are properties of all substances. These two properties are related to another property called density (DEN•sih•tee). **Density** is a measure of the amount of mass in a given volume. Objects containing the same amount of mass can take up different amounts of space. For example, the pile of feathers above takes up more space than the tomato. But they have the same mass. This is because the tomato is more dense. The tomato has more mass in a smaller space.

The density of a given substance remains the same no matter how much of the substance you have. For example, if you divide a piece of clay in half, both halves will have the same density as the original piece.

The tomato and the pile of feathers have similar masses, but the tomato has less volume. This means that the tomato is more dense.

🔎 **Active Reading**

13 Explain What is density?

_____

_____

_____

14 Predict Circle the item in each pair that is more dense.

Golf ball	Empty milk carton	Foam ball
Table-tennis ball	Milk carton full of milk	Baseball

How is density determined?

Units for density consist of a mass unit divided by a volume unit. Units that are often used for density are grams per cubic centimeter (g/cm³) for solids, and grams per milliliter (g/mL) for liquids. In other words, density is the mass in grams divided by the volume in cubic centimeters or milliliters.

To find an object's density (D), find its mass (m) and its volume (V). Then, use the given formula to calculate the density of the object.

$$D = \frac{m}{V}$$

The density of water is 1 g/mL (g/cm³). Any object with a density greater than 1 g/mL will sink in water and with a density less than 1 g/mL will float. Density, therefore, can be a useful thing to know. The sample problem below shows how to calculate the density of a volcanic rock called pumice.

Pumice and obsidian are two igneous volcanic rocks with very different densities.

Do the Math

Sample Problem

Pumice is an igneous volcanic rock, formed by the rapid cooling of lava. What is the density of a 49.8 g piece of pumice that has a volume of 83 cm³?

Identify

A. What do you know?

   mass = 49.8 g, volume = 83 cm³

B. What do you want to find? Density

Plan

C. Write the formula: $D = \frac{m}{V}$

D. Substitute the given values into the formula:

   $D = \frac{49.8 \text{ g}}{83 \text{ cm}^3}$

Solve

E. Divide: $\frac{49.8 \text{ g}}{83 \text{ cm}^3} = 0.6$ g/cm³

F. Check that your units agree: The given units are grams and cubic centimeters, and the measure found is density. Therefore, the units should be g/cm³. The units agree.

Answer: 0.6 g/cm³

You Try It

15 Calculate Obsidian is another type of igneous rock. What is the density of a piece of obsidian that has a mass of 239.2 g and a volume of 92 cm³?

Identify

A. What do you know?

B. What do you want to find?

Plan

C. Write the formula:

D. Substitute the given values into the formula:

Solve

E. Divide:

F. Check that your units agree:

Answer:

 **Do the Math**

Sample Problem

A basalt rock displaces 16 mL of water. The density of the rock is 3.0 g/cm³. What is the mass of the rock?

Identify

A. What do you know?

volume = 16 mL, density = 3.0 g/cm³

B. What do you want to find? Mass

Plan

C. Rearrange the formula $D = \frac{m}{V}$ to solve for mass. You can do this by multiplying each side by V.

$$D = \frac{m}{V}$$
$$m = D \cdot V$$

D. Substitute the given values into the formula. Recall that

1 mL = 1 cm³, so 16 mL = 16 cm³.

$$m = \frac{3.0 \text{ g}}{\text{cm}^3} \cdot 16 \text{ cm}^3$$

Solve

E. Multiply: $\frac{3.0 \text{ g}}{\text{cm}^3} \cdot 16 \text{ cm}^3 = 48$ g

F. Check that your units agree: The given units are g/cm³ and mL, and the measure found is mass. Therefore, the units should be g. The units agree.

Answer: 48 g

You Try It

16 Calculate A rhyolite rock has a volume of 9.5 mL. The density of the rock is 2.6 g/cm³. What is the mass of the rock?

Identify

A. What do you know?

B. What do you want to find?

Plan

C. Write the formula:

D. Substitute the given values into the formula:

Solve

E. Multiply:

F. Check that your units agree:

Answer:

Kilauea is the youngest volcano on the Big Island of Hawaii. "Kilauea" means "spewing" or "much spreading," apparently in reference to the lava flows that it erupts.

Visual Summary

To complete this summary, check the box that indicates true or false. Then, use the key below to check your answers. You can use this page to review the main concepts of the lesson.

Relating Mass, Weight, Volume, and Density

Mass is the amount of matter in an object. Weight is a measure of the gravitational force on an object.

Mass

Weight

	T	F	
17	☐	☐	An object's weight is the amount of space it occupies.
18	☐	☐	The mass of an object is equal to its weight.

Volume is the amount of space that matter in an object occupies.
To find the volume of a rectangular box, use the formula:

$$V = lwh$$

	T	F	
19	☐	☐	The volume of a solid can be expressed in units of cm^3.

Density describes the mass of a substance in a given volume.
To find the density of a substance, use the formula:

$$D = \frac{m}{V}$$

	T	F	
20	☐	☐	An object that floats in water is less dense than water.

Answers: 17 F; 18 F; 19 T; 20 T

21 Describe Write a set of instructions that describe how to find the density of an object. Write the instructions so that they work for a regularly shaped object and for an irregularly shaped object.

Lesson Review

Vocabulary

Fill in the blank with the term that best completes the following sentence.

1 _____ is the amount of space that matter in an object occupies.

2 _____ is anything that has mass and takes up space.

3 _____ is the amount of matter in an object.

4 _____ is a measure of the amount of matter in a given amount of space.

5 _____ is a measure of the gravitational force on an object.

Key Concepts

6 **Classify** Is air matter? How can you tell?

_____

_____

7 **Describe** Is it possible for an object's weight to change while its mass remains constant? Explain.

_____

_____

_____

8 **Compare** Explain why a golf ball is heavier than a table-tennis ball, even though the balls are the same size.

_____

_____

9 **Calculate** A block of wood has a mass of 120 g and a volume of 200 cm³. What is the density of the wood?

Critical Thinking

Use this table to answer the following questions.

Substance	Density (g/cm³)
Zinc (solid)	7.13
Silver (solid)	10.50
Lead (solid)	11.35

10 **Identify** Suppose that 273 g of one of the substances listed above displaces 26 mL of water. What is the substance?

_____

_____

11 **Evaluate** How many mL of water would be displaced by 408 g of lead?

_____

_____

12 **Predict** How can you determine that a coin is not pure silver if you know the mass and volume of the coin?

_____

_____

_____

_____

13 **Calculate** A truck whose bed is 2.5 m long, 1.5 m wide, and 1.0 m high is delivering sand for a sand-sculpture competition. About how many trips must the truck make to deliver 7 m³ of sand?

States of Matter

ESSENTIAL QUESTION

How do particles in solids, liquids, and gases move?

By the end of this lesson, you should be able to model the motion of particles in solids, liquids, and gases.

At these hot springs in Japan, you can find water in the form of a solid, a liquid, and a gas.

The hot springs are a favorite winter getaway for these Japanese macaques, or "snow monkeys."

Indiana Standards

6.1.1 Understand that the properties and behavior of matter can be explained by a model which depicts particles representing atoms or molecules in motion.

6.1.2 Explain the properties of solids, liquids and gases using drawings and models that represent matter as particles in motion whose state can be represented by the relative positions and movement of the particles.

Engage Your Brain

1 Describe Fill in the blank with a word or phrase that you think correctly completes the following sentences.

_____ is an example of a solid.

_____ is an example of a gas.

Unlike solids, gases can _____

_____

2 Identify Unscramble the letters below to find substances that are liquids. Write your words on the blank lines.

TWRAE _____

EICJU _____

RIVAENG _____

LIKM _____

PSAOMOH _____

Active Reading

3 Apply Use context clues to write your own definitions for the words *definite* and *occupy*.

Example sentence
Solid is the state of matter that has a <u>definite</u> shape and volume.

definite:

_____

_____

Example sentence
A larger container will allow a gas to <u>occupy</u> more space.

occupy:

_____

_____

Vocabulary Terms

- solid
- liquid
- gas

4 Identify As you read, place a question mark next to any words that you don't understand. When you finish reading the lesson, go back and review the text that you marked. If the information is still confusing, consult a classmate or a teacher.

Particles in Motion

How do particles move in solids, liquids, and gases?

All matter is made of atoms or groups of atoms that are in constant motion. This idea is the basis for the *kinetic theory of matter*. How much the particles move and how often they bump into each other determine the state of matter of the substance. This view of a movie theater helps to illustrate the differences between the particle motion in each of the three common states of matter.

In Solids, Particles Vibrate in Place

A **solid** substance has a definite volume and shape. The particles in a solid are close together and do not move freely. The particles vibrate but are fixed in place. Often, the particles in a solid are packed together to form a regular pattern like the one shown at the right.

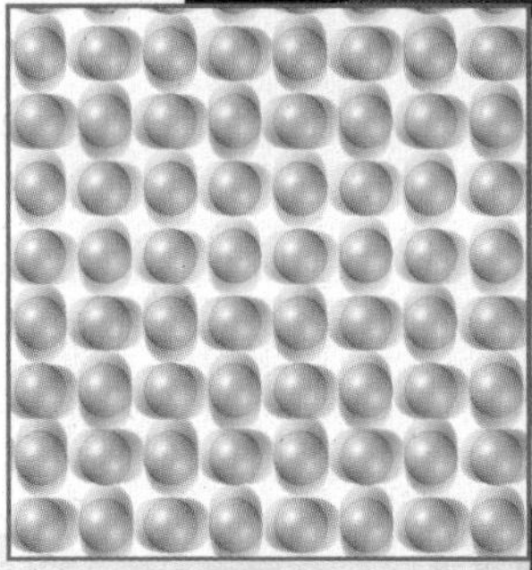

For most substances, the particles in a solid are closer together than the particles in a liquid. For example, the atoms in solid steel are closer together than the atoms in liquid steel. Water is an important exception to this rule. The molecules that make up ice actually have more space between them than the molecules in liquid water do.

Particles in a solid

5 Describe How are particles in a solid like people sitting in a movie theater?

_____

_____

_____

_____

_____

_____

In Liquids, Particles Slide Past One Another

A **liquid** substance has a definite volume but not a definite shape. Particles in a liquid, shown at the right, have more kinetic energy than particles in a solid do. The particles are attracted to one another and are close together. However, particles in a liquid are not fixed in place and can move from one place to another.

Particles in a liquid

6 Describe How are particles in a liquid like people in a movie theater lobby?

_____

_____

_____

_____

_____

In Gases, Particles Move Freely

A **gas** does not have a definite volume or shape. A substance in the gaseous state has particles with the most kinetic energy of the three states. As you can see in the model at the right, gas particles are not as close to one another and can move easily in any direction. There is much more space between gas particles than there is between particles in a liquid or a solid. The space between gas particles can increase or decrease with changes in temperature or pressure.

Particles in a gas

7 Describe How are particles in a gas like people outside of a movie theater?

_____

_____

_____

_____

Shape up!

How does particle motion affect the properties of solids, liquids, and gases?

Imagine what you would see if you put a few ice cubes into a pan on a hot stove. The hard blocks of ice would melt to form liquid water. If the pan is hot enough, the water would boil, giving off steam. Ice, liquid water, and the gaseous water in steam are all made up of the same water molecules. Yet ice looks and behaves differently than water or steam does. The kinetic theory of matter helps to explain the different properties of solids, liquids, and gases.

Active Reading **8 Identify** Underline words or phrases that describe the properties of solids, liquids, and gases.

Solids Have a Definite Volume and Shape

The fishbowl at the right contains a small toy castle. When the castle was added to the glass container, the castle kept its original size and shape. The castle, like all solid substances, has a definite shape and volume. The container does not change these properties of the toy. The particles in a solid are in fixed positions and are close together. Although the particles vibrate, they cannot move from one part of the solid to another part. As a result, a solid cannot easily change in shape or volume. If you force the particles apart, you can change the shape of a solid by breaking it into pieces. However, each of those pieces will still be a solid and have its own definite shape.

Think Outside the Book (Inquiry)

9 Model Think about the general shape and behavior of particles in solids, liquids, and gases within a container. What objects could be used as a model of particles? How could you model a container for your particles? Gather the materials and make your model. How does your model of solid, liquid, and gas particles compare to the real particles?

Liquids Have a Definite Volume but Can Change Shape

Unlike the solid toy castle, the water in this fishbowl does not have a definite shape. The water has taken the shape of the round fishbowl. If you poured this same water into a rectangular fish tank, the water would take the shape of that container. However, the water would have the same volume as it did before. It would still take up the same amount of space. Like water, all liquids have a definite volume but no definite shape. The particles in a liquid are close together, but they are not tightly attached to one another as the particles in a solid are. Instead, particles in liquids can slide past one another. As a result, liquids can flow. Instead of having a rigid form, the particles in a liquid move and fill the bottom of the container they are in.

Gases Can Change in Volume and Shape

The small bubbles in this fishbowl are filled with gas. Gases do not have a definite volume or shape. The particles in a gas are very far apart compared to the particles in a solid or a liquid. The amount of space between the particles in a gas can change more easily. If a rigid container has a certain amount of air inside and more air is pumped in, the volume of the gas does not change. The gas will still fill the entire container. Instead, the particles will become closer together. If the container is opened, the particles will spread out and mix with the air in the atmosphere.

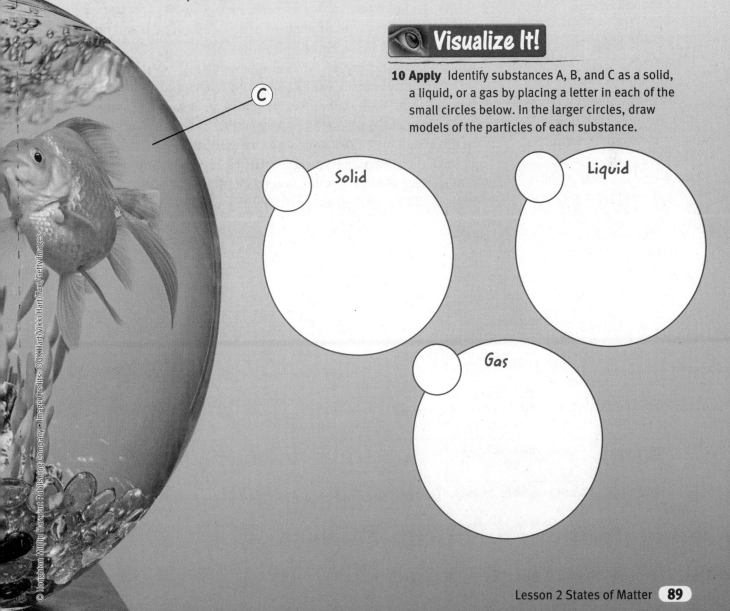

Visualize It!

10 Apply Identify substances A, B, and C as a solid, a liquid, or a gas by placing a letter in each of the small circles below. In the larger circles, draw models of the particles of each substance.

Solid

Liquid

Gas

C

Icicles grow as water drips down them and then freezes, sticking to the ice that is already there. Freezing is an example of a change of state.

What happens when substances change state?

Ice, liquid water, and water vapor are different states of the same substance. As liquid water turns into ice or water vapor, the water molecules themselves do not change. What changes are the motion of the molecules and the amount of space between them.

The Motion of the Particles Changes

The particles of a substance, even a solid, are always in motion. As a solid is heated, its particles gain energy and vibrate faster. If the vibrations are fast enough, the particles break loose and slide past one another. The process in which a solid becomes a liquid is known as *melting*. As the temperature of a liquid is lowered, its particles lose energy. Eventually, the particles move slowly enough for the attractions between them to cause the liquid to become a solid. This process is called *freezing*. Because water freezes at 0 °C, you may associate freezing with cold temperatures. But some substances are frozen at room temperature or above. For example, an aluminum can is an example of frozen aluminum. It will not melt until it reaches a temperature above 660 °C! The table below shows the most common types of state changes.

When substances lose or gain energy, one of two things can happen to the substance: its temperature can change or its state can change. But both do not happen at the same time. The energy that is added or removed during a change of state is used to break or form the attractions between particles. If you measure the temperature of boiling water, you will find that the temperature stays at 100 °C until all of the liquid has become a gas.

11 Apply Complete the table below with examples of state changes.

State change	Result	Example
Melting	A solid becomes a liquid.	
Freezing	A liquid becomes a solid.	
Boiling	A liquid becomes a gas (throughout).	
Evaporation	A liquid becomes a gas (at the liquid's surface).	A puddle dries out.
Condensation	A gas becomes a liquid.	
Sublimation	A solid becomes a gas.	Dry ice becomes a gas at room temperature.
Deposition	A gas becomes a solid.	Frost forms on a cold windowpane.

Why It Matters

Making Glass

You can see through it, drink water from it, and create objects of art with it. It's glass, a substance that has been crafted by humans for about 5,000 years! Read on to see how a few simple ingredients can become a beautiful work of art.

Glass Blowing

Glass blowing is the technique of shaping glass by blowing air into a blob of molten glass at the end of a tube. The *blowpipe* is the long, hollow tube that the glass blower uses to shape the molten glass. By blowing air through the blowpipe, a glass blower expands the open space inside the glass. This process is similar to inflating a balloon.

Glass from Sand?

Glass is made by heating a mixture of sand, soda ash, limestone, and other ingredients. Colored glass is made by adding small amounts of metal compounds. The mixture is melted in a roaring hot furnace at about 1,600 °C. Once the mixture melts, the molten glass can be shaped and allowed to cool into the solid state.

Extend

© Houghton Mifflin Harcourt Publishing Company • Image Credits: (bkgd) ©Niklas Bernstone/Johner Images Royalty-Free/Getty Images; (inset) ©James L. Amos/Photo Researchers, Inc.

Inquiry

12 Describe In your own words, describe the glass-blowing process.

13 Investigate People once thought that old glass windows are thicker at the bottom because the solid glass had flowed to the bottom over time. Research this theory and report your findings.

14 Investigate Research the various methods of making glass objects. Present your findings by doing one of the following:
• make a poster   • write a short essay
• draw a graphic novel

Visual Summary

To complete this summary, check the box that indicates true or false. Then use the key below to check your answers. You can use this page to review the main concepts of the lesson.

The particles in solids vibrate in place.

	T	F	
15	☐	☐	Solids can easily change in volume.

States of Matter

The particles in liquids slide past each other.

	T	F	
16	☐	☐	Liquids take the shape of their container.

The particles in gases move freely.

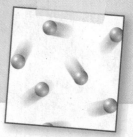

	T	F	
17	☐	☐	When the distance between gas particles increases, the volume of the gas increases.

Answers: 15 F; 16 T; 17 T

18 Describe What happens to the kinetic energy of the particles of a substance as the substance changes from a liquid to a gas?

Lesson Review

Vocabulary

Draw a line to connect the following terms to the description of their particle motion.

1 solid

2 liquid

3 gas

A particles are close together and locked in place

B particles are far apart and can move freely

C particles are close together and can slide past each other

Key Concepts

4 Define What is the kinetic theory of matter?

_____

_____

_____

_____

5 Analyze What happens to the temperature of a substance while it is changing state? Explain.

_____

_____

_____

_____

6 Analyze What could you do to change the volume of a gas?

_____

_____

_____

Critical Thinking

7 Apply Can a tank of oxygen gas ever be half empty? Explain.

_____

_____

_____

_____

Use this drawing to answer the following questions.

8 Predict This jar contains helium gas. What would happen if the lid of this jar was removed?

_____

_____

_____

_____

9 Explain How are the helium atoms in this model different from real helium atoms?

_____

_____

_____

_____

10 Infer The particles that make up a rock are constantly in motion. However, a rock does not visibly vibrate. Why do you think this is?

_____

_____

_____

_____

_____

_____

_____

Planning an Investigation

Indiana Standards

NOS 6.2 Plan and carry out investigations as a class, in small groups or independently often over a period of several class lessons.

NOS 6.4 Incorporate variables that can be changed, measured or controlled.

Scientists ask many questions and develop hypotheses about the natural world. They conduct investigations to help answer these questions. A scientist must plan an investigation carefully. The investigation should gather information that might support or disprove the hypothesis.

Tutorial
Use the following steps to help plan an investigation.

① Write a hypothesis.
The hypothesis should offer an explanation for the question that you are asking. The hypothesis must also be testable. If it is not testable, rewrite the hypothesis.

② Identify and list the possible variables in your experiment.
Select the independent variable and the dependent variable. In your investigation, you will change the independent variable to see any effect it may have on the dependent variable.

③ List the materials that you will need to perform the experiment.
This list should also include equipment that you need for safety.

④ Determine the method you will use to test your hypothesis.
Clearly describe the steps you will follow. If you change any part of the procedure while you are conducting the investigation, record the change. Another scientist should be able to follow your procedure to repeat your investigation.

⑤ Analyze the results.
Your data and observations from all of your experiments should be recorded carefully and clearly to maintain credibility. Record how you analyze your results so others can review your work and spot any problems or errors in your analysis.

⑥ Draw conclusions.
Describe what the results of the investigation show. Tell whether the results support your hypothesis.

You Try It!

You are a member of a research team that is trying to design and test a system that can protect an ice cube from melting. The system also has to be small enough to fit inside a milk carton. Therefore, you need to find an answer to the following question: What type of material will minimize the rate of melting of the ice cube?

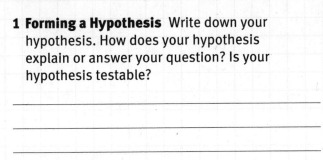

1 Forming a Hypothesis Write down your hypothesis. How does your hypothesis explain or answer your question? Is your hypothesis testable?

_____

_____

_____

_____

2 Identifying Variables List the possible variables in this experiment. Identify which variable you will be changing and which variable you will look at to see the effect.

_____

_____

_____

_____

3 Selecting Materials What equipment and tools will you need to test this variable? What might happen if you select inappropriate tools?

_____

_____

_____

_____

4 Testing Your Hypothesis What will your system look like? Will it support your testing? You may sketch the system below or on a separate page.

_____

_____

5 Planning Your Procedure What steps will you need to follow in order to test your hypothesis? What kinds of measurements will you collect? What kind of graphic organizer will you use to record your information?

_____

_____

_____

_____

6 Drawing Conclusions What conclusions can you draw from your data? Was your hypothesis useful?

_____

_____

_____

_____

Take It Home

Look closely at objects and materials in your home. Write a list of things that help to prevent the transfer of thermal energy. Design an investigation using one or more of these items to learn more about the job they do. Record your observations. Evaluate your results to see if they might point to a further investigation or an improvement to a product. Present your results in a pamphlet.

Changes of State

ESSENTIAL QUESTION

How does matter change from one state to another?

By the end of this lesson, you should be able to describe changes of state in terms of the attraction and motion of particles.

Solid ice in icebergs melts into liquid water. Water vapor in the air is water in a gaseous state.

Indiana Standards

6.1.3 Using a model in which matter is composed of particles in motion, investigate that when substances undergo a change in state, mass is conserved.

1 Identify What states of matter can you see in the photo at the right?

_____

_____

_____

_____

2 Apply What change of state do you think might be occurring in this photo?

_____

_____

_____

_____

_____

Active Reading

3 Distinguish Many scientific words, such as *freezing*, also have everyday meanings. Use context clues to write your own definition for each meaning of the word *freezing*.

Example Sentence
You wear a heavy coat when it is <u>freezing</u> cold outside.

freezing:

_____

_____

Example Sentence
<u>Freezing</u> water turns to ice.

freezing:

_____

_____

Vocabulary Terms

- freezing
- melting
- evaporation
- boiling
- condensation
- sublimation
- deposition

4 Identify This list contains the vocabulary terms you'll learn in this lesson. As you read, circle the definition of each term.

Matter Matters

How can matter change from one state to another?

Matter can gain or lose energy from its surroundings. For example, when matter absorbs heat energy, the particles that make it up move faster. When matter loses heat energy, its particles move more slowly. If the energy of the particles changes enough, the matter can change state. Changes of state can be observed in nature. For example:

- The particles of ice in a frozen lake absorb heat energy from the sun. If they gain enough energy, the ice will begin to melt and form liquid water.
- Liquid water in oceans and rivers can also absorb heat energy from the sun. Once the particles in the liquid have gained enough energy, the liquid water can change into a gas. As this happens, the gaseous water escapes into the air.
- When the particles that make up gaseous water lose a certain amount energy, the gas can change into a liquid or a solid. This change of state is responsible for the formation of clouds. Clouds are made up of small water droplets or ice crystals that are suspended in the air.

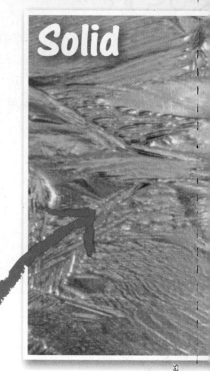

Solid

👁 Visualize It!

5 Identify Fill in the blanks to describe the changes of state that each arrow represents.

A The arrow shows that a liquid can change to a solid and a solid can change to a _____

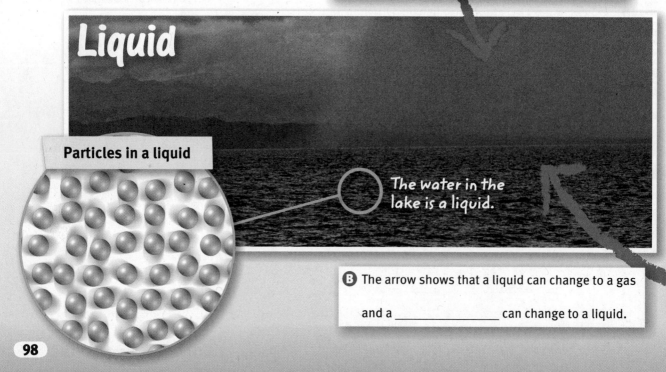

Liquid

Particles in a liquid

The water in the lake is a liquid.

B The arrow shows that a liquid can change to a gas and a _____ can change to a liquid.

98

© Houghton Mifflin Harcourt Publishing Company • Image Credits: (b) ©Photodisc/Getty Images; (t) ©Frank Cezus/Photographer's Choice/Getty Images

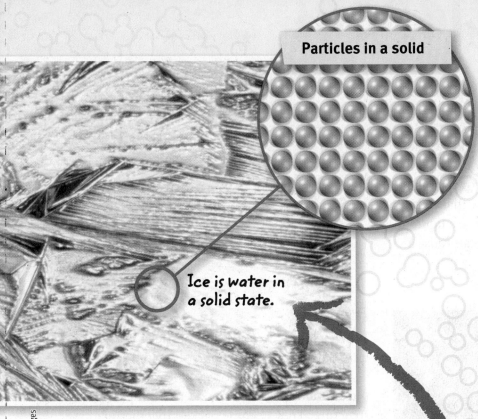

Particles in a solid

Ice is water in a solid state.

6 Apply Imagine a teapot that is full of water. As it heats up on the stove, steam comes out of the spout. Describe the states of matter that are involved.

_____

_____

_____

_____

_____

_____

_____

_____

C The arrow shows that a gas can change to a _____ and a _____ can change to a gas.

Particles in a gas

Gas

Water vapor, which is not visible, is water in a gaseous state.

Solid Science!

How do solids and liquids change state?

Remember that the particles in a liquid can slide past one another, while those in a solid can only vibrate. Particles that can slide past one another have more kinetic energy than those that cannot. Therefore, removing energy can cause a liquid to change into a solid. Adding energy can cause a solid to change into a liquid.

Solids can change to liquids. Liquids can change to solids.

Solid   Liquid

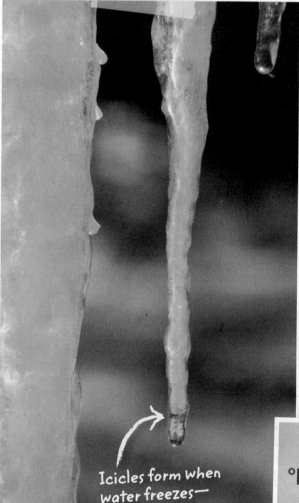

Icicles form when water freezes— at a temperature of 0 °C (32 °F).

Freezing

When a liquid is cooled, the particles that make it up have less kinetic energy than they did before. The attractive forces between them cause the particles to lock into place, forming a rigid structure. They become packed together in a solid. This process is **freezing**, and the temperature at which it occurs is the *freezing point*. Freezing only occurs once enough kinetic energy has been removed from the system.

The freezing point of water is 0 °C (32 °F). At that temperature, liquid water changes into a solid such as ice or snow.

Active Reading **7 Apply** Which water particles have more kinetic energy, those in a bowl of ice or those in a bowl of water? How do you know?

_____

_____

_____

Melting

When the temperature of a substance is increased, its particles have greater kinetic energy. The particles are able to move faster and overcome some of their attraction to one another. If the distances between particles become great enough, the particles are able to slide past one another and the matter changes from a solid to a liquid. This process is called **melting**. The temperature at which matter changes from a solid to a liquid is the *melting point*.

The melting point of water is 0 °C (32 °F). At that temperature, solid ice melts and forms liquid water. Notice that the freezing point and the melting point of water are the same temperature.

Ice is not the only solid that melts. For example, almost all metals are solid at room temperature, but at very high temperatures, they melt and become liquid. The aluminum used to make soda cans, for example, melts at 660 °C (1221 °F). That fact is useful in manufacturing. Metals like aluminum can be melted into liquid form and poured into the desired shape. When the metal cools, it becomes solid again.

Active Reading **8 Identify** What is the freezing and melting point of water?

_____

_____

9 Infer What is the freezing point of aluminum? How do you know?

_____

_____

_____

_____

_____

Melted aluminum can be cooled, pressed, and shaped to make soda cans.

Dropping in on Liquids

How do liquids and gases change state?

The particles in a liquid have less kinetic energy than those in a gas. They can only slide around each other. The particles in a gas have a great deal of kinetic energy. Therefore, they move very quickly. Adding energy can cause a liquid to change into a gas, while removing energy can cause a gas to change to a liquid.

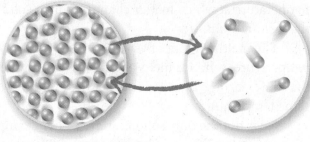

Liquids change to gases. Gases change to liquids.

Liquid   Gas

Evaporation and Boiling

Once again, temperature is crucial. When the temperature of a liquid is increased, the particles that make it up gain kinetic energy. Some particles may gain enough kinetic energy to become gaseous and escape from the surface of the liquid. This process is called **evaporation**. Evaporation happens at a range of temperatures, but it occurs more rapidly at higher temperatures.

Boiling is a rapid change from the liquid to gaseous state. It is so rapid that bubbles of gas form in the liquid. The temperature at which this occurs is the *boiling point*.

The boiling point of water is 100 °C (212 °F). The boiling point of aluminum is 2,467 °C (4,473 °F). Yes, it's true. At very high temperatures, aluminum metal boils and becomes a gas.

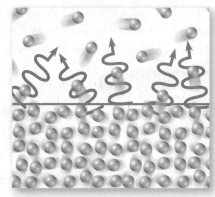

When water particles gain enough energy, they change from a liquid to a gas and escape through the surface of the liquid.

Active Reading **10 Compare** How are evaporation and boiling alike? How are they different?

_____

_____

_____

Bubbles form as water boils—at a temperature of 100 °C (212 °F).

°F   °C

210   100

200

                90
190

© Houghton Mifflin Harcourt Publishing Company • Image Credits: (bl) ©Ken Lax/Photo Researchers, Inc.

Gaseous water vapor condenses into liquid water on the cold glass.

Condensation

Temperature changes can also cause a gas to become a liquid. As the temperature of a gas is lowered, the movement of the particles is slowed. The attraction between the particles overcomes their motion, and a liquid is formed. This process is **condensation**.

You can easily see condensed water on the side of a cold glass or pitcher, especially on a hot day. The gaseous water vapor in the air quickly changes to liquid water when its particles come in contact with the cold glass surface.

Active Reading 11 **Explain** What happens to the particles in a gas during condensation?

_____

_____

_____

12 **Graph** Make a graph that shows the boiling point in degrees Celsius of the three liquids listed.

Liquid	Boiling Point (°C)
Water	100
Rubbing Alcohol	82
Acetic Acid	118

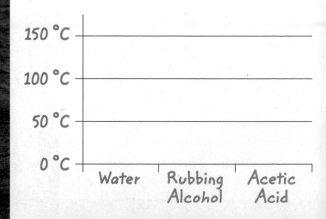

It's a Gas!

How do gases and solids change state?

We see condensed water on cold glass all the time. We see frozen water, melted ice, and rain. Those things are so common, we take them for granted. But we don't typically notice solids changing to gases, or gases changing to solids. Yet those changes of state do occur—in some everyday ways that may surprise you.

Look at this diagram. To change from a solid to a gas, the particles have to gain a great deal of kinetic energy.

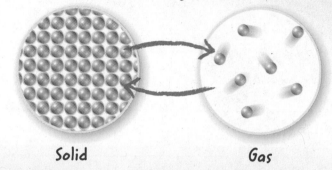

Solids can change to gases.
Gases can change to solids.

Solid

Gas

Active Reading 13 **Identify** As you read these two pages, underline examples of sublimation and deposition.

Sublimation

Have you ever seen something shipped in solid dry ice to keep it cold? If you have, you may have noticed that the solid seems to disappear without leaving a puddle. That's because dry ice changes from solid to gas with no liquid state in between. The process is called **sublimation**. It happens when particles escape into the air directly from the surface of a solid.

Both temperature and pressure changes can cause sublimation. Dry ice sublimes as it grows warmer. Snow and ice sublime at below-freezing temperatures. To see sublimation in action, hang a wet cloth outside on a freezing day. First, the water in the cloth freezes. Then, the solid ice sublimes into the air.

Particles escape from the surface of the mothball directly into the air.

Ice formed on wet clothes can sublime directly into the air.

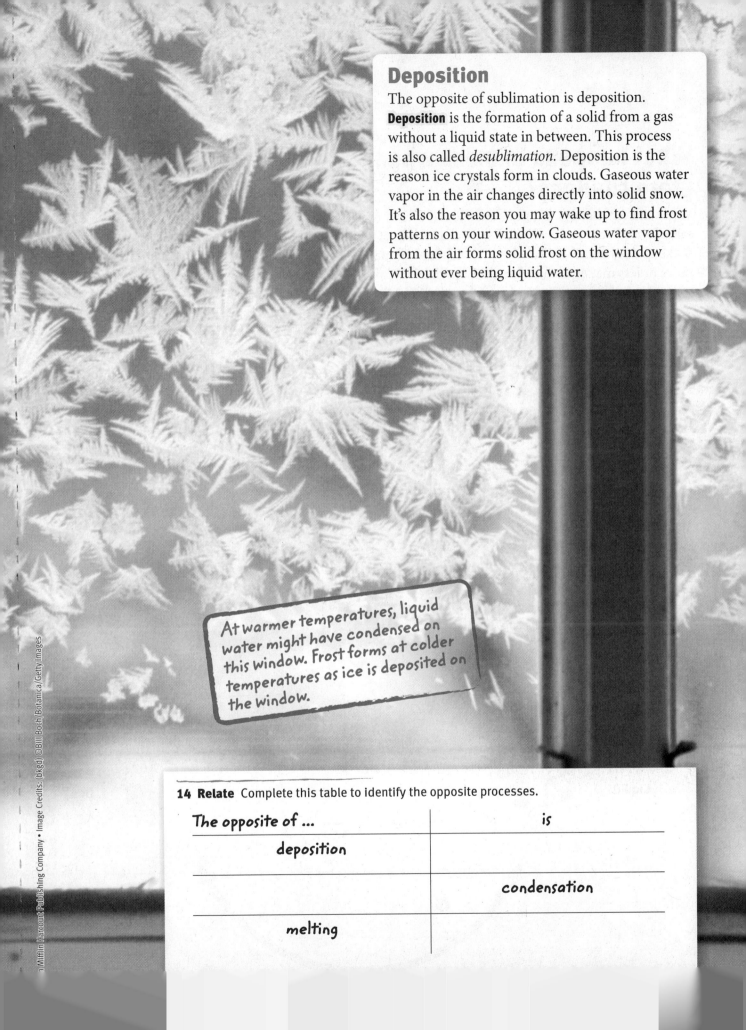

Deposition

The opposite of sublimation is deposition. **Deposition** is the formation of a solid from a gas without a liquid state in between. This process is also called *desublimation*. Deposition is the reason ice crystals form in clouds. Gaseous water vapor in the air changes directly into solid snow. It's also the reason you may wake up to find frost patterns on your window. Gaseous water vapor from the air forms solid frost on the window without ever being liquid water.

At warmer temperatures, liquid water might have condensed on this window. Frost forms at colder temperatures as ice is deposited on the window.

14 Relate Complete this table to identify the opposite processes.

The opposite of ...	is
deposition	
	condensation
melting	

Mass Matters

What happens to mass when state changes?

When matter changes from one state to another, it remains the same kind of matter. Its physical state changes, but its chemical makeup does not. But what about the amount of matter? Is there more or less matter in one state than another?

Active Reading

15 Compare When an ice cube melts into water, how do the mass of the ice cube and the water compare?

_____

_____

Water's Mass Doesn't Change

Suppose you place some ice in a sealed container. You heat the ice to the melting point. It becomes liquid water. Then, you heat it to the boiling point so that it forms a gas. At each stage, you measure the mass of the water. You would find no difference. The gaseous water would measure the same as the liquid water or the solid ice.

The size and number of particles do not change. Only the movement of the particles and the distance between them change in the three states of matter.

Visualize It!

16 Apply Label the types of state changes that are taking place at each stage. Draw the missing model for the gas state.

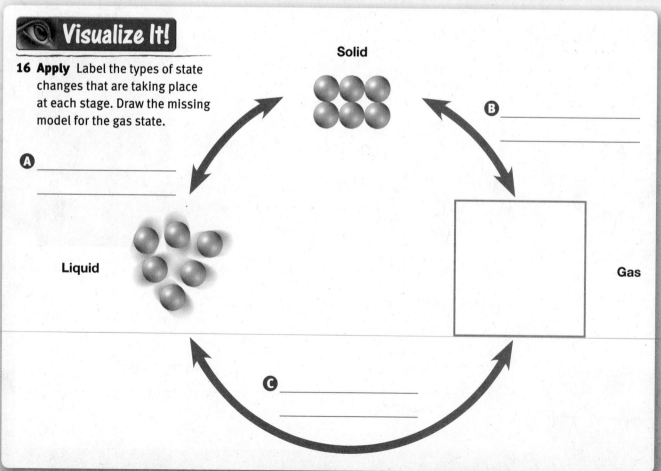

Ⓐ _____

_____

Ⓑ _____

_____

Ⓒ _____

_____

Solid

Liquid

Gas

All Mass Stays the Same

Does the same thing happen with metals or gases in the air? Yes. No matter what the state of matter of a substance is at room temperature, its mass stays the same when it changes to a different state. For example, carbon dioxide—which at room temperature is a gas in the air—can be made solid at a temperature of −78.5 °C (−109.3 °F). The solid is called dry ice. If you measured the carbon dioxide gas and the dry ice formed from it, the mass would be the same.

The same holds true for metals such as aluminum. A single aluminum can has a mass of about 15 grams. When a can is melted into its liquid form, its mass is still 15 grams. Even the gas form of an aluminum can has the same mass, 15 grams.

17 Predict How would the mass of an aluminum can compare with the mass of the liquid metal used to make it? Explain your answer.

_____

_____

_____

_____

These students are weighing a solid aluminum can full of liquid soda.

Visual Summary

To complete this summary, answer the question in each box. Then, use the key below to check your answers. You can use this page to review the main concepts of the lesson.

Changes of State

A solid can change state to a liquid or a gas.

18 What process changes a solid to a gas?

_____

19 What process changes a solid to a liquid?

_____

A liquid can change state to a gas or a solid.

20 What two processes change a liquid to a gas?

_____

21 What process changes a liquid to a solid?

_____

A gas can change state to a solid or a liquid.

22 What process changes a gas to a solid?

_____

23 What process changes a gas to a liquid?

_____

Mass is conserved when a substance changes state.

24 During a state change, physical state changes but _____ makeup does not.

Answers: 18. sublimation; 19. melting; 20. evaporation and boiling; 21. freezing; 22. deposition; 23. condensation 24. chemical

---

25 Synthesize When 300 grams of dry ice sublimes, how many grams of gaseous carbon dioxide does it form? Explain how you know.

Lesson Review

Vocabulary

Fill in the blank with the term that best completes the following sentences.

1 Sublimation is a change of

_____ to gas.

2 Condensation is a change from gas

to _____

3 The opposite of _____ is freezing.

Key Concepts

4 Compare Explain how evaporation and boiling are alike.

_____

_____

_____

5 Contrast Explain how deposition is different from sublimation.

_____

_____

_____

_____

6 Describe What happens to the particles in matter during a change from a liquid to a solid?

_____

_____

_____

_____

7 Calculate The water in a puddle has a mass of 1,500 grams. The sun comes out and the puddle evaporates. How many grams of water vapor enter the air from the puddle?

Critical Thinking

The following diagrams show three different states of the same substance. Use these diagrams to answer the following questions.

A
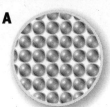

B
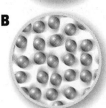

C
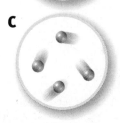

8 Identify What state of matter does each diagram represent?

_____

_____

9 Predict What is the quickest way to change B to C? Explain your answer.

_____

_____

_____

10 Analyze If mass does not change when the state of matter changes, why do you see more particles in B than in C?

_____

_____

_____

_____

My Notes

Unit 2 Summary

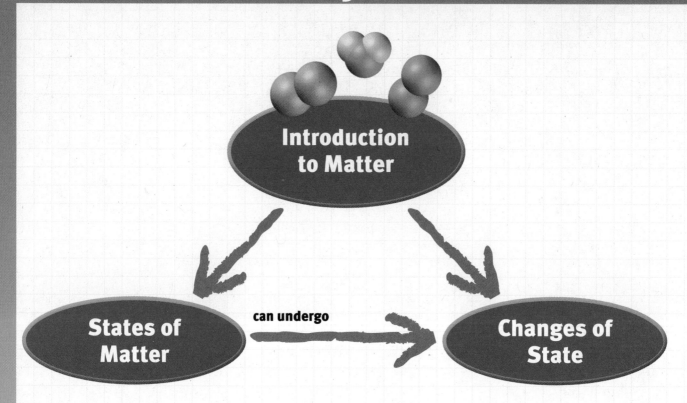

1 **Interpret** The Graphic Organizer above shows that matter can change state. Pick one change of state and describe what happens when it occurs.

_____

_____

_____

_____

2 **Contrast** What is the difference between mass and weight?

_____

_____

3 **Apply** How could you use a fish tank to find the volume of an irregularly shaped object?

_____

_____

_____

_____

_____

4 **Summarize** Describe the motion of the particles that make up oxygen gas.

_____

_____

_____

_____

ISTEP+ Review

Name _____

Multiple Choice

1 The density of a substance equals its mass divided by its volume. Talia listed the density of some common materials at 20 °C.

Material	Density (g/cm³)
gasoline	0.70
mercury	13.6
milk	1.03
water	0.998

If Talia has 10 grams of each material, which material has the GREATEST volume?

A. gasoline

B. mercury

C. milk

D. water

2 Susie used a double-pan balance to measure the mass of an object by comparing it to a reference mass. She recorded the mass as 125 grams.

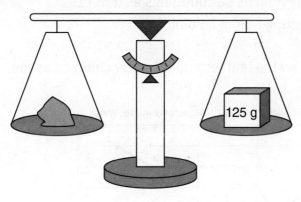

What value will Susie record for the mass of the object if she takes the same measurement on the moon, where the gravitational force is about one-sixth of Earth's gravity?

A. 0 grams

B. 21 grams

C. 125 grams

D. 750 grams

3 Tyson draws a model to show how the particles in a liquid appear.

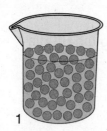  

Which model (or models) above could be Tyson's drawing of particles in a LIQUID?

A. model 1

B. model 3

C. model 1 and model 2

D. model 1, model 2, and model 3

4 Freezing temperatures can destroy citrus crops. Citrus growers sometimes spray water on the fruit to protect it from freezing. How can spraying the trees with water protect the fruit?

A. the temperature of the water changes as it freezes

B. the water releases energy to its surroundings as it freezes

C. the water takes in energy from its surroundings as it freezes

D. ice coats the fruit, protecting it from cold air

5 The diagram below shows how the temperature of water changes as the water changes states.

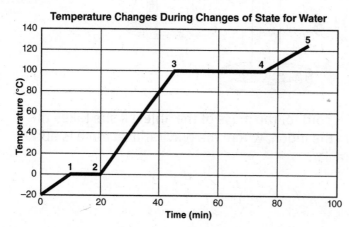

How is the motion of the particles changing between point 2 and point 3?

A. The attractions that hold the particles in place are breaking apart, and the particles begin to slide past each other.

B. The particles begin to vibrate in place faster.

C. The attractions that hold the particles together are breaking apart, and the particles begin to move freely.

D. The particles slide past each other faster.

6 Which properties of all SOLIDS are based on the motion and position of their particles?

   A. a changing shape and a changing volume

   B. a changing shape and a definite volume

   C. a definite shape and a changing volume

   D. a definite shape and a definite volume

7 A student added water to ice-cube trays until each cell was about half full. After the water froze, he noticed that the ice cubes filled more of each cell in the trays than the liquid water had. Which is a good EXPLANATION for this observation?

   A. Water gains volume when it freezes, but its mass does not change.

   B. Water gains both mass and volume when it freezes.

   C. Water loses mass and gains volume when it freezes.

   D. Water gains mass and loses volume when it freezes.

8 Dr. Suri placed a dog on the scale at the veterinary clinic and recorded a reading of 8 pounds. EXPLAIN what this reading means.

   A. The dog's mass is equal to 8 pounds.

   B. The weight of the dog as measured by the scale is 8 pounds.

   C. The volume of the dog is exactly 8 pounds.

   D. The dog has an average density of 8 lb/ft3.

9 Maria says that mass is conserved during evaporation. Her cousin Juan says that mass is conserved during boiling. Which student is CORRECT?

   A. only Maria is correct

   B. only Juan is correct

   C. both Maria and Juan are correct

   D. neither Maria nor Juan is correct

10 Dew forms when water vapor in the air condenses and forms water droplets on grass and other surfaces. When the air warms up, the dew "disappears." Which statement BEST explains what happens to the dew?

   A. The dew boils, losing mass during this change of state.

   B. The dew boils, forming an equal mass of water vapor.

   C. The dew evaporates, losing mass during this change of state.

   D. The dew evaporates, forming an equal mass of water vapor.

ISTEP+ Review

Constructed Response

11 Solid dry ice changes directly into carbon dioxide gas.

Name and describe the change of state dry ice undergoes.

_____

_____

Compare the original mass of dry ice with the mass of carbon dioxide gas that forms and explain how you know.

_____

_____

Extended Response

12 In a famous experiment, Greek philosopher Archimedes determined that an object that had an irregular shape was made of gold by measuring its density.

What MEASUREMENTS are needed to determine density?

_____

_____

Describe a PROCEDURE to make the measurements needed to determine the density of the object.

_____

_____

Describe how to calculate the density of the object from these measurements.

_____

_____

How can you use the calculated value for density to determine whether an object is gold?

_____

_____

UNIT 3
Energy

Core Standard

Understand that there are different forms of energy with unique characteristics.

Core Standard

Apply a form of energy to design and construct a simple mechanical device.

This maglev train in Shanghai uses magnets to lift and propel itself.

What do you think?

All trains use some form of energy to move from one place to the next. What forms of energy have been used to help transport large groups of people?

Unit 3
Energy

Lesson 1
Kinetic and Potential Energy 120
6.1.4, 6.1.5, 6.1.6, 6.4.3

Focus on Engineering 130
6.4.1, 6.4.2, 6.4.3

Lesson 2
Forms of Energy 132
6.1.5, 6.1.7

Unit Summary.................... 142

ISTEP+ Review 143

Indiana Standards

As citizens of the constructed world, students will participate in the design process. Students will learn to use materials and tools safely and employ the basic principles of the engineering design process in order to find solutions to problems.

DP 6.1 Identify a need or problem to be solved.

CITIZEN SCIENCE

From Here to There

For hundreds of years, people have been thinking of the best ways to transport large groups of people across land, air, and water. All of these transportation methods use energy to go from place to place. Different types of trains use different energy sources: some were powered by animals, some are powered by steam and coal, and many are now powered by electricity. Today, scientists continue to research new energy sources to power trains.

Horse-Drawn Trains
Some of the very earliest trains used horses as their main source of energy. Horses would pull large train cars that were connected to tracks.

Steam Trains

The invention of the steam engine dramatically changed train transportation. A steam engine burns coal or wood to heat water into steam. The steam then moves parts in the engine.

Electric Trains

The invention of the electric train allowed for a cleaner method of transportation that could be used underground. Electric trains use electrical energy from either an overhead electric cable, as shown above, or from an electric rail beneath the train.

What's Next?

1 Think About It

What are some other sources of energy that could be used to power new trains?

_____

_____

_____

_____

_____

2 Ask a Question

Where are some likely places that trains with new energy sources could be built? Why?

_____

_____

_____

_____

3 Conduct Research

Research a new type of train that uses innovative energy sources, such as magnetic levitation or hydrogen fuel cells. How are these trains different from the three kinds of trains discussed above?

_____

_____

_____

_____

_____

Take It Home

Describe what you have learned to adults at home. Then, have them help as you create an advertising brochure that explains the advantages and disadvantages of the new type of train that you have researched.

Kinetic and Potential Energy

ESSENTIAL QUESTION

How is mechanical energy conserved?

By the end of this lesson, you should be able to describe how mechanical energy is conserved through the transformation between kinetic and potential energy.

As this girl juggles, the balls fly up and down. As each ball moves, one type of energy changes into another.

Indiana Standards

6.1.4 Recognize that objects in motion have kinetic energy and objects at rest have potential energy.

6.1.5 Describe with examples that potential energy exists in several different forms (gravitational potential energy, elastic potential energy and chemical potential energy, among others).

6.1.6 Compare and contrast potential and kinetic energy and how they can be transformed within a system from one form to another.

6.4.3 Describe the transfer of energy amongst energy interactions.

Engage Your Brain

1 Describe Fill in the blank with the word or phrase that you think correctly completes the following sentences.

A running cat has _____ energy than a walking cat.

A balloon in the air has more energy than

_____

_____

Conservation of energy means that energy is

_____

_____

_____

2 Explain Draw a sketch that shows two uses of energy. Write a caption to go with your sketch.

Active Reading

3 Apply Many scientific words, such as *energy*, also have everyday meanings. Use context clues to write your own definition for each meaning of the word *energy*.

Example Sentence
I am tired today and don't have much <u>energy</u>.

Energy:

_____

_____

Example Sentence
Make sure to turn off the lights when you're done to save <u>energy</u>.

Energy:

_____

_____

_____

Vocabulary Terms
- energy
- kinetic energy
- potential energy
- mechanical energy
- law of conservation of energy

4 Identify This list contains the vocabulary terms you'll learn in this lesson. As you read, circle the definition of each term.

Exciting Energy!

What is energy?

Energy is the ability to cause change. It is measured in units called joules. Energy takes many different forms and has many different effects. For example, you use energy provided by the food you eat to do different activities. Your body uses energy by converting it to other forms. If you are exercising, sitting, or even thinking, then you are using energy. All forms of energy have one thing in common—they can cause changes to occur.

Just about everything that you see happening around you involves energy. In the photo of the amusement park below, there are many examples of energy uses. The lights on the Ferris wheel use energy. The rides use energy as they move. The speakers use energy as they broadcast music.

Think Outside the Book

5 **Discuss** You have probably used the word *energy* before. With a partner or as a class, discuss how the scientific definition of *energy* relates to the daily use of the word.

The lights on the Ferris wheel use energy.

The rides use energy as they move.

Visualize It!

6 **Identify** List four examples of energy being used in this photo.

_____

_____

_____

_____

What are two types of energy?

Imagine that you are biking up a hill. You would be using many different types of energy. You would use one type of energy to go up the hill. As the bike goes up the hill, it gains a second type of energy that you can use to go down the hill. These two types of energy are called kinetic energy and potential energy.

Kinetic Energy

Kinetic energy (kuh•NET•ik) is the energy of motion. All moving objects have kinetic energy. Like all forms of energy, kinetic energy has the ability to cause change. For example, as a hammer moves toward a nail, it has kinetic energy. This kinetic energy can be used to move the nail into a piece of wood. A change has occurred. First, the nail was outside of the wood. Then it was inside of the wood.

The amount of kinetic energy that an object has depends on two things: mass and speed. The more mass a moving object has, the more kinetic energy it has. If there are two objects moving at the same speed, then the one with more mass will have more kinetic energy. For example, if a car and a bike are both moving at the same speed, then the car will have more kinetic energy because it has more mass.

Kinetic energy also depends on speed. The faster an object moves, the more kinetic energy it has. If there are two objects with the same mass, then the one going faster will have more kinetic energy. For example, a cheetah has more kinetic energy when it is running than it does when it is walking.

Active Reading **7 Apply** A bowling ball and a soccer ball are both moving at the same speed. Which one has more kinetic energy? Why?

_____

_____

_____

This running cheetah has more kinetic energy than the walking cheetah because it is moving faster.

Potential Energy

Not all energy has to do with motion. Some energy is stored energy, or potential energy. **Potential energy** is the stored energy that an object has due to its position, condition, or chemical composition. Like kinetic energy, stored potential energy has the ability to cause change. For example, a book held in your hands has potential energy. If you drop it, its position will change.

One type of potential energy is called gravitational potential energy. Gravity is the force that pulls objects toward Earth's center. When you lift an object, you transfer energy to the object and give the object gravitational potential energy. Any object above the ground has gravitational potential energy. The skydivers in this photo have gravitational potential energy as they ride in the plane.

The amount of gravitational potential energy that an object has depends on its mass and its height above the ground. Gravitational potential energy increases as an object's distance from the ground, or from its lowest possible position, increases. A skydiver has more gravitational potential energy on the plane than she does after she jumps out and gets closer to the ground. Gravitational potential energy also increases as mass increases. If there are two skydivers on the plane, the one with more mass will have more gravitational potential energy.

There are other types of potential energy. Energy can be stored in springs or elastic bands. Chemical potential energy, such as the energy stored in food, depends on chemical composition. It results from the bonds between atoms. When chemical bonds of molecules are broken, and their atoms are rearranged through a series of chemical changes, energy is released.

Active Reading **8 Apply** Which has more gravitational potential energy: a bird on the ground or the same bird in a tree? Why?

_____

_____

_____

_____

As these skydivers fall, their gravitational potential energy decreases.

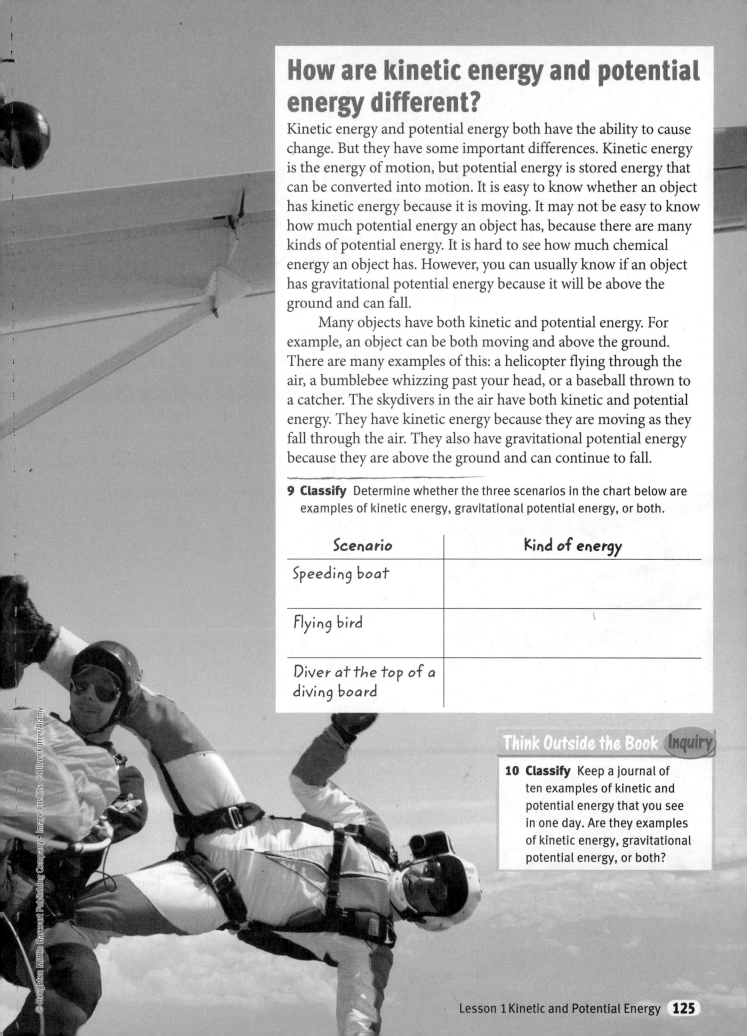

How are kinetic energy and potential energy different?

Kinetic energy and potential energy both have the ability to cause change. But they have some important differences. Kinetic energy is the energy of motion, but potential energy is stored energy that can be converted into motion. It is easy to know whether an object has kinetic energy because it is moving. It may not be easy to know how much potential energy an object has, because there are many kinds of potential energy. It is hard to see how much chemical energy an object has. However, you can usually know if an object has gravitational potential energy because it will be above the ground and can fall.

Many objects have both kinetic and potential energy. For example, an object can be both moving and above the ground. There are many examples of this: a helicopter flying through the air, a bumblebee whizzing past your head, or a baseball thrown to a catcher. The skydivers in the air have both kinetic and potential energy. They have kinetic energy because they are moving as they fall through the air. They also have gravitational potential energy because they are above the ground and can continue to fall.

9 Classify Determine whether the three scenarios in the chart below are examples of kinetic energy, gravitational potential energy, or both.

Scenario	Kind of energy
Speeding boat	
Flying bird	
Diver at the top of a diving board	

Think Outside the Book (Inquiry)

10 Classify Keep a journal of ten examples of kinetic and potential energy that you see in one day. Are they examples of kinetic energy, gravitational potential energy, or both?

Add It Up!

What is mechanical energy?

The skater in the picture has both kinetic energy and potential energy. There are many times when these two types of energy are found together. **Mechanical energy** (meh•KAN•ih•kuhl) is the kinetic energy plus the potential energy due to position.

Gravitational potential energy is one type of energy of position. An object compressing a spring also has potential energy of position. Both of these are mechanical potential energies. Add together an object's mechanical potential energies and its kinetic energy to get its mechanical energy. Often, you can add just the object's kinetic and gravitational potential energies.

At any point on the half-pipe shown in the photograph, the mechanical energy of the skater is equal to the sum of his kinetic energy and his gravitational potential energy. At any point where his kinetic energy is zero, then his mechanical energy is equal to potential energy. When he is both moving and above his lowest point, his mechanical energy is the sum of both kinds of energy.

As the skater moves up the ramp, he gains height but loses speed. The kinetic energy he loses is equal to the potential energy that he gains. **D**

At the bottom of the ramp, the skater's kinetic energy is greatest because he is going the fastest. His potential energy is at its lowest because he is closer to the ground than at any other point on the ramp. **C**

What is the law of conservation of energy?

The **law of conservation of energy** states that energy can be neither created nor destroyed. It can only be transformed. The mechanical energy of an object always remains the same unless some of it is transformed into other forms of energy, such as heat through friction. If no energy is transformed, the mechanical energy of an object stays the same.

As a skater rolls down the ramp, the amounts of kinetic and potential energy change. However, the law of conservation of energy requires that the total—or mechanical energy—stays the same, assuming no energy is converted into other forms. In order for the mechanical energy to stay the same, some potential energy changes into kinetic energy. At other times, some kinetic energy changes into potential energy. The picture below shows the skater's mechanical energy at four key places: the top of the ramp, between the top and the bottom of the ramp, the bottom of the ramp, and between the bottom and top of the ramp.

11 Identify As you read, underline examples in the text where kinetic energy changes into potential energy or where potential energy changes into kinetic energy.

At the top of the ramp, the skater has potential energy because gravity can pull him downward. He has no speed, so he has no kinetic energy.

Ⓐ

As the skater moves closer to the ground, he loses potential energy, but gains the same amount of kinetic energy. As he rolls down the ramp, his potential energy decreases because his distance from the ground decreases. His kinetic energy increases because his speed increases.

Ⓑ

12 Analyze Do you think that the skater has any gravitational potential energy at point C? Why?

_____

_____

_____

_____

_____

_____

_____

_____

_____

Visual Summary

To complete this summary, fill in the blanks with the correct word or phrase. Then, use the answer key to check your answers. You can use this page to review the main concepts of the lesson.

Energy is the ability to cause change.

13 Kinetic energy is the energy of
_____

14 Potential energy is the energy of
_____

Kinetic and Potential Energy

Mechanical energy is conserved. Ball A has the most potential energy. As it rolls down the hill, its potential energy is converted to kinetic energy. Ball B has both kinetic and potential energy. At the bottom of the hill, most of the ball's energy is kinetic.

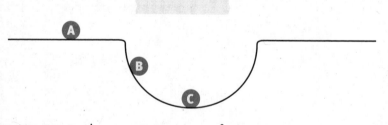

15 Mechanical energy is the sum of
_____

Answers: 13 motion; 14 position or chemical composition; 15 kinetic energy and potential energy

16 Apply Explain how the law of conservation of energy might apply to energy use that you observe in your daily life.

Lesson Review

Vocabulary

Fill in the blank with the term that best completes the following sentences.

1 Energy is the ability to _____

_____

2 _____ is an object's total kinetic and potential energy.

3 The law of conservation of energy states that

_____

_____

_____

Key Concepts

4 Describe List two ways you use energy. How does each example involve a change?

_____

_____

_____

_____

_____

5 Identify What are two factors that determine an object's kinetic energy?

_____

_____

6 Identify What are two factors that determine an object's gravitational potential energy?

_____

_____

7 Describe How does the law of conservation of energy affect the total amount of energy in any process?

_____

_____

_____

_____

Critical Thinking

Use the illustration below to answer the following questions.

8 Apply At which position would the skater have the most kinetic energy?

_____

9 Apply At which position would the skater have the most potential energy?

_____

10 Synthesize At which position would the skater's kinetic energy begin to change into potential energy? Explain.

_____

_____

_____

_____

11 Incorporate How have your ideas about energy and its forms changed after reading this lesson? Provide an example to describe how you would have thought about energy compared to how you think about it now.

_____

_____

_____

_____

_____

Focus on ENGINEERING

Indiana Standards

6.4.1 Understand how to apply potential or kinetic energy to power a simple device.

6.4.2 Construct a simple device that uses potential or kinetic energy to perform work.

6.4.3 Describe the transfer of energy amongst energy interactions.

The Right Tool

How is energy used to power a simple device?

Potential energy is transformed into kinetic energy all around us. Kinetic energy and potential energy are used in tools. These tools help us to perform everyday tasks. To use these tools, you transfer kinetic or potential energy to the tools, then the tools transfer energy to objects.

Hammer
When a hammer swings down to hit a nail, its potential energy is converted into kinetic energy. That kinetic energy is transferred to the nail, driving it into the wood.

Lever
The potential energy of a lever is converted into kinetic energy. This kinetic energy is transferred to the lid as it is lifted off a can of paint.

1 Summarize For each of the tools below, describe how energy is used and what sort of tasks can be done with that energy.

Tool	How Energy Is Used	Task Performed
Lever		
Hammer		
Wrench		

© Houghton Mifflin Harcourt Publishing Company • Image Credits: (bkg) ©Pete Saloutos/Getty Images; (l) ©E. R. Degginger/Photo Researchers, Inc.; (t) ©moodboard/Corbis

2 Design Can you design another tool that uses kinetic and potential energy conversions to accomplish a specific task? Draw a picture of it, then write a caption describing how the tool uses energy.

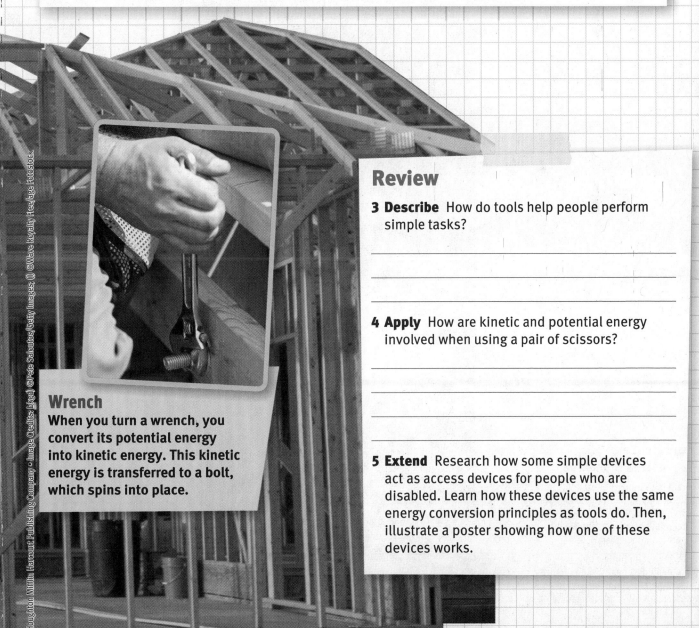

Wrench
When you turn a wrench, you convert its potential energy into kinetic energy. This kinetic energy is transferred to a bolt, which spins into place.

Review

3 Describe How do tools help people perform simple tasks?

_____

_____

_____

4 Apply How are kinetic and potential energy involved when using a pair of scissors?

_____

_____

_____

_____

5 Extend Research how some simple devices act as access devices for people who are disabled. Learn how these devices use the same energy conversion principles as tools do. Then, illustrate a poster showing how one of these devices works.

Forms of Energy

ESSENTIAL QUESTION

What are some different forms of energy?

By the end of this lesson, you should be able to describe the different forms that energy can take.

Fireworks use chemical energy to produce sound, light and heat energy. The Ferris wheel uses electrical energy to produce light energy and sound energy.

Indiana Standards

6.1.5 Describe with examples that potential energy exists in several different forms (gravitational potential energy, elastic potential energy, and chemical potential energy, among others).

6.1.7 Explain that energy may be manifested as heat, light, electricity, mechanical motion, and sound and is often associated with chemical reactions.

Engage Your Brain

1 Identify Unscramble the letters below to find different forms of energy. Write your words on the blank lines

EEIIYCLTRCL

_____

THEA

_____

LEMHCICA YRGNEE

_____

DOSUN

_____

GIHLT

_____

2 Apply Draw a sketch that shows a way that you have used energy or have seen energy being used. Below your sketch, label what form of energy you think is being used.

Active Reading

3 Synthesize Use context clues to write your own definition for the words *bond* and *transform*.

Example Sentence
To separate a water molecule into hydrogen and oxygen, we use heat to break the <u>bonds</u> between the atoms.

bond:

_____

_____

Example Sentence
The fire <u>transformed</u> the forest into a charred wasteland.

transform:

_____

_____

Vocabulary Terms

- elastic potential energy
- chemical potential energy
- heat
- light
- sound
- electical energy

4 Apply As you learn the definition of each vocabulary term in this lesson, create your own definition or sketch to help you remember the meaning of the term.

High Energy!

What are some forms of energy?

You know some basic information about energy, but there is still a lot more to learn. For example, energy comes in many different forms.

Potential and Kinetic Energy

Kinetic energy is the energy of motion. Potential energy is stored energy due to an object's position or condition. Potential energy can exist in several different forms. A ball at the top of a hill has gravitational potential energy. A stretched rubber band has elastic potential energy. It's not unusual for an object to have both potential and kinetic energy. As gravity causes the ball to roll down the hill, the ball's potential energy is changed into kinetic energy. Mechanical energy is the sum of the potential and kinetic energy in the moving parts of a system.

Active Reading **5 Classify** A baseball is hit out of the stadium. As it flies through the air, does it have kinetic energy, potential energy, or both? Explain your answer.

_____

_____

_____

_____

Elastic Potential Energy

Objects such as rubber bands and springs can bend and stretch. They are elastic. As an elastic object is stretched or bent, **elastic potential energy** is stored in the object. If the object is released, it snaps back to its original shape. The potential energy is released.

Think Outside the Book

6 Identify As you read about different forms of energy in this lesson, keep a list of examples of them. For each example, decide which form of energy it is. Write a sentence or two explaining your reasoning. When you have finished the lesson, do research to determine whether your identifications were correct.

Chemical Potential Energy

Most objects contain **chemical potential energy**. Chemical potential energy is energy that is stored in the bonds between the atoms that make up an object or substance.

All matter is made up of atoms. Atoms can join together to form molecules. For example, a molecule of water is made up of two hydrogen atoms and one oxygen atom. When the bonds that hold those three atoms together are broken, energy is released. When wood burns, the chemical potential energy in its bonds is released as light and heat.

In a sense, chemical potential energy keeps you alive. The food you eat contains chemical potential energy. Digestion is the process of making that energy usable. When you move your arm, the chemical potential energy in your body is transformed into kinetic energy. Some of the chemical potential energy from your food is converted into heat, which can keep you warm when it is cold.

Active Reading **7 Analyze** How do you know that chemical potential energy is potential energy?

_____

_____

A forest fire releases a lot of chemical potential energy.

A charged battery converts stored chemical energy into electrical energy. These remote-controlled cars use the electrical energy to produce the mechanical energy they need to race.

Heat and Light Energy

Energy comes in different forms. **Heat** is a form of energy that moves from an object or area with a higher temperature to one with a lower temperature. **Light** is a form of energy we can see.

Many materials give off light energy when they get hot. For example, most metals will glow if they are heated enough. Heat energy is released by chemical reactions, such as rusting, without releasing light energy. Lightning bugs and other animals that light up, transform chemical energy into light energy.

Hot coils give off heat and light energy.

Sound Energy

Energy travels in different ways. **Sound** is a form of kinetic energy that travels in waves. Sound waves are formed when something vibrates, or moves back and forth very quickly. Picture a stereo speaker surrounded by air. When certain parts of the speaker vibrate, they bump against air molecules. The back-and-forth motion of the speaker parts moves air molecules in patterns. These patterns are sound waves.

Sound travels through gases, such as air. It also travels through liquids and solids. That's why you can hear things when your head is underwater. That's why you can hear someone knocking on the other side of a door.

Active Reading 9 **Analyze** There are no gases, liquids, or solids in a vacuum. Can you hear something vibrating in a vacuum? Why or why not?

_____

_____

_____

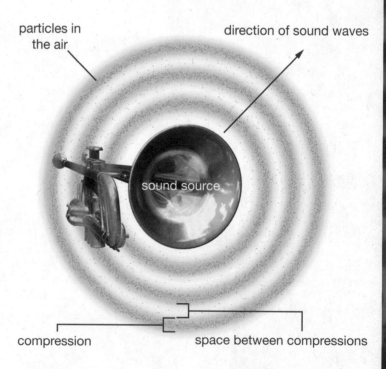

particles in the air

direction of sound waves

sound source

compression

space between compressions

Sound energy travels in waves, traveling outward from the sound source.

Electrical Energy

We use electricity every day. **Electrical energy** is the result of electric charges having energy. Electricity may be produced at power plants. There, generators transform mechanical energy into electrical energy. Batteries transform chemical potential energy into electrical energy.

These transformations work both ways. Light bulbs transform electrical energy into light energy. A fan transforms electrical energy into kinetic energy. A space heater transforms electrical energy into heat.

 **Visualize It!**

10 Categorize Name the different forms of energy shown in this picture.

Visual Summary

To complete this summary, fill in the blanks with the correct word or phrase. Then, use the key below to check your answers. You can use this page to review the main concepts of the lesson.

Forms of Energy

It's not unusual for an object to have both potential and kinetic energy.

11 Kinetic energy is the energy of _____

12 Potential energy is energy that is _____

One type of energy can be transformed into another form of energy.

13 Batteries transform _____ energy into _____ energy.

Energy can be transformed into more than one other type of energy.

14 The coils shown here give off both energy in the form of heat and _____ energy.

Sound energy travels in waves through a solid, liquid, or gas.

15 Sound energy travels through solids, liquids, and gases in the form of _____

Answer Key: 11. motion; 12. stored; 13. chemical; electrical; 14. light; 15. waves

16 Explain Give two new examples of how one form of energy can be transformed into another form.

Lesson Review

Vocabulary

Draw a line to connect the following terms to their definitions.

1 chemical energy

2 heat

3 light

4 sound

5 electrical energy

A energy that moves from an object or area with a higher temperature to one with a lower temperature

B energy associated with moving electric charges

C energy that is stored in the bonds between atoms

D energy we can see

E energy that travels in waves

Key Concepts

6 Apply An athlete places an ice pack on her sprained ankle. In which direction does energy in the form of heat move? How do you know?

_____

_____

_____

_____

7 Identify Which of the following contains chemical potential energy: a head of lettuce, an apple, a tree trunk, a book? How do you know?

_____

_____

_____

8 Describe Whales can communicate with each other over vast distances underwater. Tell what happens when sound waves travel through water from one whale to the other.

_____

_____

_____

_____

Critical Thinking

Use the graph to answer questions 9 and 10.

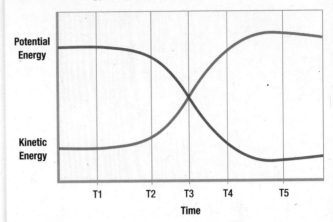

Mechanical Energy in Spencer's Bicycle

9 Analyze At what point was Spencer at the bottom of a hill? How do you know?

_____

_____

_____

10 Infer Did Spencer pedal the bike when he reached the bottom of a hill? How do you know?

_____

_____

_____

11 Apply Think about the different forms of energy present in your classroom right now. Identify one example each of chemical, heat, light, sound, electrical energy, and elastic potential energy. For each one, describe its source.

_____

_____

_____

_____

_____

_____

My Notes

Unit 3 **Summary**

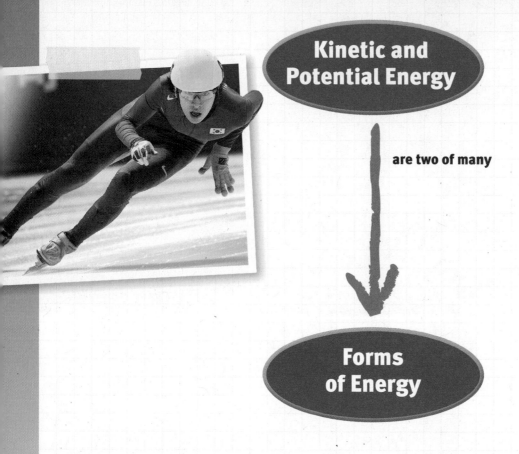

Kinetic and Potential Energy

are two of many

Forms of Energy

---

1 Interpret The Graphic Organizer above shows that kinetic and potential energy are forms of energy. Name three other forms of energy.

_____

_____

_____

_____

2 Distinguish What is the difference between kinetic energy, potential energy, and mechanical energy?

_____

_____

_____

_____

_____

_____

3 Describe Give an example of chemical energy being changed into another form of energy.

_____

_____

_____

_____

4 Apply What is the relationship between the amount of electrical energy that enters a light bulb and the heat energy and light energy given off by the bulb?

_____

_____

_____

_____

_____

Name _____

Multiple Choice

1 At what point in the upward and downward motion of a yo-yo's arc is its kinetic energy the greatest?

   A. when you hold it in your hand

   B. when it first begins to drop

   C. as it nears the end of its drop

   D. when it starts rolling back up

2 A group of sheep are grazing in a field. As they eat, the sheep break down the molecules in the grass, which releases energy. Which form of energy is stored in the grass?

   A. chemical energy   **C.** nuclear energy

   B. elastic energy   **D.** heat energy

3 Ms. Lewis is a chemist mixing two solutions together. A chemical reaction takes place, and the solution becomes warm. Which statement BEST describes what has happened?

   A. Energy has been created in the form of heat energy.

   B. Energy has been transferred from one form to another.

   C. More energy has been created than has been destroyed.

   D. The chemical energy of the solution has been destroyed.

4 The Wilson family put some solar-powered night-lights in their back yard. The lights turn on at dark. They run all night from a battery that charges during the day. What transfer of energy stores the energy that powers the lights?

   A. electromagnetic to thermal

   B. chemical to mechanical

   C. electromagnetic to chemical

   D. electrical to thermal

5 A rock sitting on top of a hill has energy due to its position. What is this energy called?

   A. chemical energy   **C.** gravitational potential energy

   B. kinetic energy   **D.** elastic potential energy

6 When a pendulum is released, it swings back and forth. It continues moving without any additional push until it is slowed by friction from the air around it. This image shows positions of a pendulum during its swing.

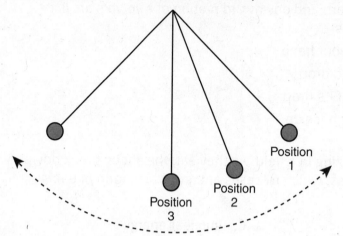

At which point does the pendulum weight have the GREATEST amount of mechanical energy?

A. Position 1

B. Position 2

C. Position 3

D. Mechanical energy does not change.

7 The illustration below shows the path of a ball when thrown into the air.

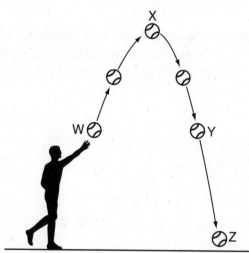

What energy does the ball have at the point labeled Y?

A. kinetic energy only

B. potential energy only

C. kinetic energy and elastic potential energy

D. kinetic energy and gravitational potential energy

8 The illustration below shows a slingshot.

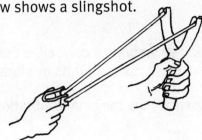

What is the source of the potential energy present in this picture?

A. the person

C. the Y-shaped stick

B. the rubber band

D. the rock held in the rubber band

Constructed Response

9 The illustration below shows a scale of the frequencies of electromagnetic radiation from the sun and their wavelengths.

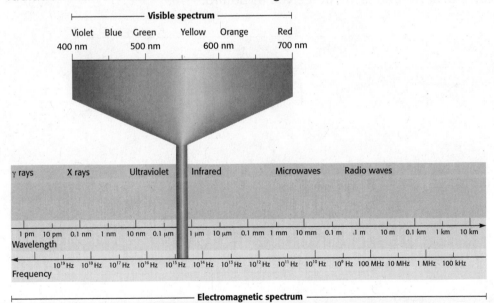

What are TWO things that you know about ultraviolet light?

1 _____

2 _____

What are TWO things you know about light with wavelengths between 400 nm and 700 nm?

1 _____

2 _____

Extended Response

10 Several musical instruments, including cymbals, a cowbell, a triangle, a handbell, a kettle drum, and a snare drum make sounds by vibrating.

Choose THREE instruments and describe how they make vibrations.

Instrument 1 _____

_____

Instrument 2 _____

_____

Instrument 3 _____

_____

Describe how these vibrations are perceived as sound.

_____

_____

UNIT 4
The Solar System

A brass orrery shows the rotation of planets around the sun.

What do you think?

For hundreds of years, scientists have created models to help us understand the solar system. What are some different ways in which scientists have modeled the solar system?

The Human Orrery models the solar system.

Unit 4
The Solar System

Lesson 1
**Historical Models of
the Solar System**.................. 150
6.2.3

People in Science................ 160

Lesson 2
Gravity and the Solar System ... 162
6.2.2

Think Science.................... 176
NOS 6.8

Lesson 3
The Sun........................... 178
6.2.3

Lesson 4
The Terrestrial Planets........... 190
6.2.4

People in Science................ 204

Lesson 5
The Gas Giant Planets........... 206
6.2.4

Lesson 6
**Small Bodies in
the Solar System**................. 218
6.2.4

Unit Summary.................... 234

ISTEP+ Review.............. 235

Indiana Standards

As citizens of the constructed world, students will
participate in the design process. Students will learn to use
materials and tools safely and employ the basic principles
of the engineering design process in order to find solutions
to problems.

DP 6.10 Communicate the solution including evidence using
mathematical representations (graphs, data tables), drawings or
prototypes.

CITIZEN SCIENCE
Solar System Discoveries

Today's knowledge of the solar system is the
result of discoveries that have been made over
the centuries. Discoveries will continue to
change our view of the solar system.

Moons of Jupiter, 1610
On January 7, 1610, Galileo used
a telescope he had improved
and discovered the four largest
moons of Jupiter. The moons are
some of the largest objects in
our solar system!

*Ganymede is the largest
of Jupiter's moons.*

Comet Hyakutake

Comet Hyakutake, 1996

Amateur astronomer Yuji Hyakutake discovered Comet Hyakutake on January 31, 1996, using a pair of powerful binoculars. This comet will approach Earth only once every 100,000 years.

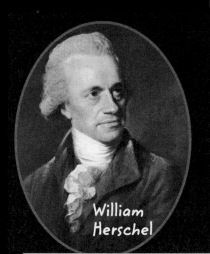

William Herschel

Uranus, 1781

British astronomer Sir William Herschel discovered Uranus on March 13, 1781. It was the first planet discovered with a telescope. Our knowledge of the solar system expanded in ways people had not expected.

Neptune, 1846

Mathematics helped scientists discover the planet Neptune. Astronomers predicted Neptune's existence based on irregularities in its orbit. On September 23, 1846, Neptune was discovered by telescope almost exactly where it was mathematically predicted to be.

Neptune

Take It Home Future Explorations

① Think About It

What are some recent discoveries that have been made about the solar system?

_____
_____
_____
_____

• Will crewed missions to distant places in the solar system ever be possible? Justify your answer.

_____
_____
_____
_____
_____

② Ask Some Questions

Research efforts, such as NASA's Stardust spacecraft, to learn more about how space is being explored now.

• How is information being transmitted back to Earth?

_____
_____

③ Make A Plan

Design a poster to explain why humans are exploring the solar system. Be sure to include the following information:

• How we are using technology for exploration
• Why it benefits all of us to learn about the solar system

Historical Models
of the Solar System

ESSENTIAL QUESTION

How have people modeled the solar system?

By the end of this lesson, you should be able to compare various historical models of the solar system.

The Earth-centered model of the solar system was accepted for almost 1,400 years. It was replaced by the sun-centered model of the solar system, which is shown in this 17th-century illustration.

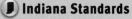

Indiana Standards

6.2.3 Understand that the sun, an average star where nuclear reactions occur, is the central and largest body in the solar system.

Engage Your Brain

1 Predict Check T or F to show whether you think each statement is true or false.

T	F	
☐	☑	The sun and planets circle Earth.
☑	☑	Most early astronomers placed the sun at the center of the solar system.
☑	☐	The planets orbit the sun in ellipses.
☐	☐	The telescope helped to improve our understanding of the solar system.

2 Evaluate What, if anything, is wrong with the model of the solar system shown below?

_____

_____

_____

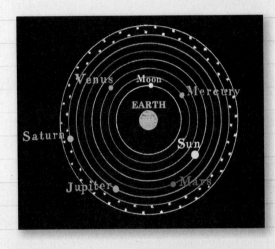

Active Reading

3 Synthesis You can often define an unknown word if you know the meaning of its word parts. Use the word parts and sentence below to make an educated guess about the meaning of the word *heliocentric*.

Word part	Meaning
helio-	sun
-centric	centered

Example sentence
The <u>heliocentric</u> model of the solar system was first proposed by Aristarchus.

heliocentric:

_____

_____

_____

Vocabulary Terms

- solar system
- heliocentric
- geocentric
- parallax

4 Apply As you learn the definition of each vocabulary term in this lesson, create your own definition or sketch to help you remember the meaning of the term.

What is the Center

What is the solar system?

The **solar system** is the sun and all of the bodies that orbit the sun. Our current model of the solar system is the *sun-centered* or *heliocentric* (hee•lee•oh•SEN•trik) model. In the **heliocentric** model, Earth and the other planets orbit the sun. The earliest models for the solar system assumed that the Earth was at the center of the solar system, with the sun, moon, and planets circling it. These models, which used Earth as the center, are called *Earth-centered* or **geocentric** (jee•oh•SEN•trik) models. The heliocentric model was not generally accepted until the work of Copernicus and Kepler in the late 16th to early 17th centuries.

Active Reading

5 Identify As you read the text, underline the definitions of geocentric and heliocentric.

Who proposed some early models of the solar system?

Until Galileo improved on the telescope in 1609, people observed the heavens with the naked eye. To observers, it appeared that the sun, the moon, the planets, and the stars moved around Earth each day. This caused them to conclude that Earth was not moving. If Earth was not moving, then Earth must be the center of the solar system and all other bodies revolved around it.

This geocentric model of the solar system became part of ancient Greek thought beginning in the 6th century BCE. Aristotle was among the first thinkers to propose this model.

Think Outside the Book

6 Research Use different sources to research a geocentric model of the solar system from either ancient Greece, ancient China, or Babylon. Write a short description of the model you choose.

Aristotle (384–322 BCE)

Aristotle

Aristotle (AIR•ih•staht'l) was a Greek philosopher. Aristotle thought Earth was the center of all things. His model placed the moon, sun, planets, and stars on a series of circles that surrounded Earth. He thought that if Earth went around the sun, then the relative positions of the stars would change as Earth moves. This apparent shift in the position of an object when viewed from different locations is known as **parallax** (PAIR•uh•laks). In fact, the stars are so far away that parallax cannot be seen with the naked eye.

of the Solar System?

Aristarchus

Aristarchus (air•i•STAHR•kuhs) was a Greek astronomer and mathematician. Aristarchus is reported to have proposed a heliocentric model of the solar system. His model, however, was not widely accepted at the time. Aristarchus attempted to measure the relative distances to the moon and sun. This was a major contribution to science. Aristarchus's ratio of distances was much too small but was important in the use of observation and geometry to solve a scientific problem.

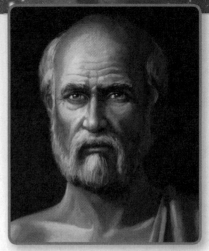

Aristarchus (about 310–230 BCE)

Aristotle thought that if Earth were moving, the positions of the stars should change as Earth moved. In fact, stars are so far away that shifts in their positions can only be observed by telescope.

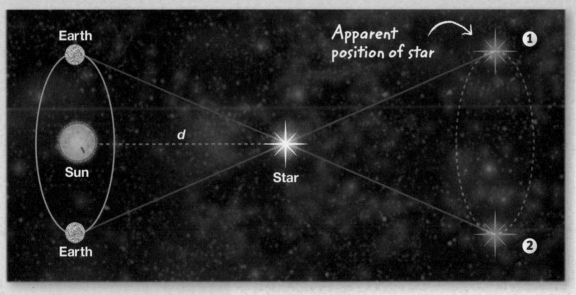

Diagram showing the shift in apparent position of a star at two different times of year seen from a telescope on Earth. A star first seen at point 1 will be seen at point 2 six months later.

 **Visualize It!**

7 Predict If a star appears at position 1 during the summer, during which season will it appear at position 2?

_____

_____

_____

Ptolemy

Ptolemy (about 100–170 CE)

Ptolemy (TOHL•uh•mee) was an astronomer, geographer, and mathematician who lived in Alexandria, Egypt, which was part of ancient Rome. His book, the *Almagest*, is one of the few books that we have from these early times. It was based on observations of the planets going back as much as 800 years. Ptolemy developed a detailed geocentric model that was used by astronomers for the next 14 centuries. He believed that a celestial body traveled at a constant speed in a perfect circle. In Ptolemy's model, the planets moved on small circles that in turn moved on larger circles. This "wheels-on-wheels" system fit observations better than any model that had come before. It allowed prediction of the motion of planets years into the future.

Visualize It!

8 Describe Use the diagram at the right to describe Ptolemy's geocentric model of the solar system.

_____

_____

_____

_____

_____

Think Outside the Book (Inquiry)

9 Defend As a class activity, defend Ptolemy's geocentric model of the solar system. Remember that during Ptolemy's time people were limited to what they could see with the naked eye.

Ptolemaic Model

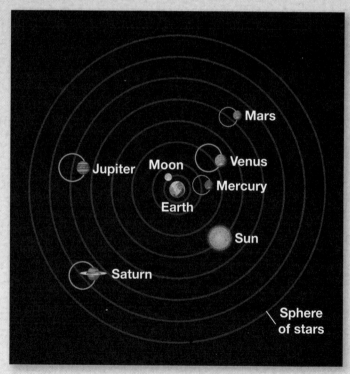

Mars

Venus

Jupiter · Moon · Mercury

Earth

Sun

Saturn

Sphere of stars

Copernicus

The Polish astronomer Nicolaus Copernicus (nik•uh•LAY•uhs koh•PER•nuh•kuhs) felt that Ptolemy's model of the solar system was too complicated. He was aware of the heliocentric idea of Aristarchus when he developed the first detailed heliocentric model of the solar system. In Copernicus's time, data was still based on observations with the naked eye. Because data had changed little since the time of Ptolemy, Copernicus adopted Ptolemy's idea that planetary paths should be perfect circles. Like Ptolemy, he used a "wheels-on-wheels" system. Copernicus's model fit observations a little better than the geocentric model of Ptolemy. The heliocentric model of Copernicus is generally seen as the first step in the development of modern models of the solar system.

Nicolaus Copernicus (1473–1543)

Copernican Model

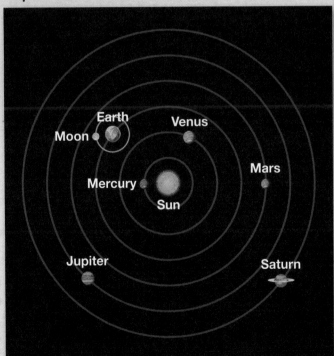

10 **Compare** How does Copernicus's model of the solar system differ from Ptolemy's model of the solar system?

Ptolemaic model	Copernican model

Johannes Kepler (1571–1630)

Active Reading

11 Identify Underline text that summarizes Kepler's three laws.

Kepler

Johannes Kepler (yoh•HAH•nuhs KEP•luhr) was a German mathematician and astronomer. After carefully analyzing observations of the planets, he realized that requiring planetary motions to be exactly circular did not fit the observations perfectly. Kepler then tried other types of paths and found that ellipses fit best.

Kepler formulated three principles, which today are known as Kepler's laws. The first law states that planetary orbits are ellipses with the sun at one focus. The second law states that planets move faster in their orbits when closer to the sun. The third law relates the distance of a planet from the sun to the time it takes to go once around its orbit.

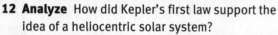

12 Analyze How did Kepler's first law support the idea of a heliocentric solar system?

_____

_____

_____

_____

Kepler's First Law

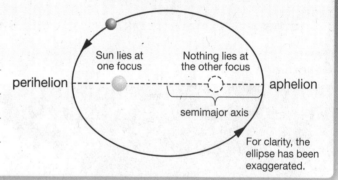

Sun lies at one focus

Nothing lies at the other focus

perihelion — — — — — — — — — — — — — — — aphelion

semimajor axis

For clarity, the ellipse has been exaggerated.

Galileo

Galileo Galilei (gahl•uh•LAY•oh gahl•uh•LAY) was a scientist who approached questions in the fashion that today we call *scientific methods*. Galileo made significant improvements to the newly invented telescope. He then used his more powerful telescope to view celestial objects. Galileo observed the moons Io, Europa, Callisto, and Ganymede orbiting Jupiter. Today, these moons are known as the Galilean satellites. His observations showed that Earth was not the only object that could be orbited. This gave support to the heliocentric model. He also observed that Venus went through phases similar to the phases of Earth's moon. These phases result from changes in the direction that sunlight strikes Venus as Venus orbits the sun.

Galileo Galilei (1564–1642)

Galileo

Galileo Galilei was an Italian mathematician, physicist, and astronomer who lived during the 16th and 17th centuries. Galileo demonstrated that all bodies, regardless of their mass, fall at the same rate. He also argued that moving objects retain their velocity unless an unbalanced force acts upon them. Galileo made improvements to telescope technology. He used his telescopes to observe sunspots, the phases of Venus, Earth's moon, the four Galilean moons of Jupiter, and a supernova.

Galileo's Telescopes

This reconstruction of one of Galileo's telescopes is on exhibit in Florence, Italy. Galileo's first telescopes magnified objects at 3 and then 20 times.

The *Galileo* Spacecraft

The *Galileo* spacecraft was launched from the space shuttle *Atlantis* in 1989. *Galileo* was the first spacecraft to orbit Jupiter. It studied the planet and its moons.

Inquiry

Extend

13 Identify What were Galileo's most important contributions to astronomy?

14 Research Galileo invented or improved upon many instruments and technologies, such as the compound microscope, the thermometer, and the geometric compass. Research one of Galileo's technological contributions.

15 Create Describe one of Galileo's experiments concerning the motion of bodies by doing one of the following:

- make a poster

- recreate the experiment

- draw a graphic novel of Galileo conducting an experiment

Visual Summary

To complete this summary, fill in the blanks with the correct word or phrase. Then use the key below to check your answers. You can use this page to review the main concepts of the lesson.

Models of the Solar System

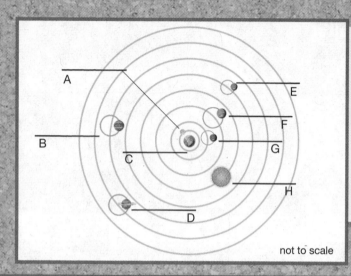

not to scale

Early astronomers proposed a geocentric solar system.

16 Label the solar system bodies as they appear in the geocentric model.

17 Which astronomers are associated with this model of the solar system?

_____

_____

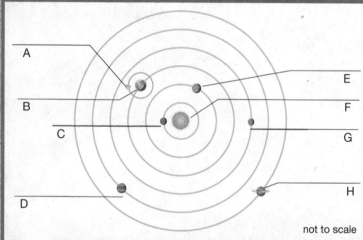

not to scale

The heliocentric solar system is the current model.

18 Label the solar system bodies as they appear in the heliocentric model.

19 Which astronomers are associated with this model of the solar system?

_____

_____

_____

_____

Answers: 16 A. moon, B. Jupiter, C. Earth, D. Saturn, E. Mars, F. Venus, G. Mercury, H. sun; 17 Aristotle, Ptolemy; 18 A. moon, B. Earth, C. Mercury, D. Jupiter, E. Venus, F. sun, G. Mars, H. Saturn; 19 Aristarchus, Copernicus, Kepler, Galileo

20 **Compare** How does the geocentric model of the solar system differ from the heliocentric model of the solar system?

Lesson Review

Vocabulary

Fill in the blank with the term that best completes the following sentences.

1 The _____ is the sun and all of the planets and other bodies that travel around it.

2 Until the time of Copernicus, most scientists thought the _____ model of the solar system was correct.

3 An apparent shift in the position of an object when viewed from different locations is called _____.

Key Concepts

In the following table, write the name of the correct astronomer next to that astronomer's contribution.

Contribution	Astronomer
4 Identify Who first observed the phases of Venus?	
5 Identify Who attempted to measure the relative distances to the moon and the sun?	
6 Identify Who replaced circles with ellipses in a heliocentric model of the universe?	
7 Identify Whose geocentric model of the solar system was accepted for 1,400 years?	
8 Identify Whose heliocentric model is seen as the first step in the development of modern models of the solar system?	

Critical Thinking

Use the illustration to answer the following question.

9 Appraise How did data gathered using Galileo's early telescope support the heliocentric model?

_____

_____

_____

_____

10 Explain How did Aristotle's inability to detect parallax lead him to propose a geocentric model of the solar system?

_____

_____

_____

_____

_____

_____

_____

Sandra Faber

ASTRONOMER

What do you do when you send a telescope into space and then find out that it is broken? You call Dr. Sandra Faber, a professor of astronomy at the University of California, Santa Cruz (UCSC). In April 1990, after the *Hubble Space Telescope* went into orbit, scientists found that the images the telescope collected were not turning out as expected. Dr. Faber's team at UCSC was in charge of a device on *Hubble* called the *Wide Field Planetary Camera*. Dr. Faber and her team decided to test the telescope to determine what was wrong.

To perform the test, they centered *Hubble* onto a bright star and took several photos. From those photos, Dr. Faber's team created a model of what was wrong. After reporting the error to NASA and presenting the model they had developed, Dr. Faber and a group of experts began to correct the problem. The group's efforts were a success and put *Hubble* back into operation so that astronomers could continue researching stars and other objects in space.

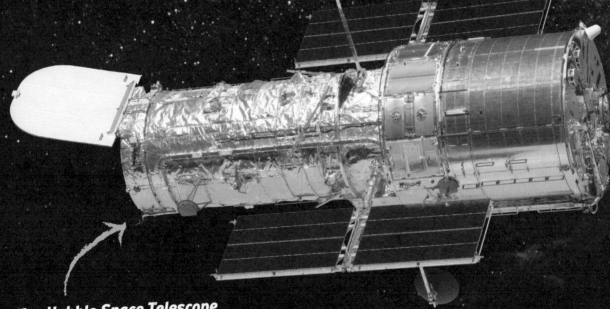

The **Hubble Space Telescope** orbits 569 km above Earth.

Language Arts Connection

Suppose you are a journalist preparing to interview Dr. Sandra Faber. List four questions you would ask her.

JOB BOARD

Astronautical Engineer

What You'll Do: Work on spacecraft that operate outside of Earth's atmosphere, like satellites or space shuttles. Other tasks include planning space missions, determining orbits of spacecraft, and designing rockets and communications systems.

Where You Might Work: Most likely with space agencies. You may also find jobs with aerospace companies or the military.

Education: All engineers must have a four-year college degree in aerospace or astronautical engineering. Many engineers go on to earn a master's degree and a doctorate. Basic engineering classes include algebra, calculus, physics, and computer programming.

Other Job Requirements: You should be able to work well with a team. You should be very careful and exact in your calculations and measurements.

Robotics Technician

What You'll Do: Help engineers build and operate robots, and work with robotic engineers on robotic tools for spacecraft. Use software to solve problems and to test equipment as part of your daily routine.

Where You Might Work: Government space agencies such as NASA, the auto industry, schools, laboratories, and manufacturing plants.

Education: Most technicians complete a two-year technical certificate. Technicians should have a strong interest in math and science. Professional certification is offered to technicians who have at least four years of work experience.

Other Job Requirements: You may also be asked to read blueprints, use microcomputers, and use oscilloscopes.

Gravity and the Solar System

ESSENTIAL QUESTION

Why is gravity important in the solar system?

By the end of this lesson, you should be able to explain the role that gravity played in the formation of the solar system and in determining the motion of the planets.

Gravity keeps objects, such as these satellites, in orbit around Earth. Gravity also affects the way in which planets move and how they are formed.

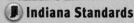

Indiana Standards

6.2.2 Recognize that gravity is a force that keeps celestial bodies in regular and predictable motion, holds objects to earth's surface and is responsible for ocean tides.

Visual Summary

To complete this summary, fill in the blanks with the correct word or phrase. Then use the key below to check your answers. You can use this page to review the main concepts of the lesson.

Models of the Solar System

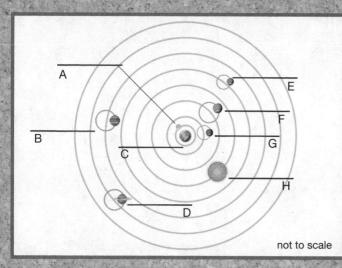

not to scale

Early astronomers proposed a geocentric solar system.

16 Label the solar system bodies as they appear in the geocentric model.

17 Which astronomers are associated with this model of the solar system?

_____

_____

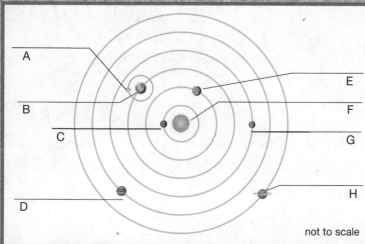

not to scale

The heliocentric solar system is the current model.

18 Label the solar system bodies as they appear in the heliocentric model.

19 Which astronomers are associated with this model of the solar system?

_____

_____

_____

_____

Answers: 16 A. moon, B. Jupiter, C. Earth, D. Saturn, E. Mars, F. Venus, G. Mercury, H. sun; 17 Aristotle, Ptolemy; 18 A. moon, B. Earth, C. Mercury, D. Jupiter, E. Venus, F. sun, G. Mars, H. Saturn; 19 Aristarchus, Copernicus, Kepler, Galileo

20 **Compare** How does the geocentric model of the solar system differ from the heliocentric model of the solar system?

Galileo

Galileo Galilei was an Italian mathematician, physicist, and astronomer who lived during the 16th and 17th centuries. Galileo demonstrated that all bodies, regardless of their mass, fall at the same rate. He also argued that moving objects retain their velocity unless an unbalanced force acts upon them. Galileo made improvements to telescope technology. He used his telescopes to observe sunspots, the phases of Venus, Earth's moon, the four Galilean moons of Jupiter, and a supernova.

Galileo's Telescopes

This reconstruction of one of Galileo's telescopes is on exhibit in Florence, Italy. Galileo's first telescopes magnified objects at 3 and then 20 times.

The *Galileo* Spacecraft

The *Galileo* spacecraft was launched from the space shuttle *Atlantis* in 1989. *Galileo* was the first spacecraft to orbit Jupiter. It studied the planet and its moons.

Inquiry

Extend

13 Identify What were Galileo's most important contributions to astronomy?

14 Research Galileo invented or improved upon many instruments and technologies, such as the compound microscope, the thermometer, and the geometric compass. Research one of Galileo's technological contributions.

15 Create Describe one of Galileo's experiments concerning the motion of bodies by doing one of the following:

- make a poster
- recreate the experiment
- draw a graphic novel of Galileo conducting an experiment

Engage Your Brain

1 Predict Check T or F to show whether you think each statement is true or false.

T F

☑ ☐ Gravity keeps the planets in orbit around the sun.

☑ ☐ The planets follow circular paths around the sun.

☑ ☐ Sir Isaac Newton was the first scientist to describe how the force of gravity behaved.

☑ ☐ The sun formed in the center of the solar system.

☑ ☐ The terrestrial planets and the gas giant planets formed from the same material.

2 Draw In the space below, draw what you think the solar system looked like before the planets formed.

Active Reading

3 Synthesize You can often define an unknown word if you know the meaning of its word parts. Use the word parts and sentence below to make an educated guess about the meaning of the word *protostellar*.

Word part	Meaning
proto-	first
-stellar	of or having to do with a star or stars

Example sentence
The <u>protostellar</u> disk formed after the collapse of the solar nebula.

protostellar:

_____

_____

Vocabulary Terms

- gravity
- orbit
- aphelion
- perihelion
- centripetal force
- solar nebula
- planetesimal

4 Apply This list contains the key terms you'll learn in this section. As you read, circle the definition of each term.

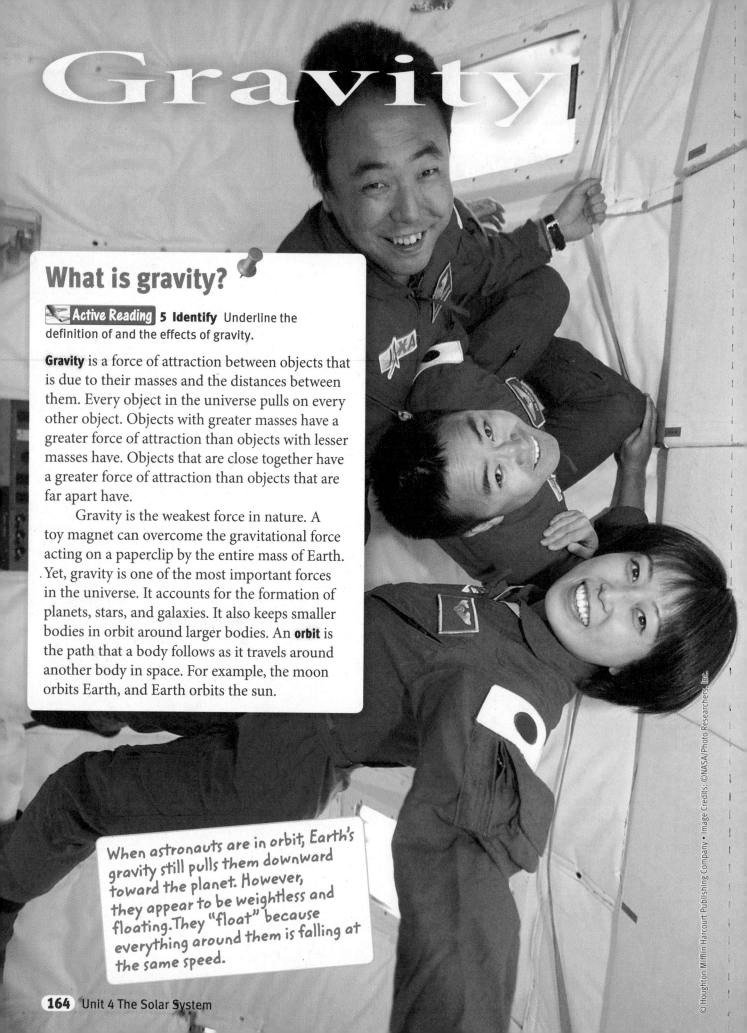

Gravity

What is gravity?

Active Reading **5 Identify** Underline the definition of and the effects of gravity.

Gravity is a force of attraction between objects that is due to their masses and the distances between them. Every object in the universe pulls on every other object. Objects with greater masses have a greater force of attraction than objects with lesser masses have. Objects that are close together have a greater force of attraction than objects that are far apart have.

Gravity is the weakest force in nature. A toy magnet can overcome the gravitational force acting on a paperclip by the entire mass of Earth. Yet, gravity is one of the most important forces in the universe. It accounts for the formation of planets, stars, and galaxies. It also keeps smaller bodies in orbit around larger bodies. An **orbit** is the path that a body follows as it travels around another body in space. For example, the moon orbits Earth, and Earth orbits the sun.

When astronauts are in orbit, Earth's gravity still pulls them downward toward the planet. However, they appear to be weightless and floating. They "float" because everything around them is falling at the same speed.

What are Kepler's laws?

The 16th-century Polish astronomer Nicolaus Copernicus (nik•uh•LAY•uhs koh•PER•nuh•kuhs) (1473–1543) changed our view of the solar system. He discovered that the motions of the planets could be best explained if the planets orbited the sun. But, like astronomers who came before him, Copernicus thought the planets followed circular paths around the sun.

Danish astronomer Tycho Brahe (TY•koh BRAH) (1546–1601) built what was at the time the world's largest observatory. Tycho used special instruments to measure the motions of the planets. His measurements were made over a period of 20 years and were very accurate. Using Tycho's data, Johannes Kepler (yoh•HAH•nuhs KEP•luhr) (1571–1630) made discoveries about the motions of the planets. We call these *Kepler's laws of planetary motion*.

Kepler found that objects that orbit the sun follow elliptical orbits. When an object follows an elliptical orbit around the sun, there is one point, called **aphelion** (uh•FEE•lee•uhn), where the object is farthest from the sun. There is also a point, called **perihelion** (perh•uh•HEE•lee•uhn), where the object is closest to the sun. Today, we know that the orbits of the planets are only slightly elliptical. However, the orbits of objects such as Pluto and comets are highly elliptical.

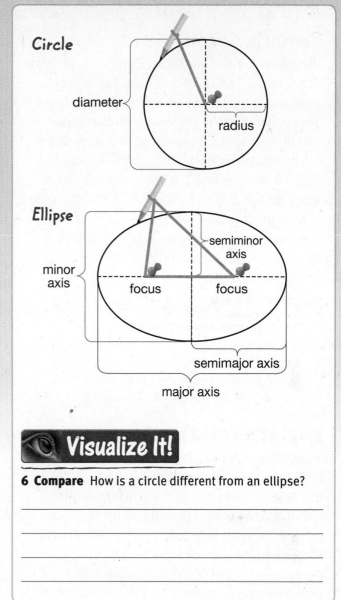

Circle

diameter

radius

Ellipse

semiminor axis

minor axis

focus   focus

semimajor axis

major axis

Visualize It!

6 Compare How is a circle different from an ellipse?

_____

_____

_____

Kepler's First Law

Kepler's careful plotting of the orbit of Mars kept showing Mars's orbit to be a deformed circle. It took Kepler eight years to realize that this shape was an ellipse. This clue led Kepler to propose elliptical orbits for the planets. Kepler placed the sun at one of the foci of the ellipse. This is Kepler's first law.

Active Reading **7 Contrast** What is the difference between Copernicus's and Kepler's description of planetary orbits?

_____

_____

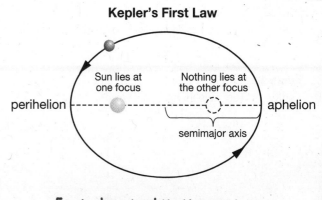

Kepler's First Law

Sun lies at one focus

Nothing lies at the other focus

perihelion   aphelion

semimajor axis

Each planet orbits the sun in an ellipse with the sun at one focus. (For clarity, the ellipse is exaggerated here.)

Kepler's Second Law

Using the shape of an ellipse, Kepler searched for other regularities in Tycho's data. He found that an amazing thing happens when a line is drawn from a planet to the sun's focus on the ellipse. At aphelion, its speed is slower. So, it sweeps out a narrow sector on the ellipse. At perihelion, the planet is moving faster. It sweeps out a thick sector on the ellipse. In the illustration, the areas of both the thin blue sector and the thick blue sector are exactly the same. Kepler found that this relationship is true for all of the planets. This is Kepler's second law.

Active Reading **8 Analyze** At which point does a planet move most slowly in its orbit, at aphelion or perihelion?

As a planet moves around its orbit, it sweeps out equal areas in equal times.

Kepler's Second Law

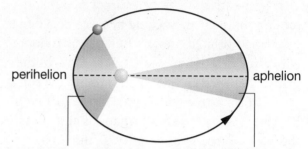

Near perihelion, a planet sweeps out an area that is short but wide.

Near aphelion, in an equal amount of time, a planet sweeps out an area that is long but narrow.

Kepler's Third Law

When Kepler looked at how long it took for the planets to orbit the sun and at the sizes of their orbits, he found another relationship. Kepler calculated the orbital period and the distance from the sun for the planets using Tycho's data. He discovered that the square of the orbital period was proportional to the cube of the planet's average distance from the sun. This law is true for each planet. This principle is Kepler's third law. When the units are years for the period and AU for the distance, the law can be written:

$$(\text{orbital period in years})^2 = (\text{average distance from the sun in astronomical units [AU]})^3$$

The square of the orbital period is proportional to the cube of the planet's average distance from the sun.

Kepler's Third Law

$$p^2 \text{ yrs} = a^3 \text{ AU}$$

perihelion | a | aphelion

9 Summarize In the table below, summarize each of Kepler's three laws in your own words.

First law	Second law	Third law

What is the law of universal gravitation?

Using Kepler's laws, Sir Isaac Newton (EYE•zuhk NOOT'n) became the first scientist to mathematically describe how the force of gravity behaved. How could Newton do this in the 1600s before the force could be measured in a laboratory? He reasoned that gravity was the same force that accounted for both the fall of an apple from a tree and the movement of the moon around Earth.

In 1687, Newton formulated the *law of universal gravitation*. The law of universal gravitation states that all objects in the universe attract each other through gravitational force. The strength of this force depends on the product of the masses of the objects. Therefore, the gravity between objects increases as the masses of the objects increase. Gravitational force is also inversely proportional to the square of the distance between the objects. Stated another way this means that as the distance between two objects increases, the force of gravity decreases.

Sir Isaac Newton
(1642–1727)

Do the Math

Newton's law of universal gravitation says that the force of gravity:
- increases as the masses of the objects increase and
- decreases as the distance between the objects increases

In these examples, M = mass, d = distance, and F = the force of gravity exerted by two bodies.

Sample Problems

A. In the example below, when two balls have masses of M and the distance between them is d, then the force of gravity is F. If the mass of each ball is increased to 2M (to the right) and the distance stays the same, then the force of gravity increases to 4F.

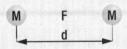 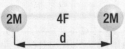

B. In this example, we start out again with a distance of d and masses of M, and the force of gravity is F. If the distance is decreased to ½ d, then the force of gravity increases to 4F.

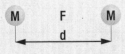

You Try It

Recall that M = mass, d = distance, and F = the force of gravity exerted by two bodies.

10 Calculate Compare the example below to the sample problems. What would the force of gravity be in the example below? Explain your answer.

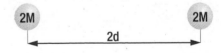

_____

_____

_____

_____

_____

How does gravity affect planetary motion?

The illustrations on this page will help you understand planetary motion. In the illustration at the right, a girl is swinging a ball around her head. The ball is attached to a string. The girl is exerting a force on the string that causes the ball to move in a circular path. The inward force that causes an object to move in a circular path is called **centripetal** (sehn•TRIP•ih•tuhl) **force**.

In the illustration at center, we see that if the string breaks, the ball will move off in a straight line. This fact indicates that when the string is intact, a force is pulling the ball inward. This force keeps the ball from flying off and moving in a straight line. This force is centripetal force.

In the illustration below, you see that the planets orbit the sun. A force must be preventing the planets from moving out of their orbits and into a straight line. The sun's gravity is the force that keeps the planets moving in orbit around the sun.

As the girl swings the ball, she is exerting a force on the string that causes the ball to move in a circular path.

Centripetal force pulls the ball inward, which causes the ball to move in a curved path.

direction centripetal force pulls the ball

direction ball would move if string broke

Center of rotation

String

path ball takes when moving around the center of rotation

Just as the string is pulling the ball inward, gravity is keeping the planets in orbit around the sun.

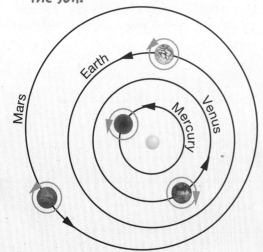

Mars

Earth

Venus

Mercury

11 Explain In the illustration at the top of the page, what does the hand represent, the ball represent, and the string represent? (Hint: Think of the sun, a planet, and the force of gravity.)

_____

_____

_____

_____

How did the solar system form?

The formation of the solar system is thought to have begun 4.6 billion years ago when a cloud of dust and gas collapsed. This cloud, from which the solar system formed, is called the **solar nebula** (SOH•ler NEB•yuh•luh). In a nebula, the inward pull of gravity is balanced by the outward push of gas pressure in the cloud. Scientists think that an outside force, perhaps the explosion of a nearby star, caused the solar nebula to compress and then to contract under its own gravity. It was in a single region of the nebula, which was perhaps several light-years across, that the solar system formed. The sun probably formed from a region that had a mass that was slightly greater than today's mass of the sun and planets.

Active Reading 12 **Define** What is the solar nebula?

A cloud of dust and gas collapsed 4.6 billion years ago, then began to spin. It may have spun around its axis of rotation once every million years.

A Protostellar Disk Formed from the Collapsed Solar Nebula

As a region of the solar nebula collapsed, gravity pulled most of the mass toward the center of the nebula. As the nebula contracted, it began to rotate. As the rotation grew faster, the nebula flattened out into a disk. This disk, which is called a *protostellar disk* (PROH•toh•stehl•er DISK), is where the central star, our sun, formed.

As a region of the solar nebula collapsed, it formed a slowly rotating protostellar disk.

The Sun Formed at the Center of the Protostellar Disk

As the protostellar disk continued to contract, most of the matter ended up in the center of the disk. Friction from matter that fell into the disk heated up its center to millions of degrees, eventually reaching its current temperature of 15,000,000 °C. This intense heat in a densely packed space caused the fusion of hydrogen atoms into helium atoms. The process of fusion released large amounts of energy. This release of energy caused outward pressure that again balanced the inward pull of gravity. As the gas and dust stopped collapsing, a star was born. In the case of the solar system, this star was the sun.

 Active Reading 13 **Identify** How did the sun form?

_____

_____

_____

_____

_____

This is an artist's conception of what the protoplanetary disk in which the planets formed might have looked like.

👁 Visualize It!

14 **Describe** Use the terms *planetesimal* and *protoplanetary disk* to describe the illustration above.

_____

_____

_____

_____

_____

_____

Planetesimals Formed in the Protoplanetary Disk

As the sun was forming, dust grains collided and stuck together. The resulting *dust granules* grew in size and increased in number. Over time, dust granules increased in size until they became roughly meter-sized bodies. Trillions of these bodies occurred in the protostellar disk. Collisions between these bodies formed larger bodies that were kilometers across. These larger bodies, from which planets formed, are called **planetesimals** (plan•ih•TES•ih•muhls). The protostellar disk had become the *protoplanetary disk*. The protoplanetary disk was the disk in which the planets formed.

Dust grains collided and stuck together.

Over time, dust granules grew to become meter-sized bodies.

Planetesimals formed from the collisions of meter-sized bodies.

Visualize It! Inquiry

15 Explain How can objects as small as dust grains become the building blocks of planets?

_____

_____

_____

_____

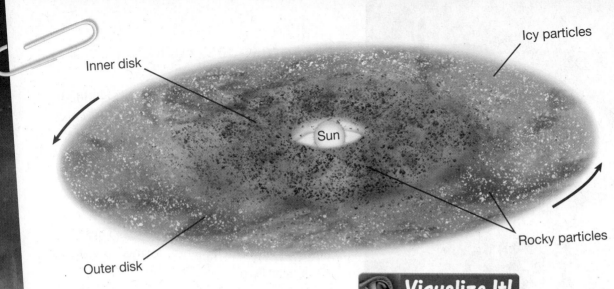

Inner disk

Icy particles

Sun

Outer disk

Rocky particles

Temperatures in the protoplanetary disk controlled the formation of the planets.

Visualize It!

16 Analyze Where did planets made mostly of gas and ice form within the protoplanetary disk?

Terrestrial planets formed when rocky planetesimals collided.

The Planets Formed from Planetesimals

The inner part of the protoplanetary disk was so hot that only rocks and metals were in solid form. Therefore, rocky, metallic planets formed in the inner disk. These planets formed from the collisions and mergers of rocky planetesimals. We call these inner planets the *terrestrial planets*.

In the cold outer disk, ices, gases, rocks, and metals were all found. At first, massive planets made of icy and rocky planetesimals may have formed. The gravity of these planets was so strong that they captured gas and other matter as they grew. Therefore, planets that formed in the outer disk have rocky or metallic cores and deep atmospheres of gas and ice. We call these outer planets the *gas giant planets*.

Gas giant planets captured gas and other matter in the area of their orbits.

17 Describe In the spaces on the left, describe Steps 2 and 4 in the formation of the solar system. In the spaces on the right, draw the last two steps in the formation of the solar system.

Steps in the Formation of the Solar System

Step 1 *The Solar Nebula Collapses*

A cloud of dust and gas collapses. The balance between the inward pull of gravity and the outward push of pressure in the cloud is upset. The collapsing cloud forms a rotating protostellar disk.

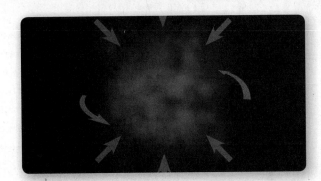

Step 2 *The Sun Forms*

_____
_____
_____
_____

Step 3 *Planetesimals Form*

Dust grains stick together and form dust granules. Dust granules slowly increase in size until they become meter-sized objects. These meter-sized objects collide to form kilometer-sized objects called *planetesimals*.

Step 4 *Planets Form*

_____
_____
_____
_____

Visual Summary

To complete this summary, fill in the blank with the correct word or phrase. Then use the key below to check your answers. You can use this page to review the main concepts of the lesson.

The Law of Universal Gravitation

Mass affects the force of gravity.

18 The strength of the force of gravity depends on the product of the _____ of two objects. Therefore, as the masses of two objects increase, the force that the objects exert on one another _____.

Distance affects the force of gravity.

19 Gravitational force is inversely proportional to the square of the _____ between two objects. Therefore, as the distance between two objects increases, the force of gravity between them _____.

Gravity affects planetary motion.

20 The sun exerts a _____, indicated by line B, on a planet so that at point C it is moving around the sun in orbit instead of moving off in a _____ as shown at line A.

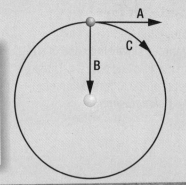

Answers: 18 masses, increases; 19 distance, decreases; 20 gravitational force or centripetal force, straight line

21 **Explain** In your own words, explain Newton's law of universal gravitation.

Lesson Review

Vocabulary

Fill in the blank with the term that best completes the following sentences.

1 Small bodies from which the planets formed are called _____

2 The path that a body follows as it travels around another body in space is its _____

3 The _____ is the cloud of gas and dust from which our solar system formed.

Key Concepts

4 Define In your own words, define the word *gravity*.

_____

_____

_____

5 Describe How did the sun form?

_____

_____

_____

_____

_____

_____

_____

6 Describe How did planetesimals form?

_____

_____

_____

_____

_____

_____

_____

Critical Thinking

Use the illustration below to answer the following question.

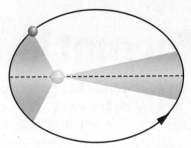

7 Identify What law is illustrated in this diagram?

_____

_____

8 Analyze How does gravity keep the planets in orbit around the sun?

_____

_____

_____

_____

_____

_____

9 Explain How do temperature differences in the protoplanetary disk explain the arrangement of the planets in the solar system?

_____

_____

_____

_____

_____

_____

_____

Determining Relevant Information

Indiana Standards

NOS 6.8 Analyze data, using appropriate mathematical manipulation as required, and use it to identify patterns and make inferences based on these patterns.

Many people and companies claim to use scientific evidence to support their ideas, arguments, or products. Some of this evidence may be strong and well-supported by scientific investigation. But some evidence may be weak and not supported by scientific investigation. Some information may seem impressive, but may not actually support the claims being made. How can you recognize the difference? How can you tell if the information is relevant?

Tutorial

The advertisement below highlights some things that you should consider as you try to identify whether information is relevant.

Grow your best Indian blanket wildflowers using new Fertilizer Formulation!

Fertilizer Formulation

We tested 20 patches of <u>Indian blanket wildflowers</u> in the Valdosta, Georgia, area. Plants that received the recommended amount of fertilizer grew an <u>average of 30% taller</u>. This fertilizer is made of <u>all-natural ingredients</u> and provides the best mixture of nutrients for any garden.

Everyone should use this fertilizer!

Limited Samples Be alert to any mention of specific times, places, or objects. Information that is relevant in one instance might not be relevant for your purpose. In this case, one type of wildflower in one place is mentioned. If you grow a different plant in a different area, this information is not relevant.

Comparisons Strong, relevant information would compare the results of two similar products or events. When a comparison is made, ask yourself what things are being compared. Relevant information might include comparisons of the results of a controlled experiment. In this advertisement, there is no mention of whether the comparison is for plants that had no fertilizer or plants that were given a similar competing fertilizer.

Unclear Connections While the all-natural ingredients may be good for plants, there is no connection made between these ingredients and how the fertilizer works or that they work better than artificial ingredients. An explanation of which ingredients the fertilizer uses and why they work better than artificial ingredients would make the connection more clear.

You Try It!

Read the following advertisement, and answer the questions below to determine which information is relevant to the claims being made.

GroBig
Soil Additive

"I've found the secret to the best wildflower garden—using GroBig Soil Additive. Now, you can have your best garden, too."
— **A. Gardener**

GroBig will work on all types of wildflowers!

Buy GroBig today, and watch your flowers grow!
$19.95 per liter

Botanists at a private nursery near Tampa, Florida, selected two tall samples of a common wildflower, the narrow-leaved sunflower. One plant received the recommended amount of GroBig Soil Additive. The other did not. After 2 weeks, the plant given GroBig Soil Additive had grown 4 cm. The other plant had grown just 2 cm. What a difference!

1 Identifying Conclusions Identify the claim that the advertisers are making.

_____

_____

_____

_____

2 Identifying Evidence What evidence or information does the writer use to support the claims? Underline two examples to support your answer. Then, identify whether the information is relevant or irrelevant.

Relevant	Irrelevant

3 Applying Concepts List three questions you would need to answer in order to support the claims being made about GroBig.

_____

_____

_____

_____

_____

_____

_____

Take It Home

Find an article or advertisement in a newspaper or magazine that contains a scientific claim and supporting information. Identify relevant or irrelevant information in the article or advertisement. Write a paragraph that summarizes the article or advertisement and its scientific evidence.

The Sun

ESSENTIAL QUESTION

What are the properties of the sun?

By the end of this lesson, you should be able to describe the structure and rotation of the sun, energy production and energy transport in the sun, and solar activity on the sun.

prominence

Different types of activity occur on the sun's surface. This loop of gas that extends outward from the sun's surface is a prominence.

Indiana Standards

6.2.3 Understand that the sun, an average star where nuclear reactions occur, is the central and largest body in the solar system.

Engage Your Brain

1 Predict Check T or F to show whether you think each statement is true or false.

T F

☑ ☐ The sun is composed mostly of hydrogen and helium.

☑ ☐ Energy is produced in the sun's core.

☑ ☑ The process by which energy is produced in the sun is known as *nuclear fission*.

☐ ☐ Energy is transferred to the surface of the sun by the processes of radiation and conduction.

☐ ☐ A dark area of the sun's surface that is cooler than the surrounding areas is called a *sunspot*.

2 Explain In your own words, explain the meaning of the word *sunlight*.

_____

_____

_____

_____

_____

_____

_____

Active Reading

3 Synthesize You can often define an unknown word if you know the meaning of its word parts. Use the word parts and sentence below to make an educated guess about the meaning of the word *photosphere*.

Word Part	Meaning
photo-	light
-sphere	ball

Example sentence
Energy is transferred to the sun's <u>photosphere</u> by convection cells.

photosphere:

_____

_____

_____

Vocabulary Terms

- **nuclear fusion**
- **sunspot**
- **solar flare**
- **prominence**

4 Apply This list contains the key terms you'll learn in this section. As you read, circle the definition of each term.

Here Comes the Sun

What do we know about the sun?

Active Reading

5 Identify As you read the text, underline different discoveries that scientists have made about the sun.

Since early in human history, people have marveled at the sun. Civilizations have referred to the sun by different names. Gods and goddesses who represented the sun were worshipped in different cultures. In addition, early astronomical observatories were established to track the sun's motion across the sky.

By the mid-19th century, astronomers had discovered that the sun was actually a hot ball of gas that is composed mostly of the elements hydrogen and helium. Scientists now know that the sun was born about 4.6 billion years ago. Every second, 4 million tons of solar matter is converted into energy. Of the light emitted from the sun, 41% is visible light, another 9% is ultraviolet light, and 50% is infrared radiation. And, perhaps most important of all, without the sun, there would be no life on Earth.

Sun Statistics	
Avg. dist. from Earth	149.6 million km
Diameter	1,390,000 km
Average density	1.41 g/cm³
Period of rotation	25 days (equator); 35 days (poles)
Avg. surface temp.	5,527 °C
Core temp.	15,000,000 °C
Composition	74% hydrogen, 25% helium, 1% other elements

Do the Math You Try It

6 Calculate The diameter of Earth is 12,756 km. How many times greater is the sun's diameter than the diameter of Earth?

_____

_____

_____

A solar flare, which is shown in this image, is a sudden explosive release of energy in the sun's atmosphere.

What is the structure of the sun?

The composition of the sun and Earth are different. However, the two bodies are similar in structure. Both are spheres. And both have a layered atmosphere and an interior composed of layers.

In the middle of the sun is the core. This is where energy is produced. From the core, energy is transported to the sun's surface through the radiative zone and the convective zone.

The sun's atmosphere has three layers—the photosphere, the chromosphere, and the corona. The sun's surface is the photosphere. Energy escapes the sun from this layer. The chromosphere is the middle layer of the sun's atmosphere. The temperature of the chromosphere rises with distance from the photosphere. The sun's outer atmosphere is the corona. The corona extends millions of kilometers into space.

7 Analyze Why is the structure of the sun different from the structure of Earth?

_____

_____

_____

_____

_____

_____

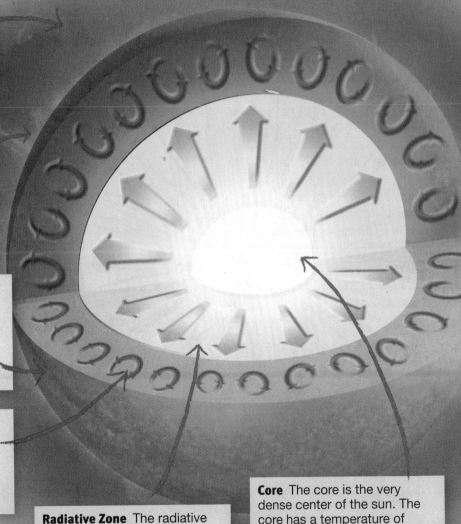

Corona The corona is the outer atmosphere of the sun. Temperatures in the corona may reach 2,000,000 °C.

Chromosphere The chromosphere is the middle layer of the sun's atmosphere. Temperatures in the chromosphere increase outward and reach a maximum of about 6,000 °C.

Photosphere The photosphere is the visible surface of the sun. It is the layer from which energy escapes into space. The photosphere has an average temperature of 5,527 °C.

Convective Zone The convective zone is the layer of the sun through which energy travels by convection from the radiative zone to the photosphere.

Radiative Zone The radiative zone is the layer of the sun through which energy is transferred away from the core by radiation.

Core The core is the very dense center of the sun. The core has a temperature of 15,000,000 °C, which is hot enough to cause the nuclear reactions that produce energy in the sun.

Let's Get Together

How does the sun produce energy?

Early in the 20th century, physicist Albert Einstein proposed that matter and energy are interchangeable. Matter can change into energy according to his famous equation $E = mc^2$. E is energy, m is mass, and c is the speed of light. Because c is such a large number, tiny amounts of matter can produce huge amounts of energy. Using Einstein's formula, scientists were able to explain the huge quantities of energy produced by the sun.

By Nuclear Fusion

Scientists know that the sun generates energy through the process of *nuclear fusion*. **Nuclear fusion** is the process by which two or more low-mass atomic nuclei fuse to form another, heavier nucleus. Nuclear fusion takes place in the core of stars. In stars that have core temperatures similar to the sun's, the fusion process that fuels the star starts with the fusion of two hydrogen nuclei. In older stars in which core temperatures are hotter than the sun's, the fusion process involves the fusion of helium into carbon.

Think Outside the Book

8 **Discussion** Einstein's equation $E = mc^2$ is probably the most famous equation in the world. With your classmates, discuss the kinds of technologies that rely on the conversion of matter to energy.

 **Visualize It!**

9 **Identify** Fill in the circles to label the particles in the diagrams.

P	Proton
N	Neutron

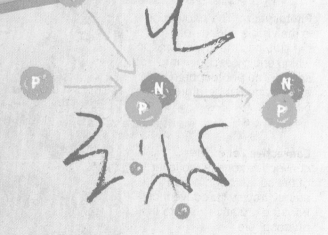

Three Steps of Nuclear Fusion in the Sun

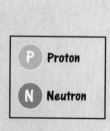

Step 1: Deuterium Two hydrogen nuclei (protons) collide. One proton emits particles and energy and then becomes a neutron. The proton and neutron combine to produce a heavy form of hydrogen called *deuterium*.

By the Fusion of Hydrogen into Helium

The most common elements in the sun are hydrogen and helium. Under the crushing force of gravity, these gases are compressed and heated in the sun's core, where temperatures reach 15,000,000 °C. In the sun's core, hydrogen nuclei sometimes fuse to form a helium nucleus. This process takes three steps to complete. This three-step process is illustrated below.

Most of the time, when protons are on a collision course with other protons, their positive charges instantly repel them. The protons do not collide. But sometimes one proton will encounter another proton and, at that exact moment, turn into a neutron and eject an electron. This collision forms a nucleus that contains one proton and one neutron. This nucleus is an isotope of hydrogen called *deuterium*. The deuterium nucleus collides with another proton and forms a variety of helium called *helium-3*. Then, two helium-3 nuclei collide and form a helium-4 nucleus that has two protons and two neutrons. The remaining two protons are released back into the sun's core.

The entire chain of fusion reactions requires six hydrogen nuclei and results in one helium nucleus and two hydrogen nuclei. There are approximately 10^{38} collisions between hydrogen nuclei taking place in the sun's core every second, which keeps the sun shining.

Active Reading

10 Identify As you read the text, underline the steps in the nuclear fusion process in the sun.

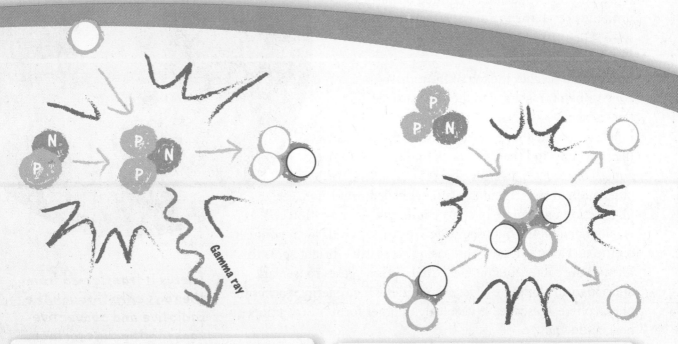

Step 2: Helium-3 Deuterium combines with another hydrogen nucleus to form a variety of helium called **helium-3**. More energy, including gamma rays, is released.

Step 3: Helium-4 Two helium-3 nuclei combine to form helium-4, which releases more energy and a pair of hydrogen nuclei (protons).

Mixing It Up

How is energy transferred to the sun's surface?

Energy is transferred to the surface of the sun by two different processes. Energy that is transferred from the sun's core through the radiative zone is transferred by the process of radiation. Energy that is transferred from the top of the radiative zone through the convective zone to the photosphere is transferred by the process of convection. Energy flow from the sun's core outward to the sun's surface by radiation and convection happens continuously.

By Radiation

When energy leaves the sun's core, it moves into the radiative zone. Energy travels through the radiative zone in the form of electromagnetic waves. The process by which energy is transferred as electromagnetic waves is called *radiation*. The radiative zone is densely packed with particles such as hydrogen, helium, and free electrons. Therefore, electromagnetic waves cannot travel directly through the radiative zone. Instead, they are repeatedly absorbed and re-emitted by particles until they reach the top of the radiative zone.

By Convection

Energy that reaches the top of the radiative zone is then transferred to the sun's surface. In the convective zone, energy is transferred by the movement of matter. Hot gases rise to the surface of the sun, cool, and then sink back into the convective zone. This process, in which heat is transferred by the circulation or movement of matter, is called *convection*. Convection takes place in convection cells. A convection cell is illustrated on the opposite page. Convection cells form *granules* on the surface of the sun. Hot, rising gases cause bright spots to form in the centers of granules. Cold, sinking gases cause dark areas to form along the edges of granules. Once energy reaches the photosphere, it escapes as visible light, other forms of radiation, heat, and wind.

Energy is transferred from the sun's core through the radiative and convective zones to the sun's surface.

The tops of convection cells form granules on the sun's surface.

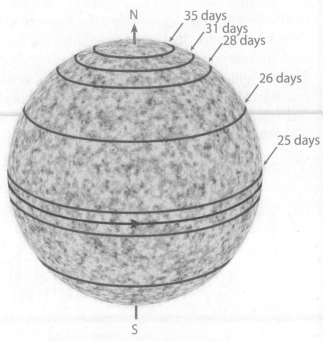

Hot, rising gases and colder, sinking gases form convection cells in the convective zone.

11 Compare How is energy transferred from the sun's core to the sun's surface in the radiative zone and in the convective zone?

Radiative zone	Convective zone

The sun's period of rotation varies with latitude.

N — 35 days
31 days
28 days
26 days
25 days

S

How does the sun rotate?

The sun rotates on its axis like other large bodies in the solar system. However, because the sun is a giant ball of gas, it does not rotate in the same way as a solid body like Earth does. Instead, the sun rotates faster at its equator than it does at higher latitudes. This kind of rotation is known as differential rotation. *Differential rotation* is the rotation of a body in which different parts of a body have different periods of rotation. Near the equator, the sun rotates once in about 25 days. However, at the poles, the sun rotates once in about 35 days.

Even stranger is the fact that the sun's interior does not rotate in the same way as the sun's surface does. Scientists think that the sun's core and radiative zone rotate together, at the same speed. Therefore, the sun's radiative zone and core rotate like Earth.

12 Define In your own words, define the term *differential rotation*.

_____

_____

_____

_____

The Ring of Fire

What is solar activity?

Solar activity refers to variations in the appearance or energy output of the sun. Solar activity includes dark areas that occur on the sun's surface known as *sunspots*. Solar activity also includes sudden explosive events on the sun's surface, which are called *solar flares*. Prominences are another form of solar activity. *Prominences* are vast loops of gases that extend into the sun's outer atmosphere.

Sunspots

Dark areas that form on the surface of the sun are called **sunspots**. They are about 1,500 °C cooler than the areas that surround them. Sunspots are places where hot, convecting gases are prevented from reaching the sun's surface.

Sunspots can appear for periods of a few hours or a few months. Some sunspots are only a few hundred kilometers across. Others have widths that are 10 to 15 times the diameter of Earth.

Sunspot activity occurs on average in 11-year cycles. When a cycle begins, the number of sunspots is at a minimum. The number of sunspots then increases until it reaches a maximum. The number then begins to decrease. A new sunspot cycle begins when the sunspot number reaches a minimum again.

Sunspots, solar flares, and prominences are three kinds of solar activity that occur on the sun's surface.

sunspot

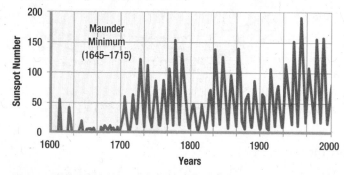

Sunspot Activity from 1600 to 2000

Maunder Minimum (1645–1715)

Sunspot Number — Years

Do the Math **You Try It**

13 Analyze The sunspot range is the difference between the maximum number of sunspots and the minimum number of sunspots for a certain period of time. To find this range, subtract the minimum number of sunspots from the maximum number of sunspots. What is the range of sunspot activity between 1700 and 1800?

_____

_____

_____

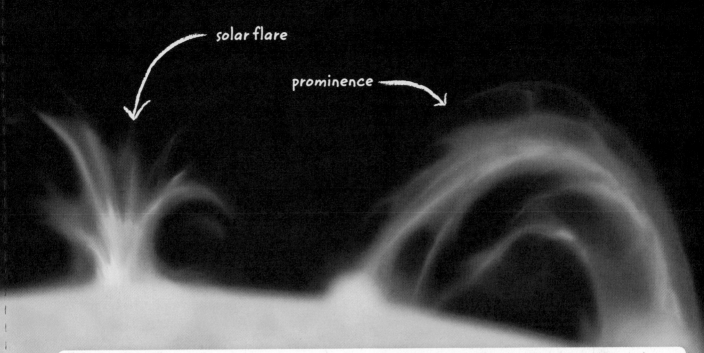

solar flare

prominence

Solar Flares

Solar flares appear as very bright spots on the sun's photosphere. A **solar flare** is an explosive release of energy that can extend outward as far as the sun's outer atmosphere. During a solar flare, enormous numbers of high-energy particles are ejected at near the speed of light. Radiation is released across the entire electromagnetic spectrum, from radio waves to x-rays and gamma rays. Temperatures within solar flares reach millions of degrees Celsius.

Prominences

Huge loops of relatively cool gas that extend outward from the photosphere thousands of kilometers into the outer atmosphere are called **prominences**. Several objects the size of Earth could fit inside a loop of a prominence. The gases in prominences are cooler than the surrounding atmosphere.

Prominences generally last from several hours to a day. However, some prominences can last for as long as several months.

14 Compare Use the Venn diagram below to compare solar flares and prominences.

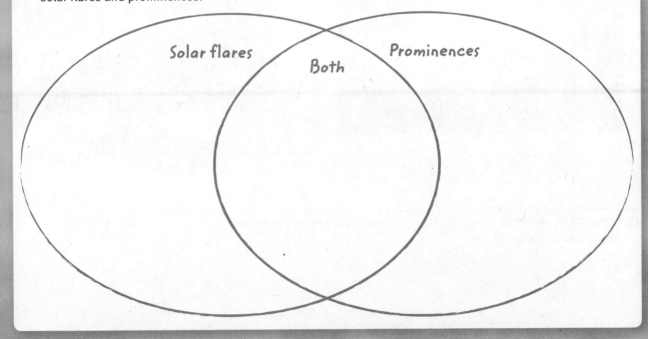

Solar flares   Both   Prominences

Visual Summary

To complete this summary, fill in the blanks with the correct word or phrase. Then use the key below to check your answers. You can use this page to review the main concepts of the lesson.

Properties of the Sun

The sun is composed of layers.

15 Identify the six layers of the sun, beginning with the innermost layer.

_____

_____

_____

_____

_____

Energy is transferred from the sun's core to the photosphere.

16 By what process is the sun's energy transported in layer A?

_____

By what process is the sun's energy transported in layer B?

_____

Answers: 15 the core, the radiative zone, the convective zone, the photosphere, the chromosphere, and the corona; 16 Layer A: radiation, Layer B: convection

17 **Describe** In your own words, describe the process of energy production by nuclear fusion in the sun.

Lesson Review

Vocabulary

Fill in the blank with the term that best completes the following sentences.

1 The process by which two or more low-mass atomic nuclei fuse to form another, heavier nucleus is called _____.

2 A _____ is a dark area on the surface of the sun that is cooler than the surrounding areas.

3 A _____ is a loop of relatively cool gas that extends above the photosphere.

Key Concepts

In the following table, write the name of the correct layer next to the definition.

Definition	Layer
4 Identify What is the layer of the sun from which energy escapes into space?	
5 Identify What is the layer of the sun in which energy is produced?	
6 Identify What is the layer of the sun through which energy is transferred away from the core by radiation?	

7 Identify What is the composition of the sun?

_____

_____

8 Explain What is the sunspot cycle?

_____

_____

_____

Critical Thinking

Use the illustration to answer the following questions.

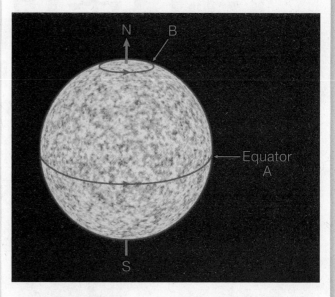

9 Determine How many days does it take for the sun to spin once on its axis at location A? How many days does it take for the sun to spin once on its axis at location B?

_____

_____

10 Compare How is the rotation of the sun different from the rotation of Earth?

_____

_____

_____

11 Explain In your own words, explain how energy is transported from the core to the surface of the sun by radiation and by convection.

_____

_____

_____

_____

The Terrestrial Planets

Mars

Earth

Venus

Mercury

ESSENTIAL QUESTION

What is known about the terrestrial planets?

By the end of this lesson, you should be able to describe some of the properties of the terrestrial planets and how the properties of Mercury, Venus, and Mars differ from the properties of Earth.

The terrestrial planets are the four planets that are closest to the sun. Distances between the planets shown here are not to scale.

sun

Indiana Standards

6.2.4 Compare and contrast the planets of the solar system with one another and with asteroids and comets with regard to their size, composition, distance from sun, surface features and ability to support life.

Engage Your Brain

1 Define Circle the term that best completes the following sentences.

Venus/Earth/Mars is the largest terrestrial planet.

Mercury/Venus/Mars has clouds that rain sulfuric acid on the planet.

Huge dust storms sweep across the surface of *Mercury/Venus/Mars*.

Venus/Earth/Mars is the most geologically active of the terrestrial planets.

Mercury/Venus/Earth has the thinnest atmosphere of the terrestrial planets.

2 Identify What are properties of Earth that make it a special place in the solar system?

_____

_____

_____

_____

Active Reading

3 Synthesize Many English words have their roots in other languages. Use the Latin words below to make an educated guess about the meaning of the word *astronomy*.

Latin word	Meaning
astrón	star
nomos	law

Example sentence
Some students who are interested in the night sky enter college to study <u>astronomy</u>.

astronomy:

_____

_____

Vocabulary Terms

- terrestrial planet
- astronomical unit

4 Apply As you learn the definition of each vocabulary term in this lesson, create your own definition or sketch to help you remember the meaning of the term.

Extreme to the Core

What are the terrestrial planets?

The **terrestrial planets** are the four small, dense, rocky planets that orbit closest to the sun. In order by distance from the sun, these planets are Mercury, Venus, Earth, and Mars. The terrestrial planets have similar compositions and consist of an outer crust, a central core, and a mantle that lies between the crust and core.

What is known about Mercury?

Mercury (MUR•kyuh•ree) is the planet about which we know the least. Until NASA's *Mariner 10* spacecraft flew by Mercury in 1974, the planet was seen as a blotchy, dark ball of rock. Today, scientists know that the planet's heavily cratered, moon-like surface is composed largely of volcanic rock and hides a massive iron core.

Mercury orbits only 0.39 AU from the sun. The letters *AU* stand for *astronomical unit*, which is the term astronomers use to measure distances in the solar system. One **astronomical unit** equals the average distance between the sun and Earth, or approximately 150 million km. Therefore, Mercury lies nearly halfway between the sun and Earth.

Active Reading

5 Identify As you read the text, underline important characteristics of the planet Mercury.

Statistics Table for Mercury

Distance from the sun	0.39 AU
Period of rotation (length of Mercury day)	58 days 15.5 h
Period of revolution (length of Mercury year)	88 days
Tilt of axis	0°
Diameter	4,879 km
Density	5.44 g/cm³
Surface temperature	-184 °C to 427 °C
Surface gravity	38% of Earth's gravity
Number of satellites	0

Although this may look like the moon, it is actually the heavily cratered surface of the planet Mercury.

Mercury Has the Most Extreme Temperature Range in the Solar System

On Earth, a day lasts 24 h. On Mercury, a day lasts almost 59 Earth days. What does this fact have to do with temperatures on Mercury? It means that temperatures on that part of Mercury's surface that is receiving sunlight can build for more than 29 days. When it is day on Mercury, temperatures can rise to 427 °C, a temperature that is hot enough to melt certain metals. It also means that temperatures on the part of Mercury's surface that is in darkness can fall for more than 29 days. When it is night on Mercury, temperatures can drop to –184 °C. This means that surface temperatures on Mercury can change by as much as 600 °C between day and night. This is the greatest difference between high and low temperatures in the solar system.

Think Outside the Book

6 Plan You are an astronaut who will be exploring Mercury. What equipment would you take to Mercury to help you survive?

Mercury Has a Large Iron Core

Mercury is the smallest planet in the solar system. It has a diameter of only 4,879 km at its equator. Amazingly, Mercury's central core is thought to be around 3,600 km in diameter, which accounts for most of the planet's interior. Scientists originally thought that Mercury had a core of solid iron. However, by observing changes in Mercury's spin as it orbits the sun, astronomers now think that the core is at least partially molten. Why is the core so large? Some scientists think that Mercury may have been struck by another object in the distant past and lost most of the rock that surrounded the core. Other scientists think that long ago the sun vaporized the planet's surface and blasted it away into space.

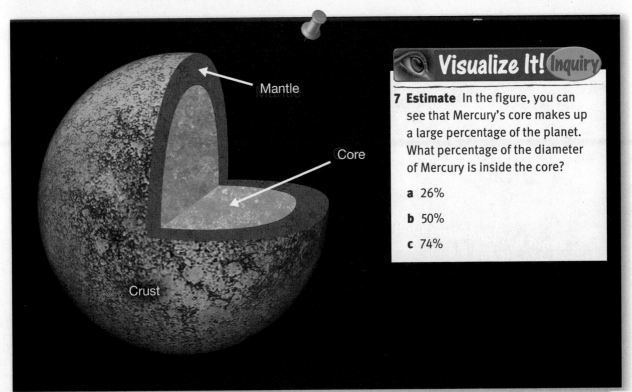

Mantle

Core

Crust

Visualize It! Inquiry

7 Estimate In the figure, you can see that Mercury's core makes up a large percentage of the planet. What percentage of the diameter of Mercury is inside the core?

a 26%

b 50%

c 74%

Harsh Planet

What is known about Venus?

Science-fiction writers once imagined Venus (VEE•nuhs) to be a humid planet with lush, tropical forests. Nothing could be further from the truth. On Venus, sulfuric acid rain falls on a surface that is not much different from the inside of an active volcano.

Active Reading

8 Identify Underline the definitions of the terms *prograde rotation* and *retrograde rotation* that appear in the text.

Venus Is Similar to Earth in Size and Mass

Venus has often been called "Earth's twin." At 12,104 km, the diameter of Venus is 95% the diameter of Earth. Venus's mass is around 80% of Earth's. And the gravity that you would experience on Venus is 89% of the gravity on Earth.

The rotation of Venus is different from the rotation of Earth. Earth has prograde rotation. *Prograde rotation* is the counterclockwise spin of a planet about its axis as seen from above the planet's north pole. Venus, however, has retrograde rotation. *Retrograde rotation* is the clockwise spin of a planet about its axis as seen from above its north pole.

Venus differs from Earth not only in the direction in which it spins on its axis. It takes more time for Venus to rotate once about its axis than it takes for the planet to revolve once around the sun. Venus has the slowest period of rotation in the solar system.

Venus has landforms such as highlands and plains, volcanoes, and impact craters.

Statistics Table for Venus

Distance from the sun	0.72 AU
Period of rotation	243 days (retrograde rotation)
Period of revolution	225 days
Tilt of axis	177.4°
Diameter	12,104 km
Density	5.20 g/cm³
Average surface temperature	465 °C
Surface gravity	89% of Earth's gravity
Number of satellites	0

Gula Mons volcano is approximately 300 km wide and 3 km high.

Impact crater Cunitz, which is 48.5 km wide, was named after Maria Cunitz, a 17th-century European astronomer and mathematician.

Venus Has Craters and Volcanoes

In 1990, the powerful radar beams of NASA's *Magellan* spacecraft pierced the dense atmosphere of Venus. This gave us our most detailed look ever at the planet's surface. There are 168 volcanoes on Venus that are larger than 100 km in diameter. Thousands of volcanoes have smaller diameters. Venus's surface is also cratered. These craters are as much as 280 km in diameter. The sizes and locations of the craters on Venus suggest that around 500 million years ago something happened to erase all of the planet's older craters. Scientists are still puzzled about how this occurred. But volcanic activity could have covered the surface of the planet in one huge outpouring of magma.

The Atmosphere of Venus Is Toxic

Venus may have started out like Earth, with oceans and water running across its surface. However, after billions of years of solar heating, Venus has become a harsh world. Surface temperatures on Venus are hotter than those on Mercury. Temperatures average around 465 °C. Over time, carbon dioxide gas has built up in the atmosphere. Sunlight that strikes Venus's surface warms the ground. However, carbon dioxide in the atmosphere traps this energy, which causes temperatures near the surface to remain high.

Sulfuric acid rains down onto Venus's surface, and the pressure of the atmosphere is at least 90 times that of Earth's atmosphere. No human—or machine—could survive for long under these conditions. Venus is a world that is off limits to human explorers and perhaps all but the hardiest robotic probes.

9 Contrast How is the landscape of Venus different from the landscape of Earth?

_____

_____

_____

_____

_____

_____

 Active Reading

10 Identify As you read the text, underline those factors that make Venus an unlikely place for life to exist.

No Place Like Home

What is special about Earth?

As far as scientists know, Earth is the only planet in the solar system that has the combination of factors needed to support life. Life as we know it requires liquid water and an energy source. Earth has both. Earth's atmosphere contains the oxygen that animals need to breathe. Matter is continuously cycled between the environment and living things. And a number of ecosystems exist on Earth that different organisms can inhabit.

Earth Has Abundant Water and Life

Earth's vast liquid-water oceans and moderate temperatures provided the ideal conditions for life to emerge and flourish. Around 3.5 billion years ago, organisms that produced food by photosynthesis appeared in Earth's oceans. During the process of making food, these organisms produced oxygen. By 560 million years ago, more complex life forms arose that could use oxygen to release energy from food. Today, the total number of species of organisms that inhabit Earth is thought to be anywhere between 5 million and 30 million.

© Houghton Mifflin Harcourt Publishing Company • Image Credits: ©Astromujoff/The Image Bank/Getty Images

Active Reading

11 Identify As you read the text, underline characteristics that make Earth special.

Statistics Table for Earth	
Distance from the sun	1.0 AU
Period of rotation	23 h 56 min
Period of revolution	365.3 days
Tilt of axis	23.45°
Diameter	12,756 km
Density	5.52 g/cm³
Temperature	-89 °C to 58 °C
Surface gravity	100% of Earth's gravity
Number of satellites	1

From space, Earth presents an entirely different scene from that of the other terrestrial planets. Clouds in the atmosphere, blue bodies of water, and green landmasses are all clues to the fact that Earth is a special place.

Earth Is Geologically Active

Earth is the only terrestrial planet whose surface is divided into tectonic plates. These plates move around Earth's surface, which causes the continents to change positions over long periods of time. Tectonic plate motion, together with weathering and erosion, has erased most surface features older than 500 million years.

Humans Have Set Foot on the Moon

Between 1969 and 1972, 12 astronauts landed on the moon. They are the only humans to have set foot on another body in the solar system. They encountered a surface gravity that is only about one-sixth that of Earth. Because of the moon's lower gravity, astronauts could not walk normally. If they did, they would fly up in the air and fall over.

Like Mercury, the moon's surface is heavily cratered. It is estimated that about 500,000 craters larger than 1 km dot the moon. There are large dark areas on the moon's surface. These are plains of solidified lava. There are also light-colored areas. These are the lunar highlands.

The moon rotates about its axis in the same time it orbits Earth. Therefore, it keeps the same side facing Earth. During a lunar day, which is a little more than 27 Earth days, the daytime surface temperature can reach 127 °C. The nighttime surface temperature can fall to −173 °C.

The moon is the only other body in the solar system where humans have been.

Statistics Table for the Moon

Distance from Earth	384,400 km (0.0026 AU)
Period of rotation	27.3 days
Period of revolution	27.3 days
Axial tilt	1.5°
Diameter	3,476 km
Density	3.34 g/cm³
Temperature	−173 °C to 127 °C
Surface gravity	16.5% of Earth's gravity

 **Visualize It!**

12 Identify In the image, circle any signs of life that you see.

Is It Alive?

What is known about Mars?

A fleet of spacecraft is now in orbit around Mars (MARZ) studying the planet. Space rovers have also investigated the surface of Mars. These remote explorers have discovered a planet with an atmosphere that is 100 times thinner than Earth's and temperatures that are little different from the inside of a freezer. They have seen landforms on Mars that are larger than any found on Earth. And these unmanned voyagers have photographed surface features on Mars that are characteristic of erosion and deposition by water.

Mars Is a Rocky, Red Planet

The surface of Mars is better known than that of any other planet in the solar system except Earth. It is composed largely of dark volcanic rock. Rocks and boulders litter the surface of Mars. Some boulders can be as large as a house. A powdery dust covers Martian rocks and boulders. This dust is the product of the chemical breakdown of rocks rich in iron minerals. This is what gives the Martian soil its orange-red color.

Think Outside the Book

13 **Debate** Research the surface features of the northern and southern hemispheres of Mars. Decide which hemisphere you would rather explore. With your class, debate the merits of exploring one hemisphere versus the other.

Statistics Table for Mars

Distance from the sun	1.52 AU
Period of rotation	24 h 37 min
Period of revolution	1.88 y
Tilt of axis	25.3°
Diameter	6,792 km
Density	3.93 g/cm³
Temperature	-140°C to 20°C
Surface gravity	37% of Earth's gravity
Number of satellites	2

Mars's northern polar ice cap is composed of carbon dioxide ice and water ice. Its size varies with the seasons.

Mars Has Interesting Surface Features

The surface of Mars varies from hemisphere to hemisphere. The northern hemisphere appears to have been covered by lava flows. The southern hemisphere is heavily cratered.

Large volcanoes are found on Mars. At 27 km high and 600 km across, Olympus Mons (uh•LIM•puhs MAHNZ) is the largest volcano and mountain in the solar system. Mars also has very deep valleys and canyons. The canyon system Valles Marineris (VAL•less mar•uh•NAIR•iss) runs from west to east along the Martian equator. It is about 4,000 km long, 500 km wide, and up to 10 km deep. It is the largest canyon in the solar system.

Mars Has a Thin Atmosphere

Mars has a very thin atmosphere that is thought to have been thicker in the past. Mars may have gradually lost its atmosphere to the solar wind. Or a body or bodies that collided with Mars may have caused much of the atmosphere to have been blown away.

Unlike Earth, Mars's atmosphere is composed mostly of carbon dioxide. During the Martian winter, temperatures at the planet's poles grow cold enough for carbon dioxide to freeze into a thin coating. During the summer, when temperatures grow warmer, this coating vanishes.

Winds on Mars can blow with enough force to pick up dust particles from the planet's surface. When this happens, giant dust storms can form. At times, these storms cover the entire planet.

Active Reading **14 Explain** What are two possible reasons why the atmosphere on Mars is so thin?

_____

_____

_____

Olympus Mons is the largest volcano in the solar system.

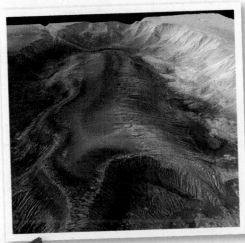

Hebes Chasma is a 6,000 m–deep depression that is located in the Valles Marineris region.

15 Compare Compare and contrast the physical properties of Mars to the physical properties of Earth.

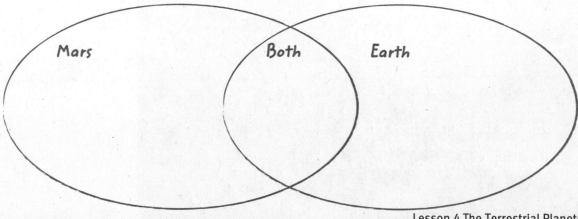

Mars   Both   Earth

Liquid Water Once Flowed on Mars

A number of features on Mars provide evidence that liquid water once flowed on the planet's surface. Many of these features have been struck by asteroids. These asteroid impacts have left behind craters that scientists can use to find the approximate dates of these features. Scientists estimate that many of these features, such as empty river basins, existed on Mars more than 3 billion years ago. Since then, little erosion has taken place that would cause these features to disappear.

In 2000, the *Mars Global Surveyor* took before-and-after images of a valley wall on Mars. Scientists observed the unmistakable trace of a liquid substance that had flowed out of the valley wall and into the valley. Since 2000, many similar features have been seen. The best explanation of these observations is that water is found beneath Mars's surface. At times, this water leaks out onto the Martian surface like spring water on Earth.

This image shows gullies on the wall of a Martian crater. Water that may be stored close to the Martian surface has run downhill into the crater.

16 Describe How do the features in the image at the right indicate that liquid water once flowed on Mars?

_____

_____

_____

_____

Water ice sits on the floor of a crater that is located about 20 degrees below Mars's north pole.

Roving Mars

The Mars Exploration Rovers *Spirit* and *Opportunity* landed safely on Mars in January 2004. The 185-kg rovers were designed to explore Mars for 90 days. However, in 2009, both rovers were still exploring Mars. They are searching for rocks and soils that indicate that water once flowed on the Martian surface. The rovers are also looking for environments in which life may have existed.

The Martian Surface
Mars's surface is made up mostly of the volcanic rock *basalt*, which is also found on Earth. Boulders of basalt cover the Martian landscape.

Testing the Rovers on Earth
Before leaving Earth, the rovers were tested under conditions that were similar to those that they would encounter on the Martian surface.

Collecting Data on Mars
The Mars rover *Spirit* took this picture of itself collecting data from the Martian surface.

Extend

Inquiry

17 Infer What advantages would a robotic explorer, such as *Spirit* or *Opportunity*, have over a manned mission to Mars?

18 Hypothesize What kind of evidence would the Mars Exploration Rovers be looking for that indicated that water once flowed on Mars?

Visual Summary

To complete this summary, write the answers to the questions on the lines. Then use the key below to check your answers. You can use this page to review the main concepts of the lesson.

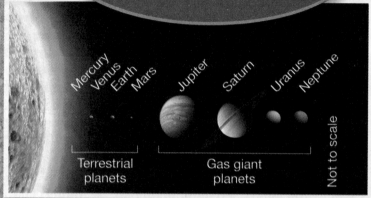

Properties
of Terrestrial Planets

Mercury Venus Earth Mars Jupiter Saturn Uranus Neptune

Terrestrial planets

Gas giant planets

Not to scale

Mercury orbits near the sun.

19 Why do temperatures on Mercury vary so much?

_____

_____

_____

Venus is covered with clouds.

20 Why is Venus's surface temperature so high?

_____

_____

_____

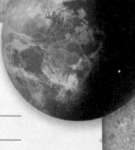

Earth has abundant life.

21 What factors support life on Earth?

_____

_____

_____

Mars is a rocky planet.

22 What makes up the surface of Mars?

_____

_____

_____

23 Compare How are important properties of Mercury, Venus, and Mars different from important properties of Earth?

Lesson Review

Vocabulary

Fill in the blanks with the terms that best complete the following sentences.

1 The _____ are the dense planets nearest the sun.

2 An _____ is equal to the distance between the sun and Earth.

Key Concepts

In the following table, write the name of the correct planet next to the property of that planet.

Properties	Planet
3 Identify Which planet has the highest surface temperature in the solar system?	
4 Identify Which planet has very large dust storms?	
5 Identify Which planet is the most heavily cratered of the terrestrial planets?	
6 Identify Which planet has the highest surface gravity of the terrestrial planets?	

7 Explain What is the difference between prograde rotation and retrograde rotation?

_____

_____

_____

_____

8 Describe What characteristics of Venus's atmosphere make the planet so harsh?

_____

_____

_____

Critical Thinking

Use this table to answer the following questions.

Planet	Period of rotation	Period of revolution
Mercury	58 days 15.5 h	88 days
Venus	243 days (retrograde rotation)	225 days
Earth	23 h 56 min	365.3 days
Mars	24 h 37 min	1.88 y

9 Analyze Which planet rotates most slowly about its axis?

_____

10 Analyze Which planet revolves around the sun in less time than it rotates around its axis?

_____

11 Analyze Which planet revolves around the sun in the shortest amount of time?

_____

12 Explain Why are the temperatures on each of the other terrestrial planets more extreme than the temperatures on Earth?

_____

_____

_____

_____

_____

_____

_____

_____

_____

A. Wesley Ward
GEOLOGIST

Geologist Dr. Wesley Ward lives in a desert region of the western United States. The living conditions are sometimes harsh, but the region offers some fascinating places to study. For a geologist like Dr. Ward, who tries to understand the geologic processes on another planet, the desert may be the only place to be.

Dr. Ward was a leading scientist on the Mars Pathfinder mission. The surface of Mars is a lot like the western desert. Dr. Ward helped scientists map the surface of Mars and plan for the Pathfinder's landing. Using data from the Pathfinder, Dr. Ward studied how Martian winds have shaped the planet's landscape. This information will help scientists better understand what conditions are like on the surface of Mars. More importantly, the information will guide scientists in choosing future landings sites. Dr. Ward's work may determine whether human beings can safely land on Mars.

You could say that Dr. Ward's scientific career has hit the big-time. He helped in the making of the Discovery Channel's documentary *Planet Storm*. The program features scientists describing weather conditions on other planets. Dr. Ward and the scientists worked with special effects artists to simulate what these conditions might feel like to astronauts.

The Mars Pathfinder rover *Sojourner* was designed to withstand the fierce Martian dust storms, such as the one shown.

Social Studies Connection

The Pathfinder is not the first attempt scientists have made to explore the surface of Mars. In fact, scientists in different countries have been exploring Mars for over 50 years. Research other missions to Mars and attempts to send rovers to Mars, and present your research in a timeline. Remember to identify where the mission started, what its goals were, and whether it achieved them.

JOB BOARD

Science Writer

What You'll Do: Research and write articles, press releases, reports, and sometimes books about scientific discoveries and issues for a wide range of readers. Science writers who write for a broad audience must work to find the stories behind the science in order to keep readers interested.

Where You Might Work: For a magazine, a newspaper, or a museum, or independently as a freelance writer specializing in science. Some science writers may work for universities, research foundations, government agencies, or non-profit science and health organizations.

Education: A bachelor's degree in a scientific field, with courses in English or writing.

Other Job Requirements: Strong communications skills. Science writers must not only understand science, but must also be able to interview scientists and to write clear, interesting stories.

Telescope Mechanic

What You'll Do: Keep telescopes at large observatories working, climbing heights of up to 30 meters to make sure the telescope's supports are in good shape, which includes welding new components, cleaning, and sweeping.

Where You Might Work: A large observatory or research institution with large telescopes, possibly in the desert.

Education: A high-school diploma with some experience performing maintenance on delicate equipment.

Other Job Requirements. Strong communications skills to consult with other mechanics and the scientists who use the telescopes. Mechanics must be able to weld and to use tools. Mechanics must also have good vision (or wear glasses to correct their vision), and be able to climb up high and carry heavy equipment.

PEOPLE IN SCIENCE NEWS

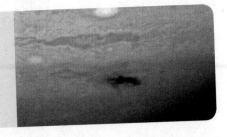

Anthony Wesley

Witnessing Impact

Anthony Wesley was sitting in his backyard in Australia on July 19, 2009, gazing at Jupiter through his custom-built telescope, when he saw a dark spot or "scar" on the planet (shown). Wesley sent his tip to the National Aeronautics and Space Administration (NASA).

NASA has much more powerful telescopes than a citizen scientist usually does. Scientists at NASA confirmed that a comet had crashed into the planet, leaving a scar. Coincidentally, this crash happened almost exactly 15 years after another comet crashed into Jupiter.

Lesson 5

The Gas Giant Planets

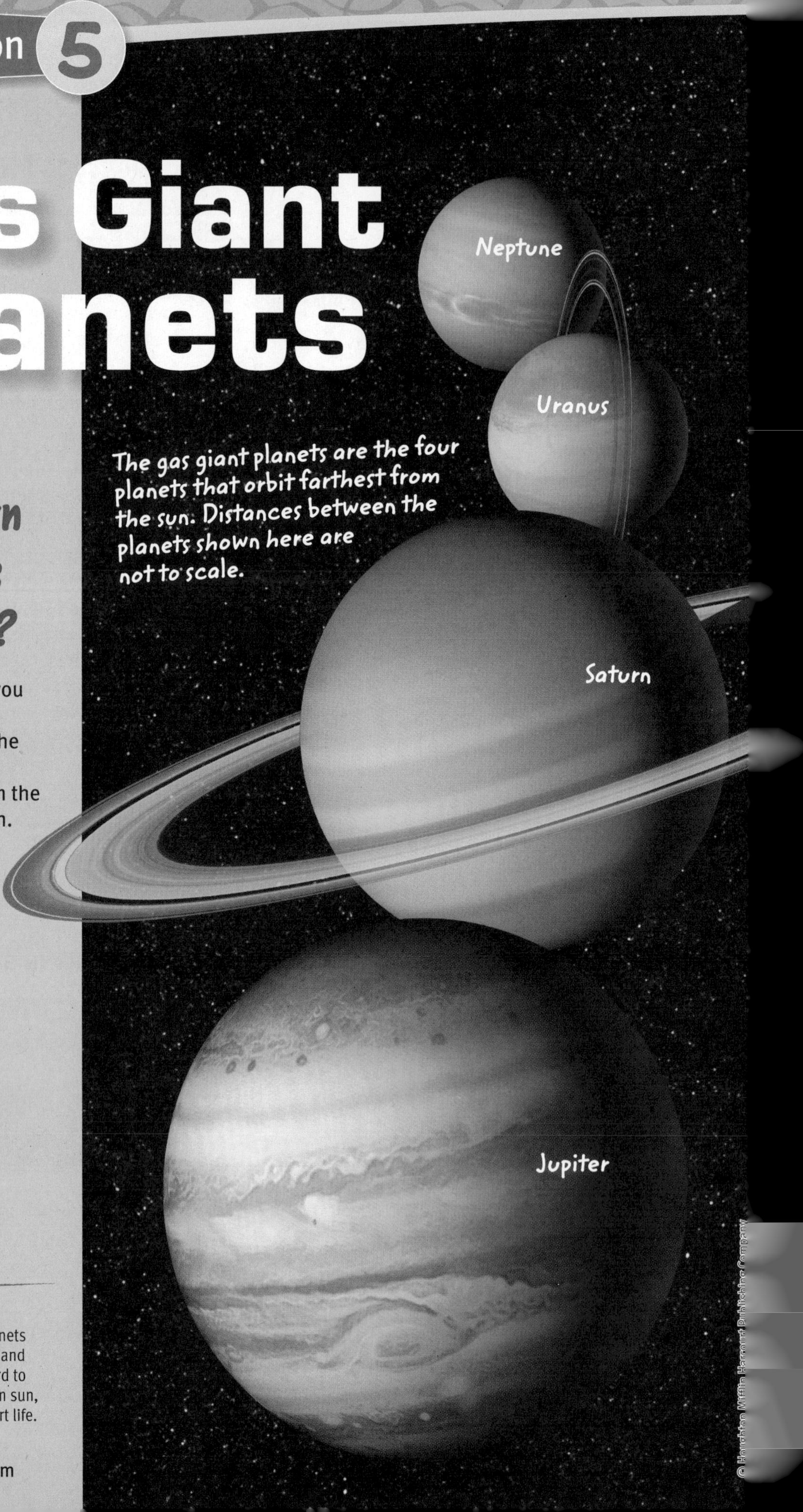
Neptune
Uranus
Saturn
Jupiter

The gas giant planets are the four planets that orbit farthest from the sun. Distances between the planets shown here are not to scale.

ESSENTIAL QUESTION

What is known about the gas giant planets?

By the end of this lesson, you should be able to describe some of the properties of the gas giant planets and how these properties differ from the physical properties of Earth.

Indiana Standards

6.2.4 Compare and contrast the planets of the solar system with one another and with asteroids and comets with regard to their size, composition, distance from sun, surface features and ability to support life.

Engage Your Brain

1 Predict Circle the term that best completes the following sentences.

Jupiter/Saturn/Uranus is the largest planet in the solar system.

Jupiter/Uranus/Neptune has the strongest winds in the solar system.

Saturn/Uranus/Neptune has the largest ring system of the gas giant planets.

Jupiter/Saturn/Neptune has more moons than any other planet in the solar system.

Jupiter/Uranus/Neptune is tilted on its side as it orbits the Sun.

2 Identify What are the objects that circle Saturn? What do you think they are made of?

_____

_____

_____

Active Reading

3 Apply Many scientific words, such as *gas*, also have everyday meanings. Use context clues to write your own definition for each meaning of the word *gas*.

Example sentence
Vehicles, such as cars, trucks, and buses, use gas as a fuel.

gas:

_____

_____

Example sentence
Gas is one of the three common states of matter.

gas:

_____

_____

_____

Vocabulary Terms

• gas giant
• planetary ring

4 Apply This list contains the key terms you'll learn in this section. As you read, circle the definition of each term.

A Giant Among

Jupiter's high winds circle the planet and cause cloud bands to form. Storms, such as the Great Red Spot shown here, form between the cloud bands.

Ganymede

Callisto

Statistics Table for Jupiter

Distance from the sun	5.20 AU
Period of rotation	9 h 55 min
Period of revolution	11.86 y
Tilt of axis	3.13°
Diameter	142,984 km
Density	1.33 g/cm³
Mean surface temperature	−150 °C
Surface gravity	253% of Earth's gravity
Number of satellites	63

Active Reading

5 Identify As you read the text, underline important physical properties of the planet Jupiter.

What is a gas giant planet?

Jupiter, Saturn, Uranus, and Neptune are the gas giant planets. They orbit far from the sun. **Gas giants** have deep, massive gas atmospheres, which are made up mostly of hydrogen and helium. These gases become denser the deeper you travel inside. All of the gas giants are large. Neptune, the smallest gas giant planet, is big enough to hold 60 Earths within its volume. The gas giant planets are cold. Mean surface temperatures range from −150 °C on Jupiter to −220 °C on Neptune.

What is known about Jupiter?

Jupiter (JOO•pih•ter) is the largest planet in the solar system. Its volume can contain more than 900 Earths. Jupiter is also the most massive planet. Its mass is twice that of the other seven planets combined. Jupiter has the highest surface gravity in the solar system at 253% that of Earth. And, although all of the gas giant planets rotate rapidly, Jupiter rotates the fastest of all. Its period of rotation is just under 10 h. Wind speeds on Jupiter are high. They can reach 540 km/h. By contrast, Earth's wind speed record is 372 km/h.

Giants!

Europa

Io

Io, Europa, Callisto, and Ganymede are Jupiter's largest moons. All four moons were named for figures in Greek mythology.

Huge Storms Travel Across Jupiter's Surface

Jupiter has some of the strangest weather conditions in the solar system. The winds on Jupiter circle the planet. Clouds are stretched into bands that run from east to west. Storms appear as white or red spots between cloud bands. The best known of these storms is the Great Red Spot. The east–west width of this storm is three times the diameter of Earth. Incredibly, this storm has been observed by astronomers on Earth for the past 350 years.

Jupiter Has the Most Moons

More than 60 moons have been discovered orbiting Jupiter. This is the greatest number of moons to orbit any planet. Jupiter's moons Io (EYE•oh), Europa (yu•ROH•puh), Callisto (kuh•LIS•toh), and Ganymede (GAN•uh•meed) are particularly large. In fact, Ganymede is larger than the planet Mercury.

Jupiter's moon Io is the most volcanically active place in the solar system. There are at least 400 active volcanoes on Io's surface. Jupiter's gravity tugs and pulls on Io. This causes the interior of Io to reach the temperature at which it melts. Lava erupts from Io's volcanoes, which throw tremendous geysers of sulfur compounds into space. Over time, the orbit of Io has become a ring of ejected gases that is visible to the Hubble Space Telescope.

Jupiter's moon Europa has an icy surface. Recent evidence suggests that an ocean of liquid water may lie beneath this surface. Because liquid water is essential for life, some scientists are hopeful that future spacecraft may discover life inside Europa.

6 Apply Io, Europa, Callisto, and Ganymede are known as the *Galilean moons*. The astronomer Galileo discovered these moons using one of the first telescopes. Why do you think that the Galilean moons were the first objects to be discovered with a telescope?

_____

_____

_____

Think Outside the Book

7 Model Select one of the following topics about weather on Jupiter to research: belts and zones; jet streams; storms. Present your findings to the rest of the class in the form of a model. Your model may be handcrafted, or may be an art piece, or may be a computer presentation.

King of the Rings!

What is known about Saturn?

Saturn (SAT•ern) is a near-twin to Jupiter. It is the second-largest gas giant planet and is made mostly of hydrogen and helium. About 800 Earths could fit inside the volume of Saturn. Amazingly, the planet's density is less than that of water.

Saturn Has a Large Ring System

The planetary ring system that circles Saturn's equator is the planet's most spectacular feature. A **planetary ring** is a disk of material that circles a planet and consists of orbiting particles. Saturn's ring system has many individual rings that form complex bands. Between bands are gaps that may be occupied by moons.

Although the rings of Saturn extend nearly 500,000 km in diameter, they are only a few kilometers thick. They consist of trillions of small, icy bodies that are a few millimeters to several hundred meters in size. The rings are mostly pieces left over from the collision of Saturn's moons with comets and asteroids.

Active Reading

8 Identify As you read the text, underline important physical properties about the planet Saturn.

Statistics Table for Saturn	
Distance from the sun	9.58 AU
Period of rotation	10 h 39 min
Period of revolution	29.5 y
Tilt of axis	26.73°
Diameter	120,536 km
Density	0.69 g/cm³
Mean surface temperature	−180 °C
Surface gravity	106% of Earth's gravity
Number of satellites	60

Saturn's rings

Saturn's southern aurora

Saturn's Moon Enceladus Has Water Geysers

In the inner solar system, liquid rock erupts from volcanoes. In some parts of the outer solar system, liquid water erupts from volcanoes. When NASA's *Cassini* spacecraft explored Saturn's moon Enceladus (en•SEL•uh•duhs), it found an icy surface. Scientists believe that Enceladus has a liquid interior beneath this icy surface. Liquid water flows up through cracks in the moon's surface. It either freezes at the surface or forms spectacular water geysers. These geysers are the largest in the solar system.

Saturn's Moon Titan Has a Dense Atmosphere

Titan (TYT'in), the largest moon of Saturn, has an atmosphere that is denser than Earth's. The moon's atmosphere is composed mostly of nitrogen and has traces of compounds such as methane and ethane. Methane clouds form in Titan's atmosphere. From these clouds, methane rain may fall. Unlike Earth, Titan has a crust of ice, which is frozen at a temperature of –180 °C.

In 2005, the *Huygens* (HY•guhnz) Titan probe descended through Titan's atmosphere. It took pictures of a surface with lakes and ponds. The liquid that fills these lakes and ponds is mostly methane.

9 Explain In your own words, write a caption for this illustration of Saturn's moon Enceladus.

_____

_____

_____

Particles that make up Saturn's ring system

Cassini Division in Saturn's ring system

10 Describe Complete this table by writing a description of each structure in Saturn's ring system.

Structure	Description
ring	
gap	
ring particles	

Just Rollin' Along

How is Uranus unique?

Active Reading **11 Identify** As you read the text, underline important physical properties of the planet Uranus.

The atmosphere of Uranus (YUR•uh•nuhs) is composed mostly of hydrogen and helium. However, the atmosphere also contains methane. The methane in Uranus's atmosphere absorbs red light, which gives the planet a blue-green color.

Uranus Is a Tilted World

Uranus's axis of rotation is tilted almost 98°. This means that unlike any other planet in the solar system, Uranus is tilted on its side as it orbits the sun. The planet's 27 moons all orbit Uranus's equator, just like the moons of other planets do. The ring system of Uranus also orbits the equator. Scientists are not sure what event caused Uranus's odd axial tilt. But computer models of the four gas giant planets as they were forming may offer an explanation. The huge gravities of Jupiter and Saturn may have caused the orbits of Uranus and Neptune to change. There may also have been many close encounters between Uranus and Neptune that could have tilted the axis of Uranus.

Statistics Table for Uranus

Distance from the sun	19.2 AU
Period of rotation	17 h 24 min (retrograde)
Period of revolution	84 y
Tilt of axis	97.8°
Diameter	51,118 km
Density	1.27 g/cm³
Mean surface temperature	−210 °C
Surface gravity	79% of Earth's gravity
Number of satellites	27

12 Predict Earth has an axial tilt of 23.5°, whereas Uranus has an axial tilt of almost 98°. If Earth had the same axial tilt as Uranus, how would the conditions be different at Earth's North and South Poles?

_____

_____

_____

_____

_____

_____

_____

_____

_____

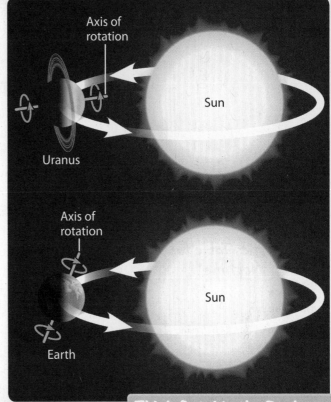

Axis of rotation

Uranus

Sun

Axis of rotation

Sun

Earth

Think Outside the Book

13 Research Astronomers are discovering planets orbiting stars in other solar systems? Find out what kinds of planets astronomers are discovering in these solar systems.

Seasons on Uranus Last 21 Years

It takes Uranus 84 years to make a single revolution around the sun. For about 21 years of that 84-year period, the north pole faces the sun and the south pole is in darkness. About halfway through that 84-year period, the poles are reversed. The south pole faces the sun and the north pole is in darkness for 21 years. So, what are seasons like on Uranus? Except for a small band near the equator, every place on Uranus has winter periods of constant darkness and summer periods of constant daylight. But, during spring and fall, Uranus has periods of both daytime and nighttime just like on Earth.

Uranus's Moon Miranda Is Active

Miranda (muh•RAN•duh) is Uranus's fifth-largest moon. It is about 470 km in diameter. NASA's *Voyager 2* spacecraft visited Miranda in 1989. Data from *Voyager 2* showed that the moon is covered by different types of icy crust. What is the explanation for this patchwork surface? The gravitational forces of Uranus pull on Miranda's interior. This causes material from the moon's interior to rise to its surface. What we see on the surface is evidence of the moon turning itself inside out.

The surface of Uranus's moon Miranda

A Blue, Windy Giant

What is known about Neptune?

Neptune (NEP•toon) is the most distant planet from the sun. It is located 30 times farther from the sun than Earth is. So, sunlight on Neptune is 900 times fainter than sunlight on Earth is. High noon on Neptune may look much like twilight on Earth.

Neptune Is a Blue Ice Giant

Neptune is practically a twin to Uranus. Neptune is almost the same size as Uranus. It also has an atmosphere that is composed of hydrogen and helium, with some methane. The planet's bluish color is caused by the absorption of red light by methane. But because Neptune does not have an atmospheric haze like Uranus does, we can see deeper into the atmosphere. So, Neptune is blue, whereas Uranus is blue-green.

When *Voyager 2* flew by Neptune in 1989, there was a huge, dark area as large as Earth in the planet's atmosphere. This storm, which was located in Neptune's southern hemisphere, was named the *Great Dark Spot*. However, in 1994, the Hubble Space Telescope found no trace of this storm. Meanwhile, other spots that may grow larger with time have been sighted in the atmosphere.

Statistics Table for Neptune	
Distance from the sun	30.1 AU
Period of rotation	16 h 7 min
Period of revolution	164.8 y
Tilt of axis	28.5°
Diameter	49,528 km
Density	1.64 g/cm³
Mean surface temperature	−220 °C
Surface Gravity	112% of Earth's gravity
Number of satellites	13

Great Dark Spot

Visualize It!

14 Predict The wind speeds recorded in Neptune's Great Dark Spot reached 2,000 km/h. Predict what kind of destruction might result on Earth if wind speeds in hurricanes approached 2,000 km/h.

_____

_____

_____

_____

Neptune Has the Strongest Winds

Where does the energy come from that powers winds as fast as 2,000 km/h? Neptune has a warm interior that produces more energy than the planet receives from sunlight. Some scientists believe that Neptune's weather is controlled from inside the planet and not from outside the planet, as is Earth's weather.

Neptune's Moon Triton Has a Different Orbit Than Neptune's Other Moons

Triton (TRYT'in) is the largest moon of Neptune. Unlike the other moons of Neptune, Triton orbits Neptune in the opposite direction from the direction in which Neptune orbits the sun. One explanation for this oddity is that, long ago, there were several large moons that orbited Neptune. These moons came so close together that one moon was ejected. The other moon, Triton, remained behind but began traveling in the opposite direction.

Triton's days are numbered. The moon is slowly spiraling inward toward Neptune. When Triton is a certain distance from Neptune, the planet's gravitational pull will begin pulling Triton apart. Triton will then break into pieces.

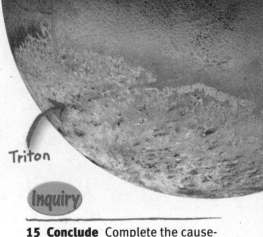

Triton

Inquiry

15 Conclude Complete the cause-and-effect chart by answering the question below.

> Triton spirals inward toward Neptune.

↓

> The gravitational pull of Neptune causes Triton to pull apart.

↓

> Triton breaks into pieces.

What do you think will happen next?

_____

_____

_____

_____

A category 5 hurricane on Earth has sustained wind speeds of 250 km/h. Some effects of the winds of a category 5 hurricane can be seen in this image.

Visual Summary

To complete this summary, write the answers to the questions on the lines. Then use the key below to check your answers. You can use this page to review the main concepts of the lesson.

Properties of Gas Giant Planets

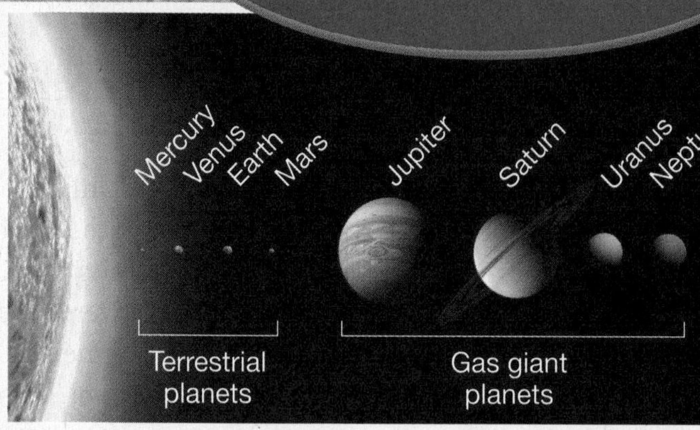

Mercury
Venus
Earth
Mars
Jupiter
Saturn
Uranus
Neptune
Terrestrial planets
Gas giant planets
Not to scale

Jupiter has cloud bands.

16 *What causes cloud bands to form on Jupiter?*

____

____

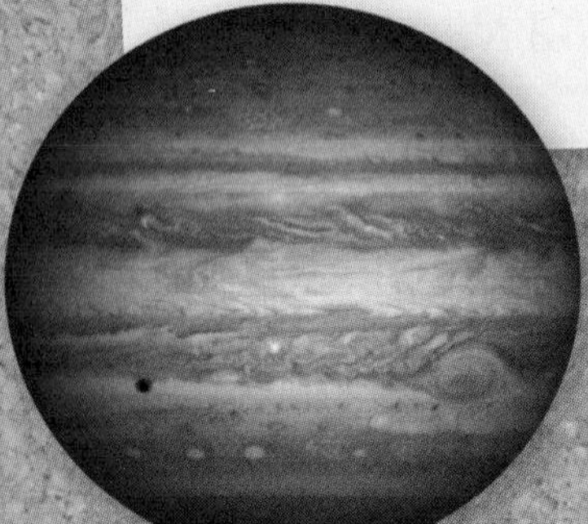

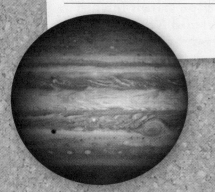

Saturn has a complex ring system.

17 *What are Saturn's rings made up of?*

____

____

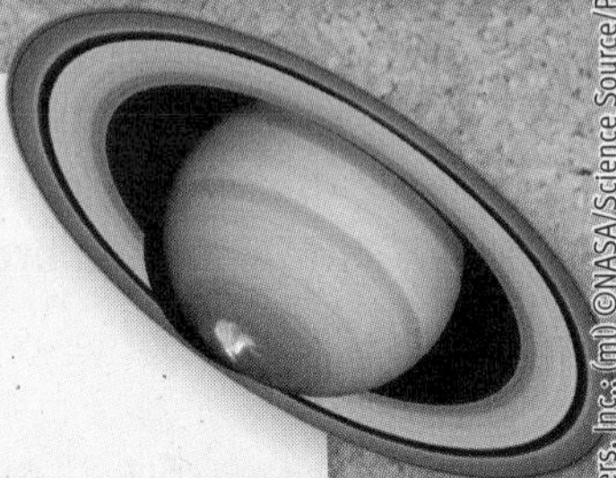

Uranus is tilted on its side.

18 *What is the tilt of Uranus's axis of rotation?*

____

____

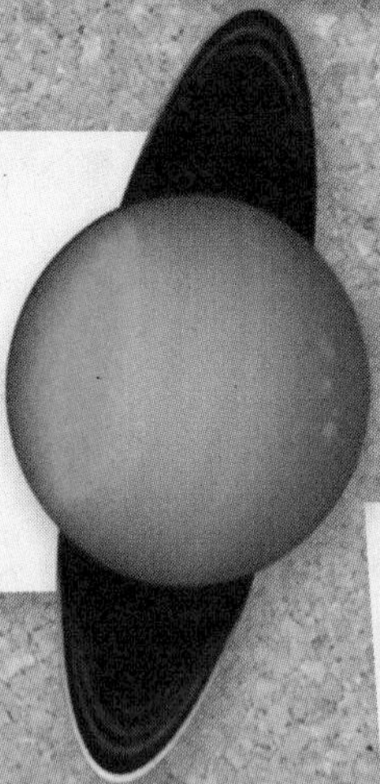

Neptune is a blue planet.

19 *What gives Neptune its bluish color?*

____

____

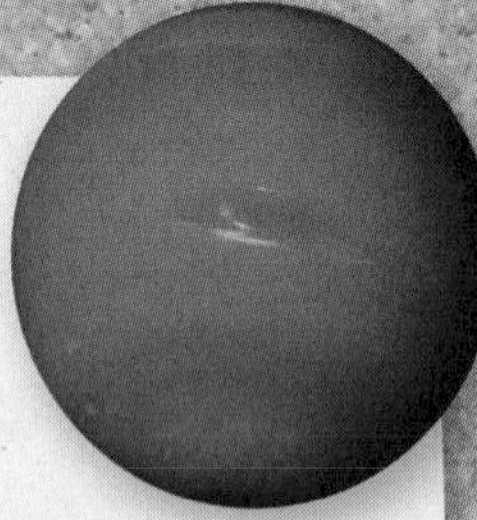

Answers: 16 The high winds on Jupiter circle the planet and cause cloud bands to form; 17 trillions of small, icy bodies; 18 almost 98° (97.8°); 19 the absorption of red light by methane in Neptune's atmosphere

20 Apply Compare the properties of the gas giant planets as a group with properties of Earth.

© Houghton Mifflin Harcourt Publishing Company • Image Credits: (t) ©The International Astronomical Union/Martin Kornmesser/Photo Researchers, Inc.; (ml) ©NASA/Science Source/Photo Researchers, Inc.; (mr) ©NASA/ESA/Space Telescope Science Institute/Science Source/Photo Researchers, Inc.; (bl) ©NASA/ESA/STSCI/E.Karkoschka/U.Arizona/Photo Researchers, Inc.; (br) ©NASA/JPL

Lesson Review

Vocabulary

Fill in the blank with the term that best completes the following sentences.

1 A large planet that has a deep, massive atmosphere is called a _____.

2 A _____ is a disk of matter that circles a planet and consists of numerous particles in orbit that range in size from a few millimeters to several hundred meters.

Key Concepts

In the following table, write the name of the correct planet next to the property of that planet.

Properties	Planet
3 Identify Which planet has a density that is less than that of water?	
4 Identify Which planet has the strongest winds in the solar system?	
5 Identify Which planet is tilted on its side as it orbits the sun?	
6 Identify Which planet is the largest planet in the solar system?	

7 Compare How does the composition of Earth's atmosphere differ from the composition of the atmospheres of the gas giant planets?

_____

_____

_____

8 Compare How do the periods of rotation and revolution for the gas giant planets differ from those of Earth?

_____

_____

_____

Critical Thinking

Use this diagram to answer the following questions.

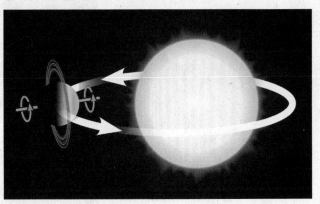

9 Identify Which planet is shown in the diagram? How do you know?

_____

_____

10 Analyze How does the axial tilt of this planet affect its seasons?

_____

_____

_____

_____

11 Analyze Why do you think the wind speeds on the gas giant planets are so much greater than the wind speeds on Earth?

_____

_____

_____

12 Compare List Earth and the gas giant planets in order from the hottest to the coldest planet. How does the temperature of each planet relate to its distance from the sun?

_____

_____

_____

_____

Small Bodies in the Solar System

ESSENTIAL QUESTION

What is found in the solar system besides the sun, planets, and moons?

By the end of this lesson, you should be able to compare and contrast the properties of small bodies in the solar system.

Comet Hale-Bopp was discovered in 1995 and was visible from Earth for 18 months. It is a long-period comet that is thought to take about 2,400 years to orbit the sun.

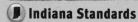

Indiana Standards

6.2.4 Compare and contrast the planets of the solar system with one another and with asteroids and comets with regard to their size, composition, distance from sun, surface features and ability to support life.

Engage Your Brain

1 Predict Check T or F to show whether you think each statement is true or false.

T	F	
☐	☐	Pluto is a planet.
☐	☐	The Kuiper Belt is located beyond the orbit of Neptune.
☐	☐	Comets are made of ice, rock, and dust.
☐	☐	All asteroids have the same composition.
☐	☐	Most meteoroids that enter Earth's atmosphere burn up completely.

2 Identify Can you identify the object that is streaking through the sky in the photograph? What do you think makes this object glow?

_____
_____
_____
_____
_____
_____
_____

Active Reading

3 Apply Many scientific words, such as *belt*, also have everyday meanings. Use context clues to write your own definition for each meaning of the word *belt*.

Example sentence
I found a <u>belt</u> to go with my new pants.

belt:
_____
_____
_____

Example sentence
Short-term comets originate in the Kuiper <u>Belt</u>.

belt:
_____
_____
_____
_____

Vocabulary Terms

- dwarf planet
- Kuiper Belt
- Kuiper Belt object
- comet
- Oort cloud
- asteroid
- meteoroid
- meteor
- meteorite

4 Apply As you learn the definition of each vocabulary term in this lesson, create your own definition or sketch to help you remember the meaning of the term.

Bigger is not better

Where are small bodies in the solar system?

Active Reading

5 Identify As you read the text, underline the names of different kinds of small bodies that are found in the solar system.

The sun, planets, and moons are not the only objects in the solar system. Scientists estimate that there are up to a trillion small bodies in the solar system. These bodies lack atmospheres and have weak surface gravity. The largest of the small bodies, the dwarf planets, are found in regions known as the *asteroid belt* and the *Kuiper Belt*. The Kuiper (KAHY•per) Belt is located beyond the orbit of Neptune. Kuiper Belt objects, as you might guess, are located in the Kuiper Belt. Comets, too, are found in the Kuiper Belt. However, comets are also located in the Oort cloud. The Oort (OHRT) cloud is a region that surrounds the solar system and extends almost halfway to the nearest star. Two other types of small bodies, asteroids and meteoroids, are located mostly between the orbits of Venus and Neptune.

Sizes and distances are not to scale.

Mercury   Venus   Earth   Mars   Ceres

Jupiter

What are dwarf planets?

In 2006, astronomers decided that Pluto would no longer be considered a planet. It became the first member of a new group of solar system bodies called *dwarf planets*. Like planets, a **dwarf planet** is a celestial body that orbits the sun and is round because of its own gravity. However, a dwarf planet does not have the mass to have cleared other bodies out of its orbit around the sun.

Five dwarf planets, made of ice and rock, have been identified. Ceres (SIR•eez), located between the orbits of Mars and Jupiter, is about 950 km in diameter and travels at around 18 km/s. Pluto, Eris (IR•is), Haumea (HOW•may•uh), and Makemake (MAH•kay•MAH•kay) are located beyond the orbit of Neptune. They range in size from about 1,500 km (Haumea) to about 2,400 km (Eris). Their orbital periods around the sun range from 250 to 560 years. All travel at speeds of between 3 km/s and 5 km/s.

© Houghton Mifflin Harcourt Publishing Company • Image Credits: (inset) ©Lynette Cook/Photo Researchers, Inc., ©NASA, ESA, and A. Feild (STScI), ©NASA, ESA, and A. Feild (STScI), ©Lynette Cook/Photo Researchers, Inc.

Active Reading

6 Describe Describe two properties of dwarf planets.

_____

_____

_____

_____

_____

_____

Saturn

Uranus

Neptune

Pluto   Haumea   Makemake   Eris

Visualize It!

7 Analyze Where in the solar system are most of the dwarf planets located?

_____

_____

_____

_____

KBOs

What are Kuiper Belt objects?

The **Kuiper Belt** is a region of the solar system that begins just beyond the orbit of Neptune and contains small bodies made mostly of ice. It extends outward to about twice the orbit of Neptune, a distance of about 55 astronomical units (AU). An AU is a unit of length that is equal to the average distance between Earth and the sun, or about 150,000,000 km. The Kuiper Belt is thought to contain matter that was left over from the formation of the solar system. This matter formed small bodies instead of planets.

A **Kuiper Belt object (KBO)** is any of the minor bodies in the Kuiper Belt outside the orbit of Neptune. Kuiper Belt objects are made of methane ice, ammonia ice, and water ice. They have average orbital speeds of between 1 km/s and 5 km/s. The first Kuiper Belt object was not discovered until 1992. Now, about 1,300 KBOs are known. Scientists estimate that there are at least 70,000 objects in the Kuiper Belt that have diameters larger than 100 km.

Quaoar is a KBO that orbits 43 AU from the sun. It is around 1,260 km in diameter and has one satellite.

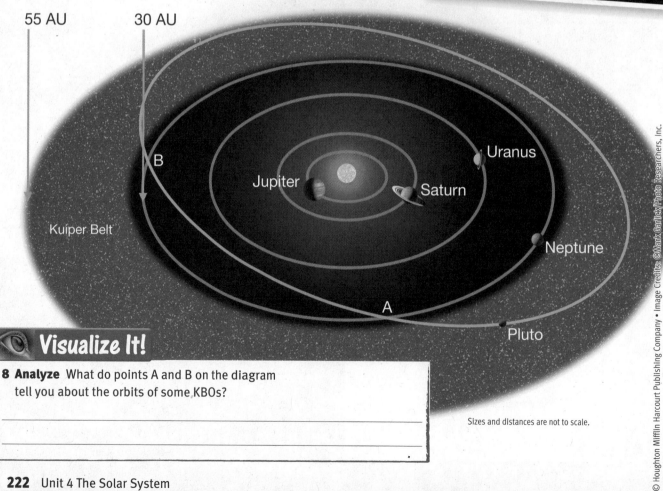

55 AU

30 AU

B

Jupiter

Uranus

Saturn

Kuiper Belt

Neptune

A

Pluto

Sizes and distances are not to scale.

Visualize It!

8 Analyze What do points A and B on the diagram tell you about the orbits of some KBOs?

_____

_____

Pluto: From Planet to KBO

From its discovery in 1930 until 2006, Pluto was considered to be the ninth planet in the solar system. However, beginning in 1992, a new group of small bodies called *Kuiper Belt objects*, or simply KBOs, began to be discovered beyond the orbit of Neptune. Not only are some of the KBOs close to Pluto in size, but some have a similar composition of rock and ice. Astronomers recognized that Pluto was, in fact, a large KBO and not the ninth planet. In 2006, Pluto was redefined as a "dwarf planet" by the International Astronomical Union (IAU).

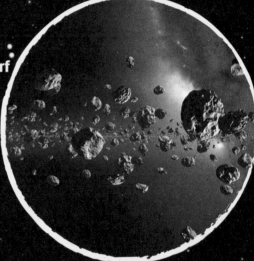

Pluto

Charon

Pluto and Charon

At 2,306 km in diameter, Pluto is the second largest KBO. It is shown in this artist's rendition with Charon (KAIR•uhn), its largest satellite. Many large KBOs have satellites. Some KBOs and their satellites, such as Pluto and Charon, orbit each other.

The Kuiper Belt

The Kuiper Belt is located between 30 AU (the orbit of Neptune) and approximately 55 AU. However, most KBOs have been discovered between 42 and 48 AU, where their orbits are not disturbed by the gravitational attraction of Neptune.

Extend

Inquiry

9 Explain Why is Pluto no longer considered a planet?

10 Research Astronomer Clyde Tombaugh discovered Pluto in 1930. Research why Tombaugh was searching beyond Neptune for "Planet X" and how he discovered Pluto.

11 Debate Research the 2006 IAU decision to redefine Pluto as a "dwarf planet." Combine this research with your research on Pluto. With your classmates, debate whether Pluto should be considered a "dwarf planet" or return to being called the ninth planet in the solar system.

What do we know about comets?

Active Reading 12 **Identify** As you read the text, underline the different parts of a comet and their properties.

A **comet** is a small body of ice, rock, and dust that follows a highly elliptical orbit around the sun. As a comet passes close to the sun, it gives off gas and dust in the form of a coma and a tail.

The speed of a comet will vary depending on how far from or how close to the sun it is. Far from the sun, a comet may travel at speeds as low as 0.32 km/s. Close to the sun, a comet may travel as fast as 445 km/s.

Comets Are Made of a Nucleus and a Tail

All comets have a *nucleus* that is composed of ice and rock. Most comet nuclei are between 1 km and 10 km in diameter. If a comet approaches the sun, solar radiation and heating cause the comet's ice to change to gas. A *coma* is a spherical cloud of gas and dust that comes off of the nucleus. The *ion tail* of a comet is gas that has been ionized, or stripped of electrons, by the sun. The solar wind—electrically charged particles expanding away from the sun—pushes the gas away from the comet's head. So, regardless of the direction a comet is traveling, its ion tail points away from the sun. A second tail made of dust and gas curves backward along the comet's orbit. This *dust tail* can be millions of kilometers long.

Visualize It!

13 Identify Use the write-on lines in the diagram to identify the structures of a comet.

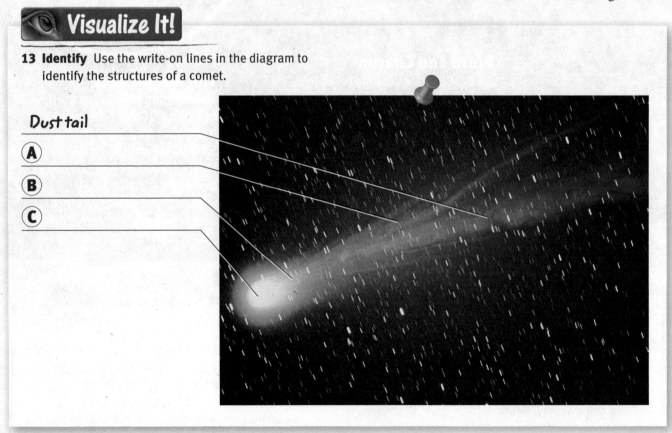

Dust tail

A

B

C

Comets Come from the Kuiper Belt and the Oort Cloud

There are two regions of the solar system where comets come from. The first region is the Kuiper Belt, which is where short-period comets originate. The second region is the Oort cloud, which is where long-period comets originate.

Collisions between objects in the Kuiper Belt produce fragments that become comets. These comets are known as *short-period comets*. Short-period comets take less than 200 years to orbit the sun. Therefore, they return to the inner solar system quite frequently, perhaps every few decades or centuries. Short-period comets also have short life spans. Every time a comet passes the sun, it may lose a layer as much as 1 m thick.

Some comets originate in the Oort cloud. The **Oort cloud** is a spherical region that surrounds the solar system and extends almost halfway to the nearest star. Comets can form in the Oort cloud when two objects collide. Comets can also form when an object in the Oort cloud is disturbed by the gravity of a nearby star and is sent into the inner solar system. Comets that originate in the Oort cloud are called *long-period comets*. Long-period comets may take up to hundreds of thousands of years to orbit the sun.

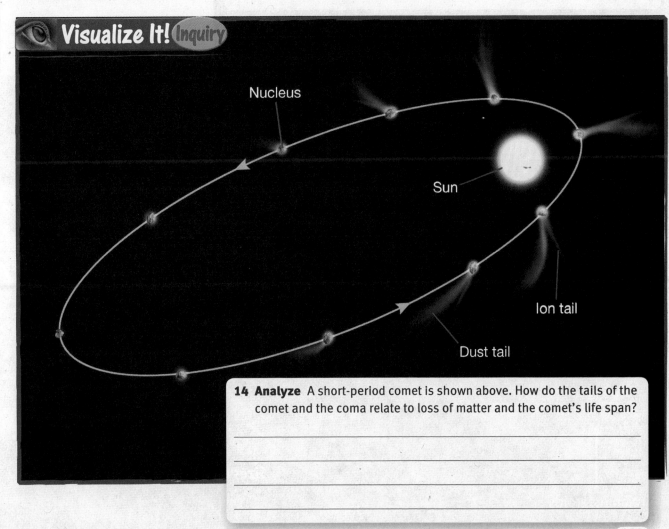

Visualize It! Inquiry

Nucleus

Sun

Ion tail

Dust tail

14 Analyze A short-period comet is shown above. How do the tails of the comet and the coma relate to loss of matter and the comet's life span?

_____

_____

_____

_____

On the rocks

What do we know about asteroids?

Active Reading **15 Identify** As you read the text, underline those places in the solar system where asteroids are located.

An **asteroid** is a small, irregularly shaped, rocky object that orbits the sun. Most asteroids are located between the orbits of Mars and Jupiter. This 300 million–km–wide region is known as the *asteroid belt*. The asteroid belt contains hundreds of thousands of asteroids, called *main-belt asteroids*. The largest main-belt asteroid by diameter is Pallas, which has a diameter of 570 km. The smallest asteroid is 4 m in diameter. Groups of asteroids are also located in the orbits of Jupiter and Neptune (called *Trojan asteroids*) and in the Kuiper Belt. Still other asteroids are called *near-Earth asteroids*. Some of these asteroids cross the orbits of Earth and Venus.

Asteroids in the asteroid belt orbit the sun at about 18 km/s and have orbital periods of 3 to 8 years. Although most asteroids rotate around their axis, some tumble end over end through space.

Visualize It!

16 Analyze Where is the asteroid belt located?

_____

_____

_____

_____

_____

_____

Asteroid Belt

Mars

Trojan Asteroids

Sizes and distances are not to scale.

Trojan Asteroids

Jupiter

Asteroids Have Different Compositions

The composition of asteroids varies. Many asteroids have dark surfaces. Scientists think that these asteroids are rich in carbon. Other asteroids are thought to be rocky and to have a core made of iron and nickel. Still other asteroids may have a rocky core surrounded largely by ice. Small, rocky asteroids have perhaps the strangest composition of all. They appear to be piles of rock loosely held together by gravity. Asteroid Itokawa (ee•TOH•kah•wah), shown below, is a rocky asteroid known as a "rubble-pile" asteroid.

Some asteroids contain economic minerals like those mined on Earth. Economic minerals that are found in asteroids include gold, iron, nickel, manganese, cobalt, and platinum. Scientists are now investigating the potential for mining near-Earth asteroids.

Itokawa is a rubble-pile asteroid. Astronomers think that the 500 m—long asteroid may be composed of two asteroids that are joined.

Thin, dusty outer core

Water-ice layer

Rocky inner core

Greetings *from* Eros!

Think Outside the Book

17 Describe Eros is a near-Earth asteroid that tumbles through space. Imagine that you are the first human to explore Eros. Write a postcard that describes what you found on Eros. Then research the asteroid and find out how close your description came to reality.

Burned Out

What do we know about meteoroids, meteors, and meteorites?

A sand grain- to boulder-sized, rocky body that travels through space is a **meteoroid**. Meteoroids that enter Earth's atmosphere travel at about 52 km/s, as measured by radar on Earth. Friction heats these meteoroids to thousands of degrees Celsius, which causes them to glow. The atmosphere around a meteoroid's path also gets hotter and glows because of friction between the meteoroid and air molecules. A bright streak of light that results when a meteoroid burns up in Earth's atmosphere is called a **meteor**. A **meteorite** is a meteoroid that reaches Earth's surface without burning up.

👁 **Visualize It!**

18 Identify Use the write-on lines below to identify the three objects that are shown.

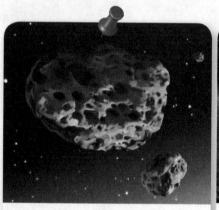

A A small, rocky body that travels through space is a

_____

B The glowing trail of a body that is burning up in Earth's atmosphere is a _____

C A body that reaches Earth's surface without burning up is a _____

A meteorite 45 m across produced kilometer-wide Barringer Crater in Arizona about 50,000 years ago.

Meteorites Reach Earth

Meteoroids come from the asteroid belt, Mars, the moon, and comets. Most of the meteoroids that enter Earth's atmosphere do not reach Earth's surface. Many meteoroids explode in the upper atmosphere. These explosions are often recorded by military satellites in orbit around Earth. Other meteoroids skip back into space after briefly crossing the upper atmosphere. However, some large meteoroids that enter Earth's lower atmosphere or strike Earth's surface can be destructive. Scientists estimate that a destructive meteorite impact occurs every 300 to 400 years.

Meteorites Have Different Compositions

Meteorites can be divided into three general groups. The first group of meteorites are the stony meteorites. They are the most common form of meteorite. Stony meteorites are made of silicate minerals, just like rocks on Earth. Some stony meteorites also contain small amounts of organic matter. A much smaller group of meteorites are the iron meteorites. Iron meteorites are composed of iron and nickel. The rarest group of meteorites are stony-iron meteorites. Stony-iron meteorites are composed of both silicate minerals and iron and nickel. All three groups of meteorites can originate from asteroids. However, some stony meteorites come from the moon and Mars.

Visualize It!

19 Describe In the boxes below, describe the composition and origin of each group of meteorite. Also, indicate how common each group of meteorite is.

Stony meteorite

_____

_____

_____

_____

Iron meteorite

_____

_____

_____

_____

Stony-iron meteorite

_____

_____

_____

_____

Visual Summary

To complete this summary, answer the questions below. Then use the key below to check your answers. You can use this page to review the main concepts of the lesson.

Small Bodies in the Solar System

Small bodies are found throughout the solar system.

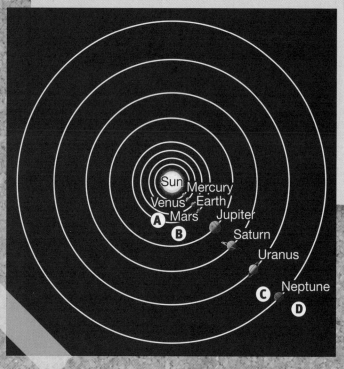

20 Enter the correct letter or letters that indicate a location for each small body in the solar system.

Asteroids	
Dwarf planets	
Kuiper Belt objects	

21 Check true or false to answer the questions below.

T	F	
☐	☐	Comets originate in the asteroid belt and the Kuiper Belt.
☐	☐	Three groups of asteroids are stony, iron, and stony-iron.
☐	☐	Most meteoroids that enter Earth's atmosphere burn up.

22 Compare Make a table in which you compare and contrast comets and asteroids in terms of composition, location in the solar system, and size.

Lesson Review

Vocabulary

Fill in the blank with the term that best completes the following sentences.

1 The _____ is a spherical region that surrounds the solar system and extends almost halfway to the nearest star.

2 A region of the solar system that extends from the orbit of Neptune to about twice the orbit of Neptune is the _____.

3 Most _____ are located between the orbits of Mars and Jupiter.

4 A meteoroid that reaches Earth's surface without burning up is a _____.

Key Concepts

In the following table, write the name of the correct body next to the property of that body.

Property	Body
5 Identify What is a minor body that orbits outside the orbit of Neptune?	
6 Identify What is a small body that follows a highly elliptical orbit around the sun?	
7 Identify What is the largest of the small bodies that are found in the solar system?	
8 Identify What is the glowing trail that results when a meteoroid burns up in Earth's atmosphere?	

Critical Thinking

Use this table to answer the following questions.

Comet	Orbital Period (years)
Borrelly	6.9
Halley	76
Hale-Bopp	2,400
Hyakutake	100,000

9 Apply Which of the comets in the table are short-period comets?

_____

_____

10 Apply Which of the comets in the table most likely originated in the Oort cloud?

_____

_____

11 Infer Why do you think that the speeds of comets increase as they near the sun?

_____

_____

_____

_____

12 Predict Why do you think that some asteroids tumble end over end through space while other asteroids rotate around their axis?

_____

_____

_____

_____

My Notes

Unit 4 Summary

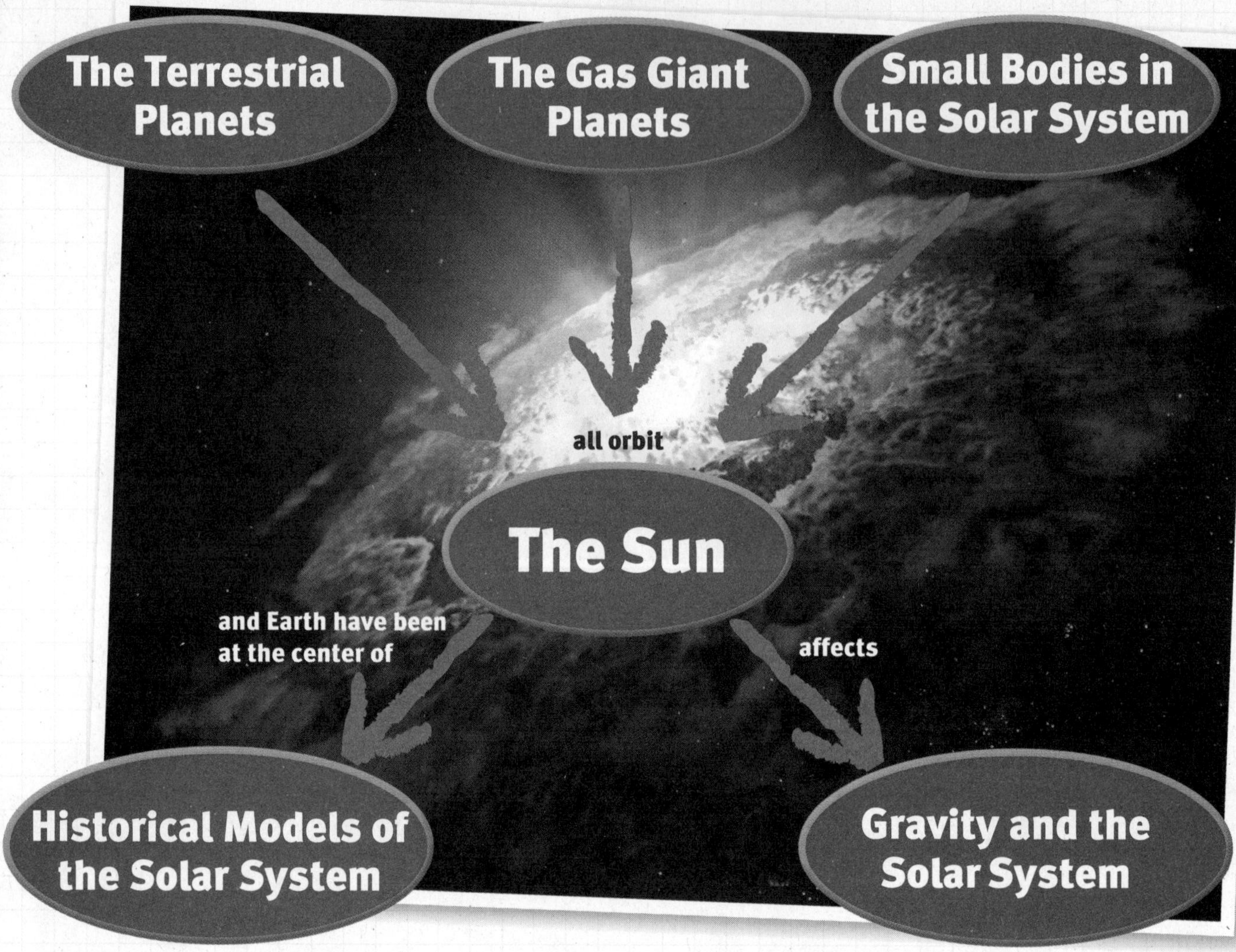

The Terrestrial Planets

The Gas Giant Planets

Small Bodies in the Solar System

all orbit

The Sun

and Earth have been at the center of

affects

Historical Models of the Solar System

Gravity and the Solar System

1 Interpret The Graphic Organizer above shows the sun at the center. Why do you think the sun has been placed at the center?

_____

_____

_____

_____

2 Compare If you were suddenly transported to another planet, how would you know if that planet was a terrestrial planet or a gas giant planet?

_____

_____

_____

_____

3 Recognize What is the importance of Newton's law of universal gravitation?

_____

_____

_____

_____

_____

4 Apply How is energy transferred to the surface of the sun?

_____

_____

_____

_____

ISTEP+ Review

Name _____

Multiple Choice

1 Copernicus challenged the ways that people of his time thought about the universe. How did Copernicus describe the motion of the sun?

   A. The sun is stationary.

   B. The sun moves around Earth.

   C. The sun moves in circles on a sphere.

   D. The sun moves in a straight line through space.

2 Galileo used a telescope to observe Venus. The diagram below explains what he saw.

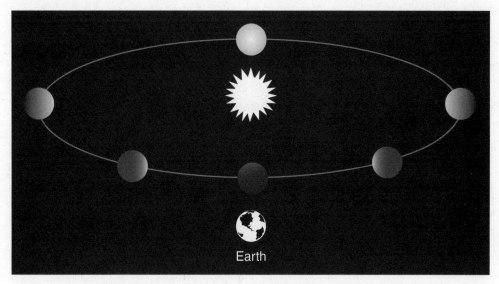

Earth

What did Galileo conclude from his observations of Venus?

   A. It is always lit.

   B. It travels around the sun.

   C. It is farther from the sun than Earth is.

   D. It has moons and the moons have phases.

3 Which of these models of the universe did Ptolemy's system support?

   A. Earth revolved around the sun.

   B. Earth was the center of the universe.

   C. The sun was the center of the universe.

   D. Earth had different paths in the universe.

ISTEP+ Review

4 What is gravity?

A. a force of attraction between objects that is due to their masses

B. an unbalanced force that makes objects move in an elliptical path

C. the rotating cloud of gas and dust from which the sun and planets formed

D. the point in the orbit of a planet at which the planet is farthest from the sun

5 The diagram below shows the effect of mass and distance on the force of gravity.

Effect of Mass on F_grav

Attract with a force of

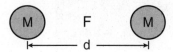

Attract with a force of

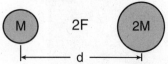

Attract with a force of

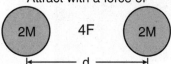

Effect of Distance on F_grav

Attract with a force of

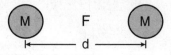

Attract with a force of

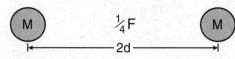

Attract with a force of

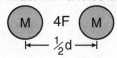

Which configuration will result in the GREATEST gravitational force?

A. small masses far apart

B. large masses far apart

C. small masses close together

D. large masses close together

6 The diagrams below illustrate principles of planetary motion. Which diagram illustrates Kepler's second law of planetary motion?

A.

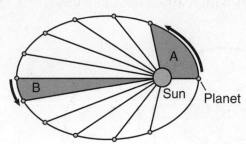

C.

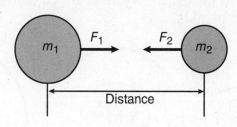

B.

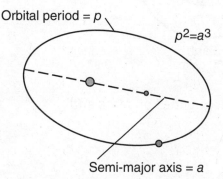

D.

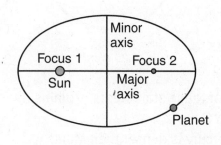

7 With which of these solar layers are solar flares MOST CLOSELY linked?

A. core

B. convective zone

C. radiative zone

D. photosphere

8 On many planets, an atmosphere acts as insulation. Mercury has almost no atmosphere. How does the lack of atmosphere affect temperatures on Mercury?

A. Temperatures vary less than they would with an atmosphere.

B. Temperatures vary more than they would with an atmosphere.

C. Temperatures would not be affected if the planet had an atmosphere.

D. Temperatures would be affected if the planet had an atmosphere, but only when the planet is closest to the sun.

9 Venus and Earth have similar gravities. Mercury and Mars have almost the same gravity, even though Mercury is much smaller. Density affects the force of gravity. The figure below contains information about the densities of four planets.

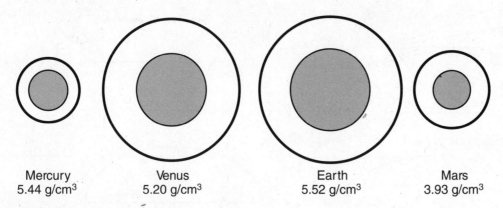

Mercury	Venus	Earth	Mars
5.44 g/cm^3	5.20 g/cm^3	5.52 g/cm^3	3.93 g/cm^3

Which of these statements explains the similar gravities on Mars and Mercury?

A. Mercury is denser than Mars.

B. Mercury is smaller than Mars.

C. Mercury is not as dense as Mars.

D. Mercury has more rocks than Mars does.

10 Which planet (or planets) has 60 or more moons?

A. Jupiter only

B. Jupiter and Saturn only

C. Jupiter, Saturn, and Neptune only

D. Jupiter, Saturn, Neptune, and Uranus

11 Where are dwarf planets located?

A. Oort cloud only

B. Kuiper Belt only

C. Oort cloud and Kuiper Belt

D. Kuiper Belt and asteroid belt

12 What is the Oort cloud made up of?

A. trillions of comets

B. dwarf planets and meteoroids

C. some comets and many asteroids

D. equal numbers of comets, asteroids, and meteoroids

13 The table below shows some physical properties of the gas giant planets.

Planet	Diameter (km)	Rotation Time	Gravity	Tilt of Axis (degrees)
Jupiter	142,984	9 hr 55 min	253% of Earth	3.13
Neptune	49,528	16 hr 7 min	112% of Earth	28.5
Saturn	120,536	10 hr 39 min	106% of Earth	26.73
Uranus	51,118	17 hr 24 min	79% of Earth	97.8

What can you conclude about the PERIOD OF ROTATION of the gas giant planets?

A. The largest gas giant planet rotates the fastest.

B. The smallest gas giant planet rotates the fastest.

C. The planet with the smallest gravity rotates the fastest.

D. The planet with the largest axial tilt rotates the fastest.

14 What is the order of the gas giant planets listed here, going FROM THE LEAST TO THE MOST gravitational force?

A. Jupiter < Uranus < Saturn < Neptune

B. Uranus < Neptune < Saturn < Jupiter

C. Neptune < Jupiter < Saturn < Uranus

D. Uranus < Saturn < Neptune < Jupiter

Constructed Response

15 The sun releases enough energy in one second to power the United States for 13 billion years.

Identify and explain the PROCESS by which the sun releases energy.

_____

_____

Draw a DIAGRAM of the layers of the sun, showing where nuclear fusion takes place and the path that energy moves before it escapes into space.

ISTEP+ Review

Extended Response

16 Venus has an unusual atmosphere – unlike that of any other planet in our solar system.

What is the composition of the atmosphere on Venus?

_____

_____

How does the atmospheric pressure on the surface of Venus compare to that on Earth?

_____

How do the clouds surrounding Venus affect its surface temperatures?

_____

_____

Using what you know about the atmosphere of Venus, explain why it is important to keep the air clean on Earth.

_____

_____

The Earth-Moon-Sun System

Core Standard

Understand the relationships between celestial bodies and the force that keeps them in regular and predictable motion.

What do you think?

Earth is affected by its sun and moon. The sun provides light and energy. The moon regulates the tides. Why is a regular tide system important?

Tide pool exposed by low tide

Unit 5
The Earth-Moon-Sun System

Lesson 1
Earth's Days, Years, and Seasons...................... 244
6.2.1, 6.2.5

Lesson 2
Moon Phases and Eclipses....... 254
6.2.1

Think Science.................. 264
NOS 6.8

Lesson 3
Earth's Tides..................... 266
6.2.2

Unit Summary.................... 278

ISTEP+ Review............. 279

Indiana Standards

As citizens of the constructed world, students will participate in the design process. Students will learn to use materials and tools safely and employ the basic principles of the engineering design process in order to find solutions to problems.

DP 6.1 Identify a need or problem to be solved.

DP 6.2 Brainstorm potential solutions.

DP 6.4 Select a solution to the need or problem.

DP 6.5 Select the most appropriate materials to develop a solution that will meet the need.

CITIZEN SCIENCE
Measuring Shadows

Do the lengths of shadows created by the sun change throughout the year? The answer to this question tells us about Earth's rotation and its orbit. Help students with an ongoing research project, called the Sun Shadows Project. The results are presented at the American Geophysical Union's Annual Conference.

1 Think About It

Students at James Monroe Middle School in Albuquerque, New Mexico, asked the following questions: The seasons change, but do the length of shadows? How could this be measured?

_____

_____

_____

Scientists in Antarctica measure shadows.

② Ask A Question

What effects do seasons have on the lengths of shadows in your area?

As a class, come up with a prediction. Then, research what students at James Monroe Middle School are doing to gather information.

Things to Consider

Some parts of the world participate in Daylight Savings Time. People move their clocks forward by an hour in the spring and back by an hour in the fall. In other parts of the world, Daylight Savings Time is not practiced. Daylight Savings Time may affect your measurements, so make sure that your group is taking measurements when shadows are the shortest.

③ Apply Your Knowledge

A List the materials your class will need to make and record the measurements to gather the information needed by the students at James Monroe Middle School.

_____

_____

_____

_____

B Decide on a time frame for your class project. Will you participate for an entire season? What factors influence your decision?

_____

_____

_____

_____

_____

_____

C Track the information gathered by your class and draw your own preliminary conclusions.

_____

_____

_____

_____

Take It Home

Who else is participating in the Sun Shadows Project? Research the various national and international groups taking part, such as the U.S. Antarctic Program.

Earth's Days, Years, and Seasons

ESSENTIAL QUESTION

How are Earth's days, years, and seasons related to the way Earth moves in space?

By the end of this lesson, you should be able to relate Earth's days, years, and seasons to Earth's movement in space.

Indiana Standards

6.2.1 Describe and model how the position, size and relative motions of the earth, moon, and sun cause day and night, solar and lunar eclipses and phases of the moon.

6.2.5 Demonstrate that the seasons in both hemispheres are the result of the inclination of the earth on its axis which in turn causes changes in sunlight intensity and length of day.

In many parts of the world, blooming flowers are one of the first signs that spring has arrived. Spring flowers start blooming with the warmer temperatures of spring, even if there is still snow on the ground.

Engage Your Brain

1 Predict Check T or F to show whether you think each statement is true or false.

T   F

☐ ☐ A day is about 12 hours long.

☐ ☐ A year is about 365 days long.

☐ ☐ When it is summer in the Northern Hemisphere, it is summer all around the world.

2 Apply Write your own caption for this photo of leaves in the space below.

_____

_____

_____

_____

_____

Active Reading

3 Synthesize The term *rotation* can be tricky to remember because it is used somewhat differently in science than it is in everyday life. In baseball, a pitching *rotation* lists the order of a team's starting pitchers. The order starts over after the last pitcher on the list has played. On the lines below, write down any other examples you can think of that use the term *rotation*.

_____

_____

_____

_____

Vocabulary Terms

- rotation
- day
- revolution
- year
- season
- equinox
- solstice

4 Apply As you learn the definition of each vocabulary term in this lesson, create your own definition or sketch to help you remember the meaning of the term.

Spinning in

What determines the length of a day?

Each planet spins on its axis. Earth's axis (ACK•sis) is an imaginary straight line that runs from the North Pole to the South Pole. The spinning of a body, such as a planet, on its axis is called **rotation**. The time it takes a planet to complete one full rotation on its axis is called a **day**.

Active Reading

5 Identify As you read, underline the places on Earth's surface at which the ends of Earth's axis would be.

The Time It Takes for Earth to Rotate Once

Earth rotates in a counterclockwise motion around its axis when viewed from above the North Pole. This means that as a location on Earth's equator rotates from west to east, the sun appears to rise in the east. The sun then appears to cross the sky and set in the west.

As Earth rotates, only one-half of Earth faces the sun at any given time. People on the half of Earth facing the sun experience daylight. This period of time in daylight is called *daytime*. People on the half of Earth that faces away from the sun experience darkness. This period of time in darkness is called *nighttime*.

Earth's rotation is used to measure time. Earth completes one rotation on its axis in 24 hours, or in one day. Most locations on Earth's surface move through daylight and darkness in that time.

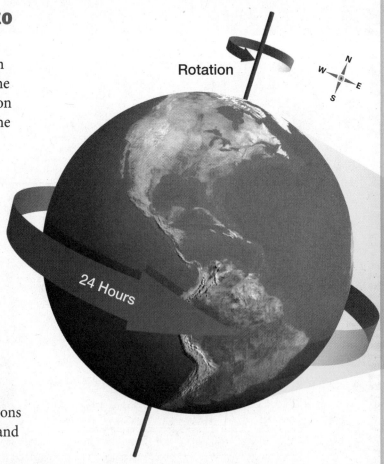

Rotation

24 Hours

Earth's motion is used to measure the length of an Earth day.

Circles

What determines the length of a year?

As Earth rotates on its axis, Earth also revolves around the sun. Although you cannot feel Earth moving, it is traveling around the sun at an average speed of nearly 30 km/s. The motion of a body that travels around another body in space is called **revolution** (reh•vuh•LOO•shun). Earth completes a full revolution around the sun in 365 ¼ days, or about one **year**. We have divided the year into 12 months, each month lasting from 28 to 31 days.

Earth's orbit is not quite a perfect circle. In January, Earth is about 2.5 million kilometers closer to the sun than it is in July. You may be surprised that this distance makes only a tiny difference in temperatures on Earth.

Think Outside the Book

6 Infer How is a leap year, in which a day is added to every fourth year, related to the time it takes Earth to revolve around the sun?

Visualize It!

7 Apply Imagine that Earth's current position is at point A below. Write the label B to show Earth's position 6 months from now in the same diagram.

This drawing is not to scale.

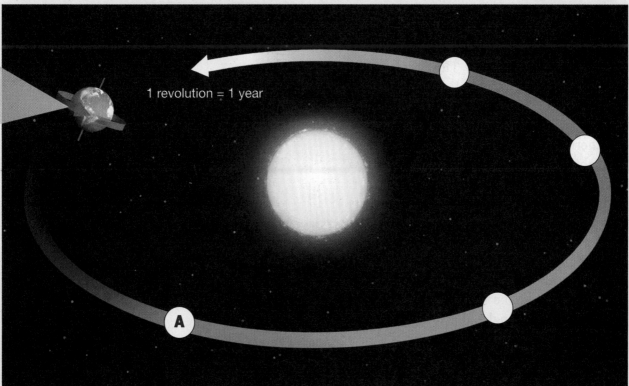

1 revolution = 1 year

A

Tilt-a-Whirl

What conditions are affected by the tilt of Earth's axis?

Earth's axis is tilted at 23.5°. Earth's axis always points toward the North Star as Earth revolves around the sun. Thus, during each revolution, the North Pole may be tilted toward the sun or away from the sun, as seen below. When the North Pole is tilted toward the sun, the Northern Hemisphere (HEHM•ih•sfeer) has longer periods of daylight than does the Southern Hemisphere. When the North Pole is tilted away from the sun, the opposite is true.

The direction of tilt of Earth's axis remains the same throughout Earth's orbit around the sun.

23.5°

23.5°

orbit

This drawing is not to scale.

Temperature

The angle at which the sun's rays strike each part of Earth's surface changes as Earth moves in its orbit. When the North Pole is tilted toward the sun, the sun's rays strike the Northern Hemisphere more directly. Thus, the region receives a higher concentration of solar energy and is warmer. When the North Pole is tilted away from the sun, the sun's rays strike the Northern Hemisphere less directly. When the sunlight is less direct, the solar energy is less concentrated and the region is cooler.

The spherical shape of Earth also affects how the sun warms up an area. Temperatures are high at point A in the diagram. This is because the sun's rays hit Earth's surface at a right angle and are focused in a small area. Toward the poles, the sun's rays hit Earth's surface at a lesser angle. Therefore, the rays are spread out over a larger area and the temperatures are cooler.

👁 Visualize It!

8 Apply Which location on the illustration of Earth below receives more direct rays from the sun?

☐ A
☐ B
☐ They receive equal amounts.

9 Identify Which location is cooler? _____

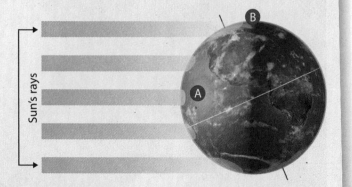

Sun's rays

Daylight Hours

All locations on Earth experience an *average* of 12 hours of light a day. However, the *actual* number of daylight hours on any given day of the year varies with location. Areas around Earth's equator receive about 12 hours of light a day. Areas on Earth's surface that are tilted toward the sun have more hours of daylight. These areas travel a longer path through the lit part of Earth than areas at the equator. Areas on Earth's surface that are tilted away from the sun have less than 12 hours of light a day. These areas travel a shorter path through the lit part of Earth, as shown below.

This drawing is not to scale.

Sun's Rays

During summer in the Northern Hemisphere, a person has already had many daylight hours by the time a person in the Southern Hemisphere reaches daylight.

About twelve hours later, the person in the Northern Hemisphere is close to daylight again, while the person in the Southern Hemisphere still has many hours of darkness left.

Midnight Sun

When it is summer in the Northern Hemisphere, the time in each day that it is light increases as you move north of the equator. Areas north of the Arctic Circle have 24 hours of daylight, called the "midnight sun," as seen in the photo. At the same time, areas south of the Antarctic Circle receive 24 hours of darkness, or "polar night." When it is winter in the Northern Hemisphere, conditions in the polar areas are reversed.

Visualize It! Inquiry

10 Synthesize Why isn't the area in the photo very warm even though the sun is up all night long?

_____

_____

_____

This composite image shows that the sun never set on this Arctic summer day.

Seasons change...

What causes seasons?

Most locations on Earth experience seasons. Each **season** is characterized by a pattern of temperature and other weather trends. Near the equator, the temperatures are almost the same year-round. Near the poles, there are very large changes in temperatures from winter to summer. We experience seasons due to the changes in the intensity of sunlight and the number of daylight hours as Earth revolves around the sun. So, both the tilt of Earth's axis and Earth's spherical shape play a role in Earth's changing seasons.

As Earth travels around the sun, the area of sunlight in each hemisphere changes. At an **equinox** (EE•kwuh•nahks), sunlight shines equally on the Northern and Southern Hemispheres. Half of each hemisphere is lit, and half is in darkness. As Earth moves along its orbit, the sunlight reaches more of one hemisphere than the other. At a **solstice** (SAHL•stis), the area of sunlight is at a maximum in one hemisphere and at a minimum in the other hemisphere.

- **September Equinox** When Earth is in this position, sunlight shines equally on both poles.
- **December Solstice** About three months later, Earth has traveled a quarter of the way around the sun, but its axis still points in the same direction into space. The North Pole leans away from the sun and is in complete darkness. The South Pole is in complete sunlight.
- **March Equinox** After another quarter of its orbit, Earth reaches another equinox. Half of each hemisphere is lit, and the sunlight is centered on the equator.
- **June Solstice** This position is opposite to the December solstice. Now the North Pole leans toward the sun and is in complete sunlight, and the south pole is in complete darkness.

The amount of sunlight an area on Earth receives changes during the year. These changes are due to Earth's tilt and position in its orbit around the sun. Equinoxes and solstices mark certain points in the range of sunlight each of Earth's hemispheres receives.

This drawing is not to scale.

March Equinox

April

May

June Solstice

11 Apply In what month does winter begin in the Southern Hemisphere?

_____

12 Infer During which solstice would the sun be at its highest point in the sky in the Northern Hemisphere?

_____

Solstices

The seasons of summer and winter begin on days called *solstices*. Each year on June 21 or 22, the North Pole's tilt toward the sun is greatest. This day is called the *June solstice*. This solstice marks the beginning of summer in the Northern Hemisphere. By December 21 or 22, the North Pole is tilted to the farthest point away from the sun. This day is the December solstice.

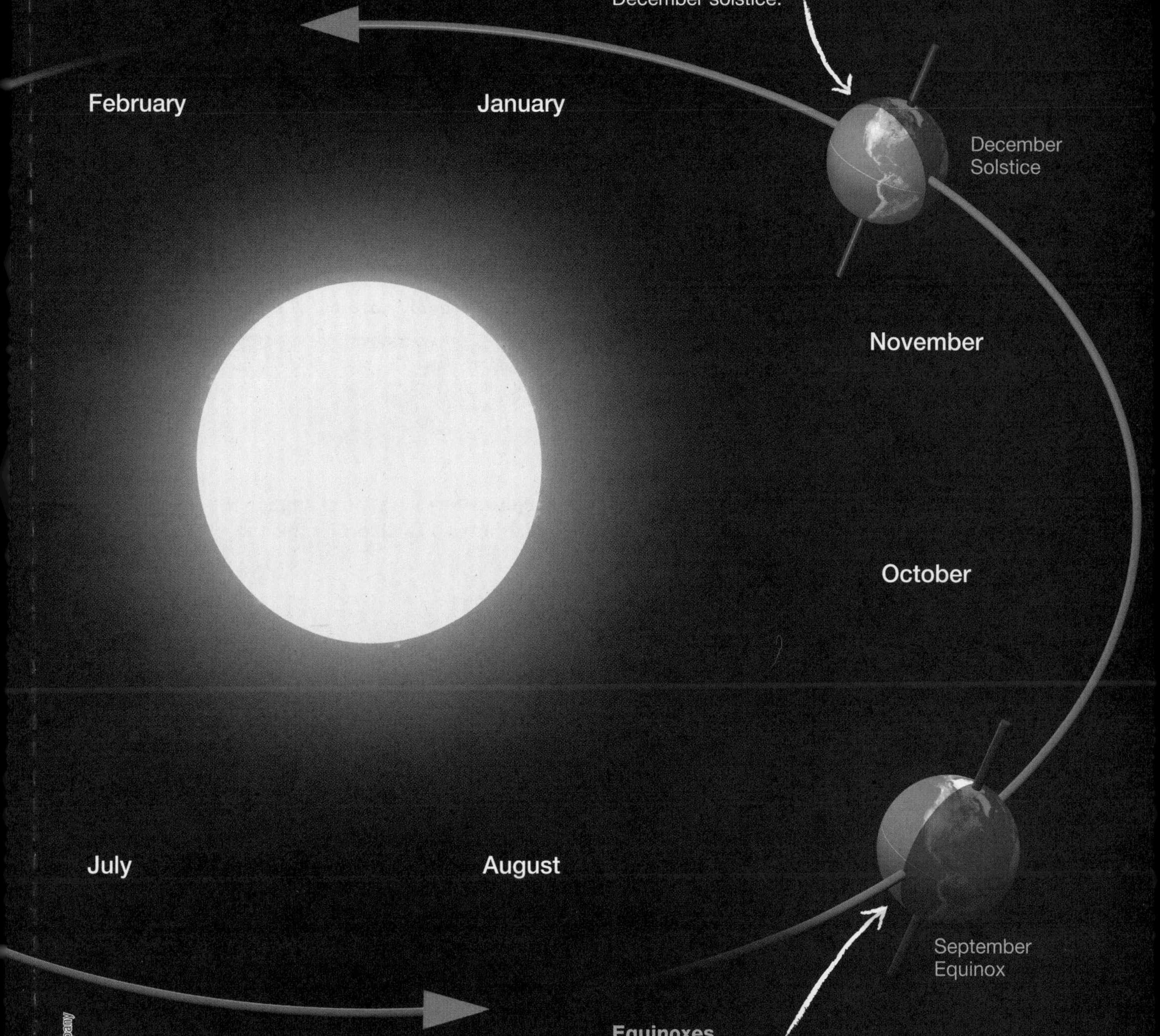

February

January

December Solstice

November

October

July

August

September Equinox

Equinoxes

The seasons fall and spring begin on days called *equinoxes*. The hours of daylight and darkness are approximately equal everywhere on Earth on these days. The *September equinox* occurs on September 22 or 23 of each year. This equinox marks the beginning of fall in the Northern Hemisphere. The March equinox on March 20 or 21 of each year marks the beginning of spring.

13 Infer In which parts of the world is an equinox most different from other days of the year?

_____

_____

Visual Summary

To complete this summary, circle the correct word. Then use the key below to check your answers. You can use this page to review the main concepts of the lesson.

The length of a day is determined by Earth's rotation.

14 It takes Earth 24 seconds/hours to make one rotation on its axis.

The length of a year is determined by Earth's revolution around the sun.

15 It takes Earth about 365 hours/days to revolve around the sun.

Earth's
Days, Years, and Seasons

Earth's tilt affects temperatures and daylight hours at different locations on Earth.

Sun's rays

16 Earth's temperatures and hours of daylight stay the most constant at the equator/poles.

This diagram shows how seasons change in the Northern Hemisphere as Earth orbits the sun.

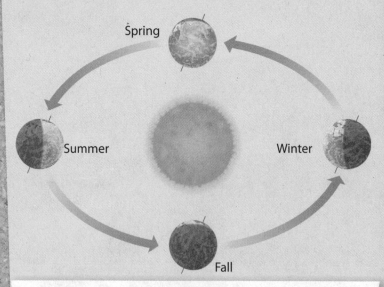

Spring

Summer

Winter

Fall

17 When it is summer in the Northern Hemisphere, it is summer/winter in the Southern Hemisphere.

Answers: 14 hours; 15 days; 16 equator; 17 winter

18 **Predict** How would conditions on Earth change if Earth stopped rotating on its axis?

Lesson Review

Vocabulary

In the space provided below, describe how each set of words are related.

1 revolution, year

_____

_____

2 rotation, day

_____

_____

3 season, equinox, solstice

_____

_____

_____

_____

_____

Key Concepts

4 Identify About how many days are in an Earth year? And how many hours in an Earth day?

_____

5 Describe How does the tilt of Earth's axis affect how the sun's rays strike Earth?

_____

_____

_____

_____

6 Synthesize How does the tilt of Earth's axis affect the number of daylight hours and the temperature of a location on Earth?

_____

_____

_____

_____

Critical Thinking

Use this image to answer the questions below.

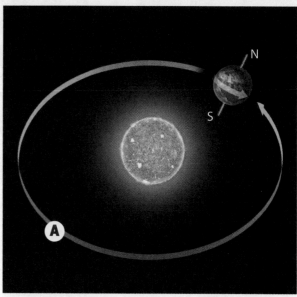

This drawing is not to scale.

7 Identify What season is the Northern Hemisphere experiencing in the image above?

_____

8 Explain How do the tilt of Earth's axis and Earth's movements around the sun cause seasons?

_____

_____

_____

_____

_____

_____

_____

_____

9 Describe If the Earth moves to point A in the image above, what season will the Northern Hemisphere experience?

Moon Phases and Eclipses

ESSENTIAL QUESTION

How do Earth, the moon, and the sun affect each other?

By the end of this lesson, you should be able to describe the effects the sun and the moon have on Earth, including gravitational attraction, moon phases, and eclipses.

Why is part of the moon orange? Because Earth is moving between the moon and the sun, casting a shadow on the moon.

Indiana Standards

6.2.1 Describe and model how the position, size and relative motions of the earth, moon, and sun cause day and night, solar and lunar eclipses and phases of the lesson.

Engage Your Brain

1 Identify Fill in the blanks with the word or phrase you think correctly completes the following sentences.

We can see the moon because it _____ the light from the sun.

The moon's _____ affects the oceans' tides on Earth.

The impact craters on the moon were created by collisions with _____, meteorites, and asteroids.

2 Describe Write your own caption for this photo in the space below.

_____

_____

_____

_____

_____

_____

Active Reading

3 Synthesize You can often define an unknown word if you know the meaning of its word parts. Use the word parts and sentence below to make an educated guess about the meaning of the word *penumbra*.

Word part	Meaning
umbra	shade or shadow
pen-, from the Latin *paene*	almost

Example sentence
An observer in the <u>penumbra</u> experiences only a partial eclipse.

Vocabulary Terms

- satellite
- gravity
- lunar phases
- eclipse
- umbra
- penumbra

4 Apply As you learn the definition of each vocabulary term in this lesson, create your own definition or sketch to help you remember the meaning of the term.

penumbra:

_____

_____

_____

'Round and 'Round They Go!

How are Earth, the moon, and the sun related in space?

Earth not only spins on its axis, but like the seven other planets in our solar system, Earth also orbits the sun. A body that orbits a larger body is called a **satellite** (SAT'l•yt). Six of the planets in our solar system have smaller bodies that orbit around each of them. These natural satellites are also called moons. Our moon is Earth's natural satellite.

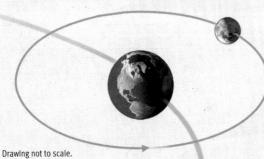

Drawing not to scale.

Earth revolves around the sun as the moon revolves around Earth.

Active Reading

5 Identify As you read, underline the reason that the moon stays in orbit around Earth.

Earth and the Moon Orbit the Sun

All bodies that have mass exert a force that pulls other objects with mass toward themselves. This force is called **gravity.** The mass of Earth is much larger than the mass of the moon, and therefore Earth's gravity exerts a stronger pull on the moon than the moon does on Earth. It is Earth's gravitational pull that keeps the moon in orbit around Earth, forming the Earth–moon system.

The Earth–moon system is itself in orbit around the sun. Even though the sun is relatively far away, the mass of the sun exerts a large gravitational pull on the Earth–moon system. This gravitational pull keeps the Earth–moon system in orbit around the sun.

The Moon Orbits Earth

The pull of Earth's gravity keeps the moon, Earth's natural satellite, in orbit around Earth. Even though the moon is Earth's closest neighbor in space, it is far away compared to the sizes of Earth and the moon themselves.

The distance between Earth and the moon is roughly 383,000 km (238,000 mi)—about a hundred times the distance between New York and Los Angeles. If a jet airliner could travel in space, it would take about 20 days to cover a distance that huge. Astronauts, whose spaceships travel much faster than jets, need about 3 days to reach the moon.

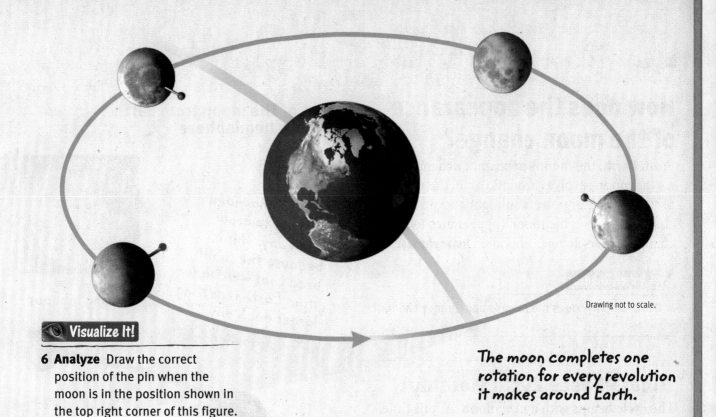

Drawing not to scale.

 Visualize It!

6 Analyze Draw the correct position of the pin when the moon is in the position shown in the top right corner of this figure.

The moon completes one rotation for every revolution it makes around Earth.

What does the moon look like from Earth?

The moon is only visible from Earth when it reflects the sunlight that reaches the moon. Although the moon is most easily seen at night, you have probably also seen it during daytime on some days. In the daytime, the moon may only be as bright as a thin cloud and can be easily missed. On some days you can see the moon during both the daytime and at night, whereas on other days, you may not see the moon at all.

When you can look at the moon, you may notice darker and lighter areas. Perhaps you have imagined them as features of a face or some other pattern. People around the world have told stories about the animals, people, and objects they have imagined while looking at the light and dark areas of the moon. The dark and light spots do not change over the course of a month because only one side of the moon faces Earth, often called the near side of the moon. This is because the moon rotates once on its own axis each time it orbits Earth. The moon takes 28.5 days or about a month to orbit Earth once.

Inquiry

7 Analyze How would the moon appear to an observer on Earth if the moon did not rotate?

_____

_____

_____

_____

It's Just a Phase!

How does the appearance of the moon change?

From Earth, the moon's appearance changes. As the moon revolves around Earth, the portion of the moon that reflects sunlight back to Earth changes, causing the moon's appearance to change. These changes are called **lunar phases.**

 **Active Reading**

8 Describe Why does the moon's appearance change?

_____

_____

Lunar Phases Cycle Monthly

The cycle begins with a new moon. At this time, Earth, the moon, and the sun are lined up, such that the near side of the moon is unlit. And so there appears to be no moon in the sky.

As the moon moves along its orbit, you begin to see the sunlight on the near side as a thin crescent shape. The crescent becomes thicker as the moon waxes, or grows. When half of the near side of the moon is in the sunlight, the moon has completed one-quarter of its cycle. This phase is called the *first quarter.*

More of the moon is visible during the second week, or the *gibbous* (GIB•uhs) *phase.* This is when the near side is more than half lit but not fully lit. When the moon is halfway through its cycle, the whole near side of the moon is in sunlight, and we see a full moon.

During the third week, the amount of the moon's near side in the sunlight decreases and it seems to shrink, or wane. When the near side is again only half in sunlight, the moon is three-quarters of the way through its cycle. The phase is called the *third quarter.*

In the fourth week, the area of the near side of the moon in sunlight continues to shrink. The moon is seen as waning crescent shapes. Finally, the near side of the moon is unlit—*new moon.*

Views of the moon from Earth's northern hemisphere

Waxing gibbous

The waxing moon appears to grow each day. This is because the sunlit area that we can see from Earth is getting larger each day.

Full moon

Waning gibbous

Think Outside the Book

9 Apply Look at the night sky and keep a moon journal for a series of nights. What phase is the moon in now?

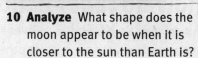
10 Analyze What shape does the moon appear to be when it is closer to the sun than Earth is?

First quarter

Waxing crescent

New moon

Drawing not to scale.

Third quarter

Waning crescent

The waning moon appears to shrink each day. When the moon is waning, the sunlit area is getting smaller. Notice above that even as the phases of the moon change, the total amount of sunlight that the moon gets remains the same. Half the moon is always in sunlight, just as half of Earth is always in sunlight.

Exploring Eclipses

How do lunar eclipses occur?

An **eclipse** (ih•KLIPS) is an event during which one object in space casts a shadow onto another. On Earth, a lunar eclipse occurs when the moon moves through Earth's shadow. There are two parts of Earth's shadow, as you can see in the diagram below. The **umbra** (UHM•bruh) is the darkest part of a shadow. Around it is a spreading cone of lighter shadow called the **penumbra** (pih•NUHM•bruh). Just before a lunar eclipse, sunlight streaming past Earth produces a full moon. Then the moon moves into Earth's penumbra and becomes slightly less bright. As the moon moves into the umbra, Earth's dark shadow seems to creep across and cover the moon. The entire moon can be in darkness because the moon is small enough to fit entirely within Earth's umbra. After an hour or more, the moon moves slowly back into the sunlight that is streaming past Earth. A total lunar eclipse occurs when the moon passes completely into Earth's umbra. If the moon misses part or all of the umbra, part of the moon stays light and the eclipse is called a partial lunar eclipse.

You may be wondering why you don't see solar and lunar eclipses every month. The reason is that the moon's orbit around Earth is tilted—by about 5°—relative to the orbit of Earth around the sun. This tilt is enough to place the moon out of Earth's shadow for most full moons and Earth out of the moon's shadow for most new moons.

This composite photo shows the partial and total phases of a lunar eclipse over several hours.

Lunar eclipse

Visualize It!

11 Identify Fill in the boxes with the type of eclipse that would occur if the moon were in the areas being pointed to.

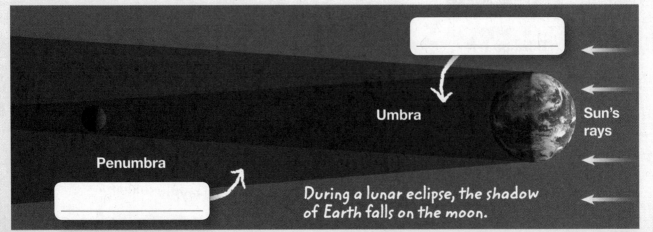

Umbra

Penumbra

Sun's rays

During a lunar eclipse, the shadow of Earth falls on the moon.

Drawing not to scale.

How do solar eclipses occur?

When the moon is directly between the sun and Earth, the shadow of the moon falls on a part of Earth and causes a solar eclipse. During a total solar eclipse, the sun's light is completely blocked by the moon, as seen in this photo. The umbra falls on the area of Earth that lies directly in line with the moon and the sun. Outside the umbra, but within the penumbra, people see a partial solar eclipse. The penumbra falls on the area that immediately surrounds the umbra.

The umbra of the moon is too small to make a large shadow on Earth's surface. The part of the umbra that hits Earth during an eclipse, is never more than a few hundred kilometers across, as shown below. So, a total eclipse of the sun covers only a small part of Earth and is seen only by people in particular parts of Earth along a narrow path. A total solar eclipse usually lasts between one to two minutes at any one location. A total eclipse will not be visible in the United States until 2017, even though there is a total eclipse somewhere on Earth about every one to two years.

Solar eclipse

During a solar eclipse, the moon passes between the sun and Earth so that the sun is partially or totally obscured.

 **Active Reading**

12 Explain Why is it relatively rare to observe a solar eclipse?

_____

_____

_____

_____

👁 **Visualize It!**

13 Describe Explain what happens during a solar eclipse.

_____

_____

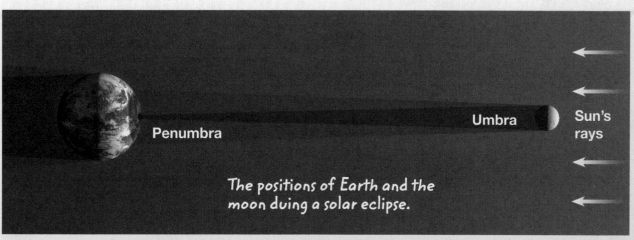

Penumbra

Umbra

Sun's rays

The positions of Earth and the moon during a solar eclipse.

Drawing not to scale.

Visual Summary

To complete this summary, circle the correct word.
Then use the key below to check your answers.
You can use this page to review the main concepts
of the lesson.

Moon Phases and Eclipses

The appearance of the moon depends on the positions of the sun, the moon, and Earth.

The Earth–moon system orbits the sun.

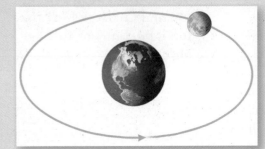

14 The moon takes about one day/month/year to orbit Earth.

Shadows in space cause eclipses.

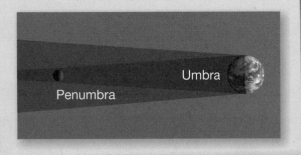

Umbra

Penumbra

15 When the moon is in Earth's umbra, a total solar/lunar eclipse is occurring.

16 The fraction of the moon that receives sunlight always/never changes.

Answers: 14 month; 15 lunar; 16 never

17 **Describe** What causes the lunar phases that we see from Earth?

Lesson Review

Vocabulary

In your own words, define the following terms.

1 gravity

_____

_____

2 satellite

_____

_____

3 umbra

_____

_____

Key Concepts

4 Describe What are two phases of a waxing moon, and how do they appear?

_____

_____

_____

_____

_____

_____

5 Identify Explain why the moon can be seen from Earth.

_____

_____

6 Describe What is the relationship between Earth, the sun, and the moon in space?

_____

_____

_____

_____

_____

Critical Thinking

Use the image below to answer the following question.

7 Identify What type of eclipse is shown in the diagram?

_____

8 Describe Where is the moon in its orbit at the time of a solar eclipse?

_____

9 Infer What phase is the moon in when there is a total solar eclipse?

_____

10 Predict Which shape of the moon will you never see during the daytime, after sunrise and before sunset? *Hint:* Consider the directions of the sun and moon from Earth.

_____

11 Synthesize If you were an astronaut in the middle of the near side of the moon during a full moon, how would the ground around you look? How would Earth, high in your sky look? Describe what is in sunlight and what is in darkness.

_____

_____

_____

_____

_____

Indiana Standards

NOS 6.8 Analyze data, using appropriate mathematical manipulation as required, and use it to identify patterns and make inferences based on these patterns.

Testing and Modifying Theories

When scientists develop a theory, they use experiments to investigate the theory. The results of experiments can support or disprove theories. If the results of several experiments do not support a theory, it may be modified.

Tutorial

Read below about the Tomatosphere Project to find out more about how theories are tested and modified. This project exposes tomato seeds to simulated Martian conditions to observe later seed germination.

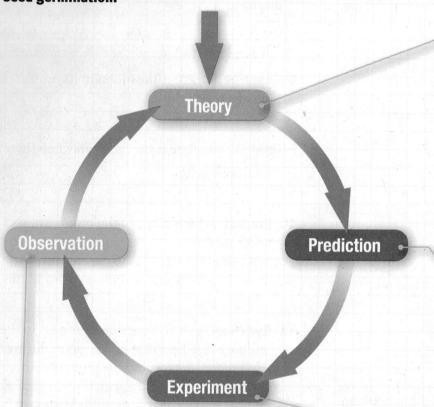

A theory is created/ modified.
Sometimes, two well-supported theories explain a single phenomenon. A theory might be modified based on new data. Scientists can figure out how to supply long-term space missions with food, water, oxygen, and other life-support needs.

A prediction is made.
Predictions are based on prior knowledge. Scientists might predict that if tomato seeds are exposed to Martian conditions, they will still be able to germinate and grow into healthy, fruit-bearing plants.

Observations are made.
Scientists evaluate their observations to see whether or not the results support their hypothesis. If any data disprove the original prediction, scientists may have to modify their theory. The results of the blind studies are gathered and analyzed to see whether exposure to harsh conditions affected the germination of the seeds.

Experiments are done.
Setting up the proper scientific procedure to test the prediction is important. In the Tomatosphere Project, a set of exposed seeds, along with a control group of regular seeds, are planted in thousands of classrooms. At least 20 of each type were planted, to ensure a large enough sample size. The type of seeds were not revealed, as part of a blind study.

You Try It!

Two scientists describe theories that try to explain the motion of galaxies. Use the information provided to answer the questions that follow.

Background

Any objects that have mass, such as Earth and you, exert a gravitational force that pulls them toward each other. An unexpected motion of an object in space, such as a galaxy, could be the result of an unseen object pulling on it. Scientists use electromagnetic radiation, such as visible, infrared, and ultraviolet light, to detect and study visible matter. However, dark matter is a hypothetical material that does not give off electromagnetic radiation that we can detect.

Scientist A

There is more dark matter than visible matter in galaxies. There is just too little visible matter to exert the force that would explain how the galaxies move. The additional force exerted by dark matter would explain the motion we see without having to change our understanding of gravitational force.

Scientist B

We must change our understanding of gravitational force. The farther away from the center of a galaxy you go, the stronger (not weaker) the gravitational force becomes. With this change, the amount of visible matter is enough to explain how the galaxies move. Dark matter is not needed.

1 Predicting Outcomes How would proof that dark matter exists affect each scientist's theory?

_____

_____

_____

_____

3 Making Inferences What evidence would require both scientists to modify their theories?

_____

_____

_____

_____

2 Predicting Outcomes If experiments fail to detect dark matter, does Scientist A's theory need to be modified? Explain why.

_____

_____

_____

_____

_____

Take It Home

Using the Internet, research a scientific theory that has been reproduced in two different experiments. Write a short report that explains how the observations helped develop the theory. How else could this theory could be investigated?

Lesson ③

Earth's Tides

ESSENTIAL QUESTION

What causes tides?

By the end of this lesson, you should be able to explain what tides are and what causes them in Earth's oceans and to describe variations in the tides.

You may wonder why this boat is sitting in such shallow water. This photo was taken at low tide, when the ocean water is below average sea level.

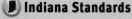

Indiana Standards

6.2.2 Recognize that gravity is a force that keeps celestial bodies in regular and predictable motion, holds objects to earth's surface, and is responsible for ocean tides.

© Houghton Mifflin Harcourt Publishing Company • Image Credits: ©Robin Whalley/LOOP IMAGES/Loop Images/Corbis

Engage Your Brain

1 Describe Fill in the blank with the word that you think correctly completes the following sentences.

The motion of the _____ around Earth is related to tides.

The daily rotation of _____ is also related to tides.

During a _____ tide, the water level is higher than the average sea level.

During a _____ tide, the water level is lower than the average sea level.

2 Label Draw an arrow to show where you think high tide might be.

Low tide ▶

Active Reading

3 Synthesize The word *spring* has different meanings. Use the meanings of the word *spring* and the sentence below to make an educated guess about the meaning of the term *spring tides*.

Meanings of *spring*
the season between winter and summer
a source of water from the ground
jump, or rise up
a coiled piece of metal

Example Sentence
During <u>spring tides</u>, the sun, the moon, and Earth are in a straight line, resulting in very high tides.

spring tides:

_____

_____

_____

Vocabulary Terms

- tide
- tidal range
- spring tide
- neap tide

4 Apply As you learn the definition of each vocabulary term in this lesson, create your own definition or sketch to help you remember the meaning of the term.

A Rising Tide of Interest

What causes tides?

Active Reading

5 Identify Underline the sentence that identifies which object is mainly responsible for tides on Earth.

The photographs below show the ocean at the same location at two different times. **Tides** are daily changes in the level of ocean water. Tides are caused by the difference in the gravitational force of the sun and the moon across Earth. This difference in gravitational force is called the *tidal force*. The tidal force exerted by the moon is stronger than the tidal force exerted by the sun because the moon is much closer to Earth than the sun is. So, the moon is mainly responsible for tides on Earth.

How often tides occur and how tidal levels vary depend on the position of the moon as it revolves around Earth. The gravity of the moon pulls on every particle of Earth. But because liquids move more easily than solids do, the pull on liquids is much more noticeable than the pull on solids is. The moon's gravitational pull on Earth decreases with the moon's distance from Earth. The part of Earth facing the moon is pulled toward the moon with the greatest force. So, water on that side of Earth bulges toward the moon. The solid Earth is pulled more strongly toward the moon than the ocean water on Earth's far side is. So, there is also a bulge of water on the side of Earth farthest from the moon.

At low tide, the water level is low, and the boats are far below the dock.

At high tide, the water level has risen, and the boats are close to the dock.

What are high tides and low tides?

The bulges that form in Earth's oceans are called high tides. *High tide* is a water level that is higher than the average sea level. Low tides form in the areas between the high tides. *Low tide* is a water level that is lower than the average sea level. At low tide, the water levels are lower because the water is in high-tide areas.

As the moon moves around Earth and Earth rotates, the tidal bulges move around Earth. The tidal bulges follow the motion of the moon. As a result, many places on Earth have two high tides and two low tides each day.

6 Identify Label the areas where high tides form and the area where the other low tide forms.

Note: Drawing is not to scale.

Moon

A _____

B _____

Earth

Low tide

C _____

This grizzly bear in Alaska is taking advantage of low tide by digging for clams.

7 Predict What happens to the bear when high tide comes in?

_____

_____

Tide Me Over

Active Reading

8 Identify As you read, underline the two kinds of tidal range.

What are two kinds of tidal ranges?

Tides are due to the *tidal force,* the difference between the force of gravity on one side of Earth and the other side of Earth. Because the moon is so much closer to Earth than the sun is, the moon's tidal force is greater than the sun's tidal force. The moon's effect on tides is twice as strong as the sun's effect. The combined gravitational effects of the sun and the moon on Earth result in different tidal ranges. A **tidal range** is the difference between the levels of ocean water at high tide and low tide. Tidal range depends on the positions of the sun and the moon relative to Earth.

Spring Tides: The Largest Tidal Range

Tides that have the largest daily tidal range are **spring tides**. Spring tides happen when the sun, the moon, and Earth form a straight line. So, spring tides happen when the moon is between the sun and Earth and when the moon is on the opposite side of Earth, as shown in the illustrations below. In other words, spring tides happen during the new moon and full moon phases, or every 14 days. During these times, the gravitational effects of the sun and moon add together, causing one pair of very large tidal bulges. Spring tides have nothing to do with the season.

Note: Drawings are not to scale.

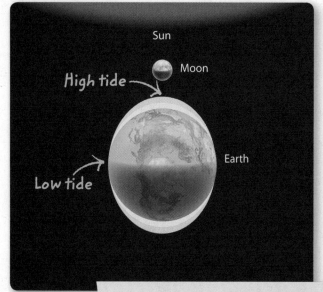
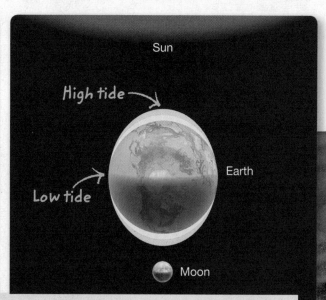

During spring tides, the tidal force of the sun on Earth adds to the tidal force of the moon. The tidal range increases.

Inquiry

9 Inquire Explain why spring tides happen twice a month.

_____

_____

© Houghton Mifflin Harcourt Publishing Company • Image Credits: ©Willard Clay/Photographer's Choice RF/Getty Images

Neap Tides: The Smallest Tidal Range

Tides that have the smallest daily tidal range are **neap tides**. Neap tides happen when the sun, Earth, and the moon form a 90° angle, as shown in the illustrations below. During a neap tide, the gravitational effects of the sun and the moon on Earth do not add together as they do during spring tides. Neap tides occur halfway between spring tides, during the first quarter and third quarter phases of the moon. At these times, the sun and the moon cause two pairs of smaller tidal bulges.

Note: Drawings are not to scale.

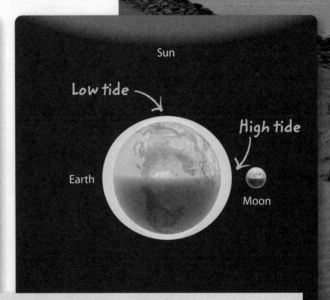

During neap tides, the gravitational effects of the sun and the moon on Earth do not add together. The tidal range decreases.

10 Compare Fill in the Venn diagram to compare and contrast spring tides and neap tides.

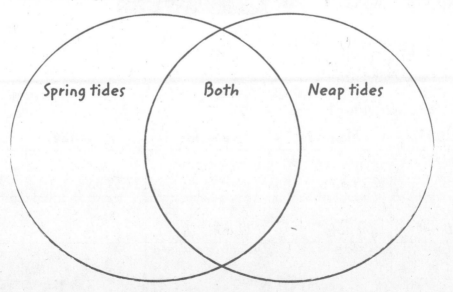

Spring tides   Both   Neap tides

What causes tidal cycles?

The rotation of Earth and the moon's revolution around Earth determine when tides occur. Imagine that Earth rotated at the same speed that the moon revolves around Earth. If this were true, the same side of Earth would always face the moon. And high tide would always be at the same places on Earth. But the moon revolves around Earth much more slowly than Earth rotates. A place on Earth that is facing the moon takes 24 h and 50 min to rotate to face the moon again. So, the cycle of high tides and low tides at that place happens 50 min later each day.

In many places there are two high tides and two low tides each day. Because the tide cycle occurs in 24 h and 50 min intervals, it takes about 6 h and 12.5 min (one-fourth the time of the total cycle) for water in an area to go from high tide to low tide. It takes about 12 h and 25 min (one-half the time of the total cycle) to go from one high tide to the next high tide.

Note: Drawings are not to scale.

Tuesday 11:00 a.m.

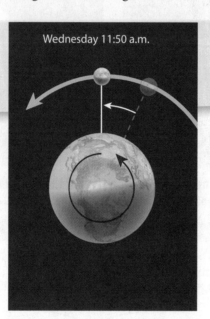

Wednesday 11:50 a.m.

The moon moves only a fraction of its orbit in the time that Earth rotates once.

Think Outside the Book Inquiry

11 **Inquire** Draw a diagram of Earth to show what Earth's tides would be like if the moon revolved around Earth at the same speed that Earth rotates.

12 **Predict** In the table, predict the approximate times of high tide and low tide for Clearwater, Florida.

Tide Data for Clearwater, Florida

Date (2009)	High tide	Low tide	High tide	Low tide
August 19	12:14 a.m.		12:39 p.m.	
August 20	1:04 a.m.	7:17 a.m.		
August 21				

Extreme Living Conditions

Some organisms living along ocean coastlines must be able to tolerate extreme living conditions. At high tide, much of the coast is under water. At low tide, much of the coast is dry. Some organisms must also survive the constant crashing of waves against the shore.

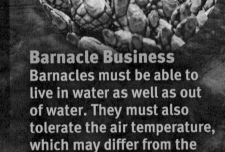

Barnacle Business
Barnacles must be able to live in water as well as out of water. They must also tolerate the air temperature, which may differ from the temperature of the water.

Ghostly Crabs
Ghost crabs live near the high tide line on sandy shores. They scurry along the sand to avoid being underwater when the tide comes in. Ghost crabs can also find cover between rocks.

Stunning Starfish
Starfish live in tidal pools, which are areas along the shore where water remains at low tide. Starfish must be able to survive changes in water temperature and salinity.

Extend
Inquiry

13 Identify Describe how living conditions change for two tidal organisms.

14 Research and Record List the names of two organisms that live in the high tide zone or the low tide zone along a coastline of your choice.

15 Describe Imagine a day in the life of an organism you researched in question 14 by doing one of the following:
- make a poster
- write a play
- record an audio story
- make a cartoon

Visual Summary

To complete this summary, fill in the blanks with the correct word. Then use the key below to check your answers. You can use this page to review the main concepts of the lesson.

In many places, two high tides and two low tides occur every day.

16 The type of tide shown here is

_____

The gravitational effects of the moon and the sun cause tides.

17 Tides on Earth are caused mainly by the

_____

Moon

Earth

Tides on Earth

Note: Drawings are not to scale.

There are two kinds of tidal ranges: spring tides and neap tides.

Sun

Moon

Earth

Sun

Moon

Earth

18 During a spring tide, the sun, moon, and Earth are in a/an

_____

19 During a neap tide, the sun, moon, and Earth form a/an

_____

Answers: 16 low tide; 17 moon; 18 straight line; 19 90° angle

20 Describe State how the moon causes tides.

Lesson Review

Vocabulary

Answer the following questions in your own words.

1 Use *tide* and *tidal range* in the same sentence.

_____

_____

_____

2 Write an original definition for *neap tide* and for *spring tide*.

_____

_____

_____

_____

Key Concepts

3 Describe Explain what tides are. Include *high tide* and *low tide* in your answer.

_____

_____

_____

_____

_____

4 Explain State what causes tides on Earth.

_____

_____

_____

5 Identify Write the alignment of the moon, the sun, and Earth that causes a spring tide.

_____

_____

6 Describe Explain why tides happen 50 min later each day.

_____

_____

_____

Critical Thinking

Use this diagram to answer the next question.

Note: Drawing is not to scale.

Last quarter moon

7 Analyze What type of tidal range will Earth have when the moon is in this position?

_____

_____

8 Apply How many days pass between the minimum and the maximum of the tidal range in any given area? Explain your answer.

_____

_____

_____

_____

_____

9 Apply How would the tides on Earth be different if the moon revolved around Earth in 15 days instead of 30 days?

_____

_____

_____

_____

_____

_____

My Notes

© Houghton Mifflin Harcourt Publishing Company

277

Unit 5 **Summary**

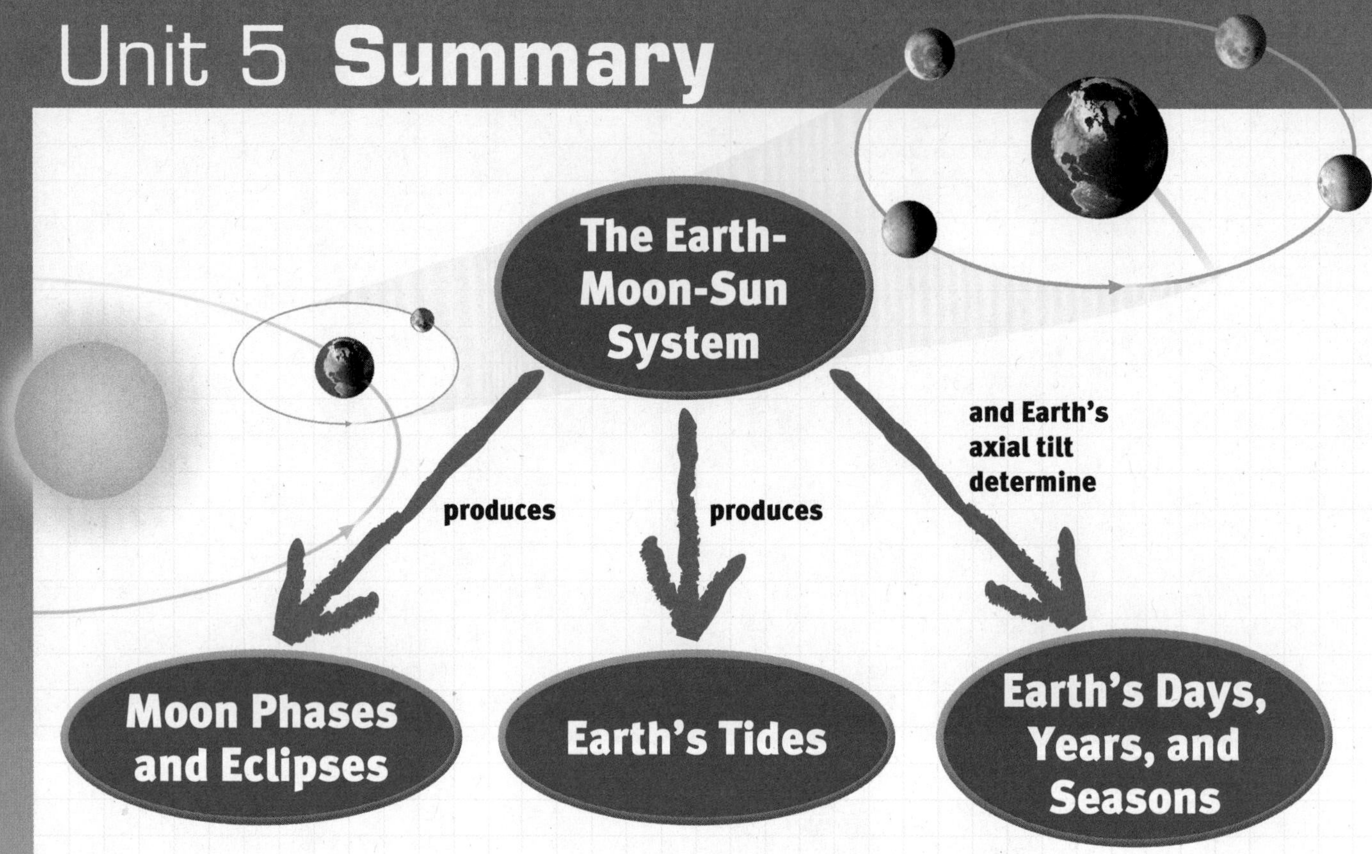

The Earth-Moon-Sun System

produces → **Moon Phases and Eclipses**

produces → **Earth's Tides**

and Earth's axial tilt determine → **Earth's Days, Years, and Seasons**

1 Interpret Review the Graphic Organizer above. What causes the moon's phases and eclipses?

_____

_____

_____

_____

_____

_____

2 Distinguish Why does the moon have a greater influence on tides on Earth than the Sun?

_____

_____

_____

3 Explain How does the tilt of Earth's axis account for differences in the area of sunlight each hemisphere receives during the summer solstice and winter solstice?

_____

_____

_____

_____

_____

_____

_____

_____

4 Recognize Why do we always see the same side of the moon from Earth?

_____

_____

_____

_____

_____

Multiple Choice

1 A region on Earth's surface always has the highest temperatures in June and the lowest temperatures in December. Which of these statements explains why the temperatures are LOWEST in December?

 A. This region is tilted the most toward the sun in December.

 B. This region is tilted the farthest away from the sun in December.

 C. This region is the farthest distance from the sun in December.

 D. This region is the nearest distance from the sun in December.

2 Which of the following is a common characteristic of WINTER compared to summer?

 A. noon sun lower in the sky

 B. higher daytime temperatures

 C. more daily hours of sunlight

 D. longer days and shorter nights

3 When it is summer, the United States receives the most direct solar energy. Why does this happen?

 A. The Northern Hemisphere is closer to the sun.

 B. The Northern Hemisphere is farther from the sun.

 C. The Northern Hemisphere is tilted toward the sun.

 D. The Northern Hemisphere is tilted away from the sun.

4 The phases of the moon are caused by the relative positions of Earth, the sun, and the moon. Lunar phases refer to the appearance of the illuminated portion of the moon as seen by an observer on Earth. When the moon is aligned with and between Earth and the sun, which phase is happening?

 A. full moon

 B. new moon

 C. first quarter moon

 D. third quarter moon

5 Although half of the moon is always illuminated, usually only a portion of the illuminated side is visible from Earth. The diagram below presents the relative positions of Earth, the sun, and the moon. The positions of the moon are labeled 1–8.

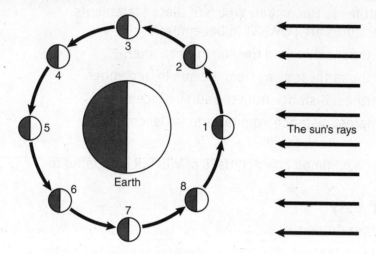

Which of the moons in the figure are in a GIBBOUS PHASE?

A. 2 and 4

B. 2 and 8

C. 4 and 6

D. 6 and 8

6 Eclipses are predictable solar system events. The answer choices below list relative positions of Earth, the sun, and the moon. Which list represents the position of Earth, the sun, and the moon during a LUNAR ECLIPSE?

A. sun, Earth, moon

B. Earth, sun, moon

C. sun, moon, Earth

D. moon, sun, Earth

7 The diagram below shows what happens during a solar system event.

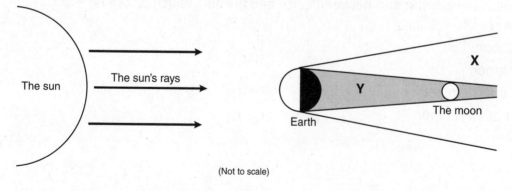

(Not to scale)

Which part of the diagram is labeled Y?

A. the umbra

B. the eclipse

C. the satellite

D. the penumbra

8 Zach is visiting Hilo, Hawaii. He wants to collect seashells, and the local people tell him that the best time to collect shells is at low tide. According to the diagram below, at about what time should Zach collect shells?

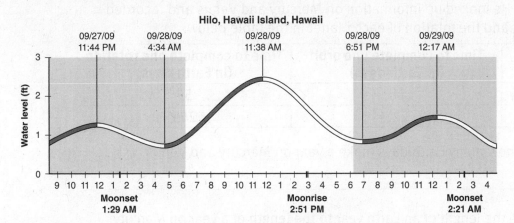

A. 9:00 a.m.

B. noon

C. 3:00 p.m.

D. 7:00 p.m.

9 How often do spring tides take place?

A. once a day

B. twice a day

C. once a month

D. twice a month

10 The tide table below shows the tidal range for a beach in Canada.

Date	High tide time	High tide height (m)	Low tide time	Low tide height (m)
June 4	6:58 a.m.	5.92	12:54 a.m.	1.87
June 5	7:51 a.m.	5.80	1:47 a.m.	1.90
June 6	8:42 a.m.	5.75	2:38 a.m.	1.87
June 7	9:30 a.m.	5.79	3:27 a.m.	1.75
June 8	10:16 a.m.	5.90	4:13 a.m.	1.56
June 9	11:01 a.m.	6.08	4:59 a.m.	1.32
June 10	11:46 a.m.	6.28	5:44 a.m.	1.05
June 11	12:32 p.m.	6.47	6:30 a.m.	0.78

Which event that happened on June 6 takes place only TWICE a month?

A. low tide

B. high tide

C. neap tide

D. spring tide

Constructed Response

11 Carter is using what he knows about Earth to find out more about other planets. He looked up information on Mercury and Venus and recorded the orbit and the rotation of each planet in the table below.

Planet	Time to complete one orbit (in Earth days)	Time to complete one rotation (in Earth days)
Mercury	88	59
Venus	225	243

Identify how many Earth days make a year on Mercury and Venus.

_____

Compare the length of an Earth year to the length of a year on Mercury and Venus.

_____

_____

Extended Response

12 Describe the daily pattern of the tides on an ocean shoreline.

_____

_____

Explain why this daily pattern of tides occurs.

_____

_____

How does the timing of the tide pattern change from one day to the next?

_____

_____

When do the highest high tides take place?

_____

_____

Ecology

Core Standard

Describe that all organisms, including humans, are part of complex systems found in all biomes (freshwater, marine, forest, desert, grassland, tundra).

Core Standard

Understand that the major source of energy for ecosystems is light produced by major nuclear reactions in the sun.

Fish and sponges in a coral reef.

What do you think?

Ecosystems consist of living things that depend on each other to survive. How might these fish depend on a coral reef? How might this bird depend on a dragonfly population?

Eastern bluebirds feed on insects.

Unit 6
Ecology

Lesson 1
Introduction to Ecology.......... 286
6.3.2, 6.3.3

| People in Science | .... 296 |

Lesson 2
Roles in Energy Transfer 298
6.3.4, 6.3.5, 6.3.6

Lesson 3
Interactions in Communities 310
6.3.1, 6.3.5

Lesson 4
**Photosynthesis and
Cellular Respiration** 320
6.3.4, 6.3.5, 6.3.6

Unit Summary.................... 334

ISTEP+ Review 335

Indiana Standards

As citizens of the constructed world, students will participate in the design process. Students will learn to use materials and tools safely and employ the basic principles of the engineering design process in order to find solutions to problems.

DP 6.1 Identify a need or problem to be solved.

CITIZEN SCIENCE

Sharing Spaces

Wetlands provide living space for many kinds of birds. Ospreys are large birds of prey that eat mostly fish. They often nest on telephone poles and other man-made structures. Yellow-rumped warblers are small birds that live in trees and eat insects and berries.

① Ask A Question

How can organisms affect each other and a whole ecosystem?

An ecosystem is made up of all the living and nonliving things in an environment. Ospreys and yellow-rumped warblers are part of the same ecosystem. With your teacher and your classmates, brainstorm ways in which ospreys and yellow-rumped warblers might affect each other.

Yellow-rumped warbler

② Think About It

Look at the photos of the ospreys in their environment. List at least two resources they need to survive and explain how the ospreys get them.

_____

_____

_____

What are two ways nonliving things could affect yellow-rumped warblers?

_____

_____

_____

Osprey nest

③ Apply Your Knowledge

A List the ways in which yellow-rumped warblers and ospreys share resources.

_____

_____

_____

B Yellow-rumped warblers have a diet that consists mainly of insects and berries. Make a list of other organisms you know that might compete with the warblers for these same food resources.

_____

_____

_____

_____

C Describe a situation that could negatively affect both the osprey population and the yellow-rumped warbler population.

_____

_____

_____

Take It Home

Are ecologists looking for people to report observations in your community? Contact a university near your community to see if you can help gather information about plants, flowers, birds, or invasive species. Then, share your results with your class.

Introduction to Ecology

ESSENTIAL QUESTION

What parts make up an ecosystem?

By the end of this lesson, you should be able to analyze the components of an ecosystem.

🅳 **Indiana Standards**

6.3.2 Describe how changes caused by organisms in the habitat where they live can be beneficial or detrimental to themselves or the native plants and animals.

6.3.3 Describe how certain biotic and abiotic factors, such as predators, quantity of light and water, range of temperatures, and soil composition, can limit the number of organisms that an ecosystem can support.

This rainforest is an ecosystem. Hornbills are organisms in the ecosystem that use the trees for shelter.

1 Describe In your own words, write a list of living or nonliving things that are in your community.

_____

_____

_____

_____

_____

_____

_____

_____

2 Relate Below, write a photo caption that compares the ecosystem shown above and the ecosystem shown on the previous page.

_____

_____

_____

_____

 Active Reading

3 Synthesize You can often define an unknown word or term if you know the meaning of its word parts. Use the word parts and sentence below to make an educated guess about the meaning of the term *abiotic factor*.

Word part	Meaning
a-	without
bio-	life

Example sentence
In an ecosystem, rocks are an example of an abiotic factor.

Vocabulary Terms

- ecology
- biotic factor
- abiotic factor
- population
- species
- community
- ecosystem
- habitat
- niche

4 Apply As you learn the definition of each vocabulary term in this lesson, create your own definition or sketch to help you remember the meaning of the term.

abiotic factor:

_____

_____

The Web of Life

How are all living things connected?

The web of life connects all organisms to each other and to the environment. Organisms need energy and matter for life. Interactions between organisms allow the exchange of energy and matter to occur. **Ecology** is the study of how organisms interact with one another and with the environment.

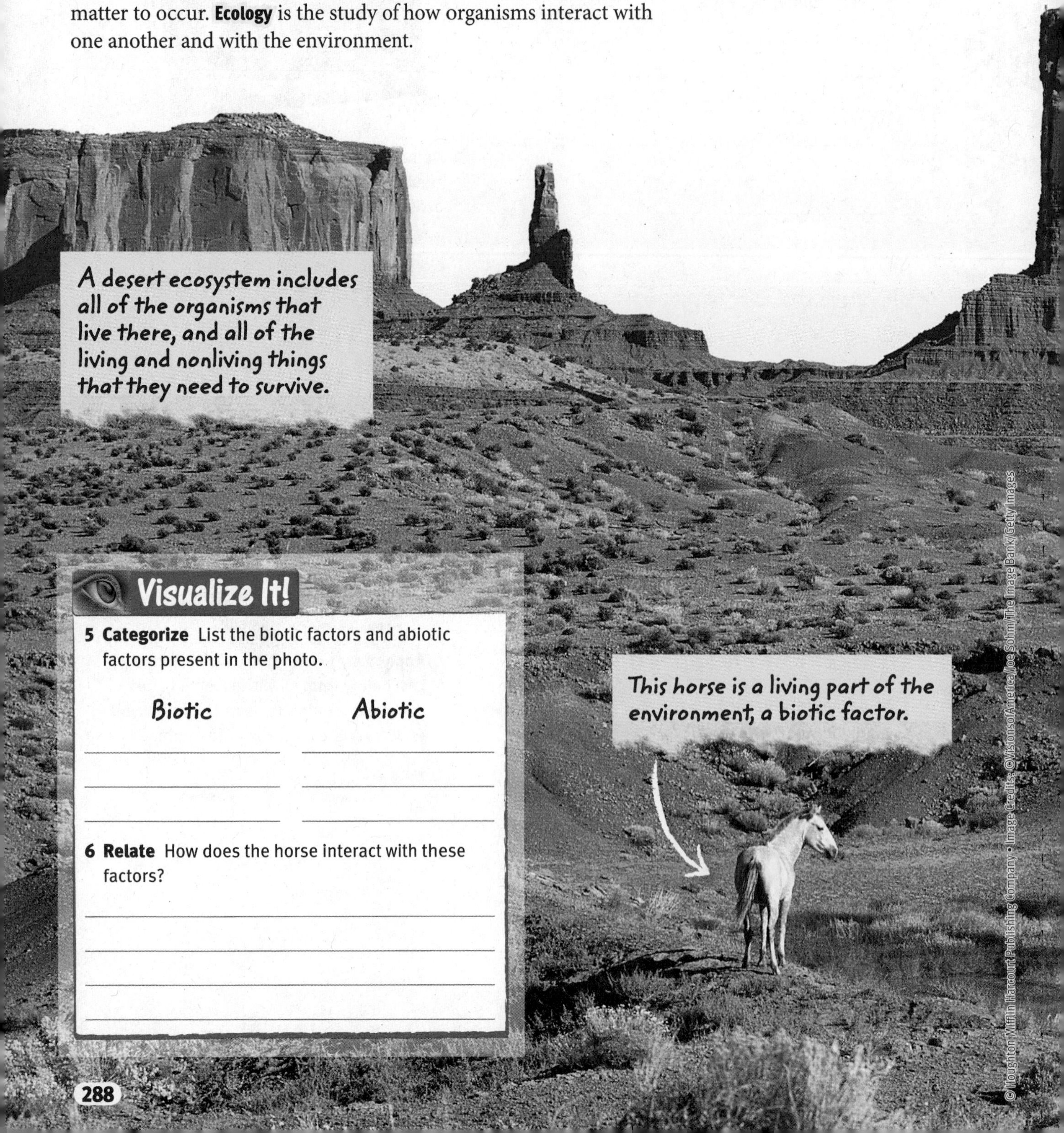

A desert ecosystem includes all of the organisms that live there, and all of the living and nonliving things that they need to survive.

👁 Visualize It!

5 Categorize List the biotic factors and abiotic factors present in the photo.

Biotic	Abiotic
_____	_____
_____	_____
_____	_____

6 Relate How does the horse interact with these factors?

_____
_____
_____
_____

This horse is a living part of the environment, a biotic factor.

Through the Living Environment

Biodiversity is the variation of living organisms, from tiny bacteria to huge whales. Each individual organism has a role to play in the flow of energy and matter. In this way, organisms are connected to all other organisms. Relationships among organisms affect each one's growth and survival. A **biotic factor** is a living part of the environment. Organisms, and how they interact, are examples of biotic factors.

The rocks and air are parts of the nonliving environment, abiotic factors.

Through the Nonliving Environment

All organisms rely on the nonliving environment for survival. An **abiotic factor** is a nonliving part of an environment, such as water, nutrients, soil, sunlight, rainfall, or temperature. Some of these are resources that organisms need to grow and survive. For example, plants use sunlight, water, and soil nutrients to make food. Similarly, some organisms rely on soil or rocks for shelter.

Abiotic factors determine where organisms can survive. The ranges of organisms that can live in an environment are limited by basic requirements in the abiotic environment. In a terrestrial environment, temperature and rainfall are important abiotic factors. In aquatic environments, temperature, salinity, and oxygen content are important abiotic factors. Changes in these basic abiotic factors cause changes in where organisms can live and how many can live there.

Active Reading **7 Infer** How does the environment determine where an organism can survive? Explain your answer.

_____

_____

_____

_____

Stay Organized!

What are all the levels of organization in the environment?

The environment can be organized into different levels. These levels range from a single organism to all of the organisms and their surroundings in an area. The levels of organization get more complex as more of the environment is considered.

Populations

A **population** is a group of individuals of the same species that live in the same place. A **species** includes organisms that are closely related and can mate to produce fertile offspring. The alligators that live in the Everglades are a population. Individuals within a population often compete with each other for food, shelter, and mates.

Population

Individual

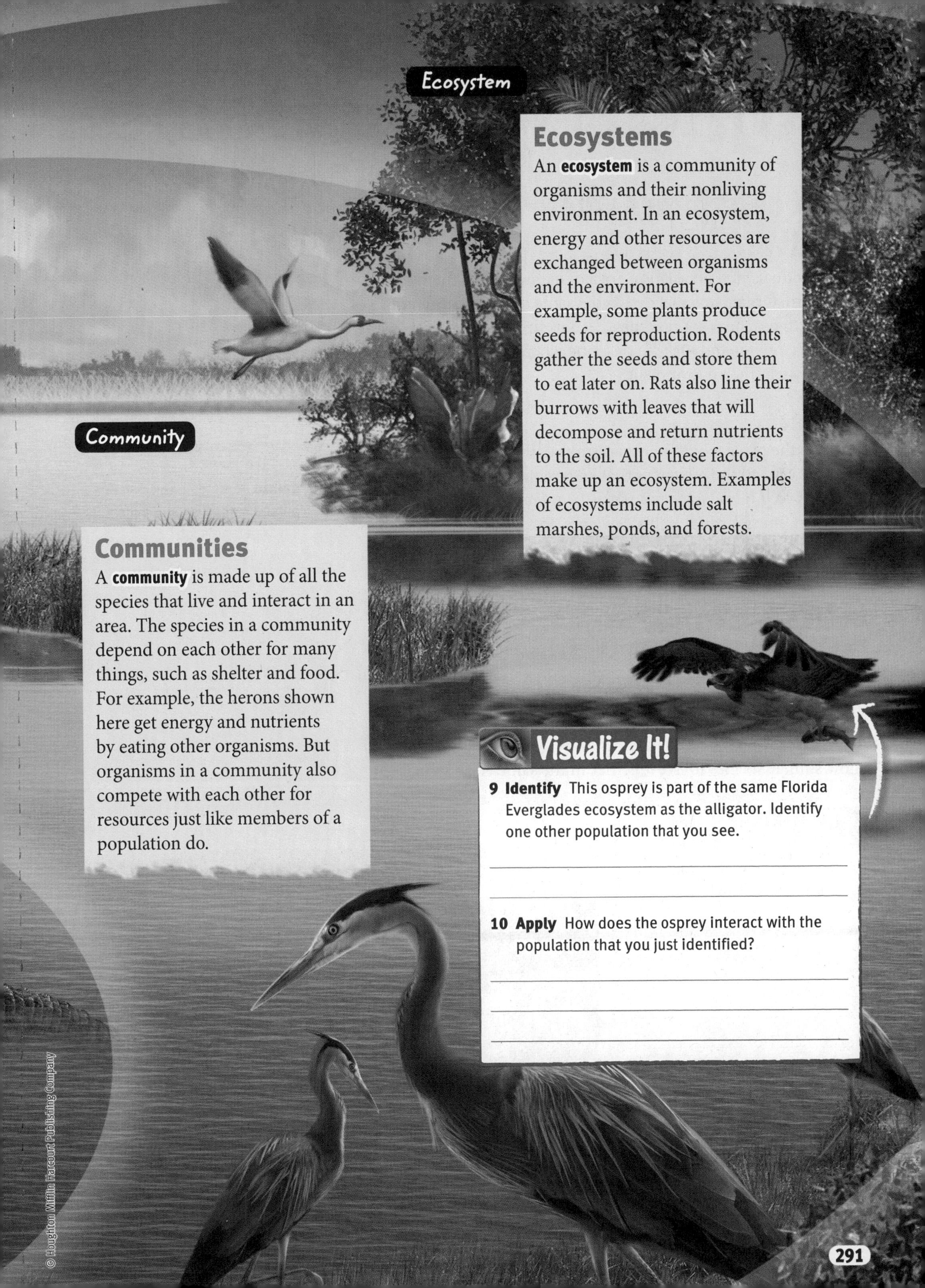

Ecosystems

An **ecosystem** is a community of organisms and their nonliving environment. In an ecosystem, energy and other resources are exchanged between organisms and the environment. For example, some plants produce seeds for reproduction. Rodents gather the seeds and store them to eat later on. Rats also line their burrows with leaves that will decompose and return nutrients to the soil. All of these factors make up an ecosystem. Examples of ecosystems include salt marshes, ponds, and forests.

Community

Communities

A **community** is made up of all the species that live and interact in an area. The species in a community depend on each other for many things, such as shelter and food. For example, the herons shown here get energy and nutrients by eating other organisms. But organisms in a community also compete with each other for resources just like members of a population do.

Visualize It!

9 Identify This osprey is part of the same Florida Everglades ecosystem as the alligator. Identify one other population that you see.

_____

_____

10 Apply How does the osprey interact with the population that you just identified?

_____

_____

_____

Home Sweet Home

What determines where a population can live?

All individuals in a population are a dynamic part of their ecosystem. Organisms that live in the same area play different roles in order to get the resources they need to survive. Ecologists use the terms *habitat* and *niche* to describe where an organism lives and its role in the environment.

Habitat

Habitat is the place where an organism usually lives. The habitat must provide all the resources that an organism needs to grow and survive. Abiotic factors, such as temperature, often determine whether a species can live in a certain place. Biotic factors, such as other organisms that live in the area, also play a role. For example, the habitat of a shark must include populations of fish it can eat.

Niche

Each population in an ecosystem plays a specific role. A population's **niche** is the role the population plays in the ecosystem, like how it gets food and interacts with other populations.

In general, two populations cannot occupy exactly the same niche. Small differences in habitats, roles, and adaptations can allow similar species to live together in the same ecosystem.

Visualize It!

12 Infer What do you think is the prairie dog's niche?

_____
_____
_____
_____
_____

Prairie dogs dig burrows in grassy plains. They eat plants and are hunted by predators like owls and foxes.

© Houghton Mifflin Harcourt Publishing Company • Image Credits: ©Raymond K. Gehman/National Geographic/Getty Images

Lizard Invasion

Green anole lizards (*Anolis carolinensis*) have been part of the South Florida ecosystem for many years. Recently a closely related lizard, the brown anole (*Anolis sagrei*), has invaded the natural habitat of the green anole. How do they avoid competing with each other for resources?

Home Base

The green anole lives on perches on the whole tree. Brown anoles mainly live on ground branches. If green and brown anoles are in the same tree, green anoles move up to avoid the ground perches. In this way they can avoid occupying the same habitat as the brown anole.

Competition Arrives

Although brown and green anoles have shifted their habitat in order to coexist, they do not live together peacefully. Brown anoles also interfere with the green anoles by eating their young.

Extend

Inquiry

13 Describe How do the anoles separate themselves to avoid competition? Draw a picture of a tree with both green and brown anoles on it.

14 Research What are other examples of two species dividing a niche or habitat?

15 Relate Infer what would happen if the habitats or niches of these species overlapped. Present your findings in a format such as a short story or a soap opera or play.

Visual Summary

To complete this summary, circle the correct word. Then use the key below to check your answers. You can use this page to review the main concepts of the lesson.

Ecology and Ecosystems

Ecology is the study of the biotic and abiotic factors in an ecosystem, and the relationships between them.

16 In a desert ecosystem, sand is an example of a biotic / abiotic factor, and cacti are an example of a biotic / abiotic factor.

Every organism has a habitat and a niche.

17 Certain types of fish live in desert ponds where they feed on other organisms from the water. In this example, the lake is a habitat / niche and filter-feeding behavior is part of a habitat / niche.

The environment can be organized into different levels, including populations, communities, and ecosystems.

18 Populations of cacti, together with sand and rocks, are included in a desert community / ecosystem.

Answers: 16 abiotic, biotic; 17 habitat, niche; 18 ecosystem

19 Predict In the desert ecosystem shown above, name a biotic factor and describe the effect on the horses if it were removed from the ecosystem.

Lesson Review

Vocabulary

1 Explain how the meanings of the terms *biotic factor* and *abiotic factor* differ._____

_____

_____

2 In your own words, write a definition for *ecology*. _____

_____

_____

3 Explain how the meanings of the terms *habitat* and *niche* differ. _____

_____

_____

_____

Key Concepts

4 List What are two ways that organisms are connected to the nonliving environment?

_____

_____

_____

5 Explain How can the environment be organized into levels from simple to complex?

_____

_____

_____

_____

6 Infer How do the populations in a community depend on each other?

_____

_____

_____

_____

7 Identify What factors determine whether a species can be present in a place?

_____

_____

_____

_____

Critical Thinking

Use this graph to answer the following question.

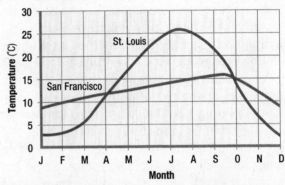

8 Calculate What is the average temperature difference in July between the two cities?

_____

9 Predict What might happen in a tropical rainforest biome if the area received very little rain for an extended period of time?

_____

_____

_____

_____

10 Infer Owls and hawks both eat rodents. They are also found in the same habitats. Since no two populations can occupy exactly the same niche, how can owls and hawks coexist?

_____

_____

_____

_____

Kenneth Krysko

ECOLOGIST

Snakes have fascinated Dr. Kenneth Krysko since he was four years old. Now he is an ecologist specializing in herpetology—the study of snakes. You can often find him in the Florida Everglades looking for Burmese pythons. He tracks these pythons to help limit the effect they have on Florida ecosystems.

Burmese pythons can grow to be 6 meters long. They are native to southeast Asia and were illegally brought to Florida as pets. Many owners released them into the wild when the snakes grew too large. The snakes breed well in Florida's subtropical climate. And they eat just about any animal they can swallow, including many native species. Dr. Krysko tracks down these invasive pythons. Through wildlife management, molecular genetics, and other areas of study, he works with other scientists to search for ways to reduce the python population.

Dr. Krysko studies many other invasive species, that is, nonnative species that can do harm in Florida ecosystems. He shares what he learns, including ways to identify and deal with invasive species with other ecologists. Along with invasion ecology, he has done research in reproduction and conservation biology. Dr. Krysko also works as a collections manager in the herpetology division at the Florida Museum of Natural History.

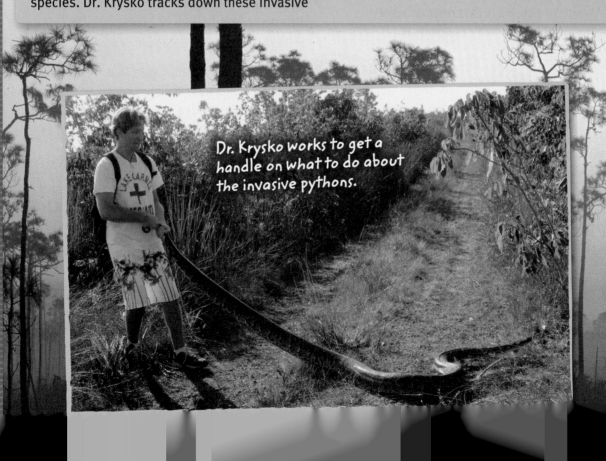

Dr. Krysko works to get a handle on what to do about the invasive pythons.

Harcourt Publishing Company • Image Credits: (bkgd) ©Willard Clay/Taxi/Getty Images; (tr) ©Dorling Kindersley/Getty Images; (bl) ©Dr. Kenneth Krysko

JOB BOARD

Park Naturalist

What You'll Do: Teach visitors at state and national parks about the park's ecology, geology, and landscape. Lead field trips, prepare and deliver lectures with slides, and create educational programs for park visitors. You may participate in research projects and track organisms in the park.

Where You Might Work: State and national parks

Education: An advanced degree in science and teacher certification

Other Job Requirements: You need to be good at communicating and teaching. Having photography and writing skills helps you prepare interesting educational materials.

Conservation Warden

What You'll Do: Patrol an area to enforce rules, and work with communities and groups to help educate the public about conservation and ecology.

Where You Might Work: Indoors and outdoors in state and national parks and ecologically sensitive areas

Education: A two-year associate's degree or at least 60 fully accredited college-level credits

Other Job Requirements: To work in the wild, good wilderness skills, map-reading, hiking, and excellent hearing are useful.

PEOPLE IN SCIENCE NEWS

Phil McCRORY

Saved by a Hair!

Phil McCrory, a hairdresser in Huntsville, Alabama, asked a brilliant question when he saw an otter whose fur was drenched with oil from the Exxon Valdez oil spill. If the otter's fur soaked up oil, why wouldn't human hair do the same? McCrory gathered hair from the floor of his salon and performed his own experiments. He stuffed hair into a pair of pantyhose and tied the ankles together. McCrory floated this bundle in his son's wading pool and poured used motor oil into the center of the ring. When he pulled the ring closed, not a drop of oil remained in the water! McCrory's discovery was tested as an alternative method for cleaning up oil spills. Many people donated their hair to be used for cleanup efforts. Although the method worked well, the engineers conducting the research concluded that hair is not as useful as other oil-absorbing materials for cleaning up large-scale spills.

Roles in Energy Transfer

ESSENTIAL QUESTION

How does energy flow through an ecosystem?

By the end of this lesson, you should be able to relate the roles of organisms to the transfer of energy in food chains and food webs.

Energy is transferred from the sun to producers, such as kelp. It flows through the rest of the ecosystem.

This fish also needs energy to live. How do you think it gets this energy? From the sun as kelp do?

Indiana Standards

6.3.4 Recognize that plants use energy from the sun to make sugar (glucose) by the process of photosynthesis.

6.3.5 Describe how all animals, including humans, meet their energy needs by consuming other organisms, breaking down their structures, and using the materials to grow and function.

6.3.6 Recognize that food provides the energy for the work that cells do and is a source of the molecular building blocks that can be incorporated into a cell's structure or stored for later use.

Engage Your Brain

1 Describe Most organisms on Earth get energy from the sun. How is energy flowing through the ecosystem pictured on the opposite page?

_____

_____

_____

_____

2 Predict List two of your favorite foods. Then, explain how the sun's energy helped make those foods available to you.

_____

_____

_____

_____

_____

Active Reading

3 Synthesize You can often define an unknown word if you know the meaning of its word parts. Use the word parts and sentences below to make an educated guess about the meaning of the words _herbivore_ and _carnivore_.

Word part	Meaning
-vore	to eat
herbi-	plant
carni-	meat

Example sentence
A koala bear is an <u>herbivore</u> that eats eucalyptus leaves.

herbivore:

_____

_____

_____

Example sentence
A great white shark is a <u>carnivore</u> that eats fish and other marine animals.

carnivore:

_____

_____

_____

Vocabulary Terms

- producer
- decomposer
- consumer
- herbivore
- carnivore
- omnivore
- food chain
- food web

4 Apply As you learn the definition of each vocabulary term in this lesson, create your own definition or sketch to help you remember the meaning of the term.

Get Energized!

How do organisms get energy?

Energy is all around you. Chemical energy is stored in the bonds of molecules and holds molecules together. The energy from food is chemical energy in the bonds of food molecules. All living things need a source of chemical energy to survive.

![Active Reading] **6 Identify** As you read, underline examples of producers, decomposers, and consumers.

Producers Convert Energy Into Food

A **producer**, also called an autotroph, uses energy to make food. Most producers use sunlight to make food in a process called photosynthesis. The sun powers most life on Earth. In photosynthesis, producers use light energy to make food from water, carbon dioxide, and nutrients found in water and soil. The food contains chemical energy and can be used immediately or stored for later use. All green plants, such as grasses and trees, are producers. Algae and some bacteria are also producers. The food that these producers make supplies the energy for other living things in an ecosystem.

Decomposers Break Down Matter

An organism that gets energy and nutrients by breaking down the remains of other organisms is a **decomposer**. Fungi, such as the mushrooms on this log, and some bacteria are decomposers. Decomposers are nature's recyclers. By converting dead organisms and animal and plant waste into materials such as water and nutrients, decomposers help move matter through ecosystems. Decomposers make these simple materials available to other organisms.

This plant is a producer. Producers make food using light energy from the sun.

These mushrooms are decomposers. They break down the remains of plants and animals.

Consumers Eat Other Organisms

A **consumer** is an organism that eats other organisms. Consumers use the energy and nutrients stored in other living organisms because they cannot make their own food. A consumer that eats only plants, such as a grasshopper or bison, is called an **herbivore**. A **carnivore**, such as a badger or this wolf, eats other animals. An **omnivore** eats both plants and animals. A *scavenger* is a specialized consumer that feeds on dead organisms. Scavengers, such as the turkey vulture, eat the leftovers of the meals of other animals or eat dead animals.

This wolf is a consumer. It eats other organisms to get energy.

Consumers

Visualize It!

7 List Beside each image, place a check mark next to the word that matches the type of consumer the animal is.

Name: Hedgehog
What I eat: leaves, earthworms, insects

What am I?
☐ herbivore
☐ omnivore
☐ carnivore

Name: Moose
What I eat: grasses, fruits

What am I?
☐ herbivore
☐ omnivore
☐ carnivore

Name: Komodo dragon
What I eat: insects, birds, mammals

What am I?
☐ herbivore
☐ omnivore
☐ carnivore

8 Infer Explain how carnivores might be affected if the main plant species in a community were to disappear.

_____

_____

_____

Energy Transfer

How is energy transferred among organisms?

Organisms change energy from the environment or from their food into other types of energy. Some of this energy is used for the organism's activities, such as breathing or moving. Some of the energy is saved within the organism to use later. If an organism is eaten or decomposes, the consumer or decomposer takes in the energy stored in the original organism. Only chemical energy that an organism has stored in its tissues is available to consumers. In this way, energy is transferred from organism to organism.

Active Reading **9 Infer** When a grasshopper eats grass, only some of the energy from the grass is stored in the grasshopper's body. How does the grasshopper use the rest of the energy?

_____

_____

This tree gets its energy from the sun.

This ant eats plants like the mesquite tree, and other insects.

10 Identify By what process does this tree get its energy?

_____

_____

11 Apply What type of energy is this ant consuming?

_____

_____

Energy Flows Through a Food Chain

A **food chain** is the path of energy transfer from producers to consumers. Energy moves from one organism to the next in one direction. The arrows in a food chain represent the transfer of energy, as one organism is eaten by another. Arrows represent the flow of energy from the body of the consumed organism to the body of the consumer of that organism.

Producers form the base of food chains. Producers transfer energy to the first, or primary, consumer in the food chain. The next, or secondary, consumer in the food chain consumes the primary consumer. A tertiary consumer eats the secondary consumer. Finally, decomposers recycle matter back to the soil.

Visualize It!

The photographs below show a typical desert food chain. Answer the following four questions from left to right based on your understanding of how energy flows in a food chain.

This hawk eats the lizard. It is at the top of the food chain.

13 Predict If nothing ever eats this hawk, what might eventually happen to the energy that is stored in its body?

_____

_____

This lizard eats mostly insects.

12 Apply What does the arrow between the ant and the lizard represent?

_____

_____

World Wide Webs

How do food webs show energy connections?

Few organisms eat just one kind of food. So, the energy and nutrient connections in nature are more complicated than a simple food chain. A **food web** is the feeding relationships among organisms in an ecosystem. Food webs are made up of many food chains.

The next page shows a coastal food web. Most of the organisms in this food web live in the water. The web also includes some birds that live on land and eat fish. Tiny algae called phytoplankton form the base of this food web. Like plants on land, phytoplankton are producers. Tiny consumers called zooplankton eat phytoplankton. Larger animals, such as fish and squid, eat zooplankton. At the top of each chain are top predators, animals that eat other animals but are rarely eaten. In this food web, the killer whale is a top predator. Notice how many different energy paths lead from phytoplankton to the killer whale.

Active Reading

14 Identify Underline the type of organism that typically forms the base of the food web.

Visualize It!

15 Apply Complete the statements to the right with the correct organism names from the food web.

ENERGY

Energy flows up the food web when _____ eat puffins.

Puffins are connected to many organisms in the food web.

ENERGY

Puffins get energy by eating

_____ ,

_____ ,

and _____ .

Food Web

The top predator is shown at the top of the food web. What is the top predator in this food web?

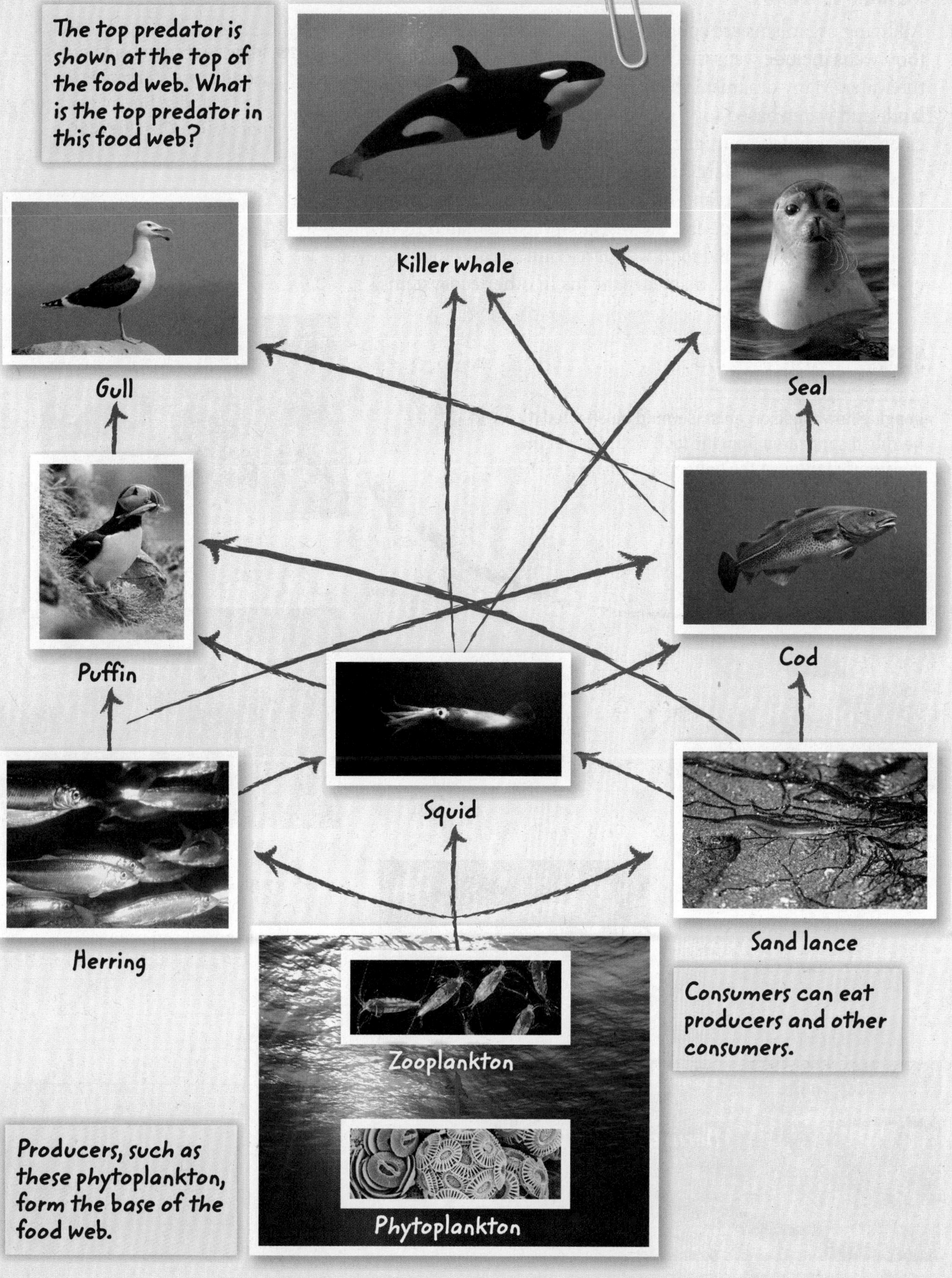

Killer whale

Seal

Gull

Cod

Puffin

Squid

Herring

Sand lance

Consumers can eat producers and other consumers.

Zooplankton

Phytoplankton

Producers, such as these phytoplankton, form the base of the food web.

How are organisms connected by food webs?

All living organisms are connected by global food webs. Global food webs include webs that begin on land and webs that begin in the water. Many organisms have feeding relationships that connect land- and water-based food webs. For example, algae might be eaten by a fish, which might then be eaten by a bird.

Food webs that start on land may also move into the water. Many insects that eat plants on land lay their eggs in the water. Some fish eat these eggs and the insect larvae that hatch from them. Because the global food webs are connected, removing even one organism can affect many organisms in other ecosystems.

18 Infer Gulls don't eat herring but they are still connected by the food web. How might gull populations be affected?

_____
_____
_____
_____

Visualize It!

Imagine how these organisms would be affected if herring disappeared from the food web. Answer the questions starting at the bottom of the page.

☐ Gull

☐ Puffin

☐ Cod

☐ Squid

Herring

16 Identify Put a check mark next to the organisms that eat herring.

17 Predict With no herring to eat, how might the eating habits of cod change?

_____
_____
_____
_____
_____
_____
_____

Dangerous Competition

Sometimes species are introduced into a new area. These invasive species often compete with native species for energy resources, such as sunlight and food.

Full Coverage
The kudzu plant was introduced to stop soil erosion, but in the process it outgrew all the native plants, preventing them from getting sunlight. Sometimes it completely covers houses or cars!

Destructive Zebras
The zebra mussel is one of the most destructive invasive species in the United States. They eat by filtering tiny organisms out of the water, often leaving nothing for the native mussel species.

Across the Grass
The walking catfish can actually move across land to get from one pond to another! As a result, sometimes the catfish competes with native species for food.

Extend

Inquiry

19 Relate Describe how the competition between invasive and native species might affect a food web.

20 Describe Give an example of competition for a food resource that may occur in an ecosystem near you.

21 Illustrate Provide an illustration of your example of competition in a sketch or a short story. Be sure to include the important aspects of food webs that you learned in the lesson.

Visual Summary

To complete this summary, circle the correct word. Then use the key below to check your answers. You can use this page to review the main concepts of the lesson.

Energy Transfer
in Ecosystems

Organisms get energy in different ways.

- Producers make their own food.
- Consumers eat other living organisms.
- Decomposers break down dead organisms.

22 Herbivores, carnivores, and omnivores are three types of producers / consumers / decomposers.

Food chains and food webs describe the flow of energy in an ecosystem.

23 All food chains start with producers / consumers / decomposers.

Answers: 22 consumers; 23 producers

24 Predict Describe the effects on global food webs if the sun's energy could no longer reach Earth.

Food Web

Lesson Review

Vocabulary

Fill in the blanks with the term that best completes the following sentences.

1 _____ is the primary source of energy for most ecosystems.

2 A _____ eats mostly dead matter.

3 A _____ contains many food chains.

4 _____ is the process by which light energy from the sun is converted to food.

Key Concepts

5 Describe What are the roles of producers, consumers, and decomposers in an ecosystem?

_____

_____

_____

_____

_____

6 Apply What types of organisms typically make up the base, middle, and top of a food web?

_____

_____

_____

_____

_____

7 Describe Identify the two types of global food webs and describe how they are connected.

_____

_____

_____

_____

_____

Use the figure to answer the following questions.

8 Apply Describe the flow of energy in this food chain. Be sure to use the names of the organisms and what role they serve in the food chain (producer, consumer, or decomposer). If an organism is a consumer, identify whether it is an herbivore, carnivore, or omnivore.

_____

_____

_____

_____

9 Apply What do the arrows represent in the figure above?

_____

_____

_____

Critical Thinking

10 Predict Give an example of a decomposer, and explain what would happen if decomposers were absent from a forest ecosystem.

_____

_____

_____

_____

11 Predict How would a food web be affected if a species disappeared from an ecosystem?

_____

_____

_____

_____

_____

Interactions in Communities

ESSENTIAL QUESTION

How do organisms interact?

By the end of this lesson, you should be able to predict the effects of different interactions in communities.

These birds, called tickbirds, eat ticks and flies on a rhinoceros. This behavior helps the rhino. The ticks are also parasites that sometimes drink the rhino's blood!

Indiana Standards

6.3.1 Describe specific relationships (predator/prey, consumer/producer or parasite/host) between organisms and determine whether these relationships are competitive or mutually beneficial.

6.3.5 Describe how all animals, including humans, meet their energy needs by consuming other organisms, breaking down their structures, and using the materials to grow and function.

Engage Your Brain

1 Predict Check T or F to show whether you think each statement is true or false.

T F

☐ ☐ Different animals can compete for the same food.

☐ ☐ Parasites help the organisms that they feed on.

☐ ☐ Some organisms rely on each other for necessities such as food or shelter.

☐ ☐ Organisms can defend themselves against predators that try to eat them.

2 Explain Draw an interaction between two living things that you might observe while on a picnic. Write a caption to go with your sketch.

Active Reading

3 Synthesize You can often define an unknown word if you know the meaning of its word parts. Use the word parts and sentence below to make an educated guess about the meaning of the word *symbiosis*.

Word part	Meaning
bio-	life
sym-	together

Example sentence
The relationship between a sunflower and the insect that pollinates it is an example of symbiosis.

symbiosis:

_____

_____

Vocabulary Terms

- predator
- prey
- symbiosis
- mutualism
- commensalism
- parasitism
- competition

4 Apply As you learn the meaning of each vocabulary term in this lesson, create your own definition or sketch to help you remember the meaning of the term.

Feeding Frenzy!

How do predator and prey interact?

Every organism lives with and affects other organisms. Many organisms must feed on other organisms in order to get the energy and nutrients they need to survive. These feeding relationships establish structure in a community.

Predators Eat Prey

In a predator–prey relationship, an animal eats another animal for energy and nutrients. The **predator** eats another animal. The **prey** is an animal that is eaten by a predator. An animal can be both predator and prey. For example, if a warthog eats a lizard, and is, in turn, eaten by a lion, the warthog is both predator and prey.

Predators and prey have adaptations that help them survive. Some predators have talons, claws, or sharp teeth, which provide them with deadly weapons. Spiders, which are small predators, use their webs to trap unsuspecting prey. Camouflage (CAM•ah•flaj) can also help a predator or prey to blend in with its environment. A tiger's stripes help it to blend in with tall grasses so that it can ambush its prey, and the wings of some moths look just like tree bark, which makes them difficult for predators to see. Some animals defend themselves with chemicals. For example, skunks and bombardier beetles spray predators with irritating chemicals.

Active Reading

5 Identify As you read, underline examples of predator–prey adaptations.

This lion is a predator. The warthog is its prey.

Adaptations of Predators and Prey

Most organisms wouldn't last a day without their adaptations. This bald eagle's vision and sharp talons allow it to find and catch prey.

sharp talons

Predators and Prey Populations Are Connected

Predators rely on prey for food, so the sizes of predator and prey populations are linked together very closely. If one population grows or shrinks, the other population is affected. For example, when there are a lot of warthogs to eat, the lion population may grow because the food supply is plentiful. As the lion population grows, it requires more and more food, so more and more warthogs are hunted by the lions. The increased predation may cause the warthog population to shrink. If the warthog population shrinks enough, the lion population may shrink due to a shortage in food supply. If the lion population shrinks, the warthog population may grow due to a lack of predators.

This lion is hunting down the antelope. If most of the antelope are killed, the lions will have less food to eat.

6 Compare Fill in the Venn diagram to compare and contrast predators and prey.

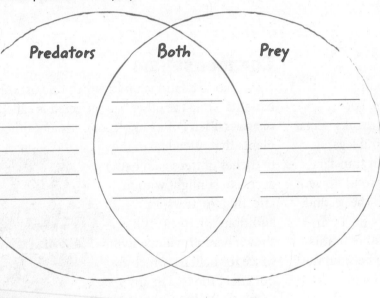

Predators   Both   Prey

Think Outside the Book

7 Apply Choose a predator and think about what it eats and how it hunts. Then do one of the following:
- Write a nomination for the predator to be "Predator of the Year."
- Draw the predator and label the adaptations that help it hunt.

Don't be surprised if this "leaf" walks away—it's actually an insect.

Visualize It!

8 Analyze How might this insect's appearance help keep it from getting eaten?

_____

_____

_____

_____

Living Together

What are the types of symbiotic relationships?

A close long-term relationship between different species in a community is called **symbiosis** (sim•bee•OH•sis). In symbiosis, the organisms in the relationship can benefit from, be unaffected by, or be harmed by the relationship. Often, one organism lives in or on the other organism. Symbiotic relationships are classified as mutualism, commensalism, or parasitism.

Active Reading **9 Identify** As you read, underline examples of symbiotic relationships.

Mutualism

A symbiotic relationship in which both organisms benefit is called **mutualism**. For example, when the bee in the photo drinks nectar from a flower, it gets pollen on its hind legs. When the bee visits another flower, it transfers pollen from the first flower to the second flower. In this interaction, the bee is fed and the second flower is pollinated for reproduction. So, both organisms benefit from the relationship. In this example, the mutualism benefits the bee and the two parent plants that are reproducing.

Bees pollinate flowers. This is an example of mutualism.

Commensalism

A symbiotic relationship in which one organism benefits while the other is unaffected is called **commensalism.** For example, orchids and other plants that often live in the branches of trees gain better access to sunlight without affecting the trees. In addition, the tree trunk shown here provides a living space for lichens, which do not affect the tree in any way. Some examples of commensalism involve protection. For example, certain shrimp live among the spines of the fire urchin. The fire urchin's spines are poisonous but not to the shrimp. By living among the urchin's spines, the shrimp are protected from predators. In this relationship, the shrimp benefits and the fire urchin is unaffected.

Lichens can live on tree bark.

10 Compare How does commensalism differ from mutualism?

_____

_____

_____

_____

Think Outside the Book **Inquiry**

12 Predict Observe and take notes about how the organisms in your area interact with one another. Imagine what would happen if one of these organisms disappeared. Write down three effects that you can think of.

parasite

host

Parasitism

A symbiotic relationship in which one organism benefits and another is harmed is called **parasitism** (PAR•uh•sih•tiz•uhm). The organism that benefits is the *parasite*. The organism that is harmed is the *host*. The parasite gets food from its host, which weakens the host. Some parasites, such as ticks, live on the host's surface and feed on its blood. These parasites can cause diseases such as Lyme disease. Other parasites, such as tapeworms, live within the host's body. They can weaken their host so much that the host dies.

11 Summarize Using the key, complete the table to show how organisms are affected by symbiotic relationships.

Symbiosis	Species 1	Species 2
Mutualism	+	
	+	0
Parasitism		

Key + organism benefits
0 organism not affected
− organism harmed

Let the Games Begin!

Why does competition occur in communities?

In a team game, two groups compete against each other with the same goal in mind—to win the game. In a biological community, organisms compete for resources. **Competition** occurs when organisms fight for the same limited resource. Organisms compete for resources such as food, water, sunlight, shelter, and mates. If an organism doesn't get all the resources it needs, it could die.

Sometimes competition happens among individuals of the same species. For example, different groups of lions compete with each other for living space. Males within these groups also compete with each other for mates.

Competition can also happen among individuals of different species. Lions mainly eat large animals, such as zebras. They compete for zebras with leopards and cheetahs. When zebras are scarce, competition increases among animals that eat zebras. As a result, lions may steal food or compete with other predators for smaller animals.

Active Reading

13 Identify Underline each example of competition.

14 Predict In the table below, fill in the missing cause and effect of two examples of competition in a community.

Cause	Effect
A population of lions grows too large to share their current territory.	
	Several male hyenas compete to mate with the females present in their area.

Many organisms rely on the same water source.

Think Outside the Book

15 Apply With a classmate, discuss how competition might affect the organisms in this photo.

Strange Relationships

Glow worms? Blind salamanders? Even creepy crawlers in this extreme cave community interact in ways that help them meet their needs. How do these interactions differ from ones in your own community?

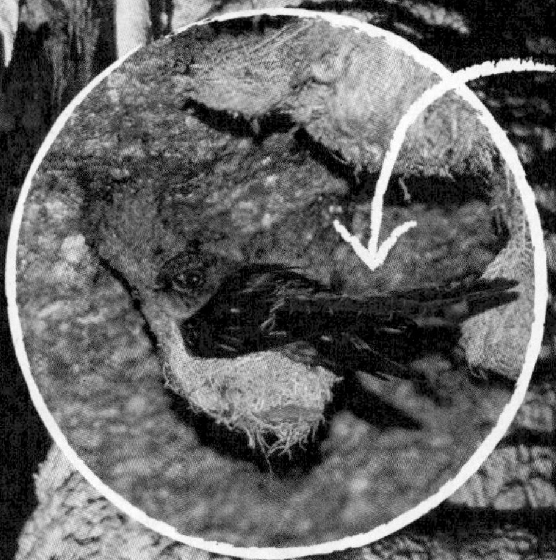

Guano Buffet

Cave swiftlets venture out of the cave daily to feed. The food they eat is recycled as bird dung, or guano, which piles up beneath the nests. The guano feeds many cave dwellers, such as insects. As a result, these insects never have to leave the cave!

A Blind Hunter

Caves are very dark and, over generations, these salamanders have lost the use of their eyes for seeing. Instead of looking for food, they track prey by following water movements.

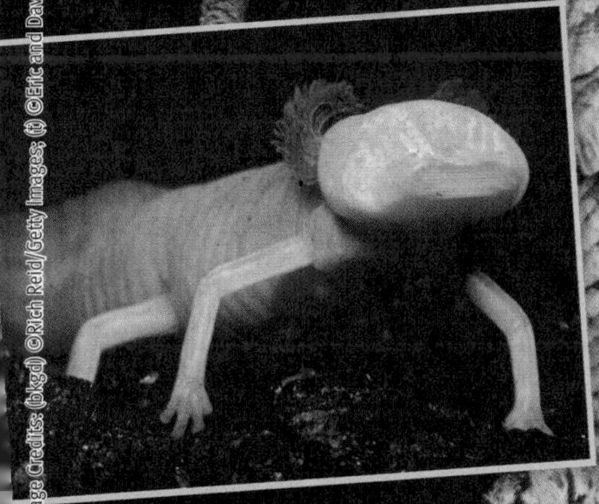

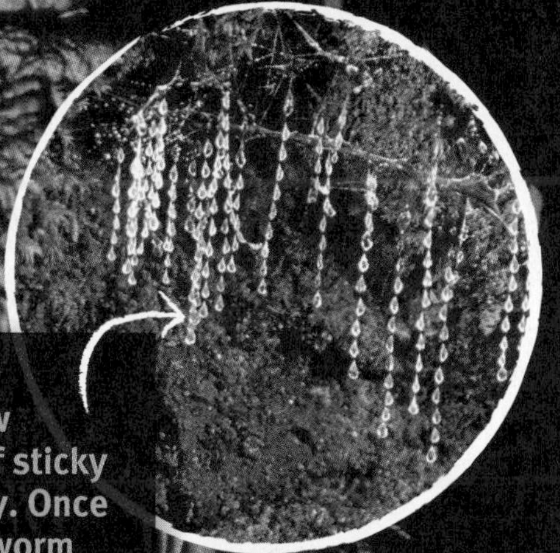

Sticky Traps

Bioluminescent glow worms make lines of sticky beads to attract prey. Once a prey is stuck, the worm pulls in the line to feast.

Extend

Inquiry

16 Identify Name the type of relationship illustrated in two of the examples shown above.

17 Research Name some organisms in your community and the interactions they have.

18 Create Illustrate two of the interactions you just described by doing one of the following:
- make a poster
- write a song
- write a play
- draw a graphic novel

Visual Summary

To complete this summary, fill in the blanks with the correct word or phrase. Then, use the key below to check your answers. You can use this page to review the main concepts of the lesson.

Organisms interact in feeding relationships.

19 Predators eat

_____

Organisms interact in symbiosis—very close relationships between two species.

Mutualism:

Commensalism:

Parasitism:

20 A parasite gets nourishment from its

_____

Interactions
in Communities

Organisms interact in competition.

21 Organisms compete for resources such as

_____

_____

_____

Competition can occur between:

Members of the same species

Members of different species

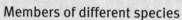

Answers: 19 prey, 20 host, 21 food, mates, shelter, and water.

22 Synthesize Explain how interactions can be both beneficial and harmful to the organisms in a community.

Lesson Review

Vocabulary

Fill in the blank with the term that best completes the following sentences.

1 A _____ is an animal that kills and eats another animal, known as prey.

2 A long-term relationship between two different species within a community is called

_____

3 _____ occurs when organisms fight for limited resources.

Key Concepts

Fill in the table below.

Example	Type of symbiosis
4 Identify Tiny organisms called mites live in human eyelashes and feed on dead skin, without harming humans.	
5 Identify Certain bacteria live in human intestines, where they get food and also help humans break down their food.	

6 Describe Think of an animal, and list two resources that it might compete for in its community. Then describe what adaptations the animal has to compete for these resources.

_____

_____

_____

_____

7 Explain What is the relationship between the size of a predator population and the size of a prey population?

_____

_____

_____

Critical Thinking

Use this graph to answer the following question.

Predator and Prey Populations Over Time

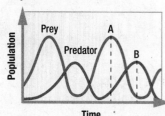

8 Analyze At which point (A or B) on this graph would you expect competition within the predator population to be the highest?

_____

9 Infer Think of a resource, and predict what happens to the resource when competition for it increases.

_____

_____

_____

10 Apply Identify a community near where you live, such as a forest, a pond, or your own backyard. Think about the interactions of the organisms in this community. Describe an interaction and identify it as predation, mutualism, commensalism, parasitism, or competition.

_____

_____

_____

_____

Lesson (4)

Photosynthesis and Cellular Respiration

ESSENTIAL QUESTION

How do cells get and use energy?

By the end of this lesson, you should be able to explain how cells capture and release energy.

Sunflowers capture light energy and change it to chemical energy, but people need to eat to get energy.

Indiana Standards

6.3.4 Recognize that plants use energy from the sun to make sugar (glucose) by the process of photosynthesis.

6.3.5 Describe how all animals, including humans, meet their energy needs by consuming other organisms, breaking down their structures, and using the materials to grow and function.

6.3.6 Recognize that food provides the energy for the work that cells do and is a source of the molecular building blocks that can be incorporated into a cell's structure or stored for later use.

Engage Your Brain

1 Predict Check T or F to show whether you think each of the following statements is true or false.

T   F

☐ ☐ All living things must eat other living things for food.

☐ ☐ Plants can make their own food.

☐ ☐ Plants don't need oxygen, only carbon dioxide.

☐ ☐ Animals eat plants or other animals that eat plants.

☐ ☐ Many living things need oxygen to release energy from food.

2 Infer Look at the photo. Describe the differences between the plants. What do you think caused these differences?

_____

_____

_____

_____

_____

_____

_____

Active Reading

3 Synthesize You can often define an unknown word if you know the meaning of its word parts. Use the word parts and sentence below to make an educated guess about the meaning of the term *chlorophyll*.

Word part	Meaning
chloro-	green
-phyll	leaf

Example sentence
Chlorophyll is a pigment that captures light energy.

chlorophyll:

_____

_____

_____

Vocabulary Terms

- photosynthesis
- chlorophyll
- cellular respiration

4 Apply As you learn the definition of each vocabulary term in this lesson, write your own definition or make a sketch to help you remember the meaning of the term.

Energize!

How do the cells in an organism function?

![Active Reading] **5 Identify** As you read, underline sources of energy for living things.

How do you get the energy to run around and play soccer or basketball? How does a tree get the energy to grow? All living things, from the tiniest single-celled bacterium to the largest tree, need energy. Cells must capture and use energy or they will die. Cells get energy from food. Some living things can make their own food. Many living things get their food by eating other living things.

Your cells use energy all the time, whether you are active or not.

Cells Need Energy

Growing, moving, and other cell functions use energy. Without energy, a living thing cannot replace cells, build body parts, or reproduce. Even when a living thing is not very active, it needs energy. Cells constantly use energy to move materials into and out of the cell. They need energy to make different chemicals. And they need energy to get rid of wastes. A cell could not survive for long if it did not have the energy for all of these functions.

![Active Reading] **6 Relate** Why do living things need energy at all times?

_____

_____

_____

Cells Get Energy from Food

The cells of all living things need chemical energy. Food contains chemical energy. Food gives living things the energy and raw materials needed to carry out life processes. When cells break down food, the energy of the chemical bonds in food is released. This energy can be used or stored by the cell. The atoms and molecules in food can be used as building blocks for the cell.

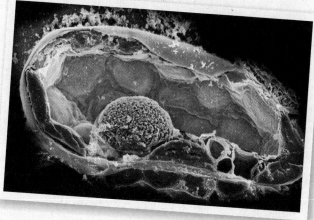

Plant cells make their own food using energy from the sun.

Living things get food in different ways. In fact, they can be grouped based on how they get food. Some living things, such as plants and many single-celled organisms, are called *producers* (proh•DOO•suhrz). Producers can make their own food. Most producers use energy from the sun. They capture and store light energy from the sun as chemical energy in food. A small number of producers, such as those that live in the deepest parts of the ocean, use chemicals to make their own food. Producers use most of the food they produce for energy. The unused food is stored in their bodies.

Many living things, such as people and other animals, are *consumers* (kun•SOO•muhrz). Consumers must eat, or consume, other living things to get food. Consumers may eat producers or other consumers. The cells of consumers break down food to release the energy it contains. A special group of consumers is made up of *decomposers* (dee•cum•POH•zhurhz). Decomposers break down dead organisms or the wastes of other organisms. Fungi and many bacteria are decomposers.

7 Compare Use the Venn diagram below to describe how producers and consumers get energy.

Producers

Both

Use chemical energy

Consumers

Cooking with Chloroplasts

How do plant cells make food?

Nearly all life on Earth gets energy from the sun. Plants make food with the energy from the sun. So, plants use energy from the sun directly. Animals use energy from the sun indirectly when they eat a plant or another animal.

In a process called **photosynthesis** (foh•toh•SYN•thuh•sys), plants use energy from sunlight, carbon dioxide, and water to make sugars. Plants capture light energy from the sun and change it to chemical energy in sugars. These sugars are made from water and carbon dioxide. In addition to sugars, photosynthesis also produces oxygen gas. The oxygen gas is given off into the air.

Active Reading

8 Identify What is the source of energy for nearly all life on Earth?

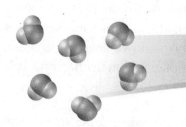

Visualize It!

Photosynthesis In many plants, photosynthesis takes place in the leaf. Chlorophyll, which is located in chloroplasts, captures light energy from the sun. This light energy is converted to chemical energy in sugars.

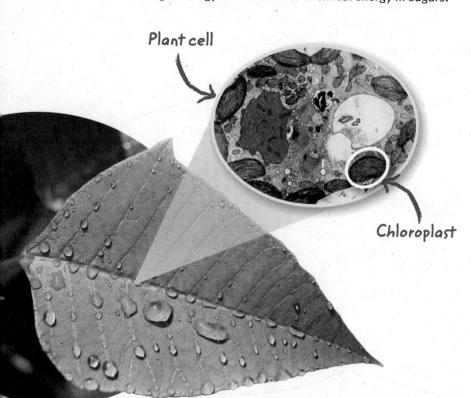

Plant cell

Chloroplast

Water

Carbon dioxide

© Houghton Mifflin Harcourt Publishing Company • Image Credits: (c) ©Biophoto Associates/Photo Researchers, Inc.; (bl) ©Oleg Shpak/Alamy

Capturing Light Energy

Energy from sunlight powers the process of photosynthesis. The light energy is converted to chemical energy, which is stored in the bonds of the sugar molecules made during photosynthesis.

Photosynthesis takes place in organelles called *chloroplasts* (KLOHR•oh•plahstz). These organelles are found only in the cells of plants and other organisms that undergo photosynthesis. They are not found in animal or fungal cells. Chloroplasts contain a green pigment called **chlorophyll** (KLOHR•oh•fill). Chlorophyll captures energy from sunlight. This energy is used to combine carbon dioxide (CO_2) and water (H_2O), forming the sugar glucose ($C_6H_{12}O_6$) and oxygen gas (O_2). Photosynthesis is a series of reactions summarized by the following chemical equation:

$$6CO_2 + 6 H_2O + \text{light energy} \longrightarrow C_6H_{12}O_6 + 6O_2$$

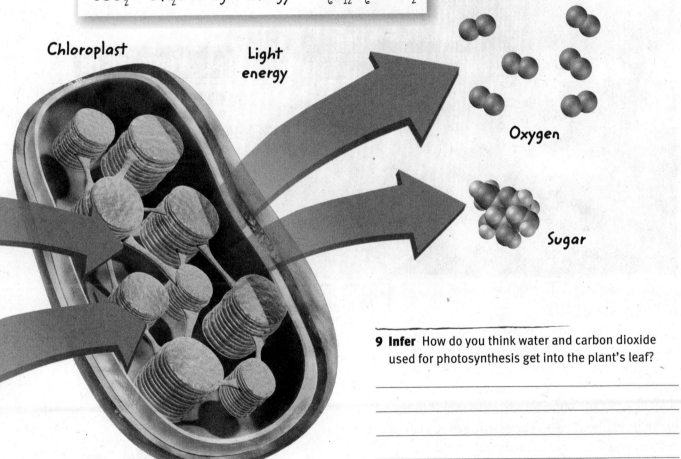

Chloroplast

Light energy

Oxygen

Sugar

9 Infer How do you think water and carbon dioxide used for photosynthesis get into the plant's leaf?

_____

_____

_____

_____

Storing Chemical Energy

Glucose (GLOO•kohs) is a sugar that stores chemical energy. It is the food that plants make. Plant cells break down glucose for energy. Excess sugars are stored in the body of the plant. They are often stored as starch in the roots and stem of the plant. When another organism eats the plant, the organism can use these stored sugars for energy.

Mighty Mitochondria

How do cells get energy from food?

When sugar is broken down, energy is released. It is stored in a molecule called *adenosine triphosphate (ATP)*. ATP powers many of the chemical reactions that enable cells to survive. The process of breaking down food to produce ATP is called **cellular respiration** (SELL•yoo•lahr ress•puh•RAY•shuhn).

Active Reading

10 Identify As you read, underline the starting materials and products of cellular respiration.

Mitochondria are found in both plant cells and animal cells.

Mitochondrion

Visualize It!

Cellular Respiration During cellular respiration, cells use oxygen gas to break down sugars and release energy.

Using Oxygen

Cellular respiration takes place in the cytoplasm and cell membranes of prokaryotic cells. In eukaryotic cells, cellular respiration takes place in organelles called *mitochondria* (singular, *mitochondrion*). Mitochondria are found in both plant and animal cells. The starting materials of cellular respiration are glucose and oxygen.

In eukaryotes, the first stage of cellular respiration takes place in the cytoplasm. Glucose is broken down into two 3-carbon molecules. This releases a small amount of energy. The next stage takes place in the mitochondria. This stage requires oxygen. Oxygen enters the cell and travels into the mitochondria. As the 3-carbon molecules are broken down, energy is captured and stored in ATP.

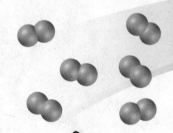

Oxygen

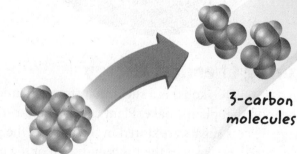

Sugar from photosynthesis

3-carbon molecules

Releasing Energy

The products of cellular respiration are chemical energy (ATP), carbon dioxide, and water. The carbon dioxide formed during cellular respiration is released by the cell. In many animals, the carbon dioxide is carried to the lungs and exhaled during breathing.

Some of the energy produced during cellular respiration is released as heat. However, much of the energy produced during cellular respiration is transferred to ATP. ATP can be carried throughout the body. When ATP is broken down, the energy released is used for cellular activities. The steps of cellular respiration can be summarized by the following equation:

$$C_6H_{12}O_6 + 6O_2 \rightarrow 6CO_2 + 6H_2O + \text{chemical energy (ATP)}$$

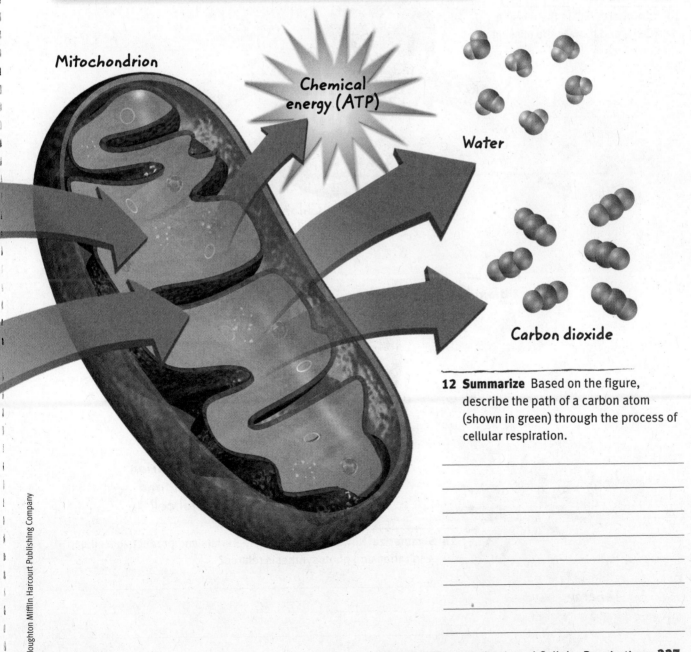

Mitochondrion

Chemical energy (ATP)

Water

Carbon dioxide

12 Summarize Based on the figure, describe the path of a carbon atom (shown in green) through the process of cellular respiration.

_____

_____

_____

_____

_____

_____

_____

_____

Merry-Go-Round!

How are photosynthesis and cellular respiration connected?

Most of the oxygen in the atmosphere was made during photosynthesis. Nearly all organisms use this oxygen during cellular respiration. They produce carbon dioxide and release it into the environment. In turn, plants use the carbon dioxide to make sugars. So, photosynthesis and respiration are linked, each depending on the products of the other.

(A) _____
energy

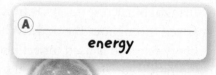

👁 Visualize It!

13 Synthesize Fill in the missing labels, and draw in the missing molecules.

(D) _____

Used in

Produces

Chloroplast
(in plant cells)

Oxygen

Carbon
dioxide

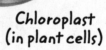

(B) _____

Produces

Used in

Mitochondrion
(in plant and
animal cells)

14 Summarize How are the starting materials and products of cellular respiration and photosynthesis related?

_____
_____
_____

(C) _____
energy

© Houghton Mifflin Harcourt Publishing Company

Out of Air

When there isn't enough oxygen, living things can get energy by anaerobic respiration (AN•uh•roh•bick ress•puh•RAY•shuhn). *Anaerobic* means "without oxygen." Like cellular respiration, anaerobic respiration produces ATP. However, it does not produce as much ATP as cellular respiration.

Rising to the Top
Fermentation is a type of anaerobic respiration. Many yeasts rely on fermentation for energy. Carbon dioxide is a product of fermentation. Carbon dioxide causes bread to rise, and gives it air pockets.

Feel the Burn!
The body uses anaerobic respiration during hard exercise, such as sprinting. This produces lactic acid, which can cause muscles to ache after exercise.

Extend

Inquiry

15 Compare What products do both cellular and anaerobic respiration have in common?

16 Research Blood delivers oxygen to the body. If this is the case, why does the body rely on anaerobic respiration during hard exercise? Research the reasons why the body switches between cellular and anaerobic respiration.

17 Compare Research and compare cellular respiration and fermentation. How are they similar? How do they differ? Summarize your results by doing one of the following:
- make a poster
- write a brochure
- draw a comic strip
- make a table

Visual Summary

To complete this summary, check the box that indicates true or false. Then, use the key below to check your answers. You can use this page to review the main concepts of the lesson.

Cells get and use energy

Living things need energy to survive.

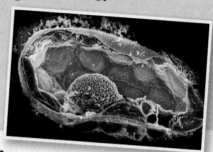

	T	F	
18	☐	☐	Organisms get energy from food.
19	☐	☐	A producer eats other organisms.

Plants make their own food.

	T	F	
20	☐	☐	Photosynthesis is the process by which plants make their own food.
21	☐	☐	Chlorophyll captures light energy during photosynthesis.

Cells release energy from food during cellular respiration.

	T	F	
22	☐	☐	Carbon dioxide is required for cellular respiration.
23	☐	☐	Cellular respiration takes place in chloroplasts.

Photosynthesis and cellular respiration are interrelated.

	T	F	
24	☐	☐	The products of photosynthesis are the starting materials of cellular respiration.

Answers: 18 T; 19 F; 20 T; 21 T; 22 F; 23 F; 24 T

25 Identify Describe how the cells in your body get energy and then use that energy.

Lesson Review

Vocabulary

Fill in the blank with the term that best completes the following sentences.

1 _____ takes place in organelles called *chloroplasts*.

2 Light energy is captured by the green pigment _____

3 Cells use oxygen to release energy during _____

Key Concepts

Use the figure to answer the following questions.

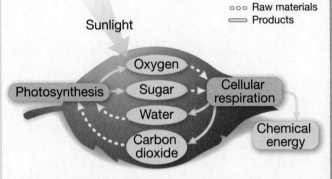

4 Identify What are the starting materials and products of photosynthesis and cellular respiration?

_____

_____

_____

_____

_____

5 Relate What does the diagram above reveal about the connections between photosynthesis and cellular respiration?

_____

_____

_____

_____

6 Contrast How do plants and animals get their energy in different ways?

_____

_____

_____

_____

Critical Thinking

7 Infer Does your body get all its energy from the sun? Explain.

_____

_____

_____

_____

_____

8 Synthesize Could cellular respiration happen without photosynthesis? Explain your reasoning.

_____

_____

_____

_____

9 Apply Plants don't move around, so why do they need energy?

_____

_____

_____

_____

_____

My Notes

Unit 6 **Summary**

Introduction to Ecology

Interactions in Communities

Photosynthesis and Cellular Respiration

include feeding relationships that lead to

are the basis of

Roles in Energy Transfer

1 Interpret The Graphic Organizer above shows that energy transfer is an important part of an ecosystem. Give an example of an energy transfer in a land ecosystem.

_____

_____

_____

_____

_____

2 Explain Do organisms compete for abiotic resources? Explain.

_____

_____

_____

3 Compare How might photosynthesis and cellular respiration be considered inverse processes?

_____

_____

_____

_____

_____

_____

4 Synthesize How could introduced species disrupt existing feeding relationships?

_____

_____

_____

_____

Multiple Choice

1 Earth's environments include both biotic and abiotic factors that living things need to survive. The figure shows a coastal mangrove ecosystem that has both biotic and abiotic factors.

Which of the following are both ABIOTIC FACTORS in the ecosystem?

A. water and pelican

B. sun and rocks

C. pelican and crab

D. snail and water

2 Purple loosestrife is a nonnative plant species that grows in Indiana. It produces thousands of seeds and spreads quickly. Which of the following is a NEGATIVE effect that purple loosestrife could have on other organisms in its habitat?

A. It provides places for animals in the habitat to hide.

B. It provides a new source of food for animals in the habitat.

C. It replaces native plants that animals depend on for food or shelter.

D. It contributes nutrients to the soil so that soil organisms can grow.

3 Ecosystems have producers, decomposers, and consumers. Carnivores and omnivores are both consumers. Which of the following is a characteristic of omnivores that makes them DIFFERENT from carnivores?

A. Omnivores eat only plant materials.

B. Omnivores always eat live animals.

C. Omnivores eat both plants and animals.

D. Omnivores are able to produce their own food.

4 Remoras are small fish that attach to sharks but do not harm them. When sharks tear prey apart, remoras eat the leftovers. What statement about the relationship between remoras and sharks is TRUE?

A. Remoras and sharks have a predator-prey relationship.

B. The relationship is an example of mutualism.

C. The relationship is an example of parasitism.

D. The relationship is an example of commensalism.

5 Green plants produce their own food during photosynthesis. Which of these statements about photosynthesis is TRUE?

A. Water is one product of photosynthesis.

B. Oxygen is one product of photosynthesis.

C. Chlorophyll is one product of photosynthesis.

D. Carbon dioxide is one product of photosynthesis.

6 Breathing involves taking in oxygen and releasing carbon dioxide. How does the oxygen affect the process of cellular respiration?

A. Oxygen and ATP combine to produce energy in the form of carbon dioxide.

B. Oxygen and glucose combine to produce energy in the form of ATP molecules.

C. Oxygen and hydrogen combine to produce energy in the form of ATP molecules.

D. Oxygen and carbon dioxide combine to produce energy in the form of ATP molecules.

7 The products from photosynthesis provide the raw materials for cellular respiration. What products of photosynthesis are STARTING MATERIALS for cellular respiration?

A. glucose and oxygen

B. heat and ATP

C. carbon dioxide and water

D. light energy and chlorophyll

8 Kristine exercises regularly. The process of cellular respiration makes it possible for Kristine to run on the treadmill and to lift weights. What do her cells do during cellular respiration?

    A. convert kinetic energy into chemical energy

    B. absorb light energy through the chlorophyll in their chloroplasts

    C. combine water and carbon dioxide to produce oxygen and glucose

    D. break down food molecules to release energy in the form of ATP

Constructed Response

9 The food web shows some of the organisms in a temperate forest.

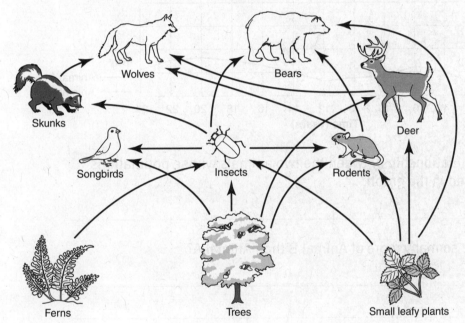

Identify THREE OMNIVORES in this food web.

1 _____

2 _____

3 _____

Identify the original source of energy for this food web.

_____

Describe the process by which it supports the food web.

_____

_____

Extended Response

10 The graph shows two different animal populations over a period of time.

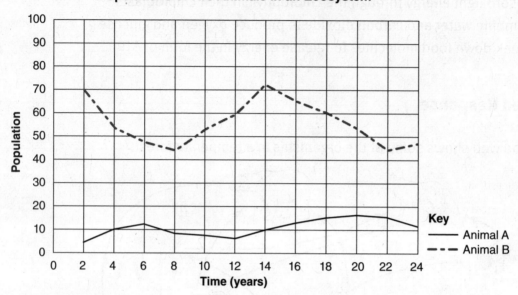

Populations of Two Animals in an Ecosystem

Describe the relationship between the two animals whose populations are represented in the graph.

_____

Why are there so many more of Animal B than Animal A?

_____

_____

Explain what might happen to the population of Animal B if Animal A were to disappear.

_____

_____

Explain might happen to the population of Animal A if Animal B were to disappear.

_____

_____

The Design Process

Look at your surroundings and you will see examples of objects, systems, and techniques that were created through the design process. Objects such as buildings, clothing, cars, and cellular phones are all products that were designed to meet a need. Systems must be designed to make these products efficiently. Techniques, or methods for using a device, are also designed.

The design process involves a series of steps that lead to the development of a new object, system, or technique. The process diagram below shows the basic steps of the design process. As you can see, the design process, like scientific methods, often involves repeated steps that can be completed in different orders.

The design process always begins by clearly identifying the need or problem to be solved. As much information as possible is needed before imagining possible solutions. Planning involves choosing a solution and making a list of materials necessary to create the solution. Once the planning is complete, then the *prototype,* or working model, is made and tested. Finally, the prototype is presented for review, evaluated, and improved as needed.

Indiana Standards

As citizens of the constructed world, students will participate in the design process. Students will learn to use materials and tools safely and employ the basic principles of the engineering design process in order to find solutions to problems.

DP 6.1 Identify a need or problem to be solved.

DP 6.2 Brainstorm potential solutions.

DP 6.3 Document the design throughout the entire design process so that it can be replicated in a portfolio/notebook with drawings including labels.

DP 6.4 Select a solution to the need or problem.

DP 6.5 Select the most appropriate materials to develop a solution that will meet the need.

DP 6.6 Create the solution through a prototype.

DP 6.7 Test and evaluate how well the solution meets the goal.

DP 6.8 Evaluate and test the design using measurement.

DP 6.9 Present evidence using mathematical representations (graphs, data tables).

DP 6.10 Communicate the solution including evidence using mathematical representations (graphs, data tables), drawings or prototypes.

DP 6.11 Redesign to improve the solution based on how well the solution meets the need.

Process Diagram

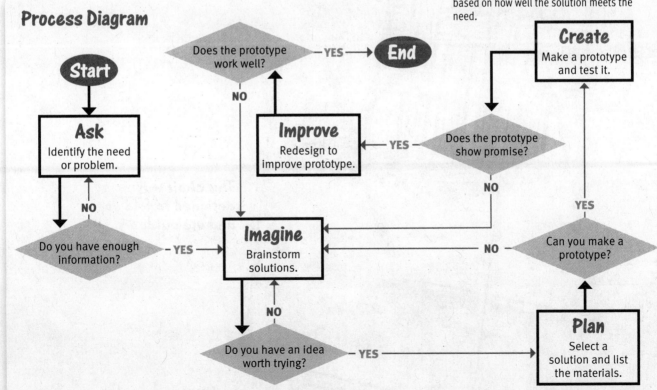

What are the steps of the design process?

While there is no single way to carry out the design process, it generally includes five basic steps. The process usually involves a team of people who are familiar with different aspects of the product design. For example, developers may explore and research a variety of possible solutions, while engineers build and test the prototype. Once the prototype is built, marketing and advertising experts might introduce the product to customers, who can provide feedback and evaluation. The product may be redesigned based on customer feedback or because of problems the developers and engineers may find during testing.

Identify a Problem

Often, new technology is designed to meet a specific need or to solve a problem. For example, an inventor might develop a wheelchair that can climb stairs to assist the disabled or a designer in the textile industry might develop flexible, lightweight, and breathable clothing to improve an athlete's performance. The goal for what the technology should achieve depends on the need or the problem to be solved.

Constraints, or restrictions, must also be considered. For example, a developer may be working with a limited amount of money or materials. There are social constraints as well. For example, an automobile must meet emissions standards so that air quality is protected.

---

1 Ask The chair below was designed to fold up. Why would a chair be designed to do this?

_____

_____

_____

_____

This chair was designed to fold up and use outdoors.

© Houghton Mifflin Harcourt Publishing Company • Image Credits: ©Burazin/Getty Images

Brainstorm Solutions

Developers must conduct research to fully understand the goal and the constraints involved in designing a product. Research might involve reading about previous related solutions that succeeded or failed, or testing and experimenting with specific aspects of an existing or proposed design. Someone developing a new bottle for soft drinks, for example, might first test how consumers react to different bottle shapes. A geneticist would research the traits of a plant before trying to modify it genetically.

Once the problem and goal are well defined, the project developer explores possible solutions. He or she may invite others to *brainstorm* solutions, a process in which people suggest as many creative ideas as they can.

2 Imagine Cool Chairs, Inc. needs suggestions for a classroom desk chair that is portable and can store materials when in use. Brainstorm with a classmate and write down some potential solutions.

_____

_____

_____

_____

Select a Solution

The developers consider the advantages and disadvantages of each solution. Solutions may involve tradeoffs, where one advantage is given up in order to gain a different advantage. For example, one design might look more appealing but be a little harder to use than another design.

Engineers design and try out different versions of a technology or a solution to determine whether it solves the problem and meets the goals and constraints. An engineer designing a bridge, for example, must make sure the bridge can support a minimum weight so that it can be used safely. Once the engineer chooses a solution, he or she makes a list of the materials necessary to create a prototype.

3 Plan What might the materials list for the chair shown below include?

_____

_____

_____

This chair changes shape and is fun to sit in.

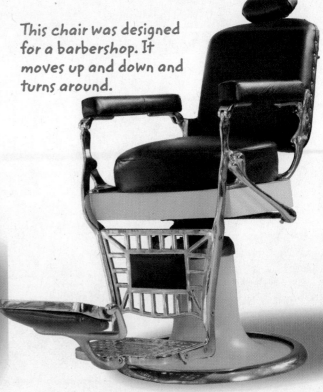

This chair was designed for a barbershop. It moves up and down and turns around.

Create a Prototype

Once engineers decide on a particular solution and develop the plans, they build a prototype. The prototype should meet the goals and constraints identified earlier in the process. The procedures and the design stages for the prototype should be clearly documented so that the prototype can be replicated by someone not involved in the initial design process.

Developers often need to share their successes, failures, and reasoning with others. They may submit details of the design process to technical journals, so that others can build on their work. They may also work with marketing and advertising experts to explain and promote the product to customers or to inform the public through news releases and advertisements.

4 Create Draw a prototype of the classroom desk chair that you plan to submit to Cool Chairs, Inc. Be sure to provide labels if necessary.

Redesign to Improve

During the testing process, engineers may encounter unexpected problems with their design. For instance, a toy designer may discover that a small part on a new toy can break off, creating a choking hazard for young children. Developers troubleshoot, or find the sources of problems, and fix them. Often, troubleshooting involves redesigning parts of the technology.

5 Improve How might you redesign the chair below to make it more student-friendly?

☐ Color _____

_____

☐ Materials _____

_____

☐ _____

_____

☐ _____

_____

This chair has a unique design.

Documenting the Design Process

Some of the objects you use every day can be redesigned to be more efficient or be improved in some way. Perhaps a new system or technique can be designed to solve a particular problem. When you redesign an existing object or design a new one, follow the steps below to document your design process.

Identify a Problem

What is the goal that the solution must achieve?

_____
_____
_____
_____

What are the constraints?

_____
_____
_____
_____

Brainstorm Solutions

In a group, or on your own, write down on a separate sheet of paper as many creative ideas for a solution as you can. Consider every idea, even those that seem strange or unrealistic.

Select a Solution

Write down the solution you think will best address the need and meet the goal you identified earlier.

_____
_____
_____

Make a list of materials you will need to develop your prototype.

_____
_____
_____
_____

Create a Prototype

In the space below, describe the prototype. Your description may be a drawing or a flowchart. Provide labels or steps where necessary.

How will you test your prototype?

_____

_____

What data will you collect in order to evaluate the design of the prototype?

_____

_____

How will you organize your data and document your procedures so that the prototype can be replicated?

_____

_____

Use the plan you have outlined above to create the prototype, test the prototype, organize the data, and communicate the results.

Redesign to Improve

How well did the solution meet the goal?

_____

_____

_____

What changes could be made to improve the design?

_____

_____

_____

_____

Look It Up!

Reference Tables R2
Mineral Properties R2
Classification of Living Things R4
Aquatic Ecosystems and Land Biomes R6
Periodic Table of the Elements R8

Reading and Study Skills R10
A How-To Manual for Active Reading R10
Using Graphic Organizers to Take Notes R12
Using Vocabulary Strategies R16

Science Skills R18
Safety in the Lab R18
Designing an Experiment R20
Using a Microscope R25
Measuring Accurately R26
Using the Metric System and SI Units R29

Math Refresher R31
Performing Calculations R31
Making and Interpreting Graphs R36

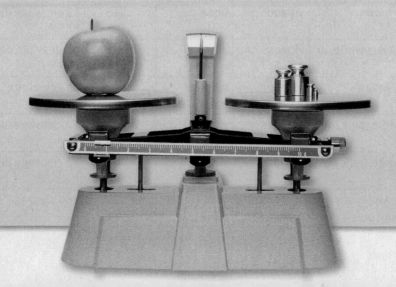

Reference Tables

Mineral Properties

Here are five steps to take in mineral identification:

1 Determine the color of the mineral. Is it light-colored, dark-colored, or a specific color?

2 Determine the luster of the mineral. Is it metallic or non-metallic?

3 Determine the color of any powder left by its streak.

4 Determine the hardness of your mineral. Is it soft, hard, or very hard? Using a glass plate, see if the mineral scratches it.

5 Determine whether your sample has cleavage or any special properties.

TERMS TO KNOW	DEFINITION
adamantine	a non-metallic luster like that of a diamond
cleavage	how a mineral breaks when subject to stress on a particular plane
luster	the state or quality of shining by reflecting light
streak	the color of a mineral when it is powdered
submetallic	between metallic and nonmetallic in luster
vitreous	glass-like type of luster

Silicate Minerals					
Mineral	Color	Luster	Streak	Hardness	Cleavage and Special Properties
Beryl	deep green, pink, white, bluish green, or yellow	vitreous	white	7.5–8	1 cleavage direction; some varieties fluoresce in ultraviolet light
Chlorite	green	vitreous to pearly	pale green	2–2.5	1 cleavage direction
Garnet	green, red, brown, black	vitreous	white	6.5–7.5	no cleavage
Hornblende	dark green, brown, or black	vitreous	none	5–6	2 cleavage directions
Muscovite	colorless, silvery white, or brown	vitreous or pearly	white	2–2.5	1 cleavage direction
Olivine	olive green, yellow	vitreous	white or none	6.5–7	no cleavage
Orthoclase	colorless, white, pink, or other colors	vitreous	white or none	6	2 cleavage directions
Plagioclase	colorless, white, yellow, pink, green	vitreous	white	6	2 cleavage directions
Quartz	colorless or white; any color when not pure	vitreous or waxy	white or none	7	no cleavage

Nonsilicate Minerals					
Mineral	**Color**	**Luster**	**Streak**	**Hardness**	**Cleavage and Special Properties**
Native Elements					
Copper	copper-red	metallic	copper-red	2.5–3	no cleavage
Diamond	pale yellow or colorless	adamantine	none	10	4 cleavage directions
Graphite	black to gray	submetallic	black	1–2	1 cleavage direction
Carbonates					
Aragonite	colorless, white, or pale yellow	vitreous	white	3.5–4	2 cleavage directions; reacts with hydrochloric acid
Calcite	colorless or white to tan	vitreous	white	3	3 cleavage directions; reacts with weak acid; double refraction
Halides					
Fluorite	light green, yellow, purple, bluish green, or other colors	vitreous	none	4	4 cleavage directions; some varieties fluoresce
Halite	white	vitreous	white	2.0–2.5	3 cleavage directions
Oxides					
Hematite	reddish brown to black	metallic to earthy	dark red to red-brown	5.6–6.5	no cleavage; magnetic when heated
Magnetite	iron-black	metallic	black	5.5–6.5	no cleavage; magnetic
Sulfates					
Anhydrite	colorless, bluish, or violet	vitreous to pearly	white	3–3.5	3 cleavage directions
Gypsum	white, pink, gray, or colorless	vitreous, pearly, or silky	white	2.0	3 cleavage directions
Sulfides					
Galena	lead-gray	metallic	lead-gray to black	2.5–2.8	3 cleavage directions
Pyrite	brassy yellow	metallic	greenish, brownish, or black	6–6.5	no cleavage

Reference Tables

Classification of Living Things

Domains and Kingdoms

All organisms belong to one of three domains: Domain Archaea, Domain Bacteria, or Domain Eukarya. Some of the groups within these domains are shown below. (Remember that genus names are italicized.)

Domain Archaea

The organisms in this domain are single-celled prokaryotes, many of which live in extreme environments.

Archaea		
Group	**Example**	**Characteristics**
Methanogens	*Methanococcus*	produce methane gas; can't live in oxygen
Thermophiles	*Sulpholobus*	require sulphur; can't live in oxygen
Halophiles	*Halococcus*	live in very salty environments; most can live in oxygen

Domain Bacteria

Organisms in this domain are single-celled prokaryotes and are found in almost every environment on Earth.

Bacteria		
Group	**Example**	**Characteristics**
Bacilli	*Escherichia*	rod shaped; some fix nitrogen; some cause disease
Cocci	*Streptococcus*	spherical shaped; cause diseases; can form spores
Spirilla	*Treponema*	spiral shaped; cause diseases, such as syphilis

Domain Eukarya

Organisms in this domain are single-celled or multicellular eukaryotes.

Kingdom Protista Many protists resemble fungi, plants, or animals, but are smaller and simpler in structure. Most are single-celled.

Protists		
Group	**Example**	**Characteristics**
Sarcodines	*Amoeba*	radiolarians; single-celled consumers
Ciliates	*Paramecium*	single-celled consumers
Flagellates	*Trypanosoma*	single-celled parasites
Sporozoans	*Plasmodium*	single-celled parasites
Euglenas	*Euglena*	single celled; photosynthesize
Diatoms	*Pinnularia*	most are single celled; photosynthesize
Dinoflagellates	*Gymnodinium*	single celled; some photosynthesize
Algae	*Volvox*	single celled or multicellular; photosynthesize
Slime molds	*Physarum*	single celled or multicellular; consumers or decomposers
Water molds	powdery mildew	single celled or multicellular; parasites or decomposers

Kingdom Fungi Most fungi are multicellular. Their cells have thick cell walls. Fungi absorb food from their environment.

Fungi		
Group	**Examples**	**Characteristics**
Threadlike fungi	bread mold	spherical; decomposers
Sac fungi	yeast; morels	saclike; parasites and decomposers
Club fungi	mushrooms; rusts; smuts	club shaped; parasites and decomposers
Lichens	British soldier	symbiotic with algae

Kingdom Plantae Plants are multicellular and have cell walls made of cellulose. Plants make their own food through photosynthesis. Plants are classified into divisions instead of phyla.

Plants		
Group	**Examples**	**Characteristics**
Bryophytes	mosses; liverworts	no vascular tissue; reproduce by spores
Club mosses	*Lycopodium*; ground pine	grow in wooded areas; reproduce by spores
Horsetails	rushes	grow in wetland areas; reproduce by spores
Ferns	spleenworts; sensitive fern	large leaves called fronds; reproduce by spores
Conifers	pines; spruces; firs	needlelike leaves; reproduce by seeds made in cones
Cycads	*Zamia*	slow-growing; reproduce by seeds made in large cones
Gnetophytes	*Welwitschia*	only three living families; reproduce by seeds
Ginkgoes	*Ginkgo*	only one living species; reproduce by seeds
Angiosperms	all flowering plants	reproduce by seeds made in flowers; fruit

Kingdom Animalia Animals are multicellular. Their cells do not have cell walls. Most animals have specialized tissues and complex organ systems. Animals get food by eating other organisms.

Animals		
Group	**Examples**	**Characteristics**
Sponges	glass sponges	no symmetry or segmentation; aquatic
Cnidarians	jellyfish; coral	radial symmetry; aquatic
Flatworms	planaria; tapeworms; flukes	bilateral symmetry; organ systems
Roundworms	*Trichina*; hookworms	bilateral symmetry; organ systems
Annelids	earthworms; leeches	bilateral symmetry; organ systems
Mollusks	snails; octopuses	bilateral symmetry; organ systems
Echinoderms	sea stars; sand dollars	radial symmetry; organ systems
Arthropods	insects; spiders; lobsters	bilateral symmetry; organ systems
Chordates	fish; amphibians; reptiles; birds; mammals	bilateral symmetry; complex organ systems

Reference Tables

Aquatic Ecosystems and Land Biomes

Aquatic Ecosystems

An ecosystem located in a body of water is called an *aquatic ecosystem*. Aquatic ecosystems are organized into freshwater ecosystems, wetlands, estuaries, and marine ecosystems.

Freshwater Ecosystem

Freshwater ecosystems are located in bodies of fresh water, such as lakes, ponds, and rivers.

Wetland

Wetlands are saturated by water for at least part of the year. Water-loving plants dominate wetlands.

Estuary

An estuary is an area where fresh water from a river mixes with salt water from an ocean.

Marine Ecosystem

Marine ecosystems, such as this coral reef, are found in the salty waters of the oceans.

Land Biomes

A *biome* is a large region characterized by a specific type of climate and certain types of plant and animal communities.

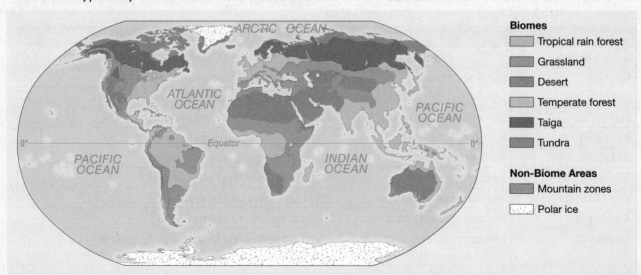

Biomes
- Tropical rain forest
- Grassland
- Desert
- Temperate forest
- Taiga
- Tundra

Non-Biome Areas
- Mountain zones
- Polar ice

Tropical

Tropical rain forest
- Warm temperatures and abundant rainfall occur all year.
- Vegetation includes lush thick forests.
- Animals that live within the thick cover of the upper-most branches of rain forest trees use loud vocalizations to defend their territory and attract mates.

Grassland

Tropical grassland
- Temperatures are warm throughout the year, with definite dry and rainy seasons.
- Vegetation includes tall grasses with scattered trees and shrubs.
- Hoofed animals, such as gazelles and other herbivores, are common in this biome.

Temperate grassland
- This biome is dry and warm during the summer; most precipitation falls as snow during the winter.
- Vegetation includes short or tall grasses, depending on the amount of precipitation.
- Many animals live underground to avoid the dry, windy conditions.

Desert

Desert
- This biome has a very dry climate.
- Plants, such as cacti, are either able to store water or have deep root systems.
- Many animals are nocternal; they limit their activies during the day to avoid exposure to the sun and heat.

Temperate

Temperate deciduous forest
- Temperatures are hot in the summer and cold in the winter; precipitation is spaced evenly over the year.
- Deciduous trees lose their leaves in the winter.
- During the winter, animals must adjust to the cold temperatures and less cover to hide themselves from predators.

Temperate rain forest
- This biome has one long wet season and a relatively dry summer.
- Evergreen conifers, which keep their leaves (needles) year-round, dominate this biome.
- Some animal species remain active during the winter; others migrate to warmer climates or hibernate.

Taiga

Taiga
- This biome has long, cold winters and short, warm summers.
- Coniferous trees dominate this biome.
- Mammals have heavy fur coats to withstand the cold winters.

Tundra

Tundra
- Subzero temperatures are common during the long winter, and there is little precipitation.
- The ground is permanently frozen; only mosses and other low-lying plants survive.
- Animal diversity is low in this biome.

Reference Tables

Periodic Table of the Elements

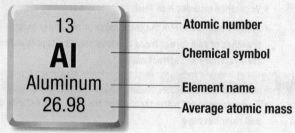

13
Al
Aluminum
26.98

— Atomic number
— Chemical symbol
— Element name
— Average atomic mass

Background

Metals
Metalloids
Nonmetals

Chemical Symbol

Solid **Na**
Liquid **Hg**
Gas ⓞ

113
Uut
Ununtrium
(284)

Unconfirmed Elements

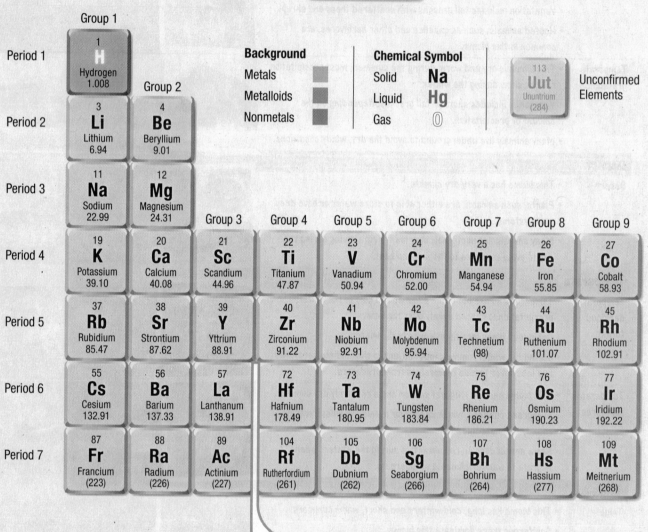

Group 1	Group 2	Group 3	Group 4	Group 5	Group 6	Group 7	Group 8	Group 9
Period 1 1 **H** Hydrogen 1.008								
Period 2 3 **Li** Lithium 6.94	4 **Be** Beryllium 9.01							
Period 3 11 **Na** Sodium 22.99	12 **Mg** Magnesium 24.31							
Period 4 19 **K** Potassium 39.10	20 **Ca** Calcium 40.08	21 **Sc** Scandium 44.96	22 **Ti** Titanium 47.87	23 **V** Vanadium 50.94	24 **Cr** Chromium 52.00	25 **Mn** Manganese 54.94	26 **Fe** Iron 55.85	27 **Co** Cobalt 58.93
Period 5 37 **Rb** Rubidium 85.47	38 **Sr** Strontium 87.62	39 **Y** Yttrium 88.91	40 **Zr** Zirconium 91.22	41 **Nb** Niobium 92.91	42 **Mo** Molybdenum 95.94	43 **Tc** Technetium (98)	44 **Ru** Ruthenium 101.07	45 **Rh** Rhodium 102.91
Period 6 55 **Cs** Cesium 132.91	56 **Ba** Barium 137.33	57 **La** Lanthanum 138.91	72 **Hf** Hafnium 178.49	73 **Ta** Tantalum 180.95	74 **W** Tungsten 183.84	75 **Re** Rhenium 186.21	76 **Os** Osmium 190.23	77 **Ir** Iridium 192.22
Period 7 87 **Fr** Francium (223)	88 **Ra** Radium (226)	89 **Ac** Actinium (227)	104 **Rf** Rutherfordium (261)	105 **Db** Dubnium (262)	106 **Sg** Seaborgium (266)	107 **Bh** Bohrium (264)	108 **Hs** Hassium (277)	109 **Mt** Meitnerium (268)

Lanthanides 58 **Ce** Cerium 140.12	59 **Pr** Praseodymium 140.91	60 **Nd** Neodymium 144.24	61 **Pm** Promethium (145)	62 **Sm** Samarium 150.36
Actinides 90 **Th** Thorium 232.04	91 **Pa** Protactinium 231.04	92 **U** Uranium 238.03	93 **Np** Neptunium (237)	94 **Pu** Plutonium (244)

Group 18

2
He
Helium
4.003

Group 13	Group 14	Group 15	Group 16	Group 17	
5	6	7	8	9	10
B	**C**	**N**	**O**	**F**	**Ne**
Boron	Carbon	Nitrogen	Oxygen	Fluorine	Neon
10.81	12.01	14.01	16.00	19.00	20.18
13	14	15	16	17	18
Al	**Si**	**P**	**S**	**Cl**	**Ar**
Aluminum	Silicon	Phosphorus	Sulfur	Chlorine	Argon
26.98	28.09	30.97	32.07	35.45	39.95

Group 10	Group 11	Group 12	Group 13	Group 14	Group 15	Group 16	Group 17	Group 18
28	29	30	31	32	33	34	35	36
Ni	**Cu**	**Zn**	**Ga**	**Ge**	**As**	**Se**	**Br**	**Kr**
Nickel	Copper	Zinc	Gallium	Germanium	Arsenic	Selenium	Bromine	Krypton
58.69	63.55	65.41	69.72	72.64	74.92	78.96	79.90	83.80
46	47	48	49	50	51	52	53	54
Pd	**Ag**	**Cd**	**In**	**Sn**	**Sb**	**Te**	**I**	**Xe**
Palladium	Silver	Cadmium	Indium	Tin	Antimony	Tellurium	Iodine	Xenon
106.42	107.87	112.41	114.82	118.71	121.76	127.6	126.9	131.29
78	79	80	81	82	83	84	85	86
Pt	**Au**	**Hg**	**Tl**	**Pb**	**Bi**	**Po**	**At**	**Rn**
Platinum	Gold	Mercury	Thallium	Lead	Bismuth	Polonium	Astatine	Radon
195.08	196.97	200.59	204.38	207.2	208.98	(209)	(210)	(222)
110	111	112	113	114	115	116		118
Ds	**Rg**	**Uub**	**Uut**	**Uuq**	**Uup**	**Uuh**		**Uuo**
Darmstadtium	Roentgenium	Ununbium	Ununtrium	Ununquadium	Ununpentium	Ununhexium		Ununoctium
(271)	(272)	(285)	(284)	(289)	(288)	(292)		(294)

63	64	65	66	67	68	69	70	71
Eu	**Gd**	**Tb**	**Dy**	**Ho**	**Er**	**Tm**	**Yb**	**Lu**
Europium	Gadolinium	Terbium	Dysprosium	Holmium	Erbium	Thulium	Ytterbium	Lutetium
151.96	157.25	158.93	162.5	164.93	167.26	168.93	173.04	174.97
95	96	97	98	99	100	101	102	103
Am	**Cm**	**Bk**	**Cf**	**Es**	**Fm**	**Md**	**No**	**Lr**
Americium	Curium	Berkelium	Californium	Einsteinium	Fermium	Mendelevium	Nobelium	Lawrencium
(243)	(247)	(247)	(251)	(252)	(257)	(258)	(259)	(262)

Reading and Study Skills

A How-To Manual for Active Reading

This book belongs to you, and you are invited to write in it. In fact, the book won't be complete until you do. Sometimes you'll answer a question or follow directions to mark up the text. Other times you'll write down your own thoughts. And when you're done reading and writing in the book, the book will be ready to help you review what you learned and prepare for tests.

Active Reading Annotations

Before you read, you'll often come upon an Active Reading prompt that asks you to underline certain words or number the steps in a process. Here's an example.

Active Reading

12 Identify In this paragraph, number the sequence of sentences that describe replication.

Marking the text this way is called **annotating,** and your marks are called **annotations.** Annotating the text can help you identify important concepts while you read.

There are other ways that you can annotate the text. You can draw an asterisk (*) by vocabulary terms, mark unfamiliar or confusing terms and information with a question mark (?), and mark main ideas with a double underline. And you can even invent your own marks to annotate the text!

Other Annotating Opportunities

Keep your pencil, pen, or highlighter nearby as you read, so you can make a note or highlight an important point at any time. Here are a few ideas to get you started.

- Notice the headings in red and blue. The blue headings are questions that point to the main idea of what you're reading. The red headings are answers to the questions in the blue ones. Together these headings outline the content of the lesson. After reading a lesson, you could write your own answers to the questions.

- Notice the bold-faced words that are highlighted in yellow. They are highlighted so that you can easily find them again on the page where they are defined. As you read or as you review, challenge yourself to write your own sentence using the bold-faced term.

- Make a note in the margin at any time. You might
  - Ask a "What if" question
  - Comment on what you read
  - Make a connection to something you read elsewhere
  - Make a logical conclusion from the text

Use your own language and abbreviations. Invent a code, such as using circles and boxes around words to remind you of their importance or relation to each other. Your annotations will help you remember your questions for class discussions, and when you go back to the lesson later, you may be able to fill in what you didn't understand the first time you read it. Like a scientist in the field or in a lab, you will be recording your questions and observations for analysis later.

Active Reading Questions

After you read, you'll often come upon Active Reading questions that ask you to think about what you've just read. You'll write your answer underneath the question. Here's an example.

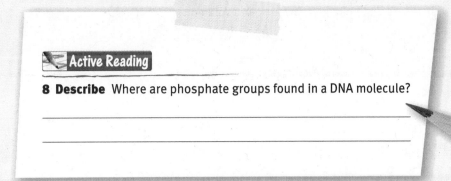

Active Reading

8 Describe Where are phosphate groups found in a DNA molecule?

_____

_____

This type of question helps you sum up what you've just read and pull out the most important ideas from the passage. In this case the question asks you to **describe** the structure of a DNA molecule that you have just read about. Other times you may be asked to do such things as **apply** a concept, **compare** two concepts, **summarize** a process, or **identify a cause-and-effect** relationship. You'll be strengthening those critical thinking skills that you'll use often in learning about science.

Reading and Study Skills

Using Graphic Organizers to Take Notes

Graphic organizers help you remember information as you read it for the first time and as you study it later. There are dozens of graphic organizers to choose from, so the first trick is to choose the one that's best suited to your purpose. Following are some graphic organizers to use for different purposes.

To remember lots of information	To relate a central idea to subordinate details	To describe a process	To make a comparison
• Arrange data in a Content Frame • Use Combination Notes to describe a concept in words and pictures	• Show relationships with a Mind Map or a Main Idea Web • Sum up relationships among many things with a Concept Map	• Use a Process Diagram to explain a procedure • Show a chain of events and results in a Cause-and-Effect Chart	• Compare two or more closely related things in a Venn Diagram

Content Frame

1 Make a four-column chart.

2 Fill the first column with categories (e.g., snail, ant, earthworm) and the first row with descriptive information (e.g., group, characteristic, appearance).

3 Fill the chart with details that belong in each row and column.

4 When you finish, you'll have a study aid that helps you compare one category to another.

Invertebrates

NAME	GROUP	CHARACTERISTICS	DRAWING
snail	mollusks	mangle	
ant	arthropods	six legs, exoskeleton	
earthworm	segmented worms	segmented body, circulatory and digestive systems	
heartworm	roundworms	digestive system	
sea star	echinoderms	spiny skin, tube feet	
jellyfish	cnidarians	stinging cells	

Combination Notes

1 Make a two-column chart.

2 Write descriptive words and definitions in the first column.

3 Draw a simple sketch that helps you remember the meaning of the term in the second column.

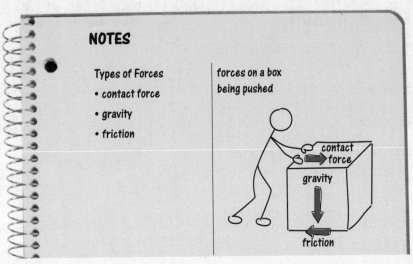

Mind Map

1 Draw an oval, and inside it write a topic to analyze.

2 Draw two or more arms extending from the oval. Each arm represents a main idea about the topic.

3 Draw lines from the arms on which to write details about each of the main ideas.

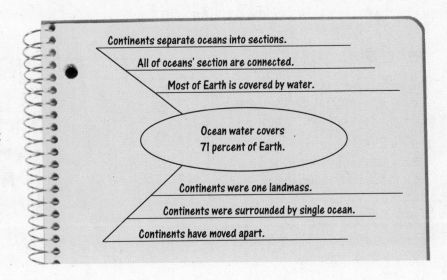

Main Idea Web

1 Make a box and write a concept you want to remember inside it.

2 Draw boxes around the central box, and label each one with a category of information about the concept (e.g., definition, formula, descriptive details)

3 Fill in the boxes with relevant details as you read.

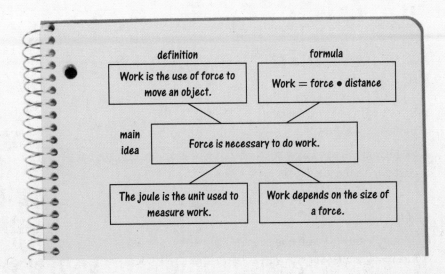

Reading and Study Skills

Concept Map

1 Draw a large oval, and inside it write a major concept.

2 Draw an arrow from the concept to a smaller oval, in which you write a related concept.

3 On the arrow, write a verb that connects the two concepts.

4 Continue in this way, adding ovals and arrows in a branching structure, until you have explained as much as you can about the main concept.

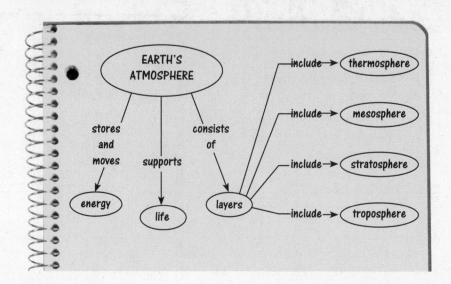

Venn Diagram

1 Draw two overlapping circles or ovals—one for each topic you are comparing—and label each one.

2 In the part of each circle that does not overlap with the other, list the characteristics that are unique to each topic.

3 In the space where the two circles overlap, list the characteristics that the two topics have in common.

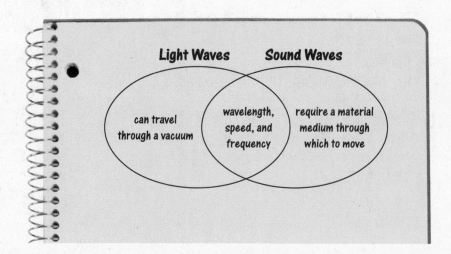

Cause-and-Effect Chart

1 Draw two boxes and connect them with an arrow.

2 In the first box, write the first event in a series (a cause).

3 In the second box, write a result of the cause (the effect).

4 Add more boxes when one event has many effects, or vice versa.

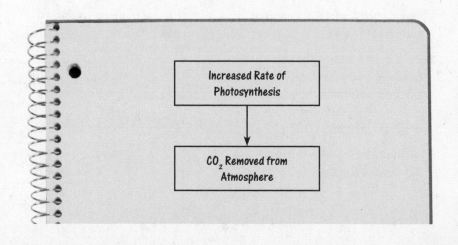

Process Diagram

A process can be a never-ending cycle. As you can see in this technology design process, engineers may backtrack and repeat steps, they may skip steps entirely, or they may repeat the entire process before a useable design is achieved.

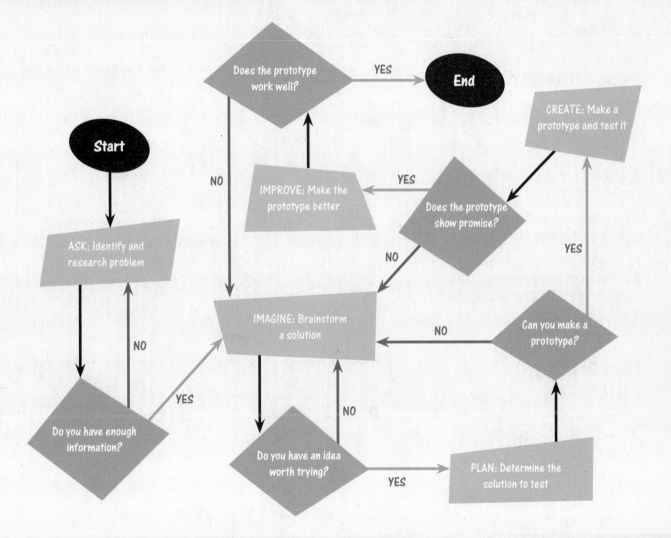

Reading and Study Skills

Using Vocabulary Strategies

Important science terms are highlighted where they are first defined in this book. One way to remember these terms is to take notes and make sketches when you come to them. Use the strategies on this page and the next for this purpose. You will also find a formal definition of each science term in the Glossary at the end of the book.

Description Wheel

1 Draw a small circle.

2 Write a vocabulary term inside the circle.

3 Draw several arms extending from the circle.

4 On the arms, write words and phrases that describe the term.

5 If you choose, add sketches that help you visualize the descriptive details or the concept as a whole.

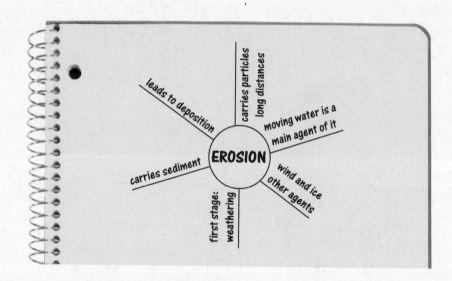

Four Square

1 Draw a small oval and write a vocabulary term inside it.

2 Draw a large rectangle around the oval, and divide the rectangle into four smaller squares.

3 Label the smaller squares with categories of information about the term, such as: definition, characteristics, examples, non-examples, appearance, and root words.

4 Fill the squares with descriptive words and drawings that will help you remember the overall meaning of the term and its essential details.

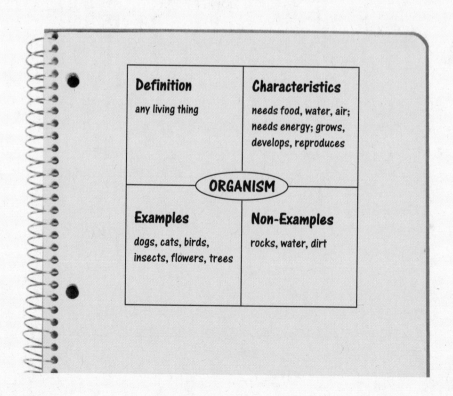

Frame Game

1 Draw a small rectangle, and write a vocabulary term inside it.

2 Draw a larger rectangle around the smaller one. Connect the corners of the larger rectangle to the corners of the smaller one, creating four spaces that frame the word.

3 In each of the four parts of the frame, draw or write details that help define the term. Consider including a definition, essential characteristics, an equation, examples, and a sentence using the term.

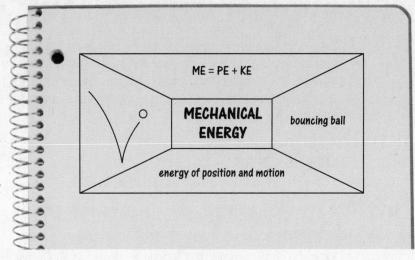

Magnet Word

1 Draw horseshoe magnet, and write a vocabulary term inside it.

2 Add lines that extend from the sides of the magnet.

3 Brainstorm words and phrases that come to mind when you think about the term.

4 On the lines, write the words and phrases that describe something essential about the term.

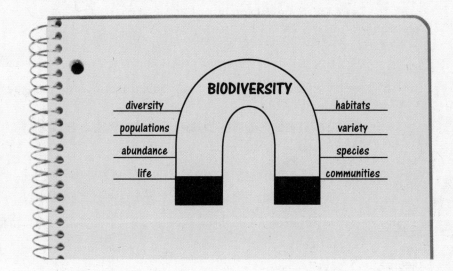

Word Triangle

1 Draw a triangle, and add lines to divide it into three parts.

2 Write a term and its definition in the bottom section of the triangle.

3 In the middle section, write a sentence in which the term is used correctly.

4 In the top section, draw a small picture to illustrate the term.

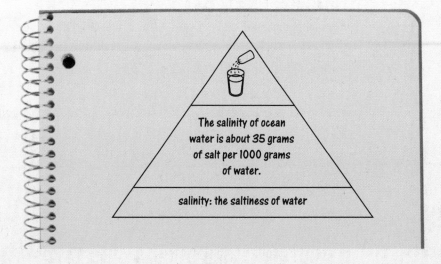

Science Skills

Safety in the Lab

Before you begin work in the laboratory, read these safety rules twice. Before starting a lab activity, read all directions and make sure that you understand them. Do not begin until your teacher has told you to start. If you or another student are injured in any way, tell your teacher immediately.

Dress Code

Eye Protection

Hand Protection

Clothing Protection

- Wear safety goggles at all times in the lab as directed.
- If chemicals get into your eyes, flush your eyes immediately.
- Do not wear contact lenses in the lab.
- Do not look directly at the sun or any intense light source or laser.
- Do not cut an object while holding the object in your hand.
- Wear appropriate protective gloves as directed.
- Wear an apron or lab coat at all times in the lab as directed.
- Tie back long hair, secure loose clothing, and remove loose jewelry.
- Do not wear open-toed shoes, sandals, or canvas shoes in the lab.

Glassware and Sharp Object Safety

Glassware Safety

Sharp Objects Safety

- Do not use chipped or cracked glassware.
- Use heat-resistant glassware for heating or storing hot materials.
- Notify your teacher immediately if a piece of glass breaks.
- Use extreme care when handling all sharp and pointed instruments.
- Cut objects on a suitable surface, always in a direction away from your body.

Chemical Safety

Chemical Safety

- If a chemical gets on your skin, on your clothing, or in your eyes, rinse it immediately (shower, faucet or eyewash fountain) and alert your teacher.
- Do not clean up spilled chemicals unless your teacher directs you to do so.
- Do not inhale any gas or vapor unless directed to do so by your teacher.
- Handle materials that emit vapors or gases in a well-ventilated area.

Electrical Safety

- Do not use equipment with frayed electrical cords or loose plugs.
- Do not use electrical equipment near water or when clothing or hands are wet.
- Hold the plug housing when you plug in or unplug equipment.

Heating and Fire Safety

- Be aware of any source of flames, sparks, or heat (such as flames, heating coils, or hot plates) before working with any flammable substances.
- Know the location of lab fire extinguishers and fire-safety blankets.
- Know your school's fire-evacuation routes.
- If your clothing catches on fire, walk to the lab shower to put out the fire.
- Never leave a hot plate unattended while it is turned on or while it is cooling.
- Use tongs or appropriate insulated holders when handling heated objects.
- Allow all equipment to cool before storing it.

Wafting

Plant and Animal Safety

- Do not eat any part of a plant.
- Do not pick any wild plants unless your teacher instructs you to do so.

- Handle animals only as your teacher directs.
- Treat animals carefully and respectfully.
- Wash your hands thoroughly after handling any plant or animal.

Cleanup

- Clean all work surfaces and protective equipment as directed by your teacher.
- Dispose of hazardous materials or sharp objects only as directed by your teacher.

- Keep your hands away from your face while you are working on any activity.
- Wash your hands thoroughly before you leave the lab or after any activity.

Electrical Safety

Heating Safety

Plant Safety

Animal Safety

Proper Waste Disposal

Hygienic Care

Science Skills

Designing an Experiment

An **experiment** is an organized procedure to study something under controlled conditions. Use the following steps of the scientific method when designing or conducting an experiment.

1 Identify a Research Problem

Every day you make **observations** by using your senses to gather information. Careful observations lead to good **questions,** and good questions can lead you to a purpose, or problem, for an experiment.

Imagine, for example, that you pass a pond every day on your way to school, and you notice green scum beginning to form on top of it. You wonder what it is and why it seems to be growing. You list your questions, and then you do a little preliminary research to find out what is already known.

You talk to others about your observations, learn that the scum is algae, and look for relvant information in books, journals, and online. You are especially interested in the data and conclusions from earlier experiments. Finally, you write the problem that you want to investigate. Your notes might look like these.

Area of Interest	Research Questions	Research Problem
Algae growth in lakes and ponds	• How do algae grow? • How do people measure algae? • What kind of fertilizer would affect the growth of algae? • Can fertilizer and algae be used safely in a lab? How?	How does fertilizer affect the presence of algae in a pond?

2 Make a Prediction

A **prediction** is a statement of what you expect will happen in your experiment. Before making a prediction, you need to decide in a general way what you will do in your procedure. You may state your prediction in an if-then format.

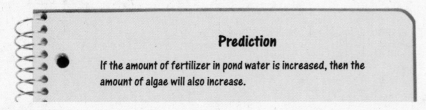

Prediction

If the amount of fertilizer in pond water is increased, then the amount of algae will also increase.

3 Form a Hypothesis

Many experiments are designed to test a hypothesis. A **hypothesis** is a tentative explanation for an expected result. You have predicted that additional fertilizer will cause additional algae growth in pond water; your hypothesis goes beyond your prediction to explain why fertilizer has that effect.

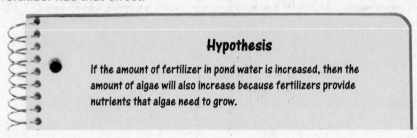

Hypothesis

If the amount of fertilizer in pond water is increased, then the amount of algae will also increase because fertilizers provide nutrients that algae need to grow.

4 Identify Variables to Test the Hypothesis

The next step is to design an experiment to test the hypothesis. The experiment may or may not support the hypothesis. Either way, the information that results from the experiment may be useful for future investigations.

Experimental Group and Control Group

An experiment to determine how two factors are related has a control group and an experimental group. The two groups are the same, except that the experimenter changes a single factor in the experimental group and does not change it in the control group.

Experimental Group: two containers of pond water with one drop of fertilizer solution added to each

Control Group: two containers of the same pond water sampled at the same time but with no fertilizer solution added

Variables and Constants

In a controlled experiment, a **variable** is any factor that can change. **Constants** are all of the variables that are kept the same in both the experimental group and the control group.

The **independent variable** is the factor that is manipulated or changed in order to test the effect of the change on another variable. The **dependent variable** is the factor that the experimenter measures to gather data about the effect.

Independent Variable	Dependent Variable	Constants
Amount of fertilizer in pond water	Amount of algae that grow	• Where and when the pond water is obtained • The type of container used • Light and temperature conditions where the water is stored

Science Skills

5 Write a Procedure

Write each step of your procedure. Start each step with a verb, or action word, and keep the steps short. Your procedure should be clear enough for someone else to use as instructions for repeating your experiment.

Procedure

1. Put on your gloves. Use the large container to obtain a sample of pond water.

2. Divide the water sample equally among the four smaller containers.

3. Use the eyedropper to add one drop of fertilizer solution to two of the containers.

4. Use the masking tape and the marker to label the containers with your initials, the date, and the identifiers "Jar 1 with Fertilizer," "Jar 2 with Fertilizer," "Jar 1 without Fertilizer," and "Jar 2 without Fertilizer."

5. Cover the containers with clear plastic wrap. Use the scissors to punch ten holes in each of the covers.

6. Place all four containers on a window ledge. Make sure that they all receive the same amount of light.

7. Observe the containers every day for one week.

8. Use the ruler to measure the diameter of the largest clump of algae in each container, and record your measurements daily.

6 Experiment and Collect Data

Once you have all of your materials and your procedure has been approved, you can begin to experiment and collect data. Record both quantitative data (measurements) and qualitative data (observations), as shown below.

Fertilizer and Algae Growth

Date and Time	Experimental Group		Control Group		Observations
	Jar 1 with Fertilizer (diameter of algae in mm)	Jar 2 with Fertilizer (diameter of algae in mm)	Jar 1 without Fertilizer (diameter of algae in mm)	Jar 2 without Fertilizer (diameter of algae in mm)	
5/3 4:00 P.M.	0	0	0	0	condensation in all containers
5/4 4:00 P.M.	0	3	0	0	tiny green blobs in jar 2 with fertilizer
5/5 4:15 P.M.	4	5	0	3	green blobs in jars 1 and 2 with fertilizer and jar 2 without fertilizer
5/6 4:00 P.M.	5	6	0	4	water light green in jar 2 with fertilizer
5/7 4:00 P.M.	8	10	0	6	water light green in jars 1 and 2 with fertilizer and jar 2 without fertilizer
5/8 3:30 P.M.	10	18	0	6	cover off jar 2 with fertilizer
5/9 3:30 P.M.	14	23	0	8	drew sketches of each container

Drawings of Samples Viewed Under Microscope on 5/9 at 100x

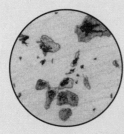
Jar 1 with Fertilizer

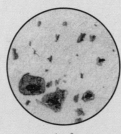
Jar 2 with Fertilizer

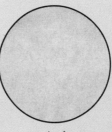
Jar 1 without Fertilizer

Jar 2 without Fertilizer

Science Skills

7 Analyze Data

After you have completed your experiments, made your observations, and collected your data, you must analyze all the information you have gathered. Tables, statistics, and graphs are often used in this step to organize and analyze the data.

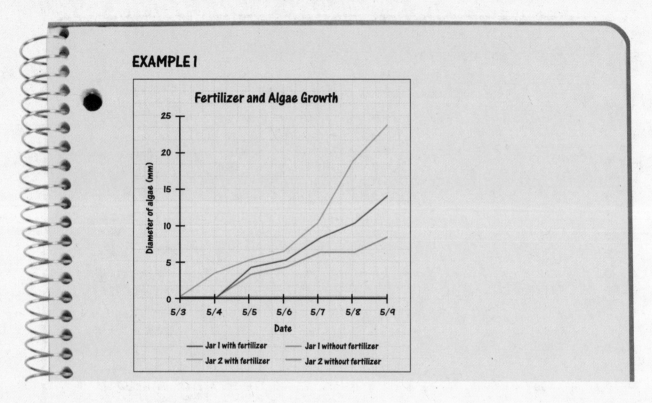

EXAMPLE 1

Fertilizer and Algae Growth

- Jar 1 with fertilizer
- Jar 1 without fertilizer
- Jar 2 with fertilizer
- Jar 2 without fertilizer

8 Make Conclusions

To draw conclusions from your experiment, first write your results. Then compare your results with your hypothesis. Do your results support your hypothesis?

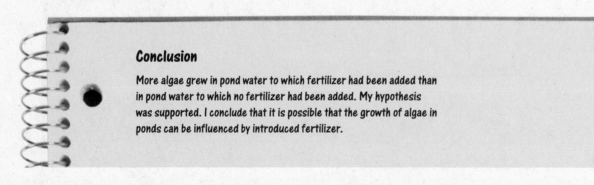

Conclusion

More algae grew in pond water to which fertilizer had been added than in pond water to which no fertilizer had been added. My hypothesis was supported. I conclude that it is possible that the growth of algae in ponds can be influenced by introduced fertilizer.

Using a Microscope

Scientists use microscopes to see very small objects that cannot easily be seen with the eye alone. A microscope magnifies the image of an object so that small details may be observed. A microscope that you may use can magnify an object 400 times—the object will appear 400 times larger than its actual size.

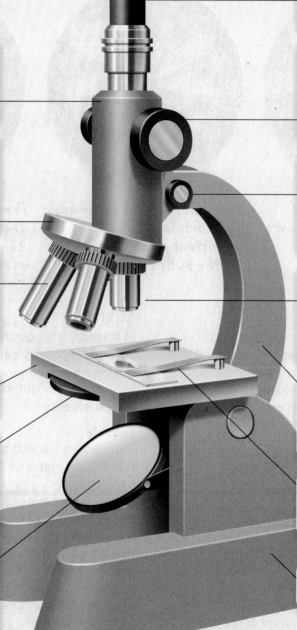

Eyepiece Objects are viewed through the eyepiece. The eyepiece contains a lens that commonly magnifies an image ten times.

Body The body separates the lens in the eyepiece from the objective lenses below.

Coarse Adjustment This knob is used to focus the image of an object when it is viewed through the low-power lens.

Nosepiece The nosepiece holds the objective lenses above the stage and rotates so that all lenses may be used.

Fine Adjustment This knob is used to focus the image of an object when it is viewed through the high-power lens.

High-Power Objective Lens This is the largest lens on the nosepiece. It magnifies an image approximately 40 times.

Low-Power Objective Lens This is the smallest lens on the nosepiece. It magnifies images about 10 times.

Stage The stage supports the object being viewed.

Arm The arm supports the body above the stage. Always carry a microscope by the arm and base.

Diaphragm The diaphragm is used to adjust the amount of light passing through the slide and into an objective lens.

Stage Clip The stage clip holds a slide in place on the stage.

Mirror or Light Source Some microscopes use light that is reflected through the stage by a mirror. Other microscopes have their own light sources.

Base The base supports the microscope.

Science Skills

Measuring Accurately

Precision and Accuracy

When you do a scientific investigation, it is important that your methods, observations, and data be both precise and accurate.

Low precision: The darts did not land in a consistent place on the dartboard.

Precision, but not accuracy: The darts landed in a consistent place, but did not hit the bull's eye.

Prescision and accuracy: The darts landed consistently on the bull's eye.

Precision

In science, *precision* is the exactness and consistency of measurements. For example, measurements made with a ruler that has both centimeter and milimeter markings would be more precise than measurements made with a ruler that has only centimeter markings. Another indicator of precision is the care taken to make sure that methods and observations are as exact and consistent as possible. Every time a particular experiment is done, the same procedure should be used. Precision is necessary because experiments are repeated several times and if the procedure changes, the results might change.

Example

Suppose you are measuring temperatures over a two-week period. Your precision will be greater if you measure each temperature at the same place, at the same time of day, and with the same thermometer than if you change any of these factors from one day to the next.

Accuracy

In science, it is possible to be precise but not accurate. *Accuracy* depends on the difference between a measurement and an actual value. The smaller the difference, the more accurate the measurement.

Example

Suppose you look at a stream and estimate that it is about 1 meter wide at a particular place. You decide to check your estimate by measuring the stream with a meter stick, and you determine that the stream is 1.32 meters wide. However, because it is difficult to measure the width of a stream with a meter stick, it turns out that your measurement was not very accurate. The stream is actually 1.14 meters wide. Therefore, even though your estimate of about 1 meter was less precise than your measurement, your estimate was actually more accurate.

Graduated Cylinders

How to Measure the Volume of a Liquid with a Graduated Cylinder

- Be sure that the graduated cylinder is on a flat surface so that your measurement will be accurate.

- When reading the scale on a graduated cylinder, be sure to have your eyes at the level of the surface of the liquid.

- The surface of the liquid will be curved in the graduated cylinder. Read the volume of the liquid at the bottom of the curve, or meniscus (muh-NIHS-kuhs).

- You can use a graduated cylinder to find the volume of a solid object by measuring the increase in a liquid's level after you add the object to the cylinder.

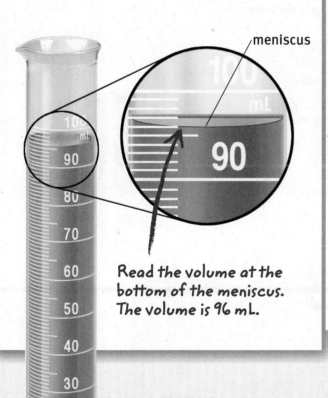

meniscus

Read the volume at the bottom of the meniscus. The volume is 96 mL.

Metric Rulers

How to Measure the Length of a Leaf with a Metric Ruler

1 Lay a ruler flat on top of the leaf so that the 1-centimeter mark lines up with one end. Make sure the ruler and the leaf do not move between the time you line them up and the time you take the measurement.

2 Look straight down on the ruler so that you can see exactly how the marks line up with the other end of the leaf.

3 Estimate the length by which the leaf extends beyond a marking. For example, the leaf below extends about halfway between the 4.2-centimeter and 4.3-centimeter marks, so the apparent measurement is about 4.25 centimeters.

4 Remember to subtract 1 centimeter from your apparent measurement, since you started at the 1-centimeter mark on the ruler and not at the end. The leaf is about 3.25 centimeters long (4.25 cm − 1 cm = 3.25 cm).

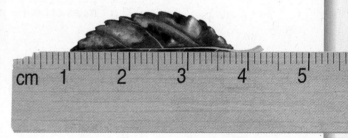

Triple Beam Balance

This balance has a pan and three beams with sliding masses, called riders. At one end of the beams is a pointer that indicates whether the mass on the pan is equal to the masses shown on the beams.

How to Measure the Mass of an Object

1 Make sure the balance is zeroed before measuring the mass of an object. The balance is zeroed if the pointer is at zero when nothing is on the pan and the riders are at their zero points. Use the adjustment knob at the base of the balance to zero it.

2 Place the object to be measured on the pan.

3 Move the riders one notch at a time away from the pan. Begin with the largest rider. If moving the largest rider one notch brings the pointer below zero, begin measuring the mass of the object with the next smaller rider.

4 Change the positions of the riders until they balance the mass on the pan and the pointer is at zero. Then add the readings from the three beams to determine the mass of the object.

300 g	position of largest rider
90 g	position of middle rider
+ 3 g	position of smallest rider
393 g	mass of beaker and water

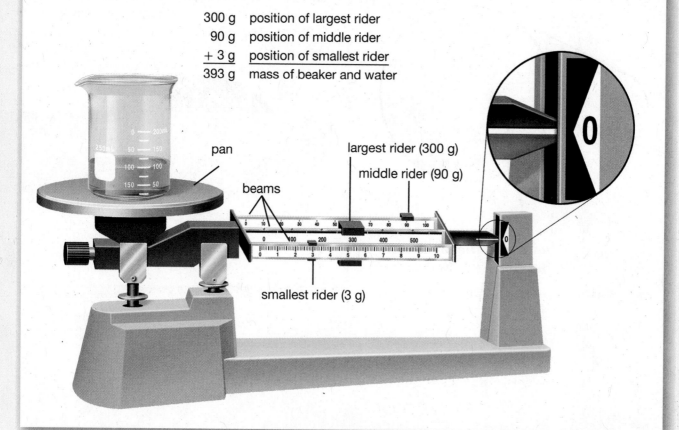

pan
beams
largest rider (300 g)
middle rider (90 g)
smallest rider (3 g)

Using the Metric System and SI Units

Scientists use International System (SI) units for measurements of distance, volume, mass, and temperature. The International System is based on powers of ten and the metric system of measurement.

Basic SI Units		
Quantity	Name	Symbol
length	meter	m
volume	liter	L
mass	gram	g
temperature	kelvin	K

SI Prefixes		
Prefix	Symbol	Power of 10
kilo-	k	1000
hecto-	h	100
deca-	da	10
deci-	d	0.1 or $\frac{1}{10}$
centi-	c	0.01 or $\frac{1}{100}$
milli-	m	0.001 or $\frac{1}{1000}$

Changing Metric Units

You can change from one unit to another in the metric system by multiplying or dividing by a power of 10.

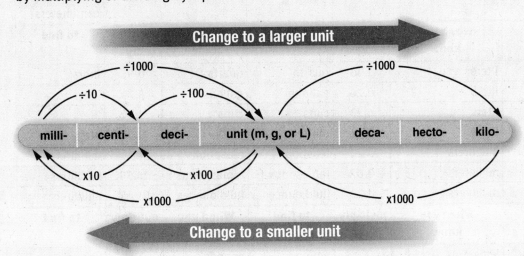

Change to a larger unit

÷1000   ÷10   ÷100   ÷1000

milli-   centi-   deci-   unit (m, g, or L)   deca-   hecto-   kilo-

x10   x100   x1000

Change to a smaller unit

Example

Change 0.64 liters to milliliters.
1 Decide whether to multiply or divide.
2 Select the power of 10.

Change to a smaller unit by multiplying

mL ◄——— x 1000 ——— L

0.64 x 1000 = 640.

ANSWER 0.64 L = 640 mL

Example

Change 23.6 grams to kilograms.
1 Decide whether to multiply or divide.
2 Select the power of 10.

Change to a larger unit by dividing

g ——— ÷ 1000 ——► kg

26.3 ÷ 1000 = 0.0263

ANSWER 23.6 g = 0.0236 kg

Science Skills

Converting Between SI and U.S. Customary Units

Use the chart below when you need to convert between SI units and U.S. customary units.

SI Unit	From SI to U.S. Customary			From U.S. Customary to SI		
Length	**When you know**	**multiply by**	**to find**	**When you know**	**multiply by**	**to find**
kilometer (km) = 1000 m	kilometers	0.62	miles	miles	1.61	kilometers
meter (m) = 100 cm	meters	3.28	feet	feet	0.3048	meters
centimeter (cm) = 10 mm	centimeters	0.39	inches	inches	2.54	centimeters
millimeter (mm) = 0.1 cm	millimeters	0.04	inches	inches	25.4	millimeters
Area	**When you know**	**multiply by**	**to find**	**When you know**	**multiply by**	**to find**
square kilometer (km²)	square kilometers	0.39	square miles	square miles	2.59	square kilometers
square meter (m²)	square meters	1.2	square yards	square yards	0.84	square meters
square centimeter (cm²)	square centimeters	0.155	square inches	square inches	6.45	square centimeters
Volume	**When you know**	**multiply by**	**to find**	**When you know**	**multiply by**	**to find**
liter (L) = 1000 mL	liters	1.06	quarts	quarts	0.95	liters
	liters	0.26	gallons	gallons	3.79	liters
	liters	4.23	cups	cups	0.24	liters
	liters	2.12	pints	pints	0.47	liters
milliliter (mL) = 0.001 L	milliliters	0.20	teaspoons	teaspoons	4.93	milliliters
	milliliters	0.07	tablespoons	tablespoons	14.79	milliliters
	milliliters	0.03	fluid ounces	fluid ounces	29.57	milliliters
Mass	**When you know**	**multiply by**	**to find**	**When you know**	**multiply by**	**to find**
kilogram (kg) = 1000 g	kilograms	2.2	pounds	pounds	0.45	kilograms
gram (g) = 1000 mg	grams	0.035	ounces	ounces	28.35	grams

Temperature Conversions

Even though the kelvin is the SI base unit of temperature, the degree Celsius will be the unit you use most often in your science studies. The formulas below show the relationships between temperatures in degrees Fahrenheit (°F), degrees Celsius (°C), and kelvins (K).

$$°C = \frac{5}{9} \ (°F - 32) \qquad °F = \frac{9}{5} \ °C + 32 \qquad K = °C + 273$$

Examples of Temperature Conversions		
Condition	**Degrees Celsius**	**Degrees Fahrenheit**
Freezing point of water	32	0
Cool day	10	50
Mild day	20	68
Warm day	30	86
Normal body temperature	37	98.6
Very hot day	40	104
Boiling point of water	100	212

Math Refresher

Performing Calculations

Science requires an understanding of many math concepts. The following pages will help you review some important math skills.

Mean

The mean is the sum of all values in a data set divided by the total number of values in the data set. The mean is also called the *average*.

Example

Find the mean of the following set of numbers: 5, 4, 7, and 8.

Step 1   Find the sum.

$$5 + 4 + 7 + 8 = 24$$

Step 1   Divide the sum by the number of numbers in your set. Because there are four numbers in this example, divide the sum by 4.

$$24 \div 4 = 6$$

Answer The average, or mean, is 6.

Median

The median of a data set is the middle value when the values are written in numerical order. If a data set has an even number of values, the median is the mean of the two middle values.

Example

To find the median of a set of measurements, arrange the values in order from least to greatest. The median is the middle value.

    13 mm   14 mm   16 mm   21 mm   23 mm   25 mm

Answer The median is 16 mm.

Mode

The mode of a data set is the value that occurs most often.

Example

To find the mode of a set of measurements, arrange the values in order from least to greatest and determine the value that occurs most often.

       13 mm, 14 mm, 14 mm, 16 mm,
       21 mm, 23 mm, 25 mm

Answer The mode is 14 mm.

A data set can have more than one mode or no mode. For example, the following data set has modes of 2 mm and 4 mm:

    2 mm   2 mm   3 mm   4 mm   4 mm

The data set below has no mode, because no value occurs more often than any other.

    2 mm   3 mm   4 mm   5 mm

Math Refresher

Ratios

A **ratio** is a comparison between numbers, and it is usually written as a fraction.

Example

Find the ratio of thermometers to students if you have 36 thermometers and 48 students in your class.

Step 1   Write the ratio.

$$\frac{36 \text{ thermometers}}{48 \text{ students}}$$

Step 2   Simplify the fraction to its simplest form.

$$\frac{36}{48} = \frac{36 \div 12}{48 \div 12} \div 12 = \frac{3}{4}$$

The ratio of thermometers to students is 3 to 4 or 3:4.

Proportions

A **proportion** is an equation that states that two ratios are equal.

$$\frac{3}{1} = \frac{12}{4}$$

To solve a proportion, you can use cross-multiplication. If you know three of the quantities in a proportion, you can use cross-multiplication to find the fourth.

Example

Imagine that you are making a scale model of the solar system for your science project. The diameter of Jupiter is 11.2 times the diameter of the Earth. If you are using a plastic-foam ball that has a diameter of 2 cm to represent the Earth, what must the diameter of the ball representing Jupiter be?

$$\frac{11.2}{1} = \frac{x}{2 \text{ cm}}$$

Step 1   Cross-multiply.

$$\frac{11.2}{1} = \frac{x}{2}$$

$$11.2 \times 2 = x \times 1$$

Step 2   Multiply.

$$22.4 = x \times 1$$

$$x = 22.4 \text{ cm}$$

You will need to use a ball that has a diameter of 22.4 cm to represent Jupiter.

Rates

A **rate** is a ratio of two values expressed in different units. A unit rate is a rate with a denominator of 1 unit.

Example

A plant grew 6 centimeters in 2 days. The plant's rate of growth was $\frac{6 \text{ cm}}{2 \text{ days}}$.

To describe the plant's growth in centimeters per day, write a unit rate.

Divide numerator and denominator by 2:

$$\frac{6 \text{ cm}}{2 \text{ days}} = \frac{6 \text{ cm} \div 2}{2 \text{ days} \div 2}$$

Simplify:

$$= \frac{3 \text{ cm}}{1 \text{ day}}$$

Answer   The plant's rate of growth is 3 centimeters per day.

Percent

A **percent** is a ratio of a given number to 100. For example, 85% = 85/100. You can use percent to find part of a whole.

Example
What is 85% of 40?

Step 1 Rewrite the percent as a decimal by moving the decimal point two places to the left.

$$0.85$$

Step 2 Multiply the decimal by the number that you are calculating the percentage of.

$$0.85 \times 40 = 34$$

85% of 40 is 34.

Decimals

To **add** or **subtract decimals**, line up the digits vertically so that the decimal points line up. Then, add or subtract the columns from right to left. Carry or borrow numbers as necessary.

Example
Add the following numbers: 3.1415 and 2.96.

Step 1 Line up the digits vertically so that the decimal points line up.

$$\begin{array}{r} 3.1415 \\ + 2.96 \\ \hline \end{array}$$

Step 2 Add the columns from right to left, and carry when necessary.

$$\begin{array}{r} 3.1415 \\ + 2.96 \\ \hline 6.1015 \end{array}$$

The sum is 6.1015.

Fractions

A **fraction** is a ratio of two nonzero whole numbers.

Example
Your class has 24 plants. Your teacher instructs you to put 5 plants in a shady spot. What fraction of the plants in your class will you put in a shady spot?

Step 1 In the denominator, write the total number of parts in the whole.

$$\frac{?}{24}$$

Step 2 In the numerator, write the number of parts of the whole that are being considered.

$$\frac{6}{24}$$

So, $\frac{6}{24}$ of the plants will be in the shade.

Math Refresher

Simplifying Fractions

It is usually best to express a fraction in its simplest form. Expressing a fraction in its simplest form is called **simplifying a fraction**.

Example

Simplify the fraction $\frac{30}{45}$ to its simplest form.

Step 1   Find the largest whole number that will divide evenly into both the numerator and denominator. This number is called the greatest common factor (GCF).

Factors of the numerator 30:
1, 2, 3, 5, 6, 10, 15, 30

Factors of the denominator 45:
1, 3, 5, 9, 15, 45

Step 2   Divide both the numerator and the denominator by the GCF, which in this case is 15.

$$\frac{30}{45} = \frac{30 \div 15}{45 \div 15} = \frac{2}{3}$$

Thus, $\frac{30}{45}$ written in its simplest form is $\frac{2}{3}$.

Adding and Subtracting Fractions

To **add** or **subtract fractions** that have the same denominator, simply add or subtract the numerators.

Examples

$\frac{3}{5} + \frac{1}{5} = ?$ and $\frac{3}{4} - \frac{1}{4} = ?$

To **add** or **subtract fractions** that have different denominators, first find the least common denominator (LCD).

Step 1   Add or subtract the numerators.

$$\frac{3}{5} + \frac{1}{5} = \frac{4}{} \text{ and } \frac{3}{4} - \frac{1}{4} = \frac{2}{}$$

Step 2   Write the sum or difference over the denominator.

$$\frac{3}{5} + \frac{1}{5} = \frac{4}{5} \text{ and } \frac{3}{4} - \frac{1}{4} = \frac{2}{4}$$

Step 3   If necessary, write the fraction in its simplest form.

$\frac{4}{5}$ cannot be simplified, and $\frac{2}{4} = \frac{1}{2}$.

Examples

$\frac{1}{2} + \frac{1}{6} = ?$ and $\frac{3}{4} - \frac{2}{3} = ?$

Step 1   Write the equivalent fractions that have a common denominator.

$$\frac{3}{6} + \frac{1}{6} = ? \text{ and } \frac{9}{12} - \frac{8}{12} = ?$$

Step 2   Add or subtract the fractions.

$$\frac{3}{6} + \frac{1}{6} = \frac{4}{6} \text{ and } \frac{9}{12} - \frac{8}{12} = \frac{1}{12}$$

Step 3   If necessary, write the frction in its simplest form.

$\frac{4}{6} = \frac{2}{3}$, and $\frac{1}{12}$ cannot be simplifed.

Multiplying Fractions

To **multiply fractions**, multiply the numerators and the denominators together, and then simplify the fraction to its simplest form.

Example

$\frac{5}{9} \times \frac{7}{10} = ?$

Step 1   Multiply the numerators and denominators.

$$\frac{5}{9} \times \frac{7}{10} = \frac{5 \times 7}{9 \times 10} = \frac{35}{90}$$

Step 2   Simplify the fraction.

$$\frac{35}{90} = \frac{35 \div 5}{90 \div 5} = \frac{7}{18}$$

Dividing Fractions

To **divide fractions,** first rewrite the divisor (the number you divide by) upside down. This number is called the reciprocal of the divisor. Then multiply and simplify if necessary.

Example

$\frac{5}{8} \div \frac{3}{2} = ?$

Step 1 Rewrite the divisor as its reciprocal.

$$\frac{3}{2} \rightarrow \frac{2}{3}$$

Step 2 Multiply the fractions.

$$\frac{5}{8} \times \frac{2}{3} = \frac{5 \times 2}{8 \times 3} = \frac{10}{24}$$

Step 3 Simplify the fraction.

$$\frac{10}{24} = \frac{10 \div 2}{24 \div 2} = \frac{5}{12}$$

Using Significant Figures

The **significant figures** in a decimal are the digits that are warranted by the accuracy of a measuring device.

When you perform a calculation with measurements, the number of significant figures to include in the result depends in part on the number of significant figures in the measurements. When you multiply or divide measurements, your answer should have only as many significant figures as the measurement with the fewest significant figures.

Examples

Using a balance and a graduated cylinder filled with water, you determined that a marble has a mass of 8.0 grams and a volume of 3.5 cubic centimeters. To calculate the density of the marble, divide the mass by the volume.

Write the formula for density: $\text{Density} = \frac{\text{mass}}{\text{volume}}$

Substitute measurements: $= \frac{8.0 \text{ g}}{3.5 \text{ cm}^3}$

Use a calculator to divide: $\approx 2.285714286 \text{ g/cm}^3$

Answer Because the mass and the volume have two significant figures each, give the density to two significant figures. The marble has a density of 2.3 grams per cubic centimeter.

Using Scientific Notation

Scientific notation is a shorthand way to write very large or very small numbers. For example, 73,500,000,000,000,000,000,000 kg is the mass of the Moon. In scientific notation, it is 7.35×10^{22} kg. A value written as a number between 1 and 10, times a power of 10, is in scientific notation.

Examples

You can convert from standard form to scientific notation.

Standard Form	Scientific Notation
720,000	7.2×10^5
5 decimal places left	Exponent is 5.
0.000291	2.91×10^{-4}
4 decimal places right	Exponent is −4.

You can convert from scientific notation to standard form.

Scientific Notation	Standard Form
4.63×10^7	46,300,000
Exponent is 7.	7 decimal places right
1.08×10^{-6}	0.00000108
Exponent is −6.	6 decimal places left

Math Refresher

Making and Interpreting Graphs

Circle Graph

A circle graph, or pie chart, shows how each group of data relates to all of the data. Each part of the circle represents a category of the data. The entire circle represents all of the data. For example, a biologist studying a hardwood forest in Wisconsin found that there were five different types of trees. The data table at right summarizes the biologist's findings.

Wisconsin Hardwood Trees	
Type of tree	**Number found**
Oak	600
Maple	750
Beech	300
Birch	1,200
Hickory	150
Total	3,000

How to Make a Circle Graph

1 To make a circle graph of these data, first find the percentage of each type of tree. Divide the number of trees of each type by the total number of trees, and multiply by 100%.

$$\frac{600 \text{ oak}}{3{,}000 \text{ trees}} \times 100\% = 20\%$$

$$\frac{750 \text{ maple}}{3{,}000 \text{ trees}} \times 100\% = 25\%$$

$$\frac{300 \text{ beech}}{3{,}000 \text{ trees}} \times 100\% = 10\%$$

$$\frac{1{,}200 \text{ birch}}{3{,}000 \text{ trees}} \times 100\% = 40\%$$

$$\frac{150 \text{ hickory}}{3{,}000 \text{ trees}} \times 100\% = 5\%$$

A Community of Wisconsin Hardwood Trees

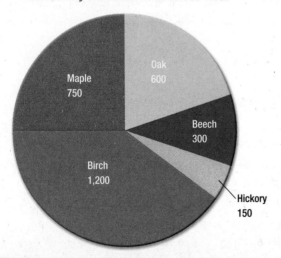

2 Now, determine the size of the wedges that make up the graph. Multiply each percentage by 360°. Remember that a circle contains 360°.

$$20\% \times 360° = 72° \qquad 25\% \times 360° = 90°$$

$$10\% \times 360° = 36° \qquad 40\% \times 360° = 144°$$

$$5\% \times 360° = 18°$$

3 Check that the sum of the percentages is 100 and the sum of the degrees is 360.

$$20\% + 25\% + 10\% + 40\% + 5\% = 100\%$$

$$72° + 90° + 36° + 144° + 18° = 360°$$

4 Use a compass to draw a circle and mark the center of the circle.

5 Then, use a protractor to draw angles of 72°, 90°, 36°, 144°, and 18° in the circle.

6 Finally, label each part of the graph, and choose an appropriate title.

Line Graphs

Line graphs are most often used to demonstrate continuous change. For example, Mr. Smith's students analyzed the population records for their hometown, Appleton, between 1910 and 2010. Examine the data at right.

Because the year and the population change, they are the variables. The population is determined by, or dependent on, the year. Therefore, the population is called the **dependent variable,** and the year is called the **independent variable**. Each year and its population make a **data pair**. To prepare a line graph, you must first organize data pairs into a table like the one at right.

Population of Appleton, 1910–2010	
Year	**Population**
1910	1,800
1930	2,500
1950	3,200
1970	3,900
1990	4,600
2010	5,300

How to Make a Line Graph

1 Place the independent variable along the horizontal (*x*) axis. Place the dependent variable along the vertical (*y*) axis.

2 Label the *x*-axis "Year" and the *y*-axis "Population." Look at your greatest and least values for the population. For the *y*-axis, determine a scale that will provide enough space to show these values. You must use the same scale for the entire length of the axis. Next, find an appropriate scale for the *x*-axis.

3 Choose reasonable starting points for each axis.

4 Plot the data pairs as accurately as possible.

5 Choose a title that accurately represents the data.

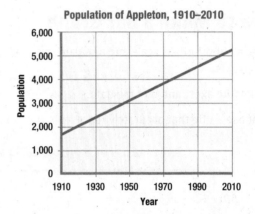

Population of Appleton, 1910–2010

How to Determine Slope

Slope is the ratio of the change in the y-value to the change in the x-value, or "rise over run."

1 Choose two points on the line graph. For example, the population of Appleton in 2010 was 5,300 people. Therefore, you can define point A as (2010, 5,300). In 1910, the population was 1,800 people. You can define point B as (1910, 1,800).

2 Find the change in the *y*-value.
(*y* at point A) − (*y* at point B) =
5,300 people − 1,800 people =
3,500 people

3 Find the change in the *x*-value.
(*x* at point A) − (*x* at point B) =
2010 − 1910 = 100 years

4 Calculate the slope of the graph by dividing the change in *y* by the change in *x*.

$$slope = \frac{change\ in\ y}{change\ in\ x}$$

$$slope = \frac{3,500\ people}{100\ years}$$

$$slope = 35\ people\ per\ year$$

In this example, the population in Appleton increased by a fixed amount each year. The graph of these data is a straight line. Therefore, the relationship is **linear**. When the graph of a set of data is not a straight line, the relationship is **nonlinear**.

Math Refresher

Bar Graphs

Bar graphs can be used to demonstrate change that is not continuous. These graphs can be used to indicate trends when the data cover a long period of time. A meteorologist gathered the precipitation data shown here for Summerville for April 1–15 and used a bar graph to represent the data.

Precipitation in Summerville, April 1–15			
Date	**Precipitation (cm)**	**Date**	**Precipitation (cm)**
April 1	0.5	April 9	0.25
April 2	1.25	April 10	0.0
April 3	0.0	April 11	1.0
April 4	0.0	April 12	0.0
April 5	0.0	April 13	0.25
April 6	0.0	April 14	0.0
April 7	0.0	April 15	6.50
April 8	1.75		

How to Make a Bar Graph

1 Use an appropriate scale and a reasonable starting point for each axis.

2 Label the axes, and plot the data.

3 Choose a title that accurately represents the data.

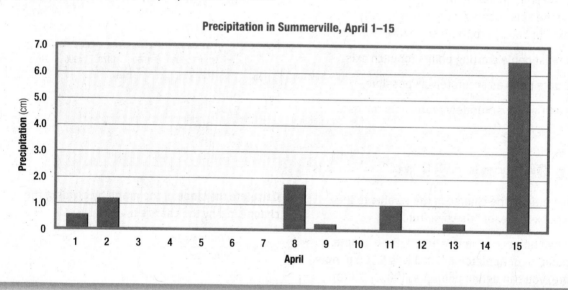

Precipitation in Summerville, April 1–15

© Houghton Mifflin Harcourt Publishing Company

Glossary

			Pronunciation Key				
Sound	**Symbol**	**Example**	**Respelling**	**Sound**	**Symbol**	**Example**	**Respelling**
ă	a	pat	PAT	ŏ	ah	bottle	BAHT'l
ā	ay	pay	PAY	ō	oh	toe	TOH
âr	air	care	KAIR	ô	aw	caught	KAWT
ä	ah	father	FAH•ther	ôr	ohr	roar	ROHR
är	ar	argue	AR•gyoo	oi	oy	noisy	NOYZ•ee
ch	ch	chase	CHAYS	ŏŏ	u	book	BUK
ĕ	e	pet	PET	ōō	oo	boot	BOOT
ĕ (at end of a syllable)	eh	settee lessee	seh•TEE leh•SEE	ou	ow	pound	POWND
ĕr	ehr	merry	MEHR•ee	s	s	center	SEN•ter
ē	ee	beach	BEECH	sh	sh	cache	CASH
g	g	gas	GAS	ŭ	uh	flood	FLUHD
ĭ	i	pit	PIT	ûr	er	bird	BERD
ĭ (at end of a syllable)	ih	guitar	gih•TAR	z	z	xylophone	ZY•luh•fohn
ī	y eye (only for a complete syllable)	pie island	PY EYE•luhnd	z	z	bags	BAGZ
				zh	zh	decision	dih•SIZH•uhn
				ə	uh	around broken focus	uh•ROWND BROH•kuhn FOH•kuhs
îr	ir	hear	HIR	ər	er	winner	WIN•er
j	j	germ	JERM	th	th	thin they	THIN THAY
k	k	kick	KIK				
ng	ng	thing	THING	w	w	one	WUHN
ngk	ngk	bank	BANGK	wh	hw	whether	HWETH•er

Glossary

A

abiotic factor an environmental factor that is not associated with the activities of living organisms (289)
factor abiótico un factor ambiental que no está asociado con las actividades de los seres vivos

accuracy (AK•yur•uh•see) a description of how close a measurement is to the true value of the quantity measured (R26)
exactitud término que describe qué tanto se aproxima una medida al valor verdadero de la cantidad medida

aphelion (uh•FEE•lee•uhn) in the orbit of a planet or other body in the solar system, the point that is farthest from the sun (165)
afelio en la órbita de un planeta u otros cuerpos en el sistema solar, el punto que está más lejos del Sol

asteroid a small, rocky object that orbits the sun; most asteroids are located in a band between the orbits of Mars and Jupiter (226)
asteroide un objeto pequeño y rocoso que se encuentra en órbita alrededor del Sol; la mayoría de los asteroides se ubican en una banda entre las órbitas de Marte y Júpiter

astronomical unit the average distance between Earth and the sun; approximately 150 million kilometers; symbol: AU (192)
unidad astronómica la distancia promedio entre la Tierra y el Sol; aproximadamente 150 millones de kilómetros; símbolo: UA

B

biome (BIE•ohm) a large region characterized by a specific type of climate and certain types of plant and animal communities (R26)
bioma una región extensa caracterizada por un tipo de clima específico y ciertos tipos de comunidades de plantas y animales

biotic factor an environmental factor that is associated with or results from the activities of living organisms (289)
factor biótico un factor ambiental que está asociado con las actividades de los seres vivos o que resulta de ellas

boiling the conversion of a liquid to a vapor when the vapor pressure of the liquid equals the atmospheric pressure (102)
ebullición la conversión de un líquido en vapor cuando la presión de vapor del líquido es igual a la presión atmosférica

C

carnivore an organism that eats animals (301)
carnívoro un organismo que se alimenta de animales

cellular respiration the process by which cells use oxygen to produce energy from food (326)
respiración celular el proceso por medio del cual las células utilizan oxígeno para producir energía a partir de los alimentos

centripetal force (sehn•TRIP•ih•tuhl) the inward force required to keep a particle or an object moving in a circular path (168)
fuerza centrípeta la fuerza hacia adentro que se requiere para mantener en movimiento una partícula o un objeto en un camino circular

chemical potential energy (KEM•ih•kuhl poh•TEN•shuhl EN•er•jee) energy that is stored in the bonds between atoms (135)
energía potencial química la energía almacenada en los enlaces que unen a los átomos

chlorophyll (KLOHR•oh•fill) a green pigment that captures light energy for photosynthesis (325)
clorofila un pigmento verde que capta la energía luminosa para la fotosíntesis

comet (KAHM•it) a small body that gives off gas and dust as it passes close to the sun; a typical comet moves in an elliptical orbit around the sun and is made of dust and frozen gases (224)
cometa un cuerpo pequeño que libera gas y polvo al pasar cerca del Sol; un cometa típico está formado por polvo y gases congelados y sigue una órbita elíptica alrededor del Sol

commensalism a relationship between two organisms in which one organism benefits and the other is unaffected (314)
comensalismo una relación entre dos organismos en la que uno se beneficia y el otro no es afectado

community all of the populations of species that live in the same habitat and interact with each other (291)
comunidad todas las poblaciones de especies que viven en el mismo hábitat e interactúan entre sí

competition (kahm•pih•TISH•uhn) ecological relationship in which two or more organisms depend on the same limited resource (316)
competencia la relación ecológica en la que dos o más organismos dependen del mismo recurso limitado

condensation (kahn•den•SAY•shuhn) the change of state from a gas to a liquid (103)
condensación el cambio de estado de gas a líquido

consumer an organism that eats other organisms or organic matter (301)
consumidor un organismo que se alimenta de otros organismos o de materia orgánica

D

data (DAY•tuh) information gathered by observation or experimentation that can be used in calculating or reasoning (29)
datos la información recopilada por medio de la observación o experimentación que puede usarse para hacer cálculos o razonar

day the time required for Earth to rotate once on its axis (246)
día el tiempo que se requiere para que la Tierra rote una vez sobre su eje

decomposer an organism that gets energy by breaking down the remains of dead organisms or animal wastes and consuming or absorbing the nutrients (300)
descomponedor un organismo que, para obtener energía, desintegra los restos de organismos muertos o los desechos de animales y consume o absorbe los nutrientes

density the ratio of the mass of a substance to the volume of the substance (81)
densidad la relación entre la masa de una sustancia y su volumen

deposition the process in which material is laid down (105)
deposición el proceso por medio del cual un material se deposita

dwarf planet a celestial body that orbits the sun, is round because of its own gravity, but has not cleared its orbital path (221)
planeta enano un cuerpo celeste que orbita alrededor del Sol, es redondo debido a su propia fuerza de gravedad, pero no ha despejado los alrededores de su trayectoria orbital

E

eclipse (ih•KLIPS) an event in which the shadow of one celestial body falls on another (258)
eclipse un suceso en el que la sombra de un cuerpo celeste cubre otro cuerpo celeste

ecology the study of the interactions of living organisms with one another and with their environment (288)
ecología el estudio de las interacciones de los seres vivos entre sí mismos y entre sí mismos y su ambiente

ecosystem a community of organisms and their abiotic, or nonliving, environment (291)
ecosistema una comunidad de organismos y su ambiente abiótico o no vivo

elastic potential energy the energy available for use when an elastic body returns to its original configuration (134)
energía potencial elástica la energía disponible para ser usada cuando un cuerpo elástico regresa a su configuración original

electrical energy the energy that is associated with charged particles because of their positions (137)
energía eléctrica la energía asociada con partículas que tienen carga debido a sus posiciones

empirical evidence (em•PIR•ih•kuhl EV•ih•duhns) the observations, measurements, and other types of data that people gather and test to support and evaluate scientific explanations (8)
evidencia empírica las observaciones, mediciones y demás tipos de datos que se recopilan y examinan para apoyar y evaluar explicaciones científicas

energy (EN•er•jee) the capacity to do work (122)
energía la capacidad de realizar un trabajo

equinox (EE•kwuh•nahks) the moment when the sun appears to cross the celestial equator (250)
equinoccio el momento en que el Sol parece cruzar el ecuador celeste

evaporation the change of state from a liquid to a gas (102)
evaporación el cambio de estado de líquido a gas

experiment (ik•SPEHR•uh•muhnt) an organized procedure to study something under controlled conditions (26)
experimento un procedimiento organizado que se lleva a cabo bajo condiciones controladas para estudiar algo

F

food chain the pathway of energy transfer through various stages as a result of the feeding patterns of a series of organisms (303)
cadena alimenticia la vía de transferencia de energía través de varias etapas, que ocurre como resultado de los patrones de alimentación de una serie de organismos

food web a diagram that shows the feeding relationships between organisms in an ecosystem (304)
red alimenticia un diagrama que muestra las relaciones de alimentación entre los organismos de un ecosistema

freezing the change of state in which a liquid becomes a solid as energy as heat is removed (100)
congelamiento el cambio de estado de líquido a sólido al eliminar calor del líquido

G

gas a form of matter that does not have a definite volume or shape (87)
gas un estado de la materia que no tiene volumen ni forma definidos

gas giant a planet that has a deep, massive atmosphere, such as Jupiter, Saturn, Uranus, or Neptune (208)
gigante gaseoso un planeta con una atmósfera masiva y profunda, como por ejemplo, Júpiter, Saturno, Urano o Neptuno

geocentric (jee•oh•SEN•trik) describes something that uses Earth as the reference point (152)
geocéntrico término que describe algo que usa a la Tierra como punto de referencia

gravity a force of attraction between objects that is due to their masses (164, 256)
gravedad una fuerza de atracción entre dos objetos debido a sus masas

H-J

habitat the place where an organism usually lives (292)
hábitat el lugar donde vive normalmente un organismo

heat the energy transferred between objects that are at different temperatures (136)
calor la transferencia de energía entre objetos que están a temperaturas diferentes

heliocentric (hee•lee•oh•SEN•trik) sun-centered (152)
heliocéntrico centrado en el Sol

herbivore an organism that eats only plants (301)
herbívoro un organismo que sólo come plantas

hypothesis (hy•PAHTH•eh•sys) a testable idea or explanation that leads to scientific investigation (28)
hipótesis una idea o explicación que conlleva a la investigación científica y que se puede probar

K

kinetic energy (kuh•NET•ik) the energy of an object that is due to the object's motion (123)
energía cinética la energía de un objeto debido al movimiento del objeto

Kuiper Belt a region of the solar system that is just beyond the orbit of Neptune and that contains small bodies made mostly of ice (222)
cinturón de Kuiper una región del Sistema Solar que comienza justo después de la órbita de Neptuno y que contiene planetas enanos y otros cuerpos pequeños formados principalmente de hielo

Kuiper Belt object one of the hundreds or thousands of minor planet-sized objects that orbit the sun in a flat belt beyond Neptune's orbit (222)
objeto del cinturón de Kuiper una región del Sistema Solar que comienza justo después de la órbita de Neptuno y que contiene planetas enanos y otros cuerpos pequeños formados principalmente de hielo

L

law a descriptive statement or equation that reliably predicts events under certain conditions (18)
ley una ecuación o afirmación descriptiva que predice sucesos de manera confiable en determinadas condiciones

law of conservation of energy the law that states that energy cannot be created or destroyed but can be changed from one form to another (127)
ley de la conservación de la energía la ley que establece que la energía ni se crea ni se destruye, sólo se transforma de una forma a otra

light (LYT) a form of radiant electromagnetic energy that can be seen by the human eye (136)
luz una forma de energía electromagnética radiante que es visible para el ojo humano

liquid the state of matter that has a definite volume but not a definite shape (87)
líquido el estado de la materia que tiene un volumen definido, pero no una forma definida

lunar phases the different appearances of the moon from Earth throughout the month (258)
fases lunares la diferente apariencia que tiene la Luna cuando se ve desde la Tierra a lo largo del mes

M

mass a measure of the amount of matter in an object (73)
masa una medida de la cantidad de materia que tiene un objeto

matter anything that has mass and takes up space (72)
materia cualquier cosa que tiene masa y ocupa un lugar en el espacio

mechanical energy (meh•KAN•ih•kuhl) the amount of work an object can do because of the object's kinetic and potential energies (126)
energía mecánica la cantidad de trabajo que un objeto realiza debido a las energías cinética y potencial del objeto

melting the change of state in which a solid becomes a liquid by adding heat (101)
fusión el cambio de estado en el que un sólido se convierte en líquido al añadir calor o al cambiar la presión

meteor a bright streak of light that results when a meteoroid burns up in Earth's atmosphere (228)
meteoro un rayo de luz brillante que se produce cuando un meteoroide se quema en la atmósfera de la Tierra

meteorite A meteoroid that reaches Earth's surface without completely burning up (228)
meteorito meteoroide que alcanza la superficie de la Tierra sin quemarse completamente.

meteoroid a relatively small, rocky body that travels through space (228)
meteoroid un cuerpo rocoso relativamente pequeño que viaja en el espacio

model a pattern, plan, representation, or description designed to show the structure or workings of an object, system, or concept (17, 44)
modelo un diseño, plan, representación o descripción cuyo objetivo es mostrar la estructura o funcionamiento de un objeto, sistema o concepto

mutualism a relationship between two species in which both species benefit (314)
mutualismo una relación entre dos especies en la que ambas se benefician

neap tide a tide of minimum range that occurs during the first and third quarters of the moon (271)
marea muerta una marea que tiene un rango mínimo, la cual ocurre durante el primer y el tercer cuartos de la Luna

niche the role of a species in its community, including use of its habitat and its relationships with other species (292)
nicho el papel que juega una especie en su comunidad, incluidos el uso de su hábitat y su relación con otras especies

nuclear fusion the process by which nuclei of small atoms combine to form a new, more massive nucleus; the process releases energy (182)
fusión nuclear el proceso por medio del cual los núcleos de átomos pequeños se combinan y forman un núcleo nuevo con mayor masa; el proceso libera energía

observation the process of obtaining information by using the senses; the information obtained by using the senses (27)
observación el proceso de obtener información por medio de los sentidos; la información que se obtiene al usar los sentidos

omnivore an organism that eats both plants and animals (301)
omnívoro un organismo que come tanto plantas como animales

Oort cloud a spherical region that surrounds the solar system, that extends from the Kuiper Belt to almost halfway to the nearest star, and that contains billions of comets (225)
nube de Oort una región esférica que rodea al Sistema Solar, que se extiende desde el cinturón de Kuiper hasta la mitad del camino hacia la estrella más cercana y contiene miles de millones de cometas

orbit the path that a body follows as it travels around another body in space (164)
órbita la trayectoria que sigue un cuerpo al desplazarse alrededor de otro cuerpo en el espacio

parallax (PAIR•uh•laks) an apparent shift in the position of an object when viewed from different locations (152)
paralaje un cambio aparente en la posición de un objeto cuando se ve desde lugares distintos

parasitism (PAIR•uh•sih•tiz•uhm) a relationship between two species in which one species, the parasite, benefits from the other species, the host, which is harmed (315)
parasitismo una relación entre dos especies en la que una, el parásito, se beneficia de la otra, el huésped, que resulta perjudicada

penumbra (pih•NUHM•bruh) the outer part of a shadow such as the shadow cast by Earth or the moon in which sunlight is only partially blocked (260)
penumbra la parte exterior de la sombra como la sombra producida por la Tierra o la Luna en la que la luz solar solamente se encuentra bloqueada parcialmente

perihelion (perh•uh•HEE•lee•uhn) the point in the orbit of a planet at which the planet is closest to the sun (165)
perihelio el punto en la órbita de un planeta en el que el planeta está más cerca del Sol

photosynthesis (foh•toh•SYN•thuh•sis) the process by which plants, algae, and some bacteria use sunlight, carbon dioxide, and water to make food (324)
fotosíntesis el proceso por medio del cual las plantas, las algas y algunas bacterias utilizan la luz solar, el dióxido de carbono y el agua para producir alimento

planetary ring a disk of matter that encircles a planet and consists of numerous particles in orbit, ranging in size from dust grains up to objects tens of meters across (210)
anillo planetario un disco de materia que rodea un planeta y está compuesto por numerosas partículas en órbita que pueden ser desde motas de polvo hasta objetos de diez metros

planetesimal (plan•ih•TES•ih•muhl) a small body from which a planet originated in the early stages of development of the solar system (171)
planetesimal un cuerpo pequeño a partir del cual se originó un planeta en las primeras etapas de desarrollo del Sistema Solar

population a group of organisms of the same species that live in a specific geographical area (290)
población un grupo de organismos de la misma especie que viven en un área geográfica específica

potential energy the energy that an object has because of the position, shape, or condition of the object (124)
energía potencial la energía que tiene un objeto debido a su posición, forma o condición

precision (pree•SIZH•uhn) the exactness of a measurement (R26)
precisión la exactitud de una medición

predator an organism that kills and eats all or part of another organism (312)
depredador un organismo que mata y se alimenta de otro organismo o de parte de él

prey an organism that is killed and eaten by another organism (312)
presa un organismo al que otro organismo mata para alimentarse de él

producer an organism that can make its own food by using energy from its surroundings (300)
productor un organismo que puede elaborar sus propios alimentos utilizando la energía de su entorno

prominence a loop of relatively cool, incandescent gas that extends above the photosphere and above the sun's edge as seen from Earth (187)
protuberancia una espiral de gas incandescente y relativamente frío que, vista desde la Tierra, se extiende por encima de la fotosfera y la superficie del Sol

R

revolution (reh•vuh•LOO•shun) the motion of a body that travels around another body in space; one complete trip along an orbit (247)
revolución el movimiento de un cuerpo que viaja alrededor de otro cuerpo en el espacio; un viaje completo a lo largo de una órbita

rotation the spin of a body on its axis (246)
rotación el giro de un cuerpo alrededor de su eje

S

satellite (SAT'l•yt) a natural or artificial body that revolves around a planet (254)
satélite un cuerpo natural o artificial que gira alrededor de un cuerpo celeste que tiene mayor masa

science the knowledge obtained by observing natural events and conditions in order to discover facts and formulate laws or principles that can be verified or tested (6)
ciencia el conocimiento que se obtiene por medio de la observación natural de acontecimientos y condiciones con el fin de descubrir hechos y formular leyes o principios que puedan ser verificados o probados

season (SEE•zuhn) a division of the year that is characterized by recurring weather conditions, and determined by both Earth's tilt relative to the sun and Earth's position in its orbit around the sun (250)
estación una de las partes en que se divide el año que se caracteriza por condiciones climáticas recurrentes y que está determinada tanto por la inclinación de la Tierra con relación al Sol como por la posición que ocupa en su órbita alrededor del Sol

solar flare an explosive release of energy that comes from the sun and that is associated with magnetic disturbances on the sun's surface (187)
erupción solar una liberación explosiva de energía que proviene del Sol y que se asocia con disturbios magnéticos en la superficie solar

solar nebula (SOH•ler NEB•yuh•luh) a rotating cloud of gas and dust from which the sun and planets formed (169)
nebulosa solar una nube de gas y polvo en rotación a partir de la cual se formaron el Sol y los planetas

solar system the sun and all of the planets and other bodies that travel around it (152)
Sistema Solar el Sol y todos los planetas y otros cuerpos que se desplazan alrededor de él

solid the state of matter in which the volume and shape of a substance are fixed (86)
sólido el estado de la materia en el cual el volumen y la forma de una sustancia están fijos

solstice (SAHL•stis) the point at which the sun is as far north or as far south of the equator as possible (250)
solsticio el punto en el que el Sol está tan lejos del ecuador como es posible, ya sea hacia el norte o hacia el sur

sound (SOWND) the movement of energy as vibrations through a medium such as a solid, water, or air (136)
sonido el movimiento de energía que atraviesa, en forma de vibraciones, un medio como el agua, el aire o un cuerpo sólido

species (SPEE•seez) a group of organisms that are closely related and can mate to produce fertile offspring (290)
especie un grupo de organismos que tienen un parentesco cercano y que pueden aparearse para producir descendencia fértil

spring tide a tide of increased range that occurs two times a month, at the new and full moons (270)
marea viva una marea de mayor rango que ocurre dos veces al mes, durante la luna nueva y la luna llena

sublimation the process in which a solid changes directly into a gas (104)
sublimación el proceso por medio del cual un sólido se transforma directamente en un gas

sunspot a dark area of the photosphere of the sun that is cooler than the surrounding areas and that has a strong magnetic field (186)
mancha solar un área oscura en la fotosfera del Sol que es más fría que las áreas que la rodean y que tiene un campo magnético fuerte

symbiosis (sim•bee•OH•sis) a relationship in which two different organisms live in close association with each other (314)
simbiosis una relación en la que dos organismos diferentes viven estrechamente asociados uno con el otro

T

terrestrial planet one of the highly dense planets nearest to the sun; Mercury, Venus, Mars, and Earth (192)
planeta terrestre uno de los planetas muy densos que se encuentran más cerca del Sol; Mercurio, Venus, Marte y la Tierra

theory the explanation for some phenomenon that is based on observation, experimentation, and reasoning; that is supported by a large quantity of evidence; and that does not conflict with any existing experimental results or observations (16)

teoría una explicación sobre algún fenómeno que está basada en la observación, experimentación y razonamiento; que está respaldada por una gran cantidad de pruebas; y que no contradice ningún resultado experimental ni observación existente

tidal range the difference in levels of ocean water at high tide and low tide (270)

rango de marea la diferencia en los niveles del agua del océano entre la marea alta y la marea baja

tide the periodic rise and fall of the water level in the oceans and other large bodies of water (268)

marea el ascenso y descenso periódico del nivel del agua en los océanos y otras masas grandes de agua

umbra a shadow that blocks sunlight, such as the conical section in the shadow of the Earth or the moon (258)

umbra una sombra que bloquea la luz solar, como por ejemplo, la sección cónica en la sombra de la Tierra o la Luna

variable (VAIR•ee•uh•buhl) any factor that can change in an experiment, observation, or model (29)

variable cualquier factor que puede modificarse en un experimento, observación o modelo

volume (VAHL•yoom) the amount of space that an object takes up, or occupies (75)

volumen la cantidad de espacio que ocupa un objeto

weight (WAYT) a measure of the gravitational force exerted on an object; its value can change with the location of the object in the universe (73)

peso una medida de la fuerza gravitacional ejercida sobre un objeto; su valor puede cambiar en función de la ubicación del objeto en el universo

year the time required for the Earth to orbit once around the sun (247)

año el tiempo que se requiere para que la Tierra le dé la vuelta al Sol una vez

Index

Page numbers for definitions are printed in **boldface** type.
Page numbers for illustrations, photographs, maps, and
charts are printed in *italics*.

A

abiotic factor, 287, **289**, 294
accuracy, R26
Active Reading, lesson opener pages,
    5, 15, 25, 39, 51, 71, 121, 151,
    163, 179, 191, 207, 219, 245,
    255, 267, 287, 299, 311, 321,
    R10–R11. *See also* **Reading Skills.**
adenosine triphosphate (ATP), 326,
    327
Almagest (Ptolemy), 154
Alvarez, Luis, 59
anaerobic respiration, 329
Andes Mountains, Peru, 28
    Anolis carolinensis, 293
annotations, R10–R11
aphelion, **165**–166, *165–166*
Aquatic Ecosystems and Land Biomes,
    R6–R7
    desert, R7
    estuary, R6
    forest, R7
    freshwater, R6
    grassland, R7
    marine, R6
    taiga, R7
    temperate, R7
    tropical, R7
    tundra, R7
    wetland, R7
Archaea (domain), R4
Aristarchus, 153, *153*
Aristotle, 152–153, *152*
asteroid, **226**
    belt, *226*
    composition of, 227
Asteroid Itokawa, 227
astronaut, *164*
astronautical engineer, 161
astronomer
    Aristarchus, 153, *153*
    Brahe, Tycho, 165
    Copernicus, Nicolaus, 155, *155*, 165
    Cunitz, Maria, 195
    Galilei, Galileo, 156–157, *156*
    Kepler, Johannes, 156, *156*, 165–
    166
    Ptolemy, 154, *154*
astronomical unit (AU), **192**, 222
astronomy, 6
Atlantis (space shuttle), 157
ATP (adenosine triphosphate), 326,
    327
AU (astronomical unit), **192**, 222, *222*
auto engineers, 55, *55*

B

Bacteria (domain), R4
bar graph, **41**, 46, R38
barnacle, 273, *273*
Barringer Crater, Arizona, *228*
bee, 314, *314*
biology, 6
bioluminescent glow worm, 317
biome, R6
    desert, R7
    grassland, R7
    taiga, R7
    temperate, R7
    tropical, R7
    tundra, R7
biotic factor, **289**, 294
boiling, *90*, **102**
boiling point, 102
botanist, 177
Brahe, Tycho, 165
brass orrery, *147*
brown anole (*Anolis segrei*), 293, *293*
Burmese python, 296, *296*

C

calculations, performing, R31–R35
    decimals, R33
    fractions, R33–R35
    mean, median, mode, R31
    percentage, R33
    proportions, R32
    rates, R32
    ratios, R32
    scientific notation, R35
    significant figures, R35
Callisto (moon of Jupiter), 156, 157,
    208, *208*
camouflage, 312
carbon dioxide, *324*, 327, *327–328*
carnivore, 299, **301**
Cassini spacecraft, 211
cell (of organisms)
    capturing and releasing energy,
    322–328 , *324–328*, 330, *330*
    energy from food for, 322–323,
    326–327, *326–327*
cellular respiration, **326**, *326–327*,
    326–327
    photosynthesis and, 328
centripetal force, **168**, *168*
Ceres (dwarf planet), 220, 221
changes of state, 108
    gases and solids, 104–105, *104*
    liquids and gases, 102–103,
    102–103

mass and, 106–107
    solids and liquids, 100–101, *100*
Charles' law, 18
Charon (moon of Pluto), 223, *223*
chemical energy, 300, 327
    storing, 325
chemical potential energy, 124, **135**
chlorophyll, 321, **325**
chloroplast, *324*, 325, *325*, 328
chromosphere, 181, *181*
circle graph, **41**, R36
Citizen Science
    Measuring Shadows, 242–243
    Sharing Spaces, 284–285
    Solar System Discoveries, 148–149
    Things Change, 2–3
classification of living things, table,
    R4–R5
climate change, 49
collapsed solar nebula, 169
colored glass, 91
coma
    of comet, 224
comet, 149, *149*, 218, **224**–225,
    224–225
    coma, 224
    dust tail, 224
    Hale-Bopp, *218*
    Hyakutake, 149, *149*
    ion tail, 224
    Kuiper Belt and Oort cloud, 225
    nucleus, 224
commensalism, **314**
community, **291**, *291*, 294
    competition, 316
    interactions in, 314–316
competition, **316**
conclusions, making, R24
condensation, *90*, **103**, 103
conservation warden, 297
constant, R21
consumer, **301**, *301*, 308, 403
control group, R21
convective zone, 181, *181*, 184, 184
converting units, R29–R31
Copernicus, Nicolaus, 155, *155*, 165
coral reef, *283*
core, of sun, 181, *181*
corona, 181, *181*
countermass, 74
crab, ghost, 273, *273*
craters
    on Venus, 195
creativity
    in designing experiments, 10
    in explaining observations, 11
Curie, Marie, *59*
customary units, converting to SI units,
    R30

D

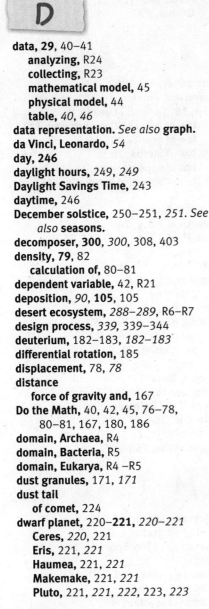

data, **29**, 40–41
  analyzing, R24
  collecting, R23
  mathematical model, 45
  physical model, 44
  table, *40*, *46*
data representation. *See also* graph.
da Vinci, Leonardo, *54*
day, 246
daylight hours, 249, *249*
Daylight Savings Time, 243
daytime, 246
December solstice, 250–251, *251. See also* seasons.
decomposer, **300**, *300*, 308, 403
density, **79**, 82
  calculation of, 80–81
dependent variable, 42, R21
deposition, *90*, **105**, *105*
desert ecosystem, *288–289*, R6–R7
design process, *339*, 339–344
deuterium, 182–183, *182–183*
differential rotation, 185
displacement, 78, *78*
distance
  force of gravity and, 167
Do the Math, 40, 42, 45, 76–78, 80–81, 167, 180, 186
domain, Archaea, R4
domain, Bacteria, R5
domain, Eukarya, R4–R5
dust granules, 171, *171*
dust tail
  of comet, 224
dwarf planet, 220–**221**, *220–221*
  Ceres, *220*, 221
  Eris, 221, *221*
  Haumea, 221, *221*
  Makemake, 221, *221*
  Pluto, 221, *221, 222, 223, 223*

E

Earth
  axis, 248
  axial tilt, 248, *248*
  motion of, 246
  orbit, 247
  period of rotation and revolution, 246–247
  planet, *190*, 196–197, *196–197*, 202, *202*, 216
  rotation, **246**, *246*
  revolution, **247**, *247*
  statistics table for, *196*
  tides, 268–272
  water and life, 196
Earth-centered model, *151*, **152**, *158. See also* geocentric model.
Earth-moon-sun system, 256–261
Earth science, 6
eclipse, **260**–261

lunar, 260, *260*
solar, 261, *261*
ecologist, 296
ecology, **288**
ecosystem, 283, **291**, *291*
  abiotic factor, 287, **289**, 289
  desert, *288–289*
  energy transfer, 308
  organisms, 284
  rainforest, *286*
Einstein, Albert, 19
  equation for energy conversion, 182
elastic potential energy, **134**
electrical energy, **137**
electromagnetic wave, 184
element, Periodic Table of the Elements, R8–R9
empirical evidence, 5, **8**, 12
Enceladus (moon of Saturn), 211, *211*
energy, **122**, 128, 320
  in cells, 322–330, *324–328*, 330, *330*
  chemical, 325
  chemical potential, 124, **135**
  elastic potential, 134
  electrical, **137**
  forms of, 134–138
  gravitational potential, 124
  heat, **136**
  kinetic, **123**, 128, 134
  kinetic vs. potential, 125
  law of conservation of, **127**
  light, **136**
  mechanical, **126**, 128
  organisms and, 300–304, 306, *300–306*, 320–330, *320*, *323–328*, 330, *330*
  plants and, 300, 302, *302*, 323–325, *323–325*, 328, *328*, 330, *330*
  potential, **124**, 128, 134
  sound, **136**
  types of, 123–124, 132
energy transfer, 308
  among organisms, 302–303
  by convection, 184
  by radiation, 184
Engage Your Brain, lesson opener pages, 5, 15, 25, 39, 51, 71, 121, 151, 163, 179, 191, 207, 219, 245, 255, 267, 287, 299, 311, 321
engineering design process, *339*, 339–342
environment
  levels of organization of, 290–291
environmental scientist, 10
equator, 249
equinox, **250**–251, *250–251*
Eris (dwarf planet), 221, *221*
Eukarya, R4–R5
Europa (moon of Jupiter), 209, *209*
evaporation, *90*, **102**, *102*
experiment, **26**
  conducting, R22–R24
  designing, R20–R24

F

Faber, Sandra, 160, *160*
fall, *251*
feeding relationships, 312, *318*
fermentation, 329
fireworks, *132*
first quarter (lunar phase), 258, *259*
Focus on Engineering, The Right Tool, 130–131
food chain, **303**, *303*
food web, 304–306, *305–306*, *308*
force. *See* centripetal force; gravitational force; gravity.
forensic technician, *55*
forest, R6–R7
freezing, 90, *90*, **100**, *100*
freezing point, 100
freshwater ecosystem, R6
full moon (lunar phase), *258*

G

Galilean moons, 209
Galilei, Galileo, 152, 156–157, *156*
  spacecraft, *157*
  telescope, *157*
Ganymede (moon of Jupiter), *148*, 156, 157, *208*, 209
gas, 87, *87*, 207
  in matter, *99*
  particle motion and, 89
  particles, *99*
gas giant planets, 172, *172*, *206*, **208**–216, *208–214*, *216*
  Jupiter, 208–209, *208–209*, 216, *216*
  properties of, 208, *216*
  Neptune, 208, 214–216, *214–216*
  Saturn, 208, 210–211, *210–211*, 216, *216*
  Uranus, 208, 212–213, *212–213*, 216, *216*
gathering data, 49
geocentric model, 152, *158*
geologist, 204
geology, 6
  law of superposition, 18, *18*
gibbous phase, 258
glass blowing, 91
glow worm, 317
glucose, 325–326
graph, 42–43, 46, 103. *See also* data representation.
  bar, **41**, 46, R38
  circle, **41**, R36
  line, 41, R37
  making and interpreting, R36–R38
  slope, R37
graphic organizers, using, R12–R15
grassland, R6–R7
gravitation
  law of universal, 167
gravitational force, 167, 174

gravitational potential energy, 124
gravity, 11, *11*, 19, *19*, 124, *162*, **164**, 167, **256**
    planetary motion, 164, 168, 174
Great Dark Spot (Neptune), 214, *214*
Great Red Spot (Jupiter), *208*, 209
green anole lizard (*Anolis carolinensis*), 293, *293*
guano, 317, *317*
Gula Mons volcano (Mars), *195*

habitat, **292**, 292, 294
Hale-Bopp (comet), *218*
Haumea (dwarf planet), 221, *221*
heat energy, **136**
Hebes Chasma, (Mars), *199*
Herschel, Sir William, 149, *149*
heliocentric model, 151–**152**, 153, 155–156, *158*
helium-**3**, 183, *183*
helium-**4**, 183, *183*
herbivore, 299, **301**
herpetology, 296
high tide, *268*, 269, *270–271*, 272, *274*
Hooke, Robert, *59*
Hubble space telescope, 160, *160*
Human Orrery, *147*
Hyakutake (comet), 149, *149*
Hyakutake, Yuji, 149
hypothesis, **28**
    forming, 24, R21
    testing, R21

IAU (International Astronomical Union), 223
icicles, *90*
Impact crater Cunitz (Mars), *195*
independent variable, 42
Inquiry Skills
    compare, 53, 83, 109, 155, 158, 165, 185, 187, 189, 199, 202, 217, 230, 271, 313–314, 323, 329
    contrast, 5, 13, 109, 165, 195, 331
    draw conclusions, 48, 95
    gathering data, 49
    hypothesize, 12, 28
    identify, 5, 9, 13, 15–16, 19–20, 23, 27, 29, 37, 39, 43, 47, 51, 54, 56–57, 71–72, 83, 85, 88, 97–98, 101, 104–105, 121–122, 127, 129, 133–134, 136–137, 139, 152, 156–157, 159, 164, 170, 175, 180, 182–183, 189, 191–192, 194–197, 203, 207–208, 210, 212, 217, 219–220, 224, 226, 228, 231, 246, 256, 268, 270, 272, 290–291, 295, 300, 302, 304, 306, 312, 314, 316–317, 319, 322, 324, 326, 327, 330, 331

    identify variables, 95
    infer, 6, 9–10, 13, 17–19, 25–26, 37, 55, 74–75, 93, 139, 201, 231, 247, 251, 289, 292, 295, 301–302, 306, 319, 321, 325, 331
    inquire, 270, 272
    interpret, 41
    investigate, 91
    model, 88, 209
    plan investigation, 32, 57, 94, 193
    predict, 5, 9, 15, 39, 49, 51, 54, 58, 79, 83, 93, 106, 109, 151, 153, 163, 179, 207, 213–214, 219, 231, 245, 252, 269, 272, 294–295, 299, 303, 306, 308–309, 311, 315–316, 321
independent variable, R21
International Astronomical Union (IAU), 223
Io (moon of Jupiter), 156, 157, 209, *209*
ion tail
    of comet, 224, *224*
iron meteorite, 229, *229*
ISTEP+ Review, 63–66, 113–116, 143–146, 235–240, 279–282, 335–338

June solstice, 250–251, *250*. See also seasons.
Jupiter
    cloud bands, 209, 216, *216*
    gas giant, 208, 216
    Great Red Spot, *208*, 209
    moons, 148, 156, 157, 209, *208–209*
    planet, *206*, 208–209, *208–209*, 216, *216*
    statistics table for, *208*
    weather, 209

Kepler, Johannes, 156, *156*, 165–166
Kepler's laws, of planetary motion, 156, *156*, 165–166, *165–166*
    first law, 156, *156*, 165, *165*
    second law, 166, *166*
    third law, 166, *166*
Kilauea, 81
kinetic energy, **123**, 125–128, 134
kingdom, R4–R5
    Animals, R5
    Fungi, R5
    Plants, R5
    Protists, R4
Krysko, Kenneth, 296, *296*
kudzu, 307, *307*
Kuiper Belt, 219–220, 222–223, *222–223*, 225
Kuiper Belt object (KBO), **220**–221, 222–223, *222–223*

Pluto, 220–221, 223, *223*
Quaoar, *222*

lab safety, R18–R19
Lavoisier, Antoine, *59*
law, **18**. *See also* scientific law.
    law of conservation of energy, **127**
    law of gravity, 11, *11*, 19, *19*
    law of inertia, 18
    law of superposition, 18, *18*
    law of universal gravitation, **167**, 174
Leakey, Mary, 54
length of a day, **246**, *246*, *252*
length of a year, **247**, *247*, *252*
lichens, 314, *314*
life science, 6
light energy, **136**
    capturing, 325, *325*
line graph, 41, R37
liquid, **87**, 87, *87*, 88–89, 92, *92*
    in particle motion, 89
    particles in, 98, *98*
    precipitation, *43*
Logan, Myra, 54
long-period comet, 225
Look It Up! Reference Section, R1–R38
low tide, *268–271*, 269, 272, *274*
lunar eclipse, 260, *260*
lunar phase, **258**–259

Magellan spacecraft, 195
main-belt asteroid, 226
Makemake (dwarf planet), 221, *221*
maps, 17
March equinox, 250, *250–251*. See also seasons.
marine ecosystem, R6
Mariner 10 spacecraft, 192
Mars
    atmosphere, 199
    composition of, 198
    carbon dioxide, *198*, 199
    liquid water, 200
    planet, *190*, 198–202, *198–202*, 216, *216*
    polar ice caps, *198*, 199
    rovers, 201, *201*, 204, *204*
    statistics table for, *198*
    surface features, 198–200, *198–200*
    water ice, 3
Mars Pathfinder mission, 204
mass, **73**, *73*, *82*
    force of gravity, 19, 167, 174
    measurement, 74, *74*
Math Refresher, R31–R38
mathematical model, 45

matter, **72**
  states of, 86–90, *92*
Mayo Clinic, 21
McCrory, Phil, 297
measurement, 7–8, 31, **46**, 71, 165,
  242–243
  of mass, 74, 82
  of space, 75
  units of, 40, 43
  of volume using a formula, 76, 82
  of volume using water
    displacement, 78
  of weight, 74, 82
measuring, R26–R27
  graduated cylinder, R27
  metric ruler, R27
  triple beam balance, R28
mechanical energy, **126**, 128
melting, 90, *90*, **101**, *101*
melting point, 101
Mercury
  temperature range of, 193
  iron core, 193
  planet, *190*, 192–193, *192–193*,
    202, *202*, 216
  statistics table for, *192*
  surface features, 192, *192*
meteor, **228**, *228*
meteorite, **228**, *228*
  composition of, 229
meteoroid, **228**, *228*
metric system, using, R29–R30
microscope
  compound light, R25
  using, R25
midnight sun, 249
Milstein, Cesar, 54
minerals,
  nonsilicate, 212–213, R3
  properties table, R2–R3
  silicate, 212, R2
Miranda, (moon of Uranus), 213, *213*
mitochondria (singular,
  mitochondrion), 326, *326*, *327*
model, **17**, **44**, 88, 209. *See also*
  mathematical model; physical
  model; scientific model.
  benefits and limitations of, 45
moon, 197, *197*, 241, *254–255*,
  256–262, *257–262*, 268–272,
  269–272, 274, *274*
  appearance of, *254–255*, 257–262,
    257–262
  gravitational effects of, 268–272,
    269–272, 274, *274*
  lunar eclipse, 260, *260*
  lunar phase, **258**, *258–259*
  statistics table for, *197*
  surface features, 197, *197*
moon phase. *See* lunar phase.
mummy, *28–29*
  DNA, 28–29
mushroom, 300, *300*
mutualism, **314**, *314*, *318*

NASA (National Aeronautics and Space
  Administration), 21, 205, 297
neap tides, **271**, *271*, 274, *274*
near-Earth asteroid, 226
Neptune
  atmosphere, 214, 216
  composition of, 214, 216
  gas giant, *216*
  Great Dark Spot, 214, *214*
  planet, 149, *149*, *206*, 214–216,
    214, *216*
  statistics table for, *214*
  weather, 214–215
new moon, 258, *259*
Newton, Sir Isaac, 2, *2*, 11, *11*, 19,
  167, *167*
Newton's law of universal gravitation,
  167, *167*, 174
niche, **292**, 294
nighttime, 246
Northern Hemisphere, 248–250, 252,
  248–252
North Pole, 246, *246*, 248–250, *248–
  251*, 252, *252*
note taking, R12–R15
nuclear fusion, **182**–183
  in sun, 182–183, *182–183*

observation, **27**
obsidian, 80, *80*
Olympus Mons (Mars), 199, *199*
Oort cloud, 220, **225**
  long-period comets, 225
orbit, **164**
organism, 300–306, 308, 322–323
  carnivore, **301**, *301*, 308
  cell function in, 322–323
  consumer, **301**, *301*, 308, 403
  decomposer, **300**, *300*, 308, 403
  herbivore, **301**, *301*, 308
  host, 315, *315*
  omnivore, **301**, *301*, 308
  parasite, 315, *315*
  predator, **312**–313, *312–313*, 318,
    318
  prey, **312**–313, *312–313*
  producer, **300**, *300*, 308, 403
  scavenger, 301
  single-celled, 323
osprey, 284–285, *285*
oxygen, 324–326, *324–327*, 328, *328*
  cellular respiration, **326**–328,
    326–328
  photosynthesis, **324**–325, 328,
    324–325, *328*

paleontologist, 14
Pangaea, 17, *17*
parallax, **152**–153, *153*
parasitism, **315**, *315*, 318, *318*
park naturalist, 297
particle accelerator, *24*
particles
  in gases, 87, *87*, 89, 92, *92*
  in liquids, 87, *87*, 89, 92, *92*
  in solids, 86, *86*, 88, 92, *92*
particle theory of light, 20, *20*
Pasteur, Louis, 3
peer review, 34
penumbra, 255, **260**, *260–262*
People in Science
  Faber, Sandra, 160, *160*
  Krysko, Kenneth, 296, *296*
  McCrory, Phil, 297
  Ward, Wesley, 204, *204*
  Wesley, Anthony, 205
perihelion, **165**–166
Periodic Table of the Elements, R8–R9
photosphere, 179, 181, *181*
photosynthesis, **324**–325, *324–325*
  and cellular respiration, 328, *328*
physical model, **44**, *44*, 46, *46*
  physical science, 6
  in scientific methods, 32
phytoplankton, 304, *305*
planet
  Earth, *190*, 196–197, *196–197*,
    202, *202*, 216
  formation of, 171–172, *172*
  gas giant, **172**, *172*, 202, 206–216,
    208–216
  Jupiter, *206*, 208–209, *208–209*,
    216, *216*
  Mercury, *190*, 192–193, *192–193*,
    202, *202*, 216
  Mars, *190*, 198–202, *198–202*,
    216, *216*
  Neptune, *206*, 214–216, *214*, *216*
  Saturn, *206–207*, 210–211, *210–
    211*, 216, *216*
  terrestrial, **172**, *172*, *190*, **192**–202,
    192–202
  Uranus, *206*, 212–213, *212–213*,
    216, *216*
  Venus, *190*, 194–195, *194–195*,
    202, *202*, 216
planetary motion, 165–166, *165–166*,
  168, *168*, 174, *174*
planetary ring system, **210**, *210–211*
planetesimals, **171**–172, *171–172*
plant cells, 323–325, *323–325*, 328
  making food, 323–325, *324–325*,
    328, *328*
plate tectonics, 16
Pluto, 221, *221*, 223, *223*
polar night, 249
population, **290**, *290*, 292, 294
potential energy, **124**–125, 128, 134
prairie dogs, *292*

precision, R26
predator, **312**–313, *312–313*, 318, *318*
predator–prey relationship, 312–313, *313*, 318
  adaptations of, 312, *312*
  population, 313
prediction making, R20
prey, **312**–313, *312–313*
procedure writing, R22
producer, **300**, *300*, 308, 403
prograde rotation, 194
prominences (sun), 178, 186–**187**, *187*
prosthetics, 54
protoplanetary disk, 171, *170–171*
  temperatures within, 172, *172*
protostellar disk, 163, 169, *169*
prototype, 341–342
Ptolemy, 154, *154*
puffins, *304*
pumice, 80, *80*

Quaoar, *222*

Radermacher, Klaus, *54*
radiation, 184
radiative zone, 181, *181*, 184, *184*
rain gauge, *43*
Reading and Study Skills, R10–R17
Reading Skills
  cause and effect, 316
  compare, 53, 83, 109, 155, 158, 165, 185, 187, 189, 199, 202, 217, 230, 271, 313–314, 323, 329
  contrast, 5, 13, 109, 165, 195, 331
  draw conclusions, 95. *See also*
    Active Reading.
reference section, R1–R38
Reference Tables, R2–R9
reflection, 20, *20*
  particle theory of light and, 20, *20*
  wave theory of light and, 20, *20*
replication, 34
retrograde rotation, 194, 212, *213*
revolution, **247**–248, *247–248*, 250, *250–251*, 252, *252*
rhinoceros, *310*
robotics technician, 161
robot, 57, *57*
rotation, 245–**246**, 252, *252*
  differential, 137, *137*
  prograde, 194
  retrograde, 194, 212, *213*
rubble-pile asteroid, 227, *227*

Salk Institute, 21
salmon, *26–27*
  in Mongolia, *27*
satellite, **256**
Saturn
  composition of, 210
  Enceladus (moon), 211, *211*
  gas giant, 210, *216*
  planet, *206–207*, 210–211, *210–211*, 216, *216*
  planetary ring, **210**, *210–211*, 216, *216*
  statistics table for, *210*
  Titan (moon), 211
  water geysers (Enceladus), 211, *211*
scavenger, 301
science, **6**, 12, 50, 52–56
  impact on society, 58
  writer, 205
Science Skills, R18–R30
science and society, 50–58
scientific explanation, 12
  empirical evidence, **8**
  evaluation of, 9
  types of, 16–18, 22
scientific investigation
  characteristics of, 36
  elements of, 29
  evaluation of, 34–35
  experiments, 26
  hypothesis, **28**
  observation, 27
  types of, 26–27, 36
scientific knowledge
  adaptability of, 22
  sources of, **21**
  theories and models, 20
scientific law, 18
scientific method, 36, **156**
  collecting and organizing data, 31
  defending conclusions, 31
  defining problem, 30
  forming hypothesis and making predictions, 30
  identifying variables, 31
  interpreting data and analyzing information, 31
  planning an investigation, 30
  used in physical science, 32
scientific model, 17, 46. *See also* model.
scientific research, 54
scientific theory, 16
scientist. *See also* **People in Science.**
  environmental, 10
seasons, 250–252, *250–252*
sea star, 273, *273*
sedimentary rock, 18
seismogram, *38*
seismograph, *38*
September equinox, 250–251, *251*. *See also* **seasons.**
short-period comet, 225, *225*

SI units,
  changing, R29
  converting to U.S. customary units, R30
  using, R29–R30
single-celled organism, 322–323
slope, R37
solar activity
  prominences, 178, 186–**187**, *187*
  solar flares, 180, 186–**187**, *187*
  sunspots, 179, **186**, *186*
solar eclipse, 261, *261*
solar flare, 180, 186–**187**, *187*
solar nebula, **169**, *169*
solar system
  Copernican model, 155, *155*
  formation of, 169–173, *169–173*
  gas giant planets, *202*, 206-216, **208**, *206–214*, 216
  geocentric model, *151*, **152**, *158*
  and gravity, 162–168, 174
  heliocentric model, *150–151*, 151–**152**, 153, 155, 157, *158*
  Ptolemaic model, 154, *154*
  small bodies, 220–230, *220–229*
  sun, 178–188, *178–181*, *184–188*
  terrestrial planets, 190–202, **192**, 204, *190–202*, *204*, 216
solid, **86**, *86*, 88, 90, 92, *92*
  ice, 88, 90, *90*, 97, 98, *98–99*, 100–101, *100*, 104, 106, 108
  matter, 86, *86*, 88, 92, *92*, *99*–100, *104*
  particle motion, 86, *86*, 88, 90, 92, *92*, 98, *98–99*, 100–101, *100*, 106
solstice, 250–251, *250–251*
sound energy, **136**, *136*, 138, *138*
Southern Hemisphere, 249–250, *249*
South Pole, 246, *246*, 248, 250–251
species, **290**–291
spontaneous generation, 3
spring, *251–252*, 267
  scale, 74, *74*
  tides, 267, **270**, *270*, 274, *274*
spring scale, 74, *74*
spring tides, 267, **270**, *270*, 274, *274*
starfish, *See* **sea star.**
states of matter, 84–90, 92, *86–90*, *92*, 96–108, *98–105*, *107–108*
stony-iron meteorite, 229
stony meteorite, 229, *229*
storms,
  on Jupiter, 209
  on Mars, 199
  on Neptune, 214, *214*
sublimation, 90, **104**, *104*, 108
sugar, 324–325, *324–325*
sulfuric acid, in atmosphere of Venus, 195
sun, 178–188, *178–181*, *184–188*
  energy production, 182–183, *182–183*
  energy transfer within, 181, *181*, 184, *184–185*, 188, *188*
  formation, 170
  midnight, 249, *249*
  prominences, 178, 186–**187**, *187*

rotation, 185, *185*
solar flares, *180*, 186–**187**, *187*
statistics table, *180*
structure, 181, *181*, 188, *188*
sunspots, 179, **186**, *186*
sun-centered model, *150–151*, 151–**152**, 153, 155, 157, 158. *See also* **heliocentric model.**
sunspots, 179, **186**, *186*
symbiosis, 311, **314**, 318
symbiotic relationships
commensalism, **314**, *318*
mutualism, **314**, *314*, *318*
parasitism, **315**, *315*, *318*

technology, 3, 30, 45, 59
tectonic plates, 197
telescope mechanic, 205
temperature, 248, *248*
in protoplanetary disk, 172, *172*
terrestrial planets, **172**, *172*, 190, **192**–202, *192–202*
Earth, 190, 196–197, *196–197*, 202, *202*, 216
formation of, 171–172, *172*
Mercury, 190, 192–193, *192–193*, 202, *202*, 216
Mars, 190, 198–202, *198–202*, 216, *216*
Venus, 190, 194–195, *194–195*, 202, *202*, 216
testable question, 6. *See also* **hypothesis.**
theory, 16. *See also* **scientific theory.**
thermometer, 7
Think Science
determining relevant information, 176–177
making conclusions from evidence, 48–49
planning an investigation, 94–95
testing and modifying theories, 264–265
third quarter (lunar phase), 258, *259*
3-carbon molecule, 326, *326–327*
tickbird, *310*
tidal cycles, 272, *272*
tidal force, 268, 270, *270*
tidal range, **270**–271, 274, *274*
tides, 266–274, **268**, *266–274*
neap tides, **271**, *271*, 274, *274*
spring tides, **267**, **270**, 274, *274*
Titan (moon of Saturn), 211
triple-beam balance, 74, *74*
Triton (moon of Neptune), 215, *215*
Trojan asteroids, 226, *226*
tundra, R6–R7
Tycho Brahe, 165

umbra, **260**–262, *260–262*
units, 73–74, 76, 78, 80–81, 82, **166**
of measurement, 40, 43
Uranus
atmosphere of, 212
Miranda moon, 213
planet, 149, *206*, 212–213, *212–213*, 216, *216*
seasons, 213
statistics table for, *212*
tilt of, *216*

variable, **29**, 95, R21
Venus
atmosphere, 195
craters and volcanoes, 195
period of rotation and revolution, *203*
planet, 190, 194–195, *194–195*, 202, *202*, 216
size and mass, 194
statistics table for, *194*
Visual Summary, 12, 22, 36, 46, 58, 82, 92, 108, 128, 138, 158, 174, 188, 202, 216, 230, 252, 262, 274, 294, 308, 318, 330
vocabulary strategies, R16–R17
volcanic rock, 80–81, *80*
volcano,
Gula Mons (Venus), *195*
Olympus Mons (Mars), 199, *199*
volume, **75**–78, 82, *75–78*
definition, **75**
formula, 76–77, *76–77*
of solid, 76–77, *76–77*
water displacement and, 78, *78*
Voyager 2 spacecraft, 213

walking catfish, 307, *307*
waning moon
crescent (lunar phase), 258, *259*
gibbous (lunar phase), 258, *258*
Ward, A. Wesley, 204, *204*
water,
displacement, 78, *78*
on Enceladus (moon of Saturn), 211, *211*
in photosynthesis, 324–325, *324–325*
on Mars, 200–201, *200*
states of matter, 86, 88–90, 98–105, *98–100*, *102–103*
wave theory of light, 20, *20*
waxing moon
crescent (lunar phase), 258, *259*
gibbous (lunar phase), 258, *258*

Wegener, Alfred, 3
weight, **73**, 82, *82*
measurement of, 74, *74*
Wesley, Anthony, 205
Why It Matters, 19, 57, 91, 157, 201, 223, 273, 293, 307, 317, 329
winter, 249, *251–252*
Wu, Chien Shiung, 54

year, **247**, *247*, 252, *252*
yellow-rumped warbler, 284, *284*

zebra mussel, 307, *307*
zooplankton, 304, *305*